Against Goliath

AGAINST GOLIATH

David Steel's Story

Weidenfeld & Nicolson
London

For my mother and father

First published in Great Britain in 1989 by
George Weidenfeld & Nicolson Ltd
91 Clapham High Street London SW4 7TA

British Library Cataloguing in Publication Data
Steel, David, *1938 Mar. 31* –
Against Goliath.
1. Great Britain. Politics – Biographies
I. Title
320'.092'4

ISBN 0–297–79678–X

Printed in Great Britain by
Butler & Tanner Ltd, Frome and London

CONTENTS

ILLUSTRATIONS

With President Sadat, 1980
The cover of *The Economist*, 5–11 December 1981
With Shirley Williams, 1981 (*Guardian*)
With the Austin 7 (*People*)
With President Mugabe, 1986, (Ministry of Information, Zimbabwe)
As Rector of Edinburgh University, 1982 (*Scotsman*)
With George Bush, 1983 (The White House, Washington)
With Billy, Tenerife, 1983, photograph by Chris Barham
Addressing the Liberal Assembly in Harrogate, November 1983
The kitchen at Ettrick Bridge, 1983
Meeting with Gorbachev, 1984, photograph by Terry Moore (Inter-Parliamentary Union)
At the Alliance Press Conference, 1987, photograph by Ros Drinkwater (*The Times*)
With David Owen, Election Campaign, 1987
Polling Day, 1987 (*Today*)
In the garden at Ettrick Bridge, 1988, photograph by Brian Randle (*Sunday Mirror*)
'Cherrydene', photographed by Eric Thorburn (*Country Homes & Interiors*)

page 115
Garland cartoon of the Liberal Party leadership contest, *Daily Telegraph*, 30 June 1976

page 131
Franklin cartoon of the LibLab pact, *Sun*, 29 June 1977

Unless otherwise acknowledged, the photographs belong to the author.

PREFACE

This story of my life has taken six months to write. Since I have rarely kept a diary I decided not to present a strictly chronological account. The reader may therefore dip into or ignore different chapters according to taste. I have been fortunate enough to enjoy a rich mixture of experiences in my first fifty years and hope the reader will share some of that sense of enjoyment. I have tried to give a candid and accurate account of public events as I witnessed and participated in them, in particular my struggle against the Goliath of the two party system, in a manner which is neither dry nor stuffy.

I am particularly grateful to David Thomson for sorting through all my papers and other records so that I had the necessary raw material on which to work. He was a research assistant to a colleague before I stole him for this task on the grounds that he had followed my footsteps in the Borders, school and university, and I cannot commend him too highly.

To Nali Dinshaw, who deserves a merit award for being able to decipher my handwriting (described in one school report simply as 'extraordinary') and who typed the whole manuscript, I wish to express my warmest thanks; and to my secretary Ann De'Ath, who has kept up some appearance of normal parliamentary office activity while surrounded by this project, I am also indebted. I also acknowledge the consideration of my leader, Paddy Ashdown, in allowing me a session free of party spokesmanship to engage in writing. People too numerous to mention have been kind enough to respond to my badgering for confirmation of my recollections or to comment on drafts of some pages. To all I extend my thanks. I trust that those I have either omitted from, or traduced in, the narrative, will forgive me.

The whole enterprise could not have been undertaken without Judy's constant cajoling, criticism, encouragement and love.

David Steel
House of Commons
June 1989

1

UPBRINGING

Early Memories of a Scottish Childhood

David Steel was shot dead outside his house in front of his wife and child. The date was 20 December 1686. Doubtless there have been times when some wished that his descendant might suffer the same fate.

The life and death of my rebellious ancestor make instructive reading. King James VI of Scotland (and I of England) claimed to be 'God's lieutenant on Earth' and hence the Church was subjected to his episcopal appointments – rather like those of a latterday prime minister. In protest against his church appointments, imposed liturgy and prohibition of church assemblies, the National Covenant was signed in Greyfriars Church, Edinburgh, in 1638 and its signatories and supporters became known as the Covenanters. Thus emboldened, an Assembly of the Church in Scotland met the same year in Glasgow, elected its own Moderator and Clerk, and laid down rules for its own government at loggerheads with Parliament and the Privy Council.

Friction between the Crown and the Covenanters continued, and increased as a result of the alliance of the Scots with the English parliamentarians in the Solemn League and Covenant of 1643. One of the bloodiest – and for the Covenanters victorious – encounters was at the battle of Philiphaugh in 1645, some six miles from my home. When Charles II came to the throne he at first accepted the Covenants, but by 1661 was reasserting his supremacy over the Church, declaring, incidentally, that 'Presbyterianism is no religion for a gentleman.' Such an outlook may explain why to this day so many of the landed and upper classes in Scotland belong to the Episcopal Church. The Solemn League and Covenant envisaged the creation of a British church on the presbyterian-puritan model.

Acts of 1661 declared adherence to the Covenant to be high treason. Ministers not appointed via the Crown and not accepting the authority of the bishops were dismissed from their pulpits. They and their congregations met in secret conventicles in the hills of Scotland. Forces were dispatched against these rebels to establish the authority of the Crown. In 1679 the Covenanters – David Steel among them – suffered a crushing defeat at the battle of Bothwell Brig. Four hundred were killed and 1,500 taken prisoner; 257 were sold as slaves to Barbados. The ship taking them from Leith ran into heavy seas in the Orkneys, whereupon the hatches were nailed down lest they should swim ashore and escape. Most of them accordingly drowned off Deerness. Altogether a cruel and bloody period.

James Barr, in his book, *The Scottish Covenanters*, makes it clear that they were neither anti-Pope nor anti-Episcopal on any theological grounds but that they 'stood for the rule of the people against the domination of an arbitrary prince. It was democracy as against tyranny.'

David Steel fled from the slaughter of the Bothwell Brig defeat and for five years was a fugitive. J. H. Thomson tells the story of his end in his book, *The Martyr Graves of Scotland*:

David Steel was tenant of Nether Skellyhill, a farm three miles to the south-east of Lesmahagow. He was at Bothwell Bridge. His name occurs on the fugitive roll of 1684. A rigorous search was made for him, and for safety he had to leave his own house, and generally passed the night in a hut, at a spot still pointed out, about four miles from Skellyhill, in the wild moorland near the source of the Nethan. In December 1686 he ventured to return home to Skellyhill. On the 20th, Lieutenant Creichton, with a party of horse and foot, came to the house. David got tidings of their approach shortly before their arrival, slipped through a back window, and ran off to hide himself in the bush-grown banks of the Nethan, a mile away. The soldiers noticed his flight, and followed him. He crossed the Logan Water where he fell, and wet the powder of the musket he had taken with him. His fall stayed his flight, but he still ran on. The soldiers, however, gained on him, and his strength began to fail. At Yondertown, a farm half a mile to the south of Skellyhill, the soldiers fired on him, and at Meadow, a little farther, they came up to him. Here he kept them at bay by presenting his musket at them, until Creichton came up and called him to surrender, with the promise of quarter and a fair trial in Edinburgh. Steel surrendered, but Creichton took him back to Skellyhill where, in the presence of his wife, Mary Weir, who, with her infant in her arms, had been earnestly watching her husband's flight, he ordered him to be shot before his own door. The dragoons refused, and rode away, but the Highlanders, less scrupulous, fired. Creichton and his men immediately set off, and, when some of the neighbours came, they found the widow gathering up the scattered brains of her husband. She bound up the shattered head with a napkin, and, as she gazed at the dead body, she said – for tradition has still preserved the words that broke from her lips – 'The archers have shot at thee, my husband, but they could not reach thy soul; it has escaped like a

2

dove far away, and is at rest. Lord, give strength to Thy handmaid that will prove she has waited for Thee, even in the way of Thy judgments.'

The body of Steel was brought to Lesmahagow, and buried at the spot now marked by a commemorative stone. It is a flat stone, seven feet long by three feet seven inches in breadth. The inscription is:

> HERE LIES
> the Body of DAVID STEEL Martyr
> who was Murdered by Chrichton for his
> Testimony to the Covenants and Work
> of Reformation and because he durst
> not own the Authority of the
> Tyrant destroying the same   He was
> shot at SKELLYHILL the 20th of Decr.
> 1686 in the 33d year of his age
>
> Be thou faithful unto Death and
> I will give thee a Crown of Life
>
> David a Shepherd first and then
> Advanced to be King of Men
> Had of his Graces in this Quarter
> This Heir, a Wand'rer now a Martyr
> Who for his Constancy and Zeal
> Still to the Back did prove true Steel
> Who for Christ's Royal Truth and Laws
> And for the Covenanted Cause
> Of SCOTLANDS famous Reformation
> Declining Tyrant's Usurpation
> By Cruel Chrichton Murder'd lies
> Whose Blood to Heaven for Vengeance cries.

In 1986 I laid a wreath on that grave at a tricentennial service in Lesmahagow churchyard. A monument to his memory stands at the site of the murder at Skellyhill farm. Four years after his death, King William came to the throne declaring he 'had no obligation to be a persecutor', since when Episcopalian and Presbyterian forms of worship have existed freely side by side, the Presbyterian being the predominant form of worship throughout Scotland.

Unfortunately no one in my family has yet had the patience or inclination to establish unambiguous proof of our direct descent either from the wretched babe in arms – who was a girl – or, from one of David's brothers, which is the oral tradition handed down in the family. Suffice to say that some two centuries later my great-grandparents Elisabeth Scott Groves and David Steel were married at Lesmahagow. He worked in the mines and gardens on the borders of Lanarkshire and Renfrewshire as an oversman: that is he had his own squad of miners who contracted with the mine owners to cut a road into a seam or to work a given yardage of a seam. There were ten children. The family had a modest lifestyle, living in one room and a kitchen. He was a staunch Liberal. In the autumn of 1987, I visited the last surviving of these ten, my great-aunt Marion, aged 102; and though almost totally blind and very deaf, she entertained me to an account of their life.

Her own aunt, great grandfather David Steel's sister Catherine, produces the only known political connection in my family history. She married James Brown, the Labour MP for South Ayrshire. He rose to become Secretary of the National Union of Scottish Mineworkers, and was elected MP for South Ayrshire in 1918. Brown maintained that his hardest task was the unveiling of the war memorial at Annbank because the first name among the local casualties of the Great War was that of his nephew, and the second that of his son. Brown had himself gone down the pits at the age of twelve, joined the miners' union at sixteen, and at twenty-two became President of the Ayrshire Miners' Union. He lived in a miner's cottage at Annbank, continued to work down the pit and was a Sunday School teacher and church elder.

His crowning honour was his appointment in 1924 by the King on the recommendation of Prime Minister Ramsay MacDonald as Lord High Commissioner to the General Assembly of the Church of Scotland, the first time in three hundred years that a commoner had represented the sovereign. He and my great great-aunt Kate took up their residence in Holyrood Palace, Edinburgh, for the two weeks' duration of the Assembly, something I always recalled when Judy and I stayed as guests at the Palace of more recent Lord High Commissioners. Afterwards they returned to the miner's cottage. He was appointed again in 1930–31 and in 1930 became a Privy Councillor. Brown was an outstanding churchman, trade unionist and parliamentarian. We still treasure a faded brown photograph of him and his wife in their carriage in Edinburgh's Royal Mile.

My own grandfather, John Scott Groves Steel, was a grocery manager in the Scottish Co-operative Wholesale Society (SCWS) complex at Burnbank, near Hamilton. (The Co-operative movement was a co-operative trading society, the dividend of which was distributed to its customers.) There he met my grandmother, Jane Scott, who was in charge of the boot and shoe department at Burnbank Co-op. She was the daughter of Andrew Scott of T. and A. Scott, who had a clothing and tailoring business in Hamilton. Some of the cloth was woven and made up on the premises. It must have been a fairly prosperous small business, for Andrew Scott bought land on the outskirts of Hamilton on which he built his own house and also a small terrace of eight houses, three of which were occupied by his daughters when they married. One of those daughters was Jane Scott, and there my father was born. Andrew Scott served on Hamilton Town Council and was a baillie (the Scottish equivalent of an alderman). I have the fondest recollection of all four of my grandparents, all of whom lived into their nineties, John Steel dying the very day I was elected to Parliament in 1965. My biographer, Peter Bartram, observed in his book in 1981 that while Mrs Thatcher was a grocer's daughter I was the grandson of a grocer's employee.

My paternal grandfather became manager of the SCWS branch at Peterhead, Aberdeenshire. There he presided over a complex of shops – a grocery, a bakery, a drapery and a shoe shop. He was also a Town Councillor and an elder of the Church. Subsequently the family moved to the outskirts of Aberdeen on his appointment as superintendent of the SCWS branches in the north of Scotland.

My own father, his elder son David, after schooling at Peterhead Academy and Robert Gordon's College, Aberdeen, went to Aberdeen University, where he graduated in Arts and then in Divinity. There he met my mother, Sheila Martin, who secured an honours degree in French and German. Her father, James Martin, who came from Dingwall, Ross-shire (where on my political travels I have been greeted by distant cousins), was a dominie all his life in various schools in Aberdeenshire, ending his days as headmaster of Skene Square school in Aberdeen. A public-spirited figure, he served on the city's education committee, was President of the City Rotary club and was made a Fellow of the Educational Institute of Scotland. I spent many childhood and teenage holidays with my maternal grandparents in Aberdeen, a city I grew to love. I was therefore sorely tempted in the last couple of years when asked to accept nomination as a candidate for the Chancellorship of Aberdeen University, but declined purely on practical grounds of geography.

Both my parents were prizewinners at school and university in their different specialities. They became engaged in my father's final year of his second degree and my mother's final year of her honours course. He was in his final year in Arts while she was a first-year student when they met. My mother maintains that she never got an opportunity to sow any wild oats – he caught her so young. After she graduated and in view of the fact that they planned to get married in a year or two, Sheila Martin took a short business training, followed by an academic post as a research assistant on the Scottish National Dictionary, which was to be completed some forty years later. Her main duties were on the business side, but she worked on one section – Char

5

to Cheese. The rest of her life she devoted to her husband and children, being also my father's secretary and typist.

On his graduation in Divinity my father was awarded a scholarship to Union Theological Seminary, New York, to work for the STM degree. He turned down the scholarship, explaining to the very understanding principal, David S. Cairns, that while he might get some further academic equipment by going to America, he felt woefully ill-equipped in his knowledge of people and in his ability to minister to them in their variety of personalities and problems. Principal Cairns finally accepted his decision and advised him to get in touch with the Church of Scotland Home Mission Committee. He did so, and along with a fellow probationer was sent to Plantation Parish, a heavily populated area with 70 per cent unemployment and appalling housing conditions, on the south side of Glasgow. Their remit was to survey the whole parish, knocking on the doors and meeting the people in their homes, and to report. This they did, one starting at one end of the parish, the other at the other end. That year, my father maintains, had the most lasting effect on his thinking. He also met George MacLeod, then minister of the neighbouring parish of Govan and later (1938) founder of the Iona Community, a Moderator of the General Assembly (1957–8) and a life peer (1967), who was very supportive and became a lifelong friend.

My parents were married in the medieval King's College chapel of the University in April 1937, and settled in the manse of my father's first parish of Denbeath in the mining town of Buckhaven, Fife, on the north shore of the Firth of Forth, where he had been ordained as minister in November 1936. It was here that I was born at noon on 31 March 1938, the first of five children.

To be precise, I was born in Kirkcaldy's Forth Park Maternity Hospital, but otherwise I have no connection with the town, famed as Adam Smith's birthplace. Indeed I recall as a child learning a long piece of doggerel about the train journey from Edinburgh to Aberdeen which referred to the stench of the town's linoleum factories:

> And ye'll ken richt well
> by the afa' smell
> the next stop's Kirkcaldy.

The English cannot pronounce the name of the place (it is 'Kirkoddy') and as we left Buckhaven before I was three, I recall almost nothing of these times.

In 1941 we moved to war-torn Clydeside as my father became minister of Bridgend Church, Dumbarton. Greenock, across the Firth of Clyde, was pounded mercilessly in German bomber raids, as was Clydebank next door on our side of the water. Dumbarton itself was not as badly hit as these. But there were innumerable air-raid warnings. My father went out as chaplain to the air-raid wardens, and my mother lifted us from our beds and carried us downstairs. Bombs fell on the town on several occasions, and there were many casualties and much damage to property. A land-mine fell in the garden of a neighbouring manse and blew out all the windows of our manse, shattering the conservatory and the greenhouse – the latter much to the disappointment of my mother who had been tending a very promising vine there. It also blew over my father while he was busy using applied science and a dustbin lid to smother a cluster of incendiary bombs that had fallen in the garden. The lid deprived the bombs of oxygen, and he claimed it was a very effective method. He met a man swiping at them with his cap, all the time uttering a volley of oaths. My father thanked the man for his help and for expressing what he too felt.

Another night a 500-pound bomb made a direct hit on a house across the road but failed to explode. We had our own air-raid shelter in the dark wine cellar of our manse, which, since it never contained wine, was made habitable with rough beds, wooden crates and candlelight. To this day I ponder the wisdom of sheltering down there for if a bomb had struck the manse we would have been trapped under a mountain of rubble. Recently I learned that in fact the manse was a former house of Denny the shipbuilder, very substantially stone-built; my father had been advised that it was the safest place in the house, and the rescue people, knowing we were there if the house was hit, would have got us out unless it was a direct hit on the cellar. I cannot remember being unduly concerned at the time. With the resilience of young children we usually slept through it all. These episodes form my earliest memories.

My father spent long hours helping the emergency services and bringing comfort to the injured or bereaved. Later in the war he served with the Church of Scotland Huts and Canteens in Europe and was away for six months. My own worst gruesome memories were of the cottage hospital where I had my tonsils removed and was made to eat cold porridge. Later my appendix joined these other troublesome organs in the same hospital.

Otherwise it was a very happy childhood. We lived in this huge, rather cold house designed for the days when ministers of the Kirk had servants. There was very little luxury on my father's stipend and my mother devoted herself to bringing up a family growing in number and size, under the austerity and rationing of wartime. My parents kept hens, and an allotment for growing vegetables; the manse outbuildings were given over to keeping cages of rabbits, not as pets but to help feed and clothe the family. I suspect the curing of the skins was not all it might have been because I can remember the smell of the coats, bonnets and glorious warm mittens which we wore. It was a time of clothing coupons: I was lucky, of course, because as the oldest I had new outfits, while my brother and sister had a mixture of hand-me-downs, both clothes and shoes. My grandparents used to mix their meagre ration of butter with their margarine to make it taste better. David Thomson, the Scottish writer notes: 'the vice of meanness condemned in every other nation is in Scotland translated into a virtue called thrift.'

To this day I still regard the 'thrift' dinned into me by my parents and grandparents as important. My children regard it as stinginess, but they have been brought up in a totally different atmosphere of conspicuous consumption and comparative financial ease. I cannot actually recall as a child, for example, ever being taken to a restaurant for a meal; my children regard that as part of their way of life. I can remember our first car at the age of about nine; they have seen fleets come and go. I go round our house complaining about lights being left on or the gas oven or central heating being turned up too high, or Judy's failure to collect the petrol tokens which add up to free gifts. This early upbringing also colours my political attitudes. I am genuinely shocked at the credit explosion which has been allowed to take place in recent years. 'Thrift' and 'saving' are words almost forgotten in current political vocabulary.

I first went to school at Dumbarton Academy, where I was taught reading, writing and arithmetic by the formidable Miss Henderson. Jackie Stewart, the racing driver, was a year ahead of me and he recalls her well, though neither of us remembers the other. At the age of five I learned to throw stones at and be pelted in return by the 'Papes'. I had no idea who these children were that went to a different school but it was part of the West of Scotland culture (and sadly still is in many places) for sectarianism on the Northern Ireland pattern to run riot. That is why I have always opposed segregated education in that province as being literally the root of all their problems, and I find it difficult to understand why the Catholic hierarchy in Scotland continue to insist on their own schools.

Although at various schools I was taught to play the piano and later the organ, my musical prowess certainly did not approach that of my mother's distinguished cousins, Bill and Jimmy Miller. Bill was leading violinist in several orchestras, while Jimmy became director of the RAF dance band during the war, appearing on occasion with his opposite number in the US Air Force band, Glenn Miller. Jimmy went on in peacetime to lead the same band as the Squadronaires, and when I was a schoolboy I had one or two of his records. An album was reissued in 1982 and in the last couple of years he has become almost a cult figure on the nostalgic radio programmes about the big band era. Perhaps it is his unconscious influence which has led me to become a life member of Ronnie Scott's jazz club in London, where I am a very occasional visitor.

I had regular scrapes involving my brother Michael, who is two years younger than me and was a more high-spirited child. On one occasion my grandfather found him chasing me round the playroom with an axe. On another he managed to let go of the string of my wooden boat which we were sailing on the banks of the Clyde and I waded in after it, only to find myself being lifted off my feet. I managed to grab it but my recklessness nearly killed me, as of course I could not swim.

Our most notorious escapade came as a result of my mother taking me go Glasgow at the age of six to be measured for my first kilt. There for the first time I saw flowersellers on the streets and inquired what they were doing there and if they kept the money people paid for the flowers. That evening Michael and I filled our little green and red wheelbarrows, given to us at Christmas, with somewhat wilted bluebells and other shrubbery flowers, and proceeded to an advantageous site at the top of a flight of steps used by pedestrians coming to our part of town. There our mother found us when she came looking for us at bedtime, happily clutching almost two shillings which we had been given by various neighbours, one being the provost (Scottish equivalent of mayor). Successfully concealing their amusement, our parents gave us a stern ticking off and sent us to return the money. To our delight the provost refused to accept his shilling, later telling our father that he had been vastly amused by the enterprise of 'the dear little boys'. There are probably government grants nowadays for such enterprise. The same kind man made the mistake one day of giving us a lift to school on his way to the Town House in his enormous car 'with two sofas' with the result that thereafter we waited for the car and thumbed a lift. Unfortunately we innocently told our parents, who promptly ordered a stop to that practice. We never thumbed a lift again, but we did watch for the car coming and walked across the road just in front of it, with the desired result.

At the end of the war my father was appointed to a post in the Church of Scotland headquarters at 121 George Street, Edinburgh. He was invited by the General Assembly's Foreign Mission Committee to become Associate Secretary, Home Organization, with the remit to increase the givings of congregations and the number of missionaries, in order to offset the serious effects of inflation and delayed retirals, both due to the war, which were having a critical impact on the church's mission. After much thought he agreed to accept the job for three years, as he was convinced that he was a parish minister, and that the five-year stint that the committee wanted was too long to be away from a parish. He led a 'normal' nine-to-five life at the office, but also travelled all over Scotland visiting presbyteries and churches. In Edinburgh we lived in a church house under the shadow of Arthur's Seat. In the postwar years we again had an allotment to grow vegetables for the family, but there was no room in the city for hens or rabbits.

I attended the local primary school, James Gillespie's Boys School in Marchmont Road, travelling first by tram and later by bicycle. I began to do rather well academically. I read a lot: I collected all of Arthur Ransome's Swallows and Amazons books. There was no television but I was a devotee of radio's *Children's Hour*, *Dick Barton Special Agent*, and the *Just William* series. Holidays consisted of either visits to the Aberdeen grandparents or family trips by car or Clyde paddle steamer to the traditional Steel family holiday ground – the Mull of Kintyre where we stayed in a series of inexpensive boarding houses or hotels, and on one occasion a caravan and tent.

The story is handed down of my great-grandfather's objection to the penny dues payable at the piers in the West of Scotland, which were all owned by the MacBrayne steamship company. Every year as he shepherded his flock off the pier at the start of the holiday at Tarbert, Loch Fyne, he would embarrass his wife and children with an altercation on the subject with the piermaster. The end was always the same. He would slam the pennies on to the counter of the kiosk and solemnly declaim a parody of Psalm 24:

> The earth belongs unto the Lord
> and all that it contains
> except the West of Scotland piers
> for they are all MacBrayne's.

My love of the unspoilt Scottish countryside as a town and city child stems from these idyllic holidays where we walked, swam in the cold sea, and were taught by my father to fish in the burns.

Life in Edinburgh was pleasant. By now there were five young Steels. In addition to my brother Michael, we now had Felicity, Jill and Ian, a large and lively family. Being the eldest I developed what I prefer to call a natural authority – for which the others had ruder descriptions. They recall with relish the occasion when a minister friend with his wife and small daughter came to stay with us, and while all the parents were at a communion service I was left in charge of both families with a series of tasks: washing the breakfast dishes, fetching in coal, laying the lunch table and so on. When they returned all had been achieved and I proudly described the list of who had done what.

'And what did you do?' inquired my mother. 'I organized it,' I answered sheepishly to the amusement of the entire household.

People sometimes ask if I had a strict upbringing. I don't think so, particularly, but by today's standards it seems so. In Edinburgh, for example, we were not allowed to play in the streets on our bicycles on Sundays. Some years ago my father and I took part in a television series, *Generation to Generation*, in which were discussed the religious views of a parent and a son or daughter. It was chaired by Joan Bakewell. My father had great difficulty in persuading her that life in a manse was not the grim affair that she imagined. She was surprised to be told that in Linlithgow we, father included, played tennis on Sunday afternoon on our bumpy grass court. We went to church every Sunday morning followed by Sunday School with perhaps Bible class in the afternoon and sometimes an evening service as well. But the Church and manse life also gave great breadth. As my father told my biographer: 'A manse child has a considerable advantage over others in that he meets all kinds of people from all strata of society in the manse. He might be meeting the Lord Lieutenant one minute and a miner the next, and he's taught to treat all people automatically the same way. Manse society is a very democratic society.'

At the age of eleven I sat an examination for a scholarship to enter George Watson's College, one of Edinburgh's prestigious direct-grant day schools. Without the scholarship there was no question of my parents affording the fees to attend. Three of us in my school managed to obtain entry and I was looking forward to it with excitement when one day my father gathered us round the table to tell his astonished children that we were off to Africa.

At the end of his three years he had been invited to accept a permanent appointment on the Foreign Mission secretariat, but he held to his conviction that he was a parish minister. Having gone around Scotland calling people to go into all the world to preach the gospel, he thought he should now offer to go himself. He was called to the largest parish of the Church of Scotland – half the size of Europe. He had been appointed minister of St Andrew's Church, Nairobi, and the parish of East Africa with the responsibility for the Scots population throughout Kenya, Uganda and Tanganyika. I didn't know where any of these places were and I was torn between the sheer drama of disappearing to Africa for four years, and doubts about leaving all my friends and hard-won scholarship behind. In fact I was given the choice of staying behind with relatives; but being only eleven I could not bear the thought of separation from the rest of the family.

Four years seems an eternity at that age. So there were lots of sad farewells when all seven of us set sail from Tilbury docks on our three-week voyage through the Mediterranean, the Suez Canal and down to Mombasa.

My father's church was based in Nairobi where he planned and built a splendid new edifice, now the very popular and crowded St Andrew's congregation of the Presbyterian Church of East Africa; but he was also responsible together with one colleague in these early days for preaching intermittently at twenty-two different places throughout the three East African territories, and he managed to arrange several of these 'safaris' during the school holidays, so that we all travelled with him. These were glorious and uncomfortable trips. The church, strapped for cash as always, had purchased what was euphemistically known as a safari car. In fact it was a Standard Vanguard van, with windows cut in the sides and a Dunlopillo mattress stuck in the back for the little Steels to sit on. Huge suitcases were piled high behind us. The East African roads were not in those days tarmac and as the car bumped and slid its way across Africa, the luggage careered forward, pinning us against the front bench seat. In these circumstances there was great competition to take turns at sitting in front between mother and father, the eldest son trying vainly to assert some rights of primogeniture.

These were memorable journeys. Both my father and his colleague were known to cover vast distances at reckless speeds, so much so that I recall the amusement in the congregation when during a national road safety week the sermon from the St Andrew's pulpit was on the text: 'It is Jehu, for he driveth furiously.' On one occasion approaching the Tanganyikan coast near Dar-es-Salaam we came round a corner in a cloud of red dust only to find a lone elephant blocking the road and tearing at the foliage with its trunk. As we shuddered to a stop (I was sitting in the back corner), I recall the terror as the animal turned and pawed the ground as though about to charge. Mother maintains that it had the largest pair of tusks of any elephant we ever saw, and we saw herds of elephants in East Africa. Wrenching one arm free from the mountain of suitcases which had descended on us I gently slid shut the side window for protection. I also asked for my camera which was in the glove box, but we were all told to be quiet. My father switched off the engine. The ear-flapping and pawing act continued until disdainfully the elephant ambled off into the bush.

On another occasion we were enjoying a family picnic by the Athi River when brother Ian, aged about three, sat on a convenient mound which turned out to be an ant-hill. Soon he was covered in crawling one-inch-long ants. The textbook solution to such a mishap is to remove clothing and plunge into the water. We pointed out that a large crocodile had just meandered past, so the ants had slowly to be brushed and picked off.

There was another encounter with ants. This time my father was the victim. Michael and I were fishing the Gura River with father. He was downstream from us fishing from the bank when he suddenly threw down his rod, dropped his khaki shorts and dashed into the river. He had ants in his pants. Our joy was unconfined. That night, sleeping in the fishing hut – which had rows of large bats hanging upside down in the roof trees – we re-enacted the scene with much laughter until father called from next door: 'Shut up, you two, and go to sleep.'

The East African territories are places of great beauty which I have since visited several times either as a politician or on holiday. Their people are an amazing variety. The Europeans came from every nationality, with the British predominant. There was a still larger Asian population, several of whom were members of St Andrew's; and the vast majority were of course African. The extraordinary feature of life in the early fifties was that all schools were racially segregated; and this remained the case right up to within a few years of Kenyan independence in 1963, when we expected these people suddenly to transform themselves into a multiracial society. The lack of any genuine social contact between young people of different races was most marked. Apart from occasional team games against other schools, it was virtually nonexistent, which as with religious segregation at home scarcely provided a foundation for good race relations.

The YMCA supervisor made a brave attempt to bridge this gap. He invited my brother Michael and me, a Dutch boy and an English boy to join a week's camp with a couple of dozen African teenagers. The condition was that we would be treated exactly the same. Not knowing quite what this meant, we accepted. It was a fascinating glimpse into a way of life of which we were totally ignorant. We carried buckets of water for about a mile from the nearest river, just like the local village women. We ate the most rudimentary stew, in which deceased ants floated to the surface, with the staple diet of tasteless posho (a maize porridge); and swam naked in the river because none of them owned swimming costumes. Sitting round the camp fire at night we talked, as all teenagers do, about life ahead.

It was against that untypical personal experience that I witnessed Kenya plunging into the Mau Mau crisis and the state of emergency in 1952. Teenage boys just older than myself were recruited into the KPR (Kenya Police Reserve). The Mau Mau engaged in terrible atrocities – mainly against fellow Africans – and this bred in some quarters a thuggish reaction. I used to listen at school to tales from sixteen- and seventeen-year-olds telling what they had done to various 'wogs' on their campaigns during the holidays. It was obvious that many of them treated other races as, by definition, inferior beings.

Significantly, a lot of these on independence made their way south to continue a racist stand in Rhodesia or South Africa. It is interesting to note, however, that after independence a group of settlers who had originally been actively opposed to Kenya's independence, signed an open letter to Rhodesian premier Ian Smith, who was threatening UDI, urging him not to do it and telling him that they had been as fearful as he was but they had stayed on in Kenya and independence was working well.

My father got a reputation for interfering in politics – though he pointed out when he left the colony in 1957 that only twenty-five of his one thousand or so speeches and sermons had any political content. He was aware of his responsibility to both church and state. He was Moderator of the Presbytery of Kenya, which meant that he was looked to for leadership in the church, by both Europeans and Africans. He was, by a minute from the Colonial Office, declared to be next in precedence (jointly with the Bishop) to the Governor. He was also Chairman of the Christian Council of Kenya, representing all the main churches. It was the Christian Council that was instrumental in the appointment of a Parliamentary Commission led by the Rt Hon. Walter Elliot MP, which produced a unanimous report justifying much of the criticism made by the churches.

In one broadcast sermon he was strongly critical of police tactics and brutality, and in particular of the indiscriminate round-ups and detentions going on in and around Nairobi, which merely generated ill-feeling and hostility. There was a frightful row, with the War Cabinet even considering his expulsion from the country. Not long after he finished his second term in Kenya and was preaching in an Edinburgh church years later, a Scot who had been the chief financial colonial servant in Kenya at the time told my father that he had to attend the Cabinet as adviser to the Finance Minister, Sir Ernest Vasy, because an important financial matter was on the agenda. Before that, however, the Cabinet discussed whether or not an expulsion order should be served on Steel. The former colonial servant said he found it very interesting; they finally decided against doing so for two reasons: (a) that he knew too much of what was going on and would be more dangerous to them in Britain than he was in Kenya; and (b) he was quite a decent chap and it would be a pity to expel him.

Ten years later Vasey asked my father if he ever saw the former chief financial civil servant, whereupon my father told him the account he had been given of the discussion of his expulsion. Vasey said: 'As a matter of fact there was a third reason; when I read the item about you on the agenda I saw the Governor privately beforehand and told him that if the decision was expulsion he would have my resignation.'

Back in the UK, Tom Driberg, MP, with characteristic hyperbole described the sermon as 'the greatest since Martin Luther'. My father was just one of many Church of Scotland ministers and missionaries to have played an important role in the development of modern Africa. The spiritual stamp of the Kirk marks many African leaders in power at the present time.

These Mau Mau days were dangerous and untrustworthy times. Sadly we had then to travel everywhere carrying a loaded revolver in the car. The government laid down for our protection that we had to have a gun or a police escort. My father refused the latter, which might suggest to Africans that he was an agent of government. I remember sitting at table in a remote farmhouse on the slopes of Mount Kenya. Our host and hostess at each end of the table had a revolver on their side plates. My father on one of his many return visits to Kenya after independence (it is a standing joke in our family that he has made more farewell appearances in St Andrew's, Nairobi, than Frank Sinatra has made anywhere) was summoned by President Kenyatta who told him: 'When I was in prison I had a transistor radio and used to listen to your sermons. They gave me hope.'

My father said, 'Sir, I held no brief for Mau Mau.'

'Of course not,' said the President. 'But you were an independent voice for truth and justice.'

To this day I have many friends in Kenya. The O'Meara brothers were my closest friends in my early teens. Rob is now an internationally successful painter. He was always top of the art class, and I was always bottom. Alan Root who used to sit alphabetically next to me in class I have not seen since, but I admire his televised balloon safaris. Roger Whittaker was a contemporary, though when the singer and I met a year or two ago in a TV studio we had to admit we didn't remember each other at all. But friends among the African and Asian communities date from my time as an MP and the development of Kenya from a white colony to a cheerful multiracial society.

Those formative years between the ages of eleven and fifteen were to provide me with the beginnings of political awareness and a deep-seated opposition to racism in all its manifestations. School itself was not a great success. I disliked the Prince of Wales school which proudly claimed to be 'Kenya's Eton'. All dayboys like me were an oppressed minority; and as I was no good at any of the many games compulsorily played, to which exaggerated importance was attached, I had a fairly miserable and uninteresting time. I frequently got into trouble, usually for dodging such activities, and was beaten by senior sadists clad in their brief authority as prefects. My physical training teacher reported: 'Fair work, his sense of humour is an asset'; while a housemaster with considerable understatement wrote: 'He has not been able to play a very full part in school games'; and another one: 'I do think he should be encouraged to take a more active part on the games field'; and as my highest accolade: 'plays a fair hockey game for the remainders'. To this day I cannot understand why grown men and women devote such passion to the collective pursuit of a ball of whatever size or shape. As leader I regularly declined to join the Tory and Labour leaders at the annual ritual of the Wembley cup final, to the fury of any dedicated football fans on my staff, although I do enjoy the local rugby 'sevens' and the occasional international at Murrayfield, especially when the majority of the team are my constituents, and in recent years an annual seat in the Royal Box at the Wimbledon tennis championship.

There were two royal visits to Kenya during my schoolboy days. The first was in 1950, when the Duke and Duchess of Gloucester came to present the Royal Charter conferring city status on Nairobi. The Duke had been Lord High Commissioner at the previous General Assembly of the Church of Scotland and agreed to lay the foundation stone of the new St Andrew's Church that was to be. It was a great occasion. Half an hour before the Duke and Duchess were due to arrive there was a tropical downpour. Every towel in the manse was used to dry the forty or so chairs for the distinguished guests, the sun came out, and all went well. There is a marble plaque in the cloisters marking the spot and commemorating the occasion.

One of the intended features of the new church was a block of marble from the holy island of Iona, cradle of Scots Christianity. It was to be in front of the communion table so that when the minister pronounced the benediction he would be standing on a symbolic piece of Scotland. The block of marble duly arrived at the port of Mombasa early in 1951, not long after the removal of the Stone of Destiny from Westminster Abbey by a group of Scottish nationalists. To the authorities a block of stone from Scotland could only mean one thing – and the Iona marble was temporarily impounded on suspicion of being the missing Coronation stone.

It was, however, in place when Princess Elizabeth and the Duke of Edinburgh came to Kenya in 1952. They visited the new St Andrew's on a Sunday morning; after the service the congregation assembled in the grounds while the royal guests walked round the church, and the Duke asked some searching questions about the reasons for the style, which my father answered apparently to his satisfaction. My brother and I bagged the blotting paper from the visitors' book with the clear marks of their signatures. (Unfortunately I don't know what happened subsequently to that precious memento.) Two days later, King George VI died and Princess Elizabeth became Queen. My father, at less than an hour's notice, was called on by the broadcasting authority, Cable and Wireless, to make the announcement of the death of the King at the beginning of the 6 o'clock news, to pay a tribute to him and to lead the listeners in a short service. Meanwhile at school we were assembled in the quadrangle to be told the news and the flag was lowered to half mast.

My school work suffered through my lack of interest. I preferred the company of my devoted pet monkey, Gibber, and Alsatian dog Duke to schoolbooks. I was giving a lacklustre performance, with little promise of improvement, and the school syllabus was geared to English rather than Scottish exams. After their six months' leave in the UK at the end of four years, my parents decided it would be better for me not to return with them, but to take up that long-postponed scholarship at Watson's. So at fifteen it was for me a sad goodbye to Africa.

Re-entry to life in Edinburgh was not too difficult. My brother Michael also obtained a scholarship to Watson's and we both entered a school where we already had some friends. My own academic record was so backward that although I entered third year in April, I had to repeat the entire year starting in the autumn, giving me a total of nearly seven years' secondary schooling. The decision for Michael to stay behind in Edinburgh as well must have been a very difficult one to take and in a strange way it left our family permanently divided – Michael and I were separated from the other three children for the next four years, and even when reunited we were the only two to go on to university. To this day I see more of him and his family than of my other brother and sisters, though this is still not very often. We do, however, always have a Christmas family reunion, which used to be at the manse but now goes round the four who have houses in Scotland – Ian lives in Yorkshire but also comes when he can. During these four years neither we nor the church could afford to pay for us to fly out to Kenya for holidays. So we stayed put. My mother, thanks to a generous family friend, paid one visit back to Scotland in four years. Our father we never saw at all during that time. We wrote and received regular weekly air letters.

We were therefore heavily dependent on friends and relations, especially my father's sister, our Aunt Lizbeth, who was a schoolteacher in Edinburgh – she came out to Kenya for a six-month holiday and taught in the first multiracial school there. We used to invade her tiny flat with oppressive regularity at weekends for food, comfort and outings. My paternal grandparents lived in a tenement flat in Leith and once a week we would go there for a meal and to play cards or watch television. On the three holidays a year we would land ourselves on them in rotation. In Aberdeen we regularly played golf with our maternal grandfather, a sport I abandoned on leaving school. Looking back on it, I don't know how they put up with such regular visitations from two teenage boys – though we were, I think, pretty well behaved.

Watson's was not a boarding school. So having been in the minority of dayboys at a boarding school, we became boarders at a day school. Some of the masters simply took a number of boys into their own homes by private arrangement. There were about four such houses. We were billeted with a genial mathematics master, William Clark, and his own family, the number of boys increasing as he moved to larger houses. Our final house was an 'official' boarding house, owned by the school, of which Mr Clark became the first housemaster and I became the first head prefect.

My abiding memory of these large Edinburgh villas was the cold in winter: linoleum on the floor in a room with huge windows, six ex-army iron beds with thin mattresses and no central heating was the order of the day. Nowadays Watson's boasts a purpose-built boarding house, catering for about eighty (which has included my daughter Catriona) with carpets and radiators, but it lacks the atmosphere which these old and smaller units provided. When I objected to the somewhat spartan furnishings in the final house, I was told we could go and buy a secondhand sofa out of our own resources. This we did for ten shillings in a saleroom in Leith. We could not afford to transport it and it was too big to get on a bus. Four of us wheeled it all the way across Edinburgh to the house.

The enforced and sudden separation from family meant that I had to find my own pursuits and recreations. My first relief was that 'games' at Watson's were not compulsory. Early on, cricket and rugby abandoned me rather than the other way round. I was allowed to take up swimming instead, which I did no better than any other sport; but at least my own indifferent performance affected nobody else. In my first week at school one of the older boys suggested that I join him in attending a meeting of the Friday evening Literary Club in the school, not so much a literary as a debating society. The school enjoyed at that time the distinction of having as former pupils the heads of both English and Scottish legal systems and the presiding officers of both Houses of Parliament: William 'Shakes' Morrison, Speaker of the House of Commons; Lord Kilmuir (David Maxwell Fyfe), Lord Chancellor; and Lord Cooper, Lord President of the Court of Session. All had been in the 'Lit' and all came back in their distinction to visit it. It became my main interest, and I never missed a meeting in my four years at Watson's, being President in my last year. The literary side of the club consisted of producing the magazine *Phoenix*. We were encouraged to take out subscriptions to the *Spectator* and I enjoyed the political commentaries of 'Taper' (Bernard Levin).

The other external influence over my life at that time was the Church. Junior boys were all frogmarched to whichever nearby kirk was convenient. Senior boys could choose, and a small group of us became regular worshippers (often twice on Sundays) at St George's West, one of Edinburgh's big city-centre churches where the minister was the Rev. Murdo Ewen Macdonald, a powerful preacher, former prisoner of war and a highlander. He conducted my confirmation and for a while in my late teens I even contemplated following my father into the ministry, but I could not see myself settling down to church life. My own Christianity is encapsulated in my father's address as Moderator in 1974 to the General Assembly of the Church of Scotland:

The Church and Christians are given too much to easy moralizing and too little to the task of converting individuals and reforming society. .... Until the Church takes the ethic of the New Testament Communism of the early Christians, according to which possessions and goods are given to all men as every man has need, the Church itself will not be taken seriously by the world.

Academically I did tolerably well, obtaining five 'Highers' and a 'Lower' at one sitting in the fifth year. I persuaded my parents to let me stay on for the sixth year to try for a bursary to Edinburgh University. But partly because of the illness of the principal teacher of English and partly because of my own inclinations, I spent most of that year enjoying myself as editor of the school weekly newspaper, *Ecce*, and magazine. I failed to get a bursary and was awarded as consolation the memorial prize for 'merit and service to the school'. This was somewhat surprising as I had had several brushes with the headmaster, leading to the suppression of one edition of the newspaper. Several years later his successor invited me to give the Founder's Day address to the schoool. My brother Michael, the year after I left, won the very prestigious Crichton bursary for medicine and went on to a glittering academic career at Edinburgh University with gold medals galore.

But mine was an incredibly rewarding four years, in which I was also involved in interschool activities through my Vice-Presidency of the Edinburgh Schools Citizenship Association, affiliated as a junior branch of the United Nations Association.

I wrote my first political editorial in support of William Douglas-Home, the Liberal candidate in the 1957 by-election in South Edinburgh, where Watson's was situated. I printed a letter the following week from a 'staunch Tory' deploring the inclusion of politics in a school newspaper. I also met someone who was to become a great friend and influence, John P. Mackintosh, then a young Labour candidate in Edinburgh, who impressively represented the Labour Party at our political evenings. The school newspaper reported a speech I made to a retiring master in which I made reference to the 'democratic principles' of the Literary Club: 'This provoked loud laughter. Members felt that, coming from dictator Steel, this was the height of hypocrisy.'

Meanwhile I was also taught to play the piano and – less successfully – the organ by Richard Telfer, later musical director of Scottish Opera. The school magazine the year after I was joint editor records in a snapshot profile:

As Junior President of the Literary Club he commands respect, as a school prefect he instils discipline, as a house prefect he rules, as Editor of *Ecce* he wields power and as vice-president of ESCA he exudes charm. A Liberal at heart, his enthusiasms embrace several seminaries: those of St George's, Lansdowne House and Leith Academy being especially favoured.

He is also something of a plutocrat, being the owner of a motor vehicle. After a period of hibernation this limousine again graces the boulevards of Edinburgh and it is understood that the motoring organizations have warned their members accordingly.

The references to the other three institutions were to girls' schools at all of whom I had passing, but not by today's standards serious, girlfriends – Watson's was at that time a boys-only school. The motor car was my first. One of my school friends, Michael and I had spent part of the previous summer serving as beaters for grouse on the Perthshire estate of the Duke of Roxburghe, whom I later encountered when in a more exalted capacity. We invested £15 of our wages in a 1932 Morris 8 which was unroadworthy, and it was on this pre-MOT test vehicle that I learned to drive. We eventually sold it for £25.

At this point, after eight years abroad, my parents were concerned about our divided family. Convinced that the emergency was ending and that, with the establishment of a united, interracial Presbyterian Church of East Africa, their work was done, they returned from Africa. After a brief sojourn in Edinburgh as locum-associate minister of St Cuthbert's, my father became minister of St Michael's, Linlithgow, about seventeen miles west of Edinburgh, and I went up to Edinburgh University.

In recounting my enjoyable five years (1957–62) at the University of Edinburgh, I had better begin with my academic career. When I left school I had little idea of what I wanted to do in later life and therefore what best to study. I thought briefly of going into the Church but felt – I think correctly – that I would have found it too cramping as an institution, though I like to think that my instinct for 'looking after the parish' found later outlet in constituency work. I thought about teaching, but I had concentrated on Latin and Greek and these did not seem likely expanding fields. 'Administration' in its vaguest sense appealed to me and the combined MA/LLB five-year course at Edinburgh seemed appropriate as combining a generality of subjects leading to specialization in law. Having acquired public speaking skills I thought I might try for the Scottish bar.

I entered cheerfully and with half-hearted diligence on the varied subjects which added up to an 'Ordinary' (i.e. general) Scottish Master of Arts degree: British History, Latin, Mathematics, Moral Philosophy, Civil Law, Constitutional Law and Jurisprudence. In only two of these – Mathematics and Moral Philosophy – did I show any academic prowess at all, achieving credits in both. In fact I became so interested in philosophy – especially Immanuel Kant and John Stuart Mill – that I decided to try to switch to an Honours MA four-year degree in the subject. While the University authorities were happy that I should do so, the student grant authority (then Edinburgh City Council) would not allow me the necessary five years of grant. Without it I could not finance my studies, so I had to stick to a legal course in which I was not really interested. My attempt to move was partly occasioned by advice from a leading QC that I should not contemplate becoming an advocate unless I had either private means or relations who were solicitors, or preferably both. Patently I had neither. Were I to seek to become a solicitor, I would have to combine my university studies with a poorly paid apprenticeship and lose my grant. I was therefore left completing a pair of degrees in which I had neither academic nor professional interest and for which I did the minimum of work consistent with obtaining the necessary passes. I graduated MA in 1960 and LLB in 1962. In the latter degree I included Scots Law, Mercantile Law, Accounting, Evidence and Pleading, Criminal Law, and Forensic Medicine. Of these only accounting was of some later obvious practical use, though Forensic Medicine was to come in handy during legislation on abortion.

Three teachers managed to leave some lasting influence. By a strange coincidence the lecturer in one term of modern British history – one of the few to draw a full theatre at 9 a.m. – was John P. Mackintosh. The Professor of Civil Law was T. B. Smith whose views on the role of Scots Law and the Act of Union are with me to this day; and Professor J. D. B. Mitchell instilled lessons on the British Constitution which remained genuinely useful in my parliamentary life. He later occupied the first chair in Britain (at Edinburgh from 1968) of European Institutions.

Freed of onerous academic demands – I think I was almost the only law student in my year *not* also in an office apprenticeship – I had plenty of spare time for university politics in both the party and student activity senses. Although they interwove, it will help to treat these separately.

The Scottish university students enjoy a right not available south of the border to a form of representation enshrined in statute. The Universities of Scotland Act of 1889 established:

regulations for the constitution and functions of a students' representative council in each university, which could frame regulations under which that council shall be entitled to make representations to the University Court.

Three first-year representatives fell to be elected from the first-year Arts faculty intake. I had opted for Edinburgh partly so that I could live at home, making up for the lost years, and partly because most of my friends from Edinburgh schools were going there. I made the somewhat arrogant assumption that if I stood I was bound to get elected because of the proportion of Edinburgh-based students who already knew me. I got my comeuppance and first lesson in campaigning. Two London students – Norman Hackett and Brian Warman – ran a vigorous joint campaign. I was elected, but only in third place. Norman has remained my longest-standing close friend ever since, while Brian was to become my Vice-President three years later. Although the elections were non-party, both were active members of the Labour Party, Norman being the nephew of George Brown and Brian later marrying the politician's daughter Frieda. Tragically Brian died of an asthmatic attack in his mid-thirties.

The three of us worked hard, Norman and Brian doing more on charities and publications. I was elected Assistant Secretary of the Students' Representative Council in my second year. In my third year I reverted to being an ordinary elected member while being President of the Liberal Club, and in my fourth year I was elected President. In that capacity I both ran the administration of the Council and chaired its meeting. I also donned my purple and gold gown of office and represented the university in debates in other Scottish universities, London and Dublin. Through these I met contemporary student debaters later to enter political life, especially from the powerful Glasgow school of debaters, including John Smith, John MacKay, Donald Dewar, David Miller and Menzies Campbell.

I unsuccessfully opposed the university's destruction of the fine Georgian George Square (Jo Grimond asserted in his memoirs that 'all the wreckers of football trains put together have never perpetrated such vandalism'); was the first student on a committee planning the new university hostels, the Pollock Halls; and had a serious row with the Principal and Vice-Chancellor, Sir Edward Appleton, over our rights to hold a ceremony in the McEwan Hall to install our elected Rector. Sir Edward backed down to the extent of permitting the ceremony without his presence and that of the Chancellor, the Duke of Edinburgh, who had both been subjected to flour bombs during the event three years previously, when the actor James Robertson-Justice had been boisterously but not riotously received. John Mackintosh, who was present at the angry meeting, said to me afterwards: 'The great thing about student politics is that it teaches you how to deal with rogues and villains.'

In pursuit of an orderly installation for Jo Grimond, I went round the university insisting – and getting away with it – that those thousands attending should wear suits and dresses and behave properly if the whole institution of the rectorship were not to be endangered by being brought into disrepute. In my farewell address to the SRC I urged student representation on the University Court, but did not welcome the advent of 'sabbatical' student politicians doing the job full-time – though as far as my professors were concerned, this is what I had done anyway.

I left my mark in one odd way: I was chairman of a committee which recommended a switch of our student publication from a fortnightly magazine to a weekly newspaper (of which I became features editor). It remains so to this day, in spite of fierce opposition at the time. I was also active in the Scottish Union of Students, being their international secretary, and attending the International Student Conference in Switzerland in 1960. I also took part in a bilateral student exchange for a fortnight at the University of Warsaw, stopping *en route* in Berlin at Easter, 1960. I think it was on that occasion that I travelled alone to visit the Communist-dominated International Union of Students' headquarters in Prague.

It was the most extraordinary, frightening train journey I have ever made. Stopping at the Czech frontier, I was aware of a military guard standing on the platform holding my passport. I was asked questions in various languages, the only one of which I recognized was German – but which I do not speak. I tried English, sign language and French. The only other language in my repertoire is Swahili. They indicated that I should remain in my compartment and the train moved off. I was alone, minus my passport, with two bench seats. I lay down on one and went to sleep. As daylight broke I woke up and was surprised to see that the corridor was full of the local peasantry, complete with various animals. I marvelled at their politeness in not entering my spacious compartment, until I attempted to leave it for a morning call of nature. I was locked in. For the next three hours I sat crosslegged, alone and passportless in the compartment while people crushed in the corridor ogled me through the glass. Fortunately someone in authority met the train in Prague and I was duly relieved.

In 1960 the first postwar delegation of Scottish students was chosen (about thirty of us) to go on a three-week exchange tour to the Soviet Union. We visited three centres: Moscow, Leningrad and Kiev. The company was interesting, including as it did Donald Dewar, now the Shadow Scottish Secretary; Donald MacCormick, now a presenter of BBC2's *Newsnight*; and George Reid, now with the Red Cross in Geneva but formerly SNP Member for Clackmannan and East Stirling. George was President of the SRC in St Andrews University and we struck up a lasting friendship. His wife Daphne by a strange coincidence was at school with Judy. The obligation to share cramped railway compartments and primitive hotel bedrooms in fours and sixes threw us together. The austerity of life in Russia was most striking. One of our number took a suitcase full of books, nylon stockings, drip-dry shirts and jazz records, from which he sold items at the black-market exchange rate late at night in his hotel room.

One evening George Reid encouraged me to leave the official programme and meet up with a Russian youth he had encountered who would show us the real night life of Moscow. We began at what passed for a nightclub, a rather bare place with white tablecloths and a string quartet. In the middle of the dance floor was a goldfish pond. I was invited to dance by a Russian girl who on the third time round this pool opened her mouth to reveal a smiling set of stainless steel teeth (rather like Oddjob in the James Bond film, *Goldfinger*) and said, 'I will give you my body for your sweater.' I was taken aback at this hitherto undisclosed attraction of Scottish knitwear. We made an excuse and left.

The next time I was on the loose in Moscow was with Michael Foot, leader of the Labour Party, but that must wait its place in this narrative.

As I've already mentioned I could only have got to university through a full student grant and my parents could not with four other children be expected to contribute to my upkeep. For all the luxuries of travel, running my motorbike and then car, I had to earn cash. I had a delightful variety of vacation jobs: driving Post Office vans in the Christmas rush; serving at Patrick Thompson's store in the January sales; and in the summer doing a number of jobs, including chauffeuring American tourists across Scotland – one of the perks of being in the SRC was grabbing the best jobs as they came in. For two summers I worked as a guide in a National Trust stately home, The Binns, near Linlithgow, the seventeenth-century home of the persecutor of my covenanting ancestors, 'Bloody Tam' Dalyell; by then it was that of a young man just down from Cambridge who was prospective Labour candidate for Roxburgh, Selkirk and Peebles, Tam Dalyell – now MP for Linlithgow. His mother was a wonderful and great eccentric who was very kind to me, though exasperated at my inability to clear up after her prodigious flower arranging. Tam appeared only occasionally, being busy campaigning in this faraway place – the Borders – of which I knew little.

My time in student administration grew parallel with my increasing interest in politics. On arrival at the university I attended a welcoming Conservative Club dance and went on to a more modest Liberal Club reception where two delightful girls, Isabel McIntyre and Janette Weatherhead, signed me up as a member. Thereafter I attended meetings regularly and learned more and more about Liberal policies from visiting speakers. I became more positively committed, being elected President of the Club in 1960. We became the largest political society in the university and won two mock elections in successive years in union debates. In 1958 and 1959 I took part in student trips to help by-election campaigns in East Aberdeenshire (Maitland Mackie was the candidate) and Galloway where the Hon. Simon Mackay, aged twenty-four, was standing. Now Lord Tanlaw, he was to became another lifetime friend. George Inglis, a minister's son from Dumfriesshire, was our Vice-President. He also had an ancient Morris 8 and we filled these two cars with our friends and sallied forth. George, like Norman Hackett, has been an internationally intermittent but close friend of mine over the years. We also attended the Scottish Liberal Party conferences and plagued our elders with resolutions on disarmament, homosexuality, capital punishment and other 'radical' topics. John MacKay was President of the Glasgow University Liberals. He became prospective Liberal candidate for Argyll and later a minister in the Scottish Office.

In the 1960 union mock election which I won for the Liberals, Norman Hackett stood for Labour and Allan Macartney (my 1983 general election opponent) for the SNP. My speeches and the subsequent Liberal 'Government' programme contained familiar themes – ending the independent nuclear deterrent while keeping the Polaris base, entry to the EEC, co-partnership in industry, home rule for Scotland and increased aid to overseas countries.

Looking at the list of those appearing on the Liberal benches in retrospect shows they were a remarkable collection: Russell Johnston, now Sir Russell, deputy leader of the Social and Liberal Democrats, had returned after national service to teacher training in the Faculty of Education – he has remained my most steadfast political friend and colleague ever since; Michael Shea, another close friend to this day, followed me as Liberal President, went into the Foreign Office and became the Queen's Press Secretary; Judy MacGregor became my wife; another who as a student served a few weeks at Her Majesty's pleasure for fiddling his post office savings book went on in later career to serve longer for defrauding his employer of a large amount; and another has since changed sex. An astonishing team, as I say.

When I retired from the Liberal Club Presidency in 1960 the student newspaper reported my last speech as 'President pulls left'. I attacked the Labour Party, especially the Labour Club President who was later to become nationally known in the Socialist Worker's Party, and declared: 'The emergence of a social democratic party may well come from a union of the Liberal Party and the Labour Right.' This was twenty years before the birth of the SDP.

By this time I had come to know Jo Grimond, whose election as Rector of the University by the students I organized. I also served on the executive of the Scottish Liberal Party and during my final year was adopted as prospective parliamentary candidate for the Pentlands division of Edinburgh at the age of twenty-two. The seat had been uncontested by us since 1950. In 1959 I had addressed my first public election meeting in support of William Douglas-Home in South Edinburgh constituency in a classroom at South Morningside school.

It was Jo Grimond who effectively matched me up with Judy. She had arranged the seventy-fifth anniversary dinner of the SRC and I was impressed. I had known her since her first year when she also sold the student magazine outside our civil law class and then sat in the back row. Later she was elected to represent the Law Faculty on the SRC. She left her mark on the university by suggesting and carrying out the production of a Law Faculty scarf worn by students to this day. But I had not previously been attracted to her because she was something of a rebel in the SRC and she regarded me as the establishment; nor was she attracted to me, her affections being engaged elsewhere.

At a private dinner Jo sat us next to each other. I found I liked her after all and she asked for a lift back to her flat. The following weekend at a student conference in St Andrews, George Reid invited me to a party and I asked her to come with me. Thereafter we didn't so much fall in love as grow in love. She had had previous attachments to the SNP and CND but had joined the Liberals after listening to a speech by Russell Johnston. She spent many hours canvassing for me in Pentlands, and we became engaged, marrying in the autumn of 1962.

That was when I finally graduated. Not knowing what career to follow, I readily accepted an offer from George Mackie to join the Scottish Liberal Party Office as assistant secretary up to the anticipated general election the following year. I had a degree, a wife and a salary of £890 a year, and Judy had a salary as a legal assistant of £750. We went to live in a rented cottage on the outskirts of Edinburgh. I was a man blissfully happy but with career prospects vague, to say the least.

2

BY-ELECTION
'It's Boy David'

J udy and I were married in the autumn of 1962 in Dunblane Cathedral. Her father, who had been awarded the CBE for his forestry work in West Africa, had a smallholding just outside Dunblane where he grew Christmas trees, kept livestock and carried on a forestry consultancy. The cathedral minister and my father jointly officiated and about a hundred guests (mostly from our large families) attended. My brother Michael was my best man. I blew my entire savings of £60 on our brief honeymoon in Skye. Thereafter we returned via various Liberal events with Jeremy Thorpe in the north of Scotland. Judy always claimed that this let her see what our married life was going to be like – a procession of Liberal rallies and bazaars.

As prospective candidate for Pentlands I worked very hard. The constituency association was small, so I set the target of fighting the four municipal wards which made up the parliamentary division. For Merchiston I persuaded a well-known Edinburgh architect, Robert Smith, who was in bed with mumps at the time, to stand and I drafted his election address. In the aftermath of the Orpington by-election, he won. We fought the other three wards, but for the safe Labour ward of Sighthill where we had only two or three members we could find no willing candidate. So Judy 'volunteered' and she polled a respectable 33 per cent in a straight fight. Outside the municipal election period we trudged round every part of the constituency delivering leaflets inviting people to public meetings in each community school, rarely attended by more than a dozen or twenty souls. I wrote regular letters to the *Scotsman* and the *Edinburgh Evening News*. In addition I had my duties as Assistant Secretary helping to gear up the party machine for the election. This took me all over Scotland to constituency meetings, one of which was the AGM in 1963 of a constituency where I had never before set foot: Roxburgh, Selkirk and Peebles.

In October 1963 Prime Minister Harold Macmillan suddenly resigned and the Earl of Home became, via the Tory 'magic circle' of consultation, Prime Minister. A by-election was about to begin in Kinross and West Perthshire and the Tory candidate, George Younger, stood down at the last minute to enable the Earl, who had renounced his peerage, to enter the House of Commons.

This was good news for us because we had a splendid local candidate, Alasdair Duncan Millar, who in the end came a creditable second. But the by-election was turned into a media circus for the world's press and television. The morning press conferences were larger than the evening public meetings. In the first week my boss, the Secretary of the Scottish Liberal Party, Arthur Purdom, who was acting as agent in the by-election, was threatened by a heart attack and I was dispatched to run the rest of the campaign.

It was a glorious shambles. The constituency was widely scattered and we had little organization. Robin Day of the BBC led a posse of distinguished Fleet Street journalists and assorted television crews, including some from Japan, at the morning press conferences, where I cheerfully tried to persuade them that we had a chance of beating the Prime Minister. It was my first chance to meet the political media. In the evenings I decided to urge the local campaigners and helpers who came in to forget about trying to cover all the scattered villages and concentrate on maintaining at least the appearance of a campaign in the towns where 80 per cent of the electorate actually lived. Willie Rushton stood as an independent on behalf of *Private Eye*. At a large and entertaining eve-of-poll meeting Rushton urged his followers to vote for our candidate and ended up with forty-five votes. At the count we were reasonably pleased with the outcome and I met Alec Douglas-Home for the first time.

This event was followed a month later by a by-election in Dumfriesshire. Again I was dispatched to manage the campaign. Even more than at Kinross we were making bricks without straw. The local Liberals kept reporting good results from Eskdalemuir – with about ninety people on the roll – while lacking canvassing organization in Dumfries burgh with 18,000 electors. Again I tried to concentrate on the towns, but we were hopelessly overwhelmed. Simon Mackay had lent me his enormous and expensive loudspeaker from his neighbouring Galloway constituency. As I travelled back from some remote outpost late at night driving rather fast, the wind blowing straight into the huge trumpet shape of the loudspeaker tore the entire contraption including my roofrack off the car and deposited it on the A74 where it smashed to pieces. This was not the only disaster of the campaign.

We had a very pleasant and worthy but nervous local candidate who on one memorable occasion made the mistake of asking George Mackie his opinion on how he had performed at the previous night's mass public meeting of fifteen. 'All right,' said George, 'but I do wish you wouldn't keep hopping from one foot to the other as though you had just shat your breeches.' As a junior employee I felt this was not the best approach to instilling confidence in our candidate. He lost his deposit. But the hard practical experience of fighting in these two rural seats was to stand me in good stead.

My job at Scottish Party Headquarters was thoroughly enjoyable, but it was not without its setbacks. One year I was to set up a fund-raising tour of Scottish cities by Kenny Ball's jazz band. It was a modest success except at Edinburgh where we had hired, at enormous expense, not just the band but the huge Palais dance hall. None of us realized that in those days it was illegal to advertise a public dance with a bar. We did so, with the result that the licence was cancelled. Those who came, soon left. The band played to about two dozen people. At the end of the week I had to meet George Mackie off a train at Waverley Station in Edinburgh. He was expecting to be told of the vast sum now swelling the party coffers. I had to break it to him that we had made a loss.

On another occasion I was detailed to drive Emlyn Hooson, QC, MP, on a journey across Scotland in my own car from St Andrews to Paisley where he was addressing Liberal events. In a raging snowstorm we stopped for petrol at Dunfermline. The snow had settled on the pumps and by accident I took on board a load of diesel. We proceeded only a further 200 yards. After two hours spent in a dingy local hotel while efforts were made to analyse the problem, we abandoned the car and with difficulty persuaded a local garage to hire out a substitute. We arrived considerably behind schedule in Paisley.

In the late summer of 1964 with an election expected at any time I acted as aide (or 'bagman' in party jargon) to the leader, on his tour of the highland constituencies. Having done the job for Jo Grimond I know what I put several subsequent bagmen through as leader, except that in those days local organization was rudimentary and it was the aide's job to co-ordinate travel, halls, publicity, accommodation etc. Great effort had been put by the Party into these highland seats. Russell Johnston was building up Inverness and George Mackie, Caithness and Sutherland, which they both indeed won in the 1964 election.

Uncertainty loomed large in two other seats. In Ross and Cromarty we had adopted a sixty-one-year-old farmer called Alasdair Mackenzie, who was unknown to the rest of the party but was a considerable figure in the county. He was a Gaelic speaker and his command of spoken English was not all that great. Apart from his radicalism, stemming from opposition to the Tory highland clearances, the rest of his Liberalism was an unknown quantity. Part of my job was to make the financial appeals at the rallies and pocket the collection to defray the expenses of the visit. When we got to Dingwall Town Hall and met Alasdair for the first time, there was a problem. He refused to make the supporting speech, saying I should do that and he would make the financial appeal at the end. Jo and I both protested that he was the candidate. He was as stubborn as a mule. I forget in what order we addressed the crowded hall of 400 or so, but Alasdair spoke for barely three minutes leaving Jo to do the rest. But of course there were questions and the Tories seized their chance. 'I'd like to address my question to the candidate,' a pukka voice declared. 'What is the Liberal policy on defence?' I clutched my chair. Jo looked as though he wished he had never come. Alasdair rose slowly to his feet, cleared his throat noisily and asserted in that halting Highland lilt: 'The Lib-er-al Par-ty will de-fend Bri-tain, the Common-wealth, and the free world.' He sat down to thunderous applause. He won the seat from the Conservatives at the election a few weeks later with a majority of 1,407. I was to think back ruefully many years later to that classically simple and accurate response to questions on defence.

The next anxious moment came on our flight to the Western Isles where our candidate was a bright young local lad, Donny B. Macleod, who was later to become a noted television personality not just in Scotland but throughout Britain in his Birmingham-based *Pebble Mill at One* programme. He died still tragically young a few years ago. Again, he was unknown to the Party.

As the plane taxied to a halt at Stornoway Airport I saw to my satisfaction a waiting photographer obviously from the *Stornoway Gazette*. Jo preceded me down the steps, I carrying the bags dutifully two paces behind. I looked anxiously for anyone resembling the expectation of our candidate. At this point Jo was greeted warmly by a man at the foot of the steps and the *Stornoway Gazette* posed them for pictures. He was Malcolm Macmillan, the Labour MP whom we had come to help oust. He was boarding the plane for the next island stop. I searched even more anxiously but in vain for our man. The media got into its car and left. Everybody else collected their bags and left. I was getting frantic with Jo putting on one of his resigned 'what have you cocked up now?' looks that I was later to bestow on others.

Eventually I admitted defeat. We started to get on to the ramshackle airport bus to go into town. A car screeched to a halt and out got Donny B. muttering a casual apology and cheerfully bidding us enter. I was furious, and when we got to our hotel took him aside: 'You bloody fool, we got the leader coming all this way at vast expense to help you and now all that will appear in your local paper is your opponent welcoming him to the island – what happened to you?'

'Och,' came the memorable reply in surprised tones, 'but the plane was on time.' I could have strangled him. I forgave him later only because he made a marvellous speech to the assembled crowd in the town hall that night. Many a time later in TV studios he would tease me about my ill-temper on that occasion. 'Never forget,' he said, 'in Gaelic there is no such word as *mañana* because we have nothing to convey such a sense of urgency.'

Over the winter of 1963, I'd had approaches from members of the Roxburgh, Selkirk and Peebles Liberal Association to abandon Pentlands and become the candidate for the Borders. It was regarded, optimistically, as a winnable seat: the major part of it, Roxburgh and Selkirk (the boundaries had been redrawn in 1955), had been held, briefly, by a Liberal in the 1950–51 Parliament. Even in the Party's worst days, our candidate had never dropped below second place, though by 1959 the gap between Tory and Liberal had widened and that between Liberal and Labour narrowed. In part, this was due to the effectiveness of Tam Dalyell as the Labour candidate. During the summer, as I showed visitors round his ancestral home of the Binns as a lowly student guide, Tam bicycled enthusiastically around the three rolling counties. His election address contained a list of all the communities he'd visited in this way.

Tam's efforts were in vain, however, and the fight for the Borders seat lay firmly between Tory and Liberal. The pressure to move was strong. The prospective Liberal candidate had just resigned: the Hon. James Tennant of the Glen, half-brother of Lord Glenconner's heir, Colin Tennant, had too many business interests. The parting was to mutual satisfaction. I was reluctant. Even apart from the two years' work I'd put in in Pentlands in building up the association, I felt very much a city product and not up to the task of representing rural interests. The by-elections in Kinross & West Perthshire and Dumfriesshire radically changed my views on that. I realized that what people needed was simply competent representation: the ability to listen, to assimilate, and to present a case. I had also found myself enormously attracted to the small towns and villages of Dumfriesshire, some of them so like their neighbours across the county boundaries in the Borders seat.

There was another potential candidate for the Borders seat, a man in his forties, John Matthew, who had impressed the selection committee: or, to be more exact, headhunting committee. They wanted me, but would accept him. But he was shortlisted for the post of bursar at Winchester School, and if offered the job would not be available as candidate.

It seems extraordinary, now, how desperately Judy and I hoped that he would not get the Winchester job, and so would end our dilemma. He did: and the dilemma continued. The Roxburgh, Selkirk and Peebles Liberals muttered that if I didn't fight for them, they might leave the seat without a candidate.

We met the delegation in the bar of the North British Hotel in Edinburgh. Andrew Haddon had been agent to the victorious Liberal in the old constituency in 1950, and at subsequent elections. He was then around sixty – in fact, I suppose they all were. He divided his time between his legal practice in Hawick and his farm in Denholm, and was and is a fount of detailed knowledge on every election campaign in the Borders since the 1930s.

Will Stewart owned a woollen mill in Galashiels. It was the only independently owned woollen mill in the town, run by his daughter and son-in-law. Jack Bryce farmed deep in the hills beyond Kelso and near the Border, and Willie Pate, who could talk with bitterness about the humiliation of the old feeing (i.e. hiring) fairs, owned farms around Galashiels. He was a great warrior, locked in desperate, unforgiving combat with the laird of Gala, Christopher Scott, also an active Liberal.

They were not just a formidable quartet: they were an attractive one. But the association itself was shaky and moribund, and they were in full agreement that many changes would need to be made. If I was going to become the candidate, I said, it would have to be on the basis that I would fight at least two elections: in that timescale, given good back-up, progress for the party nationally, and good luck, then it was a winning proposition. Riddle Dumble, who since 1970 has been my agent, became Constituency Chairman.

Telling the association in Pentlands that I was moving was a miserable business. I'd worked with good people, we'd all put in a lot of time and energy, and now they were going to have to start looking for a new candidate at short notice. George Mackie came with me to meet them, and received a censure motion at the Scottish Party Executive for his pains.

Early in January 1964 we drove down to Galashiels to the adoption meeting. How well we've got to know that forty-mile stretch of road since then. Judy complained that I was so self-effacing at the meeting that she thought they'd decide against adopting me, even at this stage. But despite this, the necessary motions were passed and my relationship with the Borders began.

The sitting MP was a man in his early sixties, Commander C. E. M. Donaldson. No one ever called him by his Christian name. He had won the seat back from the Liberals in 1951 against expectations including those of the Tories, who had hoped that the Earl of Dalkeith would eventually stand in their interest, as his uncle and father had before. Donaldson was a mild, unimpressive man, and I have to say, an easy target. He had lost credibility in the constituency over one issue above all: after speaking locally against the Beeching Report (which proposed axing the Waverley railway line, right through the Borders) he then voted in its favour in Parliament. He taught me one thing: he never responded to my constant challenges throughout 1964, and refused to share a public platform with me. Both were maddening to a young candidate.

Donaldson lived on his parliamentary salary, which at the time had just been raised from £1,750 to £3,250. He lived in London, and was never offered so much as a cottage in the constituency by any of the Tory lairds or farmers. There were strong moves to deselect him: Hector Monro, after losing the nomination for the Dumfries by-election, was approached to replace him. Fortunately for me, such moves came to nothing.

There were markedly fewer Liberal lairds and farmers than Tory ones, but such as there were had warm hearts. Before long we were offered accommodation in the Borders by Christopher Scott. There was the longer-term prospect of a three-roomed cottage by the Tweed; but in the meantime, to tide us over the summer, he could let us have a large farmhouse that had become empty.

In April we gave up the tenancy of our Edinburgh cottage and moved to Hollybush, about a mile out of Galashiels. The furniture from the cottage looked somewhat lost in it. When it was augmented by £16-worth of assorted items from a local auction sale, we managed to furnish four of its dozen or so rooms. The Party allowed me two days a week in the constituency; Judy continued working in Edinburgh. Since she didn't drive, this meant a daily bicycle trip to the station and back to catch the Edinburgh train – a twelve-hour day before setting out with me to do whatever evening function we were involved in.

So the spring and summer were spent getting to know the Borders. In the villages, I'd make three basic calls: at the manse, the schoolhouse, and the village shop. It's a reflection of how times have changed that nowadays this method of getting to know, and be known, would no longer work. As parishes have united, manses have been sold; and though village schools have on the whole been maintained, it's often the case that the schoolhouse has been sold and the headteacher commutes from the nearest town. There are fewer village shops.

I remember my first visit to one of these villages, Ettrick Bridge, because I was taken into a house to meet a bedridden lady in her late eighties, Mrs Macgowan. I was introduced as the new Liberal candidate. 'I'm so pleased to meet you, young man,' she said, 'because my brother Sandy won the

34

Border burghs for Mr Gladstone.' True enough, her brother, A. L. Brown, a wool manufacturer in Galashiels, had won the old Border burghs constituency as Liberal candidate in 1886.

In the towns I took part in the great Border traditions of the Common Ridings, which are both a means of expressing commemoration of the past and an affirmation of a present sense of community. Shepherded about them by local Liberals, I became entranced; throughout the years since then the summer weekends are marked off to give priority to them.

I had been lucky in gaining the extra time of the spring and summer. At the time of my adoption, it was expected that the 1964 election might be held in the spring. In April 1964 Sir Alec Douglas-Home announced that the parliament would run its full term until the autumn. It was just what I needed. Throughout the summer I was conscious all the time of gaining ground. But there was a long way to go. I persuaded university friends to join us in rural leafleting.

In Hawick, we heard that a local journalist had switched to the Party. She came to a Liberal coffee evening. We were warned by a longstanding worthy: 'You don't want to speak to *her*: she's a turncoat.'

'But,' I replied, 'we need to find five thousand turncoats if we're going to win this seat.'

When the election was announced, the spirit was good; but the active troops were still few and far between. Judy had three weeks' annual holiday: a week of it had gone earlier; she could only take two for the election. She never got as far as canvassing: she was needed to man the phone in the headquarters, and to do such mundane tasks as folding election addresses into envelopes. At night we charged round 1,700 square miles of the constituency as I addressed over fifty meetings. The supporting speakers were longstanding Liberals from the 1950 election and some of my university friends; I'm not sure which were more disastrous. I once arrived late at one meeting to find the audience had had two half-hour stints on proportional representation, and another where my London friend Norman Hackett had begun his answer to a questioner by saying, 'My old darling, that's a load of rubbish.' At both these meetings I arrived to a somewhat frosty reception.

Sometimes there were as many as twenty miles between meetings. Will Stewart and Andrew Haddon took it in turns to drive me, Andrew being the slower of the two. Once, along the road past Hermitage Castle in the dark, we got slower and slower in his great Armstrong-Siddeley as he recited the whole of Scott's version of the great ballad of Johnnie Armstrong. After we got back from the meetings, Judy and I would don duffle coats, mix a flour-and-water paste, and set off for a spot of illegal flyposting.

35

It was a next-day count. We spent election night at Hollybush in despair at the near-misses up and down the country. Yet I must admit that despite the despair, despite the fact that another Labour defeat would have hastened the realignment, despite my lack of enthusiasm for Harold Wilson, there was a sense of excitement at the prospect of a change of direction. Labour had won by five seats.

As for myself, I had no fantasies about a surprise win. My aim at this election had been to reduce the Tory majority by half – i.e. to bring it down to 5,000. As we walked into the count, we had no evidence of canvassing returns: only a gut feeling. 'I think,' I said to Judy, 'we might have got it down to about 3,000.'

I was being conservative. At the end of the day the result was

C. Donaldson (Conservative)	18,924
D. Steel (Liberal)	17,185
R. K. Murray (Labour)	7,007
A. J. C. Kerr (SNP)	1,093
Conservative majority	1,739

In his speech Commander Donaldson said: 'I would like to thank my Labour and Scottish Nationalist opponents for the gentlemanly way in which they have conducted the campaign.' He did not mention me.

Later in the day came the news that lifted our spirits: all three Highland seats had been won by the Liberals – Inverness by Russell Johnston, Ross and Cromarty by Alasdair Mackenzie, and Caithness and Sutherland by George Mackie. My own result was the next closest call in Scotland, and one of the bigger swings in the country to us.

My contract with the party was due to finish after the election. I was anxious to get into television, partly for its own sake and partly as a step forwards politically. I was lucky in securing a short-term contract with BBC Scotland on a new Scottish current affairs programme, *Checkpoint*. Magnus Magnusson south to BBC1's *Tonight* and everyone on the programme climbed one rung up.

We moved out of the carpetless grandeur of Hollybush to a cottage, also rented from Christopher Scott, right down on the River Tweed. The branch line from Galashiels to Selkirk passed our front door, but by then only the last few goods trains chugged along it.

Meantime the Border Tories acted with ruthless speed. As Commander Donaldson confided miserably to the newly elected MP for Ross and Cromarty, the pressure on him to stand down had become too strong to resist. He was obliged to issue a statement declaring that he would not contest the next election 'for personal reasons'. As it turned out, he could have been spared that.

The election was six weeks behind us, and I was in the studio for only my third broadcast when someone from the newsroom shouted 'Hey, David, the man you stood against at the election's died.' 'Ah yes,' I said, 'pull the other one.' It was only when I saw the typed script from the newsreader's hands that I believed it. Donaldson, who had been in perfectly good health at the election, had gone into St Thomas's Hospital for a minor operation. Under the anaesthetic, his heart failed. (In the by-election, the Tories frequently used the line, '*Poor* Commander Donaldson was a dying man.' But his retiral statement had not used the convenient excuse of ill-health.)

I refused to make any statement other than a message of condolence to Mrs Donaldson until the funeral was over. I did, and do, find premature speculation about by-election prospects after the death of an MP totally disgraceful. There is time for that in the weeks and months ahead: surely a family deserves honour paid to a memory at least until the funeral?

But my public reticence did not mean a lack of private action. The BBC told me that, since I was a candidate, I could not continue appearing weekly on television: this was before I had even been officially re-adopted. But I was on a six months' contract, which effectively meant that the BBC were forced to pay me and I became a full-time candidate. I did not have to ask Judy to give up her Edinburgh job. She had always been much more interested in politics than in law, and the prospect of working together full-time on the campaign was infinitely more appealing than continued travelling to Edinburgh for the daily office routine. She resigned her solicitor's post.

My re-adoption went without a hitch – almost. Archie Macdonald, who had been the MP in 1950–51, had, after much to-ing and fro-ing, refused the Association's invitation to stand in 1955. Now, however, he indicated that he would be willing to take up the standard again, and the young man who had achieved a creditable showing at the election could be his agent! His idea got no further than the elders of the Association to whom he put it forward.

In the October election, the Labour candidate had been Ronald King Murray, who later became MP for Leith and Lord Advocate. His share of the poll, against a national Labour tide, had fallen. The Borderers were amongst the vanguard of the realignment of the anti-Conservative vote. He, too, was re-adopted, though I warned him privately when we met by chance in Edinburgh that I was determined to win and in doing so to ensure that Labour lost their deposit.

The SNP candidate in 1964 was a total, brilliant eccentric. Anthony Kerr lived in Jedburgh, talked with a plummy Harrovian accent, could speak fourteen languages, wrote endless letters to newspapers, travelled around the countryside on a motor scooter and resembled a benign walrus; he had attracted just over a thousand votes. The SNP decided not to put up a candidate at the by-election. Anthony had other ideas. So did some other people: in a tight squeeze, his votes might make a difference. The day before nominations closed, £150 in used notes was pushed through his letter box – it was widely believed that his benefactor was not of his own political persuasion. He stood as an Independent Nationalist, now that he had precisely the sum needed for his deposit.

The Tory shortlist contained the names of two aspirants who later became MPs elsewhere – Nicky Fairbairn, who had just fought Central Edinburgh, and John Corrie, a young local farmer. But the hot favourite, and the choice, was Robin McEwen of Marchmont in Berwickshire. The Tories were euphoric at the adoption meeting. McEwen seemed to have every necessary attribute: wealth, a Border pedigree (his father had been MP for Berwickshire), intelligence, a beautiful wife and four young children. He had even been an escort of Princess Margaret, and he had contested East Edinburgh, solid Labour territory, in the Tory cause in October with no discredit. We were faintly depressed – he seemed to be the strongest candidate they could have picked.

Christopher Scott, who had known him since school, was more sanguine. I can't remember if he actually said that Robin McEwen wouldn't stay the course, but that was the impression. 'He won't *do*,' he assured us blithely. 'I know him, and I know Galashiels, and I tell you he won't *do*.'

Understanding of the Borders was something I had begun to acquire during the months before the '64 general election. The bulk of the electorate, 80 per cent or so, were in the eight mainly industrial towns, each with strong mutual rivalry partly derived from rugby and partly maintained by the different Common Ridings and festivals. The Border folk are very down to earth. As an example, I was asked by the Liberal MPs if I could acquire a fresh salmon to be presented to Lady Violet Bonham-Carter on her elevation to the peerage as Baroness Asquith in 1964. I was to put it on the night train. I went into the bar of the Galashiels Liberal Club and made inquiries. I was assured that if I slipped a fiver to one of the regulars he would be able to arrange immediate supply. He assured me that several fish were lying conveniently in the Gala Water tributary of the Tweed as it ran under a bridge in the town. I was to call at his house later in the evening, and go round the back to his garden shed – a fresh silvery fish would be lying there in a carrier basket. I then made the mistake of telling him why I wanted it. He looked aghast: 'Ye canna give the Baroness a fish wi' a cleek mark on it.' 'Nonsense,' I said, 'she won't know what a cleek mark looks like.' 'Aye, right enough.' The fish duly arrived with the mark of the wire noose visible to the discerning eye. I took it to the station, and next morning it was presented to her ladyship at a small ceremony in the House of Lords.

Apart from getting to know the Border people, I also continued a serious study of the depopulation problems of the area, spending days reading in the library in Edinburgh. I produced my analysis in the first of many political publications: *Boost for the Borders*, a twenty-page pamphlet (1964) modelled on the successful example of my colleagues' similar work in the Highlands. It received much attention locally and throughout Scotland with its well-argued case for development-area status to include areas not just of crude unemployment but of depopulation. In addition to the national issues raised in the 1964 general election, it was to form the basic policy appeal for the by-election.

Donaldson had died in December; the by-election writ wasn't moved till the beginning of March 1965. By then the party organization was in shape; my agent was Arthur Purdom, who'd been my boss at Scottish Liberal Party Headquarters and from whom I'd taken over running the Kinross and West Perthshire by-election. He was in bullish form. 'What this party needs,' he said, 'is fewer brilliant seconds and more mediocre firsts.'

Judy canvassed in the villages and most of the old peoples' homes. She *still* couldn't drive – though she had at least sat and failed her test by now. But there were enough drivers, enough canvassers, enough leaflet distributors. Hollybush, devoid of furniture, was made over as a student hostel. To this day there is a young man somewhere with the middle name of 'Roxburgh' who was conceived on the premises. The Douglas Hotel in Galashiels became the journalists' camp. At Gala House, Christopher and Anne Scott laid on a nightly supper and a roaring log fire for the MPs and candidates who'd poured in to help. There was an especially strong contingent all the way from Devon and Cornwall.

'The by-election where every night is like Hogmanay' ran one headline, and indeed there was some truth in this. The journalists were enchanted by the Borders. They were unanimous on one thing – never had they seen such packed or lively meetings. In one night at three meetings George Brown spoke to more people than actually voted Labour. All the Liberal MPs came to speak for me, but one: I had expressly refused to have Peter Bessell, MP for Bodmin. I don't know why. I didn't know him – it was a sixth sense.

I am amazed now at the temerity with which I laid down orders for the meetings. No matter how illustrious the supporting speaker, he was given the instructions. They were, as I remember them: no attacks on Sir Alec Douglas-

Home, no attacks on the Labour candidate (or for that matter on the Nationalist Anthony Kerr); no speaker to speak after me; no one but me to answer
questions. There was an unwritten rule that the supporting speaker should
endeavour not to outshine the candidate – one who signally failed to conform
to this was John MacKay. Now chief executive of the Scottish Tory Party,
he was the most fiery and radical of the young candidates. 'If I'd brought my
bagpipes,' was one of his jokes, 'I'd be able to play McEwen's lament, and
King Murray's farewell to his deposit.'

There were two especial towers of strength. There was John Bannerman,
who had fought so many gallant fights in the darkest days of Liberalism. On
no less than three occasions he had lost elections by under a couple of thousand
votes. At Inverness in 1955, he appeared to have won. The candidates and
agents had shaken hands, the declaration was about to be made, and – 'Hang
on,' said a depute returning officer, 'we haven't counted the postal votes.'
And John had lost, not won, by 966 votes.

He was a special favourite in the Borders because of his stature as a rugby
hero. In the Borders, as in Wales, rugby is a classless religion. John's sporting
analogies were apt. The week after an exciting finish to the Calcutta Cup
match, he advised the audience how to conduct themselves on polling day:
'And if you see a Tory coming in injury time – blow your whistle.'

The other person was Jeremy Thorpe. After his scheduled visits early in
the campaign, he returned at the end of the second week. It was partly that
he scented victory, and couldn't keep away: but he also knew the lassitude
that sets in in mid-campaign. He came all over the countryside with us, was
a regular supporting speaker, and simply entertained us between meetings.
Many years later, I discovered that it was at this time that he began to come
under pressure from Norman Scott, but his high humour and effervescence
never betrayed the difficulties that were beginning for him.

The Tories too had brought in the big guns, as the newspapers put it.
Judy, delighted, saw the historical parallel 500 years before. 'James II was
killed at the siege of Roxburgh by a big gun backfiring,' she told me, and I
used it. It was an apt parallel – the Tory big guns were firing off all over the
place. The late Sir Gerald Nabarro said it was no wonder there was depopulation: the previous Lord Napier and Ettrick had fourteen servants, now the
present incumbent was down to one.

Robin McEwen had had a gilded life. He was used to being in authority,
and not used to having that authority questioned. Faced at first with genuine
questioners putting reasonable queries on the Tory record or policies, he
replied antagonistically or imperiously. As verbal aggro built up, his London
barrister's intellect was no match for the cross-examination of the down-to-

earth Borderers. The word went out; not from headquarters, but from mouth to mouth – Tory baiting was a good blood sport. Squads of questioners went from hall to hall. Under the pressure, McEwen's health gave way and he retired to Marchmont while his wife Brigid gallantly continued canvassing and read his speeches.

As the climax came, the goodwill and excitement built up. Cars and council house windows sported yellow dayglo posters. The blue-clad trees of the big Tory estates, as I observed at meetings, did not have votes. In an excess of confidence, we placed our entire meagre savings of a few hundred pounds on a bet. We decided that if I didn't win, we were going to have to start our lives from scratch again, so we might as well be thorough. We would be both unemployed and broke.

James Graham, Marquis of Montrose, put it thus:

> He either fears his fate too much,
> Or his deserts are small,
> That puts it not unto the touch
> To win or lose it all.

I'd fallen out with the BBC as well during the campaign. On Arthur Purdom's advice, I'd refused to take part in an election special, thereby depriving my rivals of face-to-face camera exposure. I think it was probably a mistake: it severed relations between them and the Party for some time, and they refused to cover the count, predicting a Tory victory. I'd have liked the footage.

The final meetings were packed. The last one, traditionally, was in the Roxy cinema at Kelso after the evening film. (In general elections, we used to drive to Kelso with the ten o'clock newscaster on the car radio saying, 'The election campaign is over: the last speech has been made.' And we'd shout at it in glee, 'No it hasn't – you've forgotten the Roxy!' The platform is only two feet wide in front of the cinema screen. George Mackie spoke. John Bannerman spoke. I spoke. The chairman called for questions. A woman rose in her seat, possibly tired and emotional. 'There's just one thing I want to ken,' she said. 'Will ye be better than oor last MP? 'Cause he'd chewing gum stuck to the erse o' his troosers.'

We awoke to snow. My heart sank. Would we get the votes out? A more immediate problem turned out to be: would the voters get into the polling stations? Our friends who were official presiding officers at Newcastleton, twenty miles south of Hawick, ran into a snowdrift at 5 a.m. At 9 a.m. there was an angry queue outside Newcastleton school, and a frantic returning officer.

All over, we saw that our organization was effective and enthusiastic, while the Tories' was patchy. Their most efficient, run from a luxury caravan, was in a tiny village in the North of Peeblesshire. 'I must admit,' said Jeremy Thorpe, 'we have to hand it to them. They may have had no tellers in Hawick (the largest town in the constituency) but we'd better concede Romanno Bridge.' One scare during polling day came with the result at lunchtime of the Saffron Walden by-election held the previous day. The Liberal candidate lost his deposit, and the Tories quickly distributed pre-prepared placards to most polling stations with this news.

'Do you think it will affect us?' I asked one visiting party official from Northern Ireland.

'Saffron Walden, Saffron Walden,' he replied. 'They'll think it's just some kind of haggis.'

There were seventy-seven polling stations to cover then. Judy and I had decided to try to cover each one between the two of us. We've always managed to keep this up. Once we checked our joint day's mileage: it was 450 miles.

During polling day of the by-election, the news came to me that my grandfather had died. He had been ailing for some months, but his mind was as active as ever, and his interest in the by-election enormous. As we sat around the Scotts' log fire in the respite between the closing of the polls and going to the count, tired and confident in the knowledge of a high poll and good polling-day arrangements, it saddened the day.

Jeremy Thorpe, with his usual panache, managed to get both himself and John Bannerman into the count without passes. For John, mentor and inspirer of so many of us, it promised to be the first time he had been at a victorious count. Both Judy and I felt the same: a regret and almost a guilt that there should be coming to me, aged twenty-six and at only my second attempt, the prize, so much deserved, which had eluded him so long. (It was a special joy that his daughter Ray snatched Argyll and Bute from the Tory John MacKay in 1987.) But in that great heart there was no corner for envy or even wistfulness. 'If this laddie makes it,' he said to Jeremy, tears rolling down his face, 'it will all have been worth while.'

From the beginning it was clear we had made it. The crucial factor was the Labour vote: if I had managed to erode it still further, we were in with a chance. Voting patterns were much less fluid than they are now; but King Murray's piles of voting papers were clearly below deposit level, and that, coupled with the high turnout of 84 per cent, meant a certain win.

We sat quietly at the side of Jedburgh Town Hall, a bit shaky, and very emotional. The McEwens arrived, Brigid conservatively dressed in a dark blue silk coat and matching hat; they were cheerful and confident. With a shock I realized that no one had prepared them for the result. Had the Tory machine not forecast it? Or had they been lulled by the *Scotsman* headline, 'Roxburgh: Tories' thin blue line likely to hold'? Robin McEwen was totally shaken: it was Brigid who performed the niceties. I hardly ever met him. Some years later sitting opposite him at a local dinner I wondered how such an able man who might have made a good MP had been such a poor candidate.

The result was declared inside the hall, and then outside, opposite the graceful view of Jedburgh Abbey. It was:

D. Steel (Liberal)	21,549
R. McEwen (Conservative)	16,942
R. K. Murray (Labour)	4,936
A. J. C. Kerr (SNP)	411
Liberal majority	4,607

I was swept away, shoulder high, down the High Street to the Liberal Club. I suppose it must have been Hawick men who carried me, for they sang the chorus of a Common Riding song:

> What though her lads are wild a wee
> And ill tae keep in order,
> Of all the towns she bears the gree
> Hawick's Queen o' a' the Border!

The *Daily Express* headline next morning in bold black letters said: 'It's boy David' – the phrase coined by John Bannerman to describe my fight against the Goliaths which was to stick with me for many years to come.

SCOTTISH
DAILY EXPRESS

No. 20,159   Thursday March 25 1965   FOUNDED BY LORD BEAVERBROOK   Weather: Showers   Price 4d

Victory! David Steel salutes cheers at 2 a.m.

2 a.m. sensation:
Liberals grab Borders
with 4,607 majority

IT'S BOY DAVID!

3

CROSS-PARTY CURRENTS

Grasping the Initiative

I fought three elections in eighteen months: the October 1964 general election, the March 1965 by-election and the March 1966 general election at which I was re-elected by a more natural majority of 2,211, the Tory candidate being an able Scottish Conservative Central Office apparatchik, Ian McIntyre, who gave me a difficult few months. He had no real empathy with the Border people and later found his natural home as Controller of BBC Radio 4. The general election was a much tamer affair than the by-election and we struggled without all the outside help. Bert Clyne, who had been West Aberdeenshire's agent and one of the by-election visitors, decided to move to the Borders and become my agent, which he was in both the '66 and '70 elections before moving on to local industry. During that election we had a car cavalcade passing through the Peeblesshire village of Walkerburn when, much against my will, we made an unscheduled stop outside one of the council houses to meet the oldest inhabitant of the village, a lady in her nineties, who was at the garden gate with several of her relations. She shook my hand and spoke haltingly: 'You are the second MP I've shaken hands with in my life, and the first was Mr Gladstone.' I was thunderstruck. She had apparently been a girl of twelve and had presented Gladstone with a bouquet in the Midlothian campaign.

The Tories made a great effort to get me out. One reason for their antipathy, apart from the natural one of wishing to regain the seat, was that they blamed me for the resignation as their leader of Alec Douglas-Home to whom the Border Tories were naturally devoted. Certainly after the by-election the press and some Tory backbenchers had been severely critical, claiming that if the Tories couldn't hold a seat in natural Douglas-Home territory, with a chum of his as candidate, then they should get a new leader. In vain I pointed out he was one of the few members of the Shadow Cabinet who had played no part in the campaign, whereas Heath, Maudling, Macleod, Hogg etc. had all stumped round the Borders and addressed huge audiences. (In those days there was a tradition that party leaders did not go to by-elections.) Sir Alec had approached me in the House of Commons lobby after I took my seat and with typical courtesy had shaken me by the hand saying, 'I am naturally sorry to see you here; but now that you are here I wish you luck.' Within four months he had resigned as leader of the Conservative Party and been replaced by Edward Heath in their first-ever election of a leader by MPs.

History will not describe Alec Douglas-Home as a great Prime Minister – he was only a year in the job. But he was one of the last effective gentleman-players in politics and he had that instinctive feel for the interests of all manner of people which was common in the knights of the shires. It may have been rather patronizing but it was genuine, and infinitely preferable to the couldn't-care-less attitude of the men on the make who inhabit the Tory benches today. *Ignoblesse désoblige?*

I came to know the former '14th Earl of Home' quite well through our local Border connections and during his subsequent period as Foreign Secretary. On one occasion when we were both heading for the night-sleeper at Berwick-on-Tweed after a farmers' dinner, he insisted that we call in at his home, The Hirsel, for a glass of beer. With such a huge house and estate I expected at least footmen and silver trays. On the contrary we blundered about the deserted, darkened basement while he found some beer and drank it quickly in his frozen library, nearly missing our train in the process.

Another example of his unstuffy directness came when I had a constituent stranded in some remote and dangerous part of the world – I forget the details. I had been badgering Alec about the case. One Saturday evening we were giving a dinner party at home and I told our home help, a young girl, that I was 'not available' to anyone on the telephone. After our guests departed I asked who-all had telephoned. She told me, including Sir Alec. She had carried out my instructions to the letter and refused to get me to the telephone. Next morning, I rang The Hirsel rather early. He answered the phone himself and was obviously still in bed. I started to apologize for the previous night's failure to speak to him and he chortled: 'You Liberals certainly protect yourselves.'

His brother William, for whom I had made that first public speech, had long since abandoned both politics and the Liberal Party in favour of play-writing when I met up with him years later at a dinner in London. 'You know,' he said, 'I should have been in your shoes as leader of the Liberal Party.' This seemed an improbable claim and I asked him to explain. His logic was irrefutable. In 1959 he had sought the Liberal nomination for

Roxburgh, Selkirk and Peebles. The selection meeting was being held in a hotel in St Boswells and his friend and relative, the Earl of Dalkeith, lived nearby. Johnnie (later MP for Edinburgh North, 1960–73, and now Duke of Buccleuch) was then president of the constituency Tories and devised a sure way of stopping the potentially dangerous Douglas-Home nomination. He invited him for an early dinner beforehand, saying: 'Of course, we dress for dinner.' According to William he was plied with the best claret and arrived at the Liberal meeting slightly late and slightly the worse for wear in a bottle-green velvet dinner jacket. He failed to secure the nomination. Whatever may or may not have been 'my part in his downfall', I never found anything from Alec Douglas-Home but kindness and consideration.

I shall leave account of my life as the Borders MP, which I so much enjoy, to chapter seven. My first five years as an MP were dominated at the national level by four major themes: balance of power for the Liberals; the better government of Scotland; the fight against racism at home and in Africa; and abortion.

When I arrived in the Commons, bringing the number of Liberal MPs into double figures, the Labour Government of Harold Wilson had a majority of precisely five over all other parties. This made for an exciting parliament. I was immediately given responsibility (one of the advantages of being in a minority party) for shadowing the Ministry of Labour. There were obvious instructions to ministers to be nice to Liberals in the hope of securing our support for at least some of their legislation. Ray Gunter invited me round to see his ministry and took a paternalistic interest in my wellbeing. I made some worthy speeches on the Redundancy Payments Bill and on prices-and-incomes policy, stressing on the latter that although the Declaration of Intent had referred to 'productivity, prices, and incomes', the first word had usually been forgotten and had not been stressed sufficiently by the Government. What was lacking was the co-operative effort of management and unions throughout British industry, encouraged by the Government, which would enable restrictive practices to be scrapped, industry to be made more efficient, and higher productivity to be achieved.

In 1965, when I had been in the House less than six months, the Speaker, Sir Harry Hylton-Foster, suddenly died on 2 September. The convention is that the government in power provides the Speaker from among the ranks of its own backbenchers; but, as with all conventions, it is not binding. Thus Harold Wilson was most reluctant to reduce his Government's majority to two (and indeed one assuming Hylton-Foster's seat would be resumed by a Tory). He therefore sounded out the most senior Liberal MP, Roderic Bowen QC, Member for Cardigan, who had been in the House since 1945 and had been passed over in favour of Jo Grimond for the leadership in 1957.

The situation was a highly delicate one, promptly made worse through an unbelievably crass intervention by Peter Bessell. The Bodmin MP writes in self-criticism with some wit about the episode in *Cover-Up*. Knowing that Jo Grimond had for some time been considering retiring, he suddenly briefed the *Sunday Express* lobby correspondent that Jo might accept the Speakership. He compounded this error by going on Westward Television in Plymouth and in a maladroit interview he said not only that he thought it a good idea but that he considered himself as a possible replacement as leader. ('I thought it was only a local broadcast,' he later told his colleagues.) The story was run by ITN and the Monday press made much fun of the whole affair.

When the Liberal MPs met, I had never seen Jo so angry. We had just struggled to get up to ten members and now we were contemplating going back to nine. I took the relaxed view that since we didn't see Bowen very often and he was so senior, it wouldn't be a disaster if he did become Speaker. Bowen himself was cagey, especially when I asked if he would take one of the deputy positions – which did not require our support, but which would equally affect the arithmetic.

He declined to say. Had he made known his intention to accept that, I and some others would have proposed we back him for the Speakership which at least carried both prestige and a noncontest in his constituency. As it was, he took the minor job, Chairman of Ways and Means, and lost the next election. In public, Jo was as good-humoured as ever, declaring he was about to be offered the premiership of Greece. Labour was forced to supply Horace King as Speaker and their paper majority fell to one. Another election was inevitable.

Bessell wrote of the embarrassment he had caused the party: 'It created a gulf between me and the rest of my colleagues that was never properly bridged. Much of the magic of parliamentary life died for me that weekend and the net result was that I drew still closer to Jeremy [Thorpe].'

The party had badly fumbled the ball and let slip an opportunity to influence events. Early in March 1965 Jo Grimond had given an interview to *The Times* with some prescience dealing with the possibility that Liberals could find ourselves holding the balance at a time when the Conservatives were determined to throw the government out:

'Then my view is that either we must have some reasonably long-range agreement with the Government or a general election. We must have an agreement for a few months on some purpose we both want.
'I should be very much opposed to going back to the 1929 system, in which the

Labour Government and the Liberal Party made practically *ad hoc* decisions on the business of Government.

'I should be very much inclined to say: "We are in this difficult situation. Here are certain things both parties want to get through. We will support you on all issues, however minor, until that is done." '

In June 1965 there was furore in the party over an interview he gave to the *Guardian* and a party political broadcast. He made it clear he did not propose to approach Prime Minister Harold Wilson but was merely setting out his views in general terms. His attempt to educate the party to the realities of power was not very successful. The MPs themselves divided into three – supporters of a Lib-Lab deal (Jeremy Thorpe and I), outright opponents, and a majority of unenthusiastic acquiescents. In September I wrote an article in the *New Statesman* quoting Wilson's response to questions about a possible Lib-Lab understanding, saying: 'Let's face that situation when it arises.' I said, 'It has arisen.' Also in September, during the annual Liberal assembly and after the Speakership fiasco Jo Grimond wrote again in the *Guardian*:

I believe we could find common aims behind which a majority could unite and for which there will be real enthusiasm. But their formulation will take time. The parliamentary situation will not give us the time. The throwing of life-belts to a sinking Government is not a job I would welcome.

The Assembly was equally unhappy and divided by such speculation, with Nancy Seear giving a ringing warning about 'a-whoring after foreign women'.

As a new and junior participant, I watched the Party fail to respond to Jo's leadership while Labour, not unjustifiably, believed Jo could not deliver the necessary votes for an agreement. We sailed into the general election the following spring, saw our numbers rise to twelve and influence slip from our grasp as the Labour Government secured a majority of ninety-seven. Butler and King wrote in *The British General Election of 1966*: 'The prospect of holding the balance of power presented the Liberals with their most serious threat, and also with their greatest opportunity.' Jo's dramatic Assembly speech about our teeth being in the red meat of power seemed remote. The Liberal Party's teeth had turned out to be false, and liable to fall out when it came to chewing a particularly difficult piece.

In January 1967 Judy and I, with our baby Graeme, went to stay with the Grimonds in Orkney, where I was to address his annual Liberal supper. Just before we left his house he took me into his study and told me he didn't want me to put my foot in it in what I was about to say at the meeting, and that he ought to let me know he would be telling his colleagues next week of his intention to retire from the leadership. I was aghast but somehow got through the evening. In his memoirs Jo comments: 'I am touched that he was "shattered" (so he says) when I told him I was going to resign. He says we discussed the situation calmly. Indeed we did: he showed a positively Asquithian calm.'

On our return to London there was a quick vote among the twelve MPs with me rounding up support for Jeremy Thorpe as the best communicator and campaigner and the man most determined to pursue the Grimond strategy. There were six votes for Jeremy, three for Eric Lubbock and three for Emlyn Hooson. The other two groups declared their backing and Jeremy was elected with unanimous support. Jo's leadership was decisive in leading us back from the decaying remnants of the old party of government to the beginnings of a new radical movement. The issues he faced returned later; but without the foundation he laid, nothing I was to do in the years ahead could have been attempted. In his resignation press conference he said he regretted that there had not been a realignment of the Left while he was Liberal leader, resulting in the formation of a 'broadly based radical party', but that he did not despair of such a development in the future.

Luck had, as I've demonstrated, played a significant part in my political career. It was to do so again. Because of the spring election the state opening was in April 1966 instead of the usual November, thus giving an exceptionally long parliamentary session. In the annual ballot for private members' bills held early in the session, I drew third place. Only the top six in this annual raffle have any real chance in the parliamentary timetable of piloting a bill right through onto the statute-book. Outside the committee room where the draw takes place there lurk other MPs and pressure groups eager to press their case on the lucky winners. In addition, there is a whole raft of minor and relatively uncontroversial causes left over from the priority lists of government departments which they too are eager to press on the private member. (I recall that one such was the Plumbers' Registration Bill and I confess that to this day I don't know whether plumbers remain in a state of unregistration.)

I early on decided that third place in the ballot was too precious to be wasted either on any such minor cause which should be tabled by government or on any tilt at a gigantic windmill. Thus I declined to introduce a Scottish self-government bill on the grounds that there were plenty of other opportunities to debate that important matter, while a precious bill would fall at the first hurdle. No, it seemed right to take up one of the great social reforms. Capital punishment and divorce law reform had both been tackled. That left the more touchy topics of homosexuality and abortion, both of which bills had successfully passed through the House of Lords and were awaiting

49

champions in the Commons. The Earl of Arran, a member of my party, had pioneered the former and wished me to take it up. Beyond having been much impressed by Sir John Wolfenden, Chairman of the Royal Commission which had recommended reform, I knew little about the subject. The same was true of abortion. As a candidate in the general election I had committed myself in answer to the usual questions to support both. Could I now dodge both as sponsor? Obviously not. Roy Jenkins as Home Secretary asked me to discuss the matter with his two junior ministers, Lord Stonham and Dick Taverne. They preferred me to take on the Sexual Offences Bill, mainly on the grounds that it was a less complicated piece of legislation for a new Member.

But my mind went back to a discussion with Humphrey Berkeley, Conservative sponsor of a homosexual law reform bill in the previous session, as to why his bill had applied only to England and Wales. He replied simply: 'Nothing to do with the merits, I just don't want all those Scottish MPs staying here on Fridays to vote against it.' Opinion in Scotland and among my own constituents was firmly against it. Indeed the law in Scotland was not reformed until some years later.

By a process of elimination it looked as though I should tackle abortion. Before finally deciding, I read a movingly impressive book by Alice Jenkins, *Law for the Rich*, written at the age of seventy-two, 'only because of my hatred of preventable suffering'. There had been six previous attempts to reform the law in the Commons and two in the Lords. There was proven all-party support and there was an effective outside campaigning body, the Abortion Law Reform Association. A compelling document on the ethics of abortion had been published by the Church of England's Board of Social Responsibility, *Abortion: an ethical discussion*. I have yet to see anything which so powerfully states a positive Christian attitude to this most complex subject. The Committee Chairman was Canon Ian Ramsey, then Professor of the Philosophy of the Christian Religion at Oxford, and later during passage of my bill in the Lords, Bishop of Durham.

The Anglican committee recognized that it was 'the feeling that the interest of the mother is least well served by the existing law, and a humane anxiety for her, that lends most strength to the movement for reform of the law in this country today'. It accepted that 'the Christian moral and legal tradition recognizes implicitly that there are circumstances in which the killing of the unborn child does not come under the general condemnation attaching to murder'. It admitted that there was no certainty 'in any verifiable sense' of the relation between soul and embryo 'or of the precise moment or stage at which the relation begins to exist'. It pointed out a fact of which most Catholics and most reformers were unaware, namely that even the Catholic

Church did not regard *all* abortion as murder. 'Today', commented the report tersely, 'there has developed a casuistry to match the new medical possibilities.' It illustrated this by pointing out that even a Catholic gynaecologist would be permitted by his Church to terminate an anencephalic pregnancy (one in which the child had no brain); consequently it could not be said that the defence of the inviolability of the foetus, even in Catholic tradition, was absolute. (This did not, however, prevent the Catholic bishops in England and Wales from pronouncing: '*All* destruction of life in the womb is immoral.') 'Consequently,' the report went on, 'the concept of a human being, even within the Christian tradition is to some extent "indeterminate" and dependent upon society's value judgements.' There are certain defects so serious that we no longer think of a creature defective in this way as truly human. The probelm was to decide, given the general inviolability of the foetus, what the exceptions might be; and how the claims of the potential mother were to be weighed against the claims of the foetus when they conflicted. The committee concluded, finally, that abortion should be permissible when there was a threat not only to the mother's life, but also to her 'wellbeing' and hence inescapably to her health, if she were obliged to carry the child to term. 'Our view is that in reaching this conclusion her life and wellbeing must be seen as integrally connected with the life and wellbeing of her family.'

The report also traced the history of the thinking on abortion in the Catholic Church, pointing out that well before the time of St Augustine, Christian theologians accepted the 'theory of animation' whereby at conception the fertilized egg was vegetative only, days later developing an animal soul, and later, a rational soul. Thus the absolutist position of the Catholic Church was not always part of its doctrine.

In my whole experience of debate on the subject I have always envied those who are able to adopt positions of moral certainty such as 'To kill life in the womb is always wrong,' or 'It is a woman's right to choose.' My bill was based on neither of these assumptions, but on the more difficult one of conflicts of right. I sought to create a positive state of the law where two medical practitioners could lawfully balance the rights and conditions of the mother against the assumption of the right to develop to full life of the foetus. Indeed at the conclusion of my thirty-five-minute speech on 22 July 1966, moving the Second Reading of my bill, I drew attention to the view of my own Church of Scotland:

The Report of the Social and Moral Welfare Board of the Church of Scotland quotes a German theologian as stating that human life in every form is sacrosanct but that we have to ask ourselves what quantitative item of sacrosanctity may be attached to

51

each form of life – the ovum fertilized, the moving embryo, the born child and the mother. He said:

'A paper-thin wall separates us from sacrilege – all such decisions can be made only under saving grace – such dangers always go with freedom. Those who want to avoid the dangers do so only by setting up a rigid dogma.... So there is obviously no perfect solution. The decision has to be taken in the light of God's understanding of our human frailty.'

It is in that spirit that I have approached the drafting of the Bill, and I hope that the House will give it a Second Reading.

The bill was carried by 223 votes to 29 into its committee stage. This was a tribute to our unofficial whips, Peter Jackson (Labour) and Sir George Sinclair (Conservative), as well as Alastair Service, who led the appropriate lobbying by ALRA.

In arguing for the bill, which was largely the same as Lord Silkin's successful measure from the Lords, I pointed to the unsatisfactory and negative state of the law in both England and Wales and in Scotland. Estimates of illegal abortions varied between 40,000 and 200,000 a year. In the 1930s judges, medical bodies and women's organizations had all called for reform, leading to the appointment of a Government Inter-Departmental Committee chaired by the late Lord Birkett, who spoke of 'the urgency of the problem of the misery and heartbreak which at present prevail, of the need for clear thinking on the problem, and of the strong necessity for making the law clear and intelligible and in accordance with public opinion – the only ultimate sanction of the law'.

I also argued that if the Bill became law:

... it will become possible for a patient to consult her family doctor freely and openly about her pregnancy and about the possible termination of the pregnancy. This is an important new provision. At present the whole question is surrounded by so much whispering and so much doubt about the legality that the effect is that the last person, very often, with whom a woman wishes to discuss it is her family doctor.

And I went on to give the appalling figures of deaths of women from criminal abortion which were simply the tip of the iceberg.

In choosing sponsors of the Bill, I had two constituency neighbours, Alex Eadie (Labour, Midlothian) and Lord Lambton (Conservative, Berwick); two senior women MPs, Tory Dame Joan Vickers and Labour's Renee Short; together with my invaluable Liberal colleague, Dr Michael Winstanley. We put as many other doctors on to the Committee as possible, including Dr David Kerr, Dr John Dunwoody and Dr David Owen.

There was a long gap between the July second reading and the January start to the Committee, during which I had endless meetings with all manner of bodies for and against the bill, including a difficult but friendly session with the Catholic lobby in my own constituency. I argued with them that they seemed to accept both natural abortion and illegally induced abortion and were only upset by legally induced abortion. My Catholic friends have never satisfactorily explained this to me.

The bill as drafted came in for a lot of criticism. I was greatly influenced by going to lunch in Aberdeen with Professor Sir Dugald Baird, who persuaded me to accept amendments creating a single socio-medical clause rather than a series of individual categories. This I did, to general acceptance though amid some opposition from supporters.

The committee stage was protracted and at times bad-tempered, with extremist views expressed from both sides. I sat at the ministerial bench, with three ministers from the Home Office, the Ministry of Health and the Scottish Office alongside to give 'expert' guidance. We finished the Committee Stage after twelve weekly sittings from January to April 1967. One of the main opponents – and the most articulate – was Norman St John Stevas. I added a conscience clause to the Bill, but that apart I accepted no changes other than those we tabled as sponsors.

As we headed for the report stage, the public crescendo for and against the bill rose. There were endless public debates, rallies, radio and television programmes. As a result I was worried about being publicly identified with this one issue to the exclusion of all else. I received huge quantities of mail, some of it abusive and obscene. Some even went to Judy, who was pregnant twice during the long passage of the Bill. I could not help reflecting that those who were trumpeting the highest moral tones were associated with some of the lowest tactics.

The Report Stage on 2 June 1967 – a whole year after the first publication of the bill – ran into difficulties. There was not enough time to deal with all the amendments tabled, given the long speeches of the opponents. At this point the coincidence of support among several senior individual members of the Government was decisive. John Silkin, the Chief Whip, was the son of Lord Silkin, pilot of the previous reform bill in the Lords. Kenneth Robinson, the Minister of Health, had himself been the promoter of one of the six previous reform bills. Roy Jenkins as Home Secretary was actively and publicly in favour of reform as was Richard Crossman as Leader of the House. A decision had to be taken by the Cabinet on whether to grant extra time, but these vital few were especially influential.

I went to see Dick Crossman in his room, full of awe as a junior Member. He gave me a whisky. I rehearsed the arguments for granting time – the weight of opinion in the House, long overdue reform, campaign outside etc., etc. He absentmindedly poured a second helping – of brandy – into my whisky glass. This was no time to complain. In the cause of getting my bill, I drank the revolting mixture. We got two extra night sittings, and on the morning of 14 July I rose to move the third reading, which was approved by 167 to 83. The Bill went through another tortuous process in the Lords before receiving the Royal Assent on 27 October 1967.

Roy Jenkins paid me a generous tribute as 'a young man with a marginal constituency and without a massive party machine behind him' and others were equally laudatory. Hindell and Simms in *Abortion Law Reformed* commented:

In view of the tremendous effort which was later needed to get even the amended or watered-down version through parliament, it is very difficult to fault Steel's judgment. At the time, however, many of the reformers were extremely critical of it.

The experience achieved three things in addition to the major reform itself. It gave me detailed knowledge of parliamentary procedure, exposure to the media, and acquaintance with successful interparty co-operation. The outside campaigners and advisers had also been crucial, Vera Houghton, Diane Munday and Peter Diggory being in almost constant attendance in addition to Alastair Service. Their marshalling of opinion polls, professional bodies and MPs and peers was a marvel to behold.

The success of ALRA led during 1967 to the formation of SPUC – the Society for the Protection of the Unborn Child, or as it is irreverently known 'for the Production of Unwanted Children'. Madeleine Simms and Keith Hindell have charted the set-up of the society and some of its methods in their excellent book and so I will not repeat the details here. Over the years since, there have been abuses of the Act and on occasions I have criticized the slowness of ministers to use the power of regulation given to them under the Act. The most flagrant abuse was taxi-touting for foreign customers by profit-making private clinics. That was eventually stopped.

I have seen two abortion operations, once before my legislation at the invitation of the Royal College of Obstetricians and Gynaecologists and once since at a charitable private clinic. I am in no doubt about what is involved and still stick by my view that it has to be judged in each individual case as the lesser of two evils. Parliament has resisted every attempt to reverse the law. In the early '70s the Government set up under pressure a committee of inquiry into the working of the Act under Mrs Justice Lane. They concluded: 'We have no doubt that the gains facilitated by the Act have much outweighed any disadvantages for which it has been criticized.' Opponents of abortion use every abuse to attack the Act itself, but parliamentary and public opinion remains in support of it.

The only change I would now support is an alteration to the Infant Life Preservation Act of 1929, reducing the assumption of viability from twenty-eight weeks of pregnancy to twenty-four in the light of developments in medical science since those days.

With the Abortion Act on the statute-book in October 1967, I returned to normal political activity. I was now Commonwealth spokesman. That month I was the Liberal Member on the five-person parliamentary delegation to the United Nations General Assembly in New York. It was to be the first of many visits to the United States.

Early in 1968 I found myself embroiled in a heated parliamentary controversy over the influx of Asians from Kenya. I was one of the few MPs who knew and understood the situation. At that time Kenya had an Asian population of around 190,000 – it had always been larger than the European population in that country (the total population of Kenya at the time was ten million). Of that 190,000 some 60,000 had automatically become Kenyan citizens on independence because of their birth and a further 10,000 had chosen to acquire that citizenship in the two years following allowed under the Independence Act.

The remaining 120,000 remained British citizens. The Kenyan government at that time began a programme of 'Kenyanization' whereby public employment, trading licences etc. were increasingly granted to their own citizens. This was incorrectly called 'Africanization' by much of the British press. Although no doubt there was some racist pressure from Africans against the Asians who occupied many middle-class jobs, technically the policy of the Kenyan government was no different from that of European or American governments who favour their own nationals in employment policies. Where both successive British and Kenyan governments were culpable was in not spelling out more clearly the implications of the two-year choice available to Asians on independence. Many 'chose' British citizenship by default. Dr Jo Karanja, later Vice-President of Kenya but then their High Commissioner in London, shrewdly observed when Asians began to exercise their right to leave the country and come to Britain: 'If the people had been white there would be no problem in Britain.' Iain Macleod, who as Colonial Secretary in 1959–61 had presided over the Kenya independence constitutional settlement, declared unequivocally in an article in the *Spectator*: 'We did it. We meant to do it, and in any case we had no alternative.' This was in response to

Duncan Sandys, who had been Commonwealth Secretary at the time and who was now politically exploiting the influx and waffling about a 'loophole in the law'.

Since the maximum entitled to come was 120,000 over an indefinite period there was no real problem since in any case most of them had no wish to. What created the problem was the sudden acceleration of Kenyanization plus growing publicity and rumours that Britain might act to stop the influx, assisted by inflammatory speeches from Enoch Powell and Duncan Sandys.

On 12 February this was fuelled by an action which was utterly irresponsible – the tabling of a motion on the Commons order paper by Duncan Sandys and others calling on the Government 'to introduce immediate legislation to curtail the influx of immigrants into Britain'. *The Times* reported from Nairobi on 16 February: 'The exodus has been given momentum by the Commons motion sponsored on Monday by Duncan Sandys.' The Government failed to give assurance that the rights of British citizens would be maintained and this heightened anxiety in the Asian community that they might be left increasingly jobless and stateless.

So often in international politics major events occur because governments give the wrong signals. Thus UDI in Rhodesia might never have happened had not the British Government inadvertently signalled that any rebellion would not be met with the traditional deployment of force. Similarly the invasion of the Falklands by the Argentine junta might never have taken place had we not announced the withdrawal of HMS *Endurance*.

So in Kenya the failure of the British Government to repeat the 1962 assurance of citizenship actually increased the panic outflow. On the contrary, on 22 February the Labour administration announced that they would legislate to withdraw the automatic rights of entry to British citizens.

The intention of the bill had been to stop British citizens who were coloured from entering the country at all – in other words, to set up a racial barrier. The legislation proposed in the bill would be successful in this aim.

The second effect of the bill was to make a distinction between British citizens with regard to their right of entry into the United Kingdom. Unless they fulfilled certain conditions, they could not expect unconditional entry, but would be obliged to wait in a queue for vouchers, which were to be limited to 1,500 a year for heads of households. In other words, the British Government wished, by means of the bill, to create two forms of citizenship in the United Kingdom and Colonies, with the second type not carrying with it the right to enter the United Kingdom. This second type has been described as a form of statelessness. It was not this in the full meaning of the word, since the individuals concerned were still to remain citizens of the United

Kingdom, but they were not to have the right to enter their country – the basic right of citizenship.

The announcement of the bill confirmed the fears of the Asians in Kenya, who were now leaving at the rate of nearly 750 a day. Indeed, in the last two weeks in February 1968, i.e. the week before the actual debates on the Government bill, and during that week, 10,000 people rushed to Britain, creating problems that would not have existed if the British Government had not succumbed to the pressure from the racialists, both inside the United Kingdom itself and in Kenya, where the economy was severely disrupted by the sudden departure of many of the commercial and clerical middle class.

The 'beat-the-ban' rush to enter Britain now reached a new height. Scenes at Nairobi airport verged on the hysterical. If those who were seeing their friends off could find a seat on the plane, they also embarked without even going home to prepare, leaving their cars at the airport. There were reports of a proposed Berlin-style 'mass airlift' to beat the bill, but the leaders of the Asian community were unable to charter sufficient planes for those who wished to get to Britain. Some Asians who were unable to find seats on direct flights to London were prepared to go by longer routes to get there, and some even went via Moscow.

On the Saturday before the bill was debated in the House I proposed a resolution at the Liberal Party Council committing us to fight the bill. The Archbishop of Canterbury, Michael Ramsay, declared that the bill 'appears to involve the country in breaking its pledged word'; while the Tory MP Hugh Fraser, who had been Macleod's junior minister, wrote to *The Times*: 'For the House of Commons to be provoked into yet another breach of a solemn undertaking will be an enduring national shame.'

The official (Conservative) Opposition supported the bill, but their Shadow Home Secretary Quintin Hogg was clearly unhappy:

'I do not think that it is our fault that this has happened . . . . we have to deal with the situation whether it is our fault or not . . . I have always regarded the tenure of a British passport as something of which people can be proud and be sure . . . I am not making my argument with any kind of relish . . . . a measure which none of us like.'

In my own speech I pointed out that in the end the Government could not unilaterally withdraw rights – and indeed I was later proved correct when Idi Amin expelled our citizens from Uganda and we had no alternative but to admit them.

At the end of the debate we Liberals forced a division. It was carried by 374 (211 Labour plus 163 Tories) votes to 62 (15 Conservatives, including

Iain Macleod, 35 Labour, 10 Liberals and 2 Nationalists, plus John Pardoe and myself as tellers). By one of the strangest ironies, immediately after the division the House formally approved a resolution 'to present a parliamentary library and silver inkstand to the National Assembly of Botswana'.

Next day, contrary to all normal parliamentary procedure we plunged straight into a continuous all-night sitting on the committee stage, report stage (which was held formally) and third reading. We divided the House six times during the night, attracting 76 supporters at one stage. We also vainly fought the bill all through the House of Lords proceedings.

It was a most discreditable episode in our parliamentary history, a major concession to racism and a blot on the reputation of the Labour Party. The Home Secretary at the time was Jim Callaghan. In his recent memoirs he sought to justify the bill as necessary to 'reassure the country' following Enoch Powell's 'rivers of blood' speech, but in fact that speech was not made until *after* the 1968 Act. I was proud to be a Liberal. These events left a profound impression on me. Once again I was in the thick of parliamentary debate, joining with like-minded people of other parties. The arrival of a delegation of four leaders of the Kenya Asian community whom I helped to look after was the start of a whole series of abiding family friendships which have continued to this day – the Shahs, the de Souzas, the Mehtas and the Vadhers. I was also stirred to write my first book: *No Entry: the Background and Implications of the Commonwealth Immigrants Act, 1968.* One of my conclusions was that the British needed a Bill of Rights as a second outer wall of defence round the liberty of the subject.

The late Sixties were also a period of excitement in Scottish politics. The Liberal Party had in fact done rather better in Scotland than anywhere else. As Professor John Vincent put it in *New Society* in January 1967, by then of the twelve Liberal seats, five were in Scotland, one in Wales, three in Devon and Cornwall, and only three in urban England. We had successfully secured an electoral base in areas protesting against their neglect by the metropolis. The Party had, after the celebrated 1962 Orpington by-election, 'set their cap at the London commuter and ended up with the Ross and Cromarty crofter'. Putting it another way, what we had succeeded in doing was infusing the areas of traditional Liberalism such as my own constituency with fresh zeal and renewed efficiency. But in general and in Scotland in particular, we had not much impact in urban, especially Labour, areas.

Thus in the Glasgow Pollok by-election in March 1967 with poor administration, though an able candidate in David Miller, we polled only 735 votes, while the SNP polled over 10,000 votes. Some of us began to argue that since our Party had always steadfastly from the days of Gladstone been in favour of 'home rule all round' with a domestic parliament for Scotland, we should consider an electoral accommodation with the SNP whereby they would attack in those seats where we had little hope anyway and we would, untrammelled by their intervention, make further inroads in our areas of strength. This internal debate went on over many months but came to nothing. The SNP had – and continues to have – two basic problems. It was divided between on the one hand the home-rule fundamentalists, or fanatics, who – wild-eyed with tartan fervour – would settle for nothing less than the dismemberment of the UK and the restoration of a sovereign Scottish state, and on the other the more pragmatic nationalists, who might well harbour such illusions but were more concerned about the state of Scotland's economy and culture and the effect of London domination and centralization; they were willing to accept a democratic solution to remedy these, falling short of separation, as well as co-operation with others of similar mind. At the outer fringes some, such as the Tartan Army or the Scottish Liberation Army, were mixtures of the anarchic, the revolutionary and the plain eccentric and were a constant embarrassment to their party. Their second problem is that the SNP has never yet produced a leader of stature and of imagination to capture public opinion on a par with either Scottish Liberals like Jo Grimond or John Bannerman or the Welsh Nationalist Gwynfor Evans. (A third problem, more evident then than now, is that their membership encompassed every shade of the political spectrum from Marxist to crypto-fascist.)

This made the search for agreement difficult. On our own side George Mackie and Russell Johnston, who were the mainstay of the Scottish Liberal Party, backed by the executive, disapproved of too much activity in this direction, while Jo Grimond and I together with the other two MPs, James Davidson and Alasdair Mackenzie, were much keener to pursue the path of co-operation.

Indeed the gulf became alarmingly acrimonious when at the 1968 Liberal Assembly, being held in Edinburgh, Russell Johnston publicly rebuked Jo, which was the Liberal equivalent of swearing aloud in church. He had a point because Jo had the cavalier habit of making delphic pronouncements while not actually coming to grips with the necessary negotiations. At any rate this was a running sore in the 1966–70 Parliament.

As early as 1964 William Wolfe of the SNP suggested a joint approach which the Scottish Liberal Party rebuffed on the grounds that it, 'although autonomous, was part of the Great Britain Liberal Movement, and would not contemplate any unilateral action for Scottish self-government'. Unfortunately this was all megaphone diplomacy. Yet in the '64 election we clashed in only four of the seventy-one seats, including my own. In 1966 Ludovic Kennedy proposed a motion to the Scottish Conference putting home rule as 'the principal aim and object of our policy'; but as he ruefully observed in an article for the *Spectator* in 1967: 'To my great astonishment this resolution was carried unanimously, and thereafter, equally unanimously ignored.'

At the 1967 Conference James Davidson spiked an attempt by Ludovic Kennedy and Michael Starforth, our hard-working candidate in East Renfrewshire, to commit us to an alliance with the SNP by getting Conference to invite the SNP to indicate willingness to co-operate. Jo and I made some attempt privately to secure a deal with the SNP prior to the Hamilton by-election that autumn, but the SNP had the bit between their teeth and demanded ludicrously that a Scottish parliament should become the main priority of the UK Liberal Party.

None the less, discretion being the better part of valour, we decided not to fight Hamilton. At this point, unfortunately, I left the country for two weeks at the UN General Assembly in New York. Ludovic Kennedy decided that he would speak for the SNP candidate, Winnie Ewing, and seemed to think it necessary to resign membership of the party in order to do so. Had I been around, I would have advised him to do as he wished, since there was no Liberal standing. He wrote (living as he did near Kelso, Roxburghshire, at that time) to my constituency President, Andrew Haddon, resigning. It was a great boost to the SNP and an unnecessary blow to us, though contrary to popular belief he never joined the SNP, and has remained a consistent friend and Liberal, renewing his membership some years later.

He and George Mackie never got on – the antipathy was entirely mutual – and I was missing at a crucial moment. Winnie Ewing won the by-election and we collected none of the credit. In 1968 I published my second political pamphlet, *Out of Control*. It was an analysis of the failure of the machinery of Scottish government, tracing the history of administrative devolution in Scotland and arguing in detail that the failure to achieve corresponding legislative devolution and parliamentary control meant that Scottish government was actually less democratically responsible than Whitehall. The argument holds good today and the pamphlet received much favourable attention. As 'interim solutions' I proposed the setting up of a Scottish Select Committee and meetings of the Scottish Grand Committee in Edinburgh, neither of which, although they intermittently came to pass, has proved an unqualified success. I also suggested more meetings of the Grand Committee to include extra Scottish question sessions.

I saw none of these proposals as 'diminishing our determination to campaign for a Scottish parliament' and contributed a chapter to a powerful book edited by Neil MacCormick, *The Scottish Debate* (1970), in which I argued:

The two home-rule parties in Scotland – the Liberals and the Nationalists – could effectively campaign together on this theme of the Scots having the right to decide the future for themselves (including the right to total sovereignty and separation if so desired).

And, in eerie anticipation of arguments to surface twenty years later:

It is, moreover, worth asking whether for Scotland – small and attached as she is physically to a larger neighbour – the concept of total sovereignty has any real meaning. Our neighbours of similar size on either side of us, Denmark and Eire, have found their freedom of movement severely restricted. Eire devalued within minutes of Britain. Both have applied to join the EEC, withdrawn their applications, and then reapplied at precisely the same time as the United Kingdom Government. In theory they are sovereign states free to do as they please; in practice their sovereignty is limited by the facts of life. Hence talk by the SNP about how Scotland ought to be free to decide separately from England whether or not to go into Europe is both excellent in principle and utterly meaningless.

The strange feature of this period is that the Labour Party who both in its early years and as recently as the early fifties had been strongly pro Scottish self-government, made no moves towards recognizing Scottish public opinion, whereas the Conservative Party under Edward Heath did. The Cabinet ministers, Willie Ross (Secretary of State for Scotland) and George Thomas (Secretary of State for Wales), were both anti-devolution, while Heath set up a distinguished Tory committee under Sir Alec Douglas-Home which at least examined the question, though provided watered-down solutions. In response to that initiative, Prime Minister Harold Wilson set up a Royal Commission on the Constitution in 1968, which did not report until after he was out of office.

The SNP increased their strength in general elections from one in 1970 to seven in February 1974 and eleven in October 1974. The lack of political cohesion among the eleven (which reflected the tendency I have mentioned to cover every point of the spectrum) led to their decline in 1979 to two.

Writing reflectively in 1976, George Reid, one of their MPs (1974–9) said:

In the late nineteen-fifties, in the Scores Hotel on the seafront at St Andrews, David Steel and I had something of a clandestine meeting. He was President of the Student Council at Edinburgh, and I had the same job at the local University.

The purpose of our meeting, however, had nothing to do with academic politics. It just so happened that we were also chairmen of our respective Liberal and Labour clubs. How, we wondered, were we going to get Lib-Labbery, a contemporary social democracy, going? And when were we going to get a Scots Parliament?

In the inevitable way of things, we were stamped on by our respective party hierarchies, and we went our separate ways: David into the Scottish Liberal office on a minuscule salary, and eventually into Westminster in his sensational by-election win of March 1965. Myself, into the rather lusher pastures of television.

The opportunity for an effective political drive to secure Scottish self-government was passed over in the late sixties, fumbled in the late seventies (as I shall recount in Chapter 6), and had risen tantalizingly again in the late eighties, as I shall expand on later.

While all these theoretical discussions were going on I was also engaged at a practical level in all-party co-operation in the dynamic new charity, Shelter. Des Wilson, its energetic director, who made it an effective campaigning spearhead for the homeless, steered Shelter into being a successful propaganda unit as well as a fundraising one. Massive advertising, together with TV programmes such as the famous Wednesday Play, *Cathy Come Home* (1966), stirred the national conscience. The Labour Government was spurred into increasing the housebuilding programme (not, in retrospect, always wisely with high-rise flats) while Shelter funded many housing associations to renovate slum properties. Early on, I visited an impressive area improvement scheme in Liverpool.

Des was looking for someone to head a Scottish equivalent and asked me to become chairman. This I did with two successive directors, Ron Dick and Willy Roe, and an advisory committee which included members of all parties and of none. It was refreshing, down-to-earth, practical work with visible results.

I also attempted – less successfully – to put out feelers to members of other parties interested in cross-party co-operation on a wider basis. I helped form the short-lived Radical Action Movement. In 1968 the *Guardian* had published a depressing editorial which sounds oddly familiar today: 'Today's situation is one from which those who want a realignment on the left ought to profit. But they are not ready with a common policy or with the means to achieve a realignment. They are about to miss their chance again.'

My fellow instigators of this initiative were: Richard Holme (who had fought the East Grinstead by-election, being another 'brilliant second', a few weeks before mine); Christopher Layton, son of Lord Layton, the great Liberal economist; John Pardoe; and Terry Lacey of the Young Liberals, who later joined the Labour Party. We persuaded Peter Jackson, Labour MP for High Peak, who had worked with me on the Abortion Bill, and Ben Whitaker, Labour MP for Hampstead, who was active with me in the Anti-Apartheid Movement, to join together with non-parliamentarians like

Des Wilson from Shelter, Anthony Steel from War on Want, and Lee Chapman from Oxfam.

Our launching document was full of fine phrases such as 'a catalyst of a much wider radical movement, and to start a debate both within the Labour and Liberal parties with the aim of forging an alliance between the progressive forces of Britain'; and:

Now the opportunity for political realignment is even greater outside Parliament than within. If the Liberal Party can grasp the initiative in bringing this about, it deserves success .... This may mean a reassessment of priorities, it may mean more militant attitudes, and it will certainly mean a greater awareness of the future than of the integrity of historical tradition.

However, it turned out to be no more than a minor talking shop.

More successful was my activity in the Anti-Apartheid Movement which I had joined as a student at its inception after the Sharpeville massacre in March 1960. I became a member of the National Committee and then suddenly in 1966 I was requested to become President. Barbara Castle had been President but had to step down on entering the Government in 1964. Similarly David Ennals as President had now gone into the government in 1966. When I asked 'Why me?' the emissaries declared with remarkable frankness that they now wanted somebody who would be unlikely to be entering Government. I agreed and did the job for four years until after the 1970 election when I was succeeded by two great and godly men, Bishop Ambrose Reeves and later Archbishop Trevor Huddleston.

Chairing that disparate coalition which formed the National Committee was a difficult but rewarding experience. I also got to know people like Neil Kinnock, who sought me out as a fellow campaigner when he entered the House in the 1970 election and with whom I shared platforms. Another platform sharer was Andrew Faulds, MP, notably in a meeting at the YMCA Theatre in Edinburgh where we had to call the police to quell the riot after Andrew had leapt off the platform and threatened to thump an objectionable man who was among a group of disrupters from the League of Empire Loyalists. An amusing sequel was that Andrew stayed the night with us at Ettrick Bridge and next day he was impressed by my arranging for the Edinburgh–Birmingham express to be stopped at Hawick to pick him up. The stationmaster, a co-operative Labour supporter, said: 'That's how they did the great train robbery, you know.'

Our main public campaign was for the sports boycott, especially in the rugby and cricket so loved by the white South African regime. A breakaway group which included Peter Hain believed in 'direct action'. He set up his own organization which daubed slogans, dug up pitches, and generally made our life difficult; though I have to admit they had some effect, and I always liked Peter – sufficiently to appear as a character witness in his trial at the Old Bailey, when an unsuccessful attempt was made by South African agents to frame him for a bank robbery.

Early in 1970 an appalling prospect presented itself. The Springbok rugby tour was to include one match in my own constituency where rugby is a religion. I was going to be on the spot. I could scarcely turn a blind eye to this match at Galashiels while opposing the entire visit. My views against a racially-selected team, itself bringing politics into sport, were well known. I was on record as having said:

'There is no more feeble argument than "I disapprove of apartheid but...". There can be no "buts" in the eyes of the majority of the people in South Africa or in the rest of the world. Sporting contacts have done nothing to alleviate apartheid. They have merely depressed those struggling against it.'

My constituency association passed a motion condemning the fixture. Two days before the match I held a public meeting in Galashiels at which I invited both the Very Rev. Lord MacLeod, and my friend Menzies Campbell, clad in all his aura as a former Olympic sprinter, to support me. It was thinly attended.

I decided on an orderly protest outside the ground, persuading a few brave clergy and councillors to join me in handing out leaflets explaining why we were not attending. I was terrified of rentamobs disrupting the game and the Tories trying to blame me for them.

There were only a couple of dozen of us. It was a miserable day. I saw many of my ardent supporters slipping shamefacedly into the ground. I was spat at by some of my constituents, as I and my small band of demonstrators distributed 5,000 leaflets giving facts about apartheid to the rugby fans. My worst fears were also realized. A chanting, banner-waving mob of protesters arrived from Glasgow. They stationed themselves close to my small band and hurled insults at the four-deep lines of police and the arriving rugby fans. Fearing a violent confrontation, I persuaded them to leave when the match started, as my group planned to do. But unlike my group, which dispersed quietly, they marched four or five abreast into Galashiels, the wrong way round the one-way traffic system. Although I had played no part in their demonstration, I suffered from guilt by association. Hostility towards me from some of my constituents continued for several months. At the general election only five months later, the Conservatives did their best to revive the issue. On the eve of polling day, they distributed a leaflet throughout the constituency. It showed a pair of rugby goal posts, with a ball sailing between the uprights, the slogan on it: Convert to Conservatism. Many of my constituents did just that. My majority slumped to 550, and I had to sit through two nail-biting recounts at Jedburgh Town Hall.

My main political experience in that first full Parliament of 1966–70 had been therefore in interparty co-operation to achieve common objectives – the Abortion Act, the Kenya Asian affair, the Anti-Apartheid Movement, Shelter, the Radical Action Movement. My activity was more as a Liberal working with others outside the Liberal Party than within it to advance Liberal causes. It was to prove a formative period in my political outlook.

4

REVIVAL

'You Liberals are Different'

The general election of 1970 was a disaster for the Liberal Party, and very nearly for me too. Our share of the vote fell from 8.5 per cent to 7.4 per cent with a calamitous drop in our Commons representation from twelve MPs to just six. We were right back to the level of the mid 1950s. Total catastrophe was only narrowly averted, because Jeremy Thorpe, John Pardoe and I were all clinging on by majorities under a thousand. If we three had been wiped out it is difficult to see how the party could have survived at all, yet I have no doubt it would have somehow. The late swing to the right ousted the Labour government and very nearly destroyed us.

In my own seat my artificially high by-election majority of 4,607 had settled down to 2,211 in the 1966 general election. So I was defending a marginal seat. The Abortion Bill was not exactly a help and my opposition to the South African rugby tour a positive hindrance. (I must add in parenthesis that very few of my constituents deserted me because they held fundamentally different views on abortion. I recall hearing of one Roman Catholic couple, previously keen Liberal supporters who had become inactive, telling their priest: 'Such a shame about David Steel's bill – we used to be such keen supporters.' 'Yes indeed,' replied Father Donati. 'Mind you, I've never let it put me off voting for the lad myself'; after which the couple reappeared in my local party.)

I had in fact an anti-abortion candidate standing against me which produced unwelcome press attention, but he polled only 103 votes, and it was the rugby issue on which the Tories focused. It was a hard-fought campaign. The Tory candidate was Russell Fairgrieve, a local mill director, later MP for Aberdeenshire West and a junior Scottish Office minister. We still thought we had won until we arrived, as is my habit, late during the count. My agent, Bert Clyne, and supporters had long faces. The counting was done in batches of a thousand. As each thousand was counted the score was entered on a large sheet of paper on a table in the middle of the floor. It was therefore possible to see the running total as the night wore on.

At around 1 a.m. when I arrived, some 20,000 votes – nearly half – had been counted, and I was about a thousand behind Fairgrieve. As the other thousands were added I stayed consistently trailing. I went into a corner and began to scribble notes for my defeat speech. At the same time news was coming in over the radio of Liberal losses elsewhere: Aberdeenshire West; Birmingham Ladywood; Bodmin; Cheadle; Ross and Cromarty; Orpington; Colne Valley. It was one of my darkest hours. About half an hour later one of my stalwart helpers, John Gebbie, said to me, 'There is still hope. They haven't counted the Gala' boxes yet.' He had been watching carefully the positioning of the ballot boxes and bundles of a thousand votes in order to assess our areas of strength and weakness. Galashiels was always the strongest Liberal burgh. But Fairgrieve was a Gala' man, so I was not sure that this would follow as before. As it turned out he suffered from a syndrome well known in Scottish politics which we call: 'Ah ken't his granny' – otherwise known as a prophet without honour in his own land. Galashiels, the second largest town in the then constituency, turned out over 60 per cent for me with 40 per cent divided among the others. Fairgrieve put away his victory speech and the sheriff called the candidates and agents to the platform. I appeared to have won by 700 votes. Fairgrieve immediately demanded a recount, more out of shock and disbelief than anything else and the sheriff granted it without declaring the result, though it went round in whispers.

At the second count my majority appeared to be 1,700. By this time it was after 3 a.m. All the other overnight results were in and the nation was told on TV and radio as results programmes closed down that there was to be a second recount in my constituency. This was inevitable because of the discrepancy between the two results. But instead of just checking the bundles for the thousand error all the papers were given out again and recounted. At nearly 5 a.m. they made my majority 550. By this time I would have settled cheerfully for 1.

We staggered out into the early June dawn where hundreds of people had waited all night and the sheriff read the result as usual from the Jedburgh Town Hall steps. I had had a very nasty fright.

We came back to Parliament a depleted and dispirited band. For Jeremy as leader little had gone right in the three years since he took over from Jo Grimond in 1967. A year later there was much muttering and plotting against his leadership. The party's finances were in an appalling state, and the headquarters moved from the prestige of Smith Square to more reduced circumstances up a squalid litter-strewn lane off the Strand. In 1969 Pratap

Chitnis resigned as General Secretary as the bank overdraft neared six figures. Sir Frank Medlicott, then Party Treasurer, complained that 85 per cent of the funds which came in before the election were donated by twenty-five people, one (as I shall detail later) especially.

Our opinion poll rating rarely reached double figures in this period. In twelve of the twenty-eight by-elections fought in that Parliament – they were more frequent in those days – we lost our deposit. The only bright spot was Wallace Lawler's personal but short-lived win in the declining city centre seat of Birmingham Ladywood – from which much of our attachment to community politics was to flow. Attendance at the 1969 Assembly at Brighton was 900 compared with 1,400 at the same place in 1966.

The number of Liberal councillors declined from the post-Orpington peak; and the Party, in spite of setting a target of fighting 500 parliamentary seats, ended up fielding only 332 candidates, standing in just over half the seats.

Just before the election Jeremy had announced with typical flourish that the Party's debts had been paid and indeed he injected money into some target seats. It was a brave and vigorous campaign in the circumstances, but none of us foresaw the disaster.

It was inevitable after such a setback that we would go through a period of miserable introspection, but Jeremy was saved from any part in that by an even greater tragedy. On 29 June 1970 the Commons was summoned to elect the Speaker. At 3.30 p.m. Jeremy had made the formal speech to the Speaker, following Prime Minister Edward Heath and Leader of the Opposition Harold Wilson. After these proceedings John Pardoe, Jeremy and I were sitting in the Leader's room, mulling over our reduced dispositions, when the Superintendent in charge of police at the House knocked and put his head round the door, saw us sitting there and asked Jeremy if he would come out for a private word. He was back in seconds, followed by the police officer, and slumped into his chair, white as a sheet. 'Help me,' he said, 'it's Caroline. She's dead.' Between them the officer and Jeremy explained painfully to us.

Jeremy had come back from Devon by train with their baby son Rupert and his nanny. Caroline had stayed behind to pack up all the post-election detritus and bring her loaded estate car back to London. Emerging from a roundabout she had run straight into the front of a lorry and had been killed instantly.

This was not the last time that a fatal car crash was to have such a devastating effect on the parliamentary Liberal Party. My reaction was the same in both cases: stunned disbelief followed by acute sadness. Jeremy and Caroline had been married for only two years and though she was not well known in the party, she had become very popular among those who did know her: tall, elegant, with an infectious sense of humour and loyal enthusiasm for Jeremy's work.

John and I had quickly to come to our senses and help out. John stayed to look after Jeremy, while I grabbed a taxi and went round to his flat to break the awful news to the nanny. I can remember the scene. Rupert was sitting gurgling in his high chair and she was feeding him a boiled egg. I can't remember what I said, or how I got out of the flat without bursting into tears.

Our world of politics in all its chaos was forgotten in the midst of this dreadful happening and its aftermath. The episode was a cruel reminder of how much we depend on our wives. Both John and Jeremy had constituency houses but basically tried to pursue a normal family life in London, while I kept my home and family in the Borders. In either practice the demands on a parliamentary wife are substantial. At the inquest various theories were advanced. Caroline might have been moving flowers out of the sun on the passenger seat, or she might just have been exhausted after the election campaign and let her attention wander. It all seemed irrelevant. She was gone.

Jeremy has great resilience. The combined political and personal tragedies would have finished a lesser man. After the state opening a few days later Jo Grimond stood in for him in the Queen's Speech debate saying:

'In different and happier circumstances, my right hon. Friend the Leader of the Liberal Party would have been trying to catch your eye in this debate, Mr Deputy Speaker, but he has been struck by this appalling tragedy, a personal tragedy which, I think, has been felt more deeply in the House than any other, at least in my experience. I must start by asking to be associated with the sympathy which has been expressed to my right hon. Friend by the mover of the Address and by the Leader of the Opposition and the Prime Minister.'

Jeremy himself returned to the House three weeks later to pay a moving tribute to Iain Macleod, the new Chancellor of the Exchequer, who had died suddenly in his sleep:

'One of the supreme qualities of the House of Commons is that when misfortune strikes a colleague the House, individually and collectively, reacts as a family, and its kindness, its understanding and its readiness to share in sorrows is something which is deeply comforting, and for which I myself have cause to be moved and grateful. It is my fervent hope that Eve Macleod will be similarly sustained and helped by the feelings of the House as she faces the agony of separation.'

Jeremy, who had felt the defeat of his Chief Whip, Eric Lubbock, at Orpington most keenly, had appointed me in his place. John was to look after policy and Russell the Party in Scotland.

On my becoming Chief Whip, the Joseph Rowntree Social Service Trust came to my assistance. They had been impressed by the argument of senior figures in the Labour Party that Opposition spokesmen were ill-served in relation to the resources of government. The Trust decided to finance a series of assistants to Opposition front-bench spokesmen. (This pilot scheme was so successful that it led much later to an official scheme of 'aid to Opposition parties' which continues to this day.)

The Trust chose the people to whom assistants would be attached and helped in their recruitment. I made an early bid and was accepted. The young people appointed became known as the chocolate soldiers. I duly advertised, and interviewed a short-list in London, almost settling on Eric Flounders, whom I had met as a college Liberal President, who had an uncle as one of my constituency office-bearers and who later became consecutively an employee in the Liberal Whip's Office and then a councillor and indeed leader of the London Borough of Tower Hamlets Council. He had an impeccable Liberal pedigree.

But I also had to interview a handful of people in Edinburgh the following weekend. One of these was a young pharmacy graduate, and a member of the Labour Party, Archy Kirkwood. I took to him right away and agonized over whom I should appoint. I telephoned Pratap Chitnis, by now secretary to the Rowntree Trust, for advice and described both possibles. He said simply: 'I should avoid the Liberal if I were you – they can be awfully wearing.'

I followed his advice, which coincided with my own instincts, and Archy became a key part of my life from then on. He served four years (1970–74) as the Chief Whip's assistant, married Rosemary Chester, then secretary of the Young Liberals, moved to Ettrick Bridge to begin a career as a solicitor, was brought back by me to act as my chief assistant in 1978 during the Lib-Lab pact, and ended up after the boundary redistribution in 1983 as MP in the new next-door seat of Roxburgh and Berwickshire. He never quite lived down a newspaper description as 'David Steel's devoted 27-year-old assistant'. I grew to rely heavily on – but not always follow – his advice.

Amidst the wreckage the post-election debate began. My contribution to that debate started with an article in *Liberal News* in early July, extensively reported in the serious press. I rejected the view that we should shut up shop and the six of us join one or other of the major parties, as our enemies and some faint hearts were advocating. But with equal force I rejected the view that the party could 'plod on as before, spending the next ten years building back up to a dozen MPs only to face near annihilation again on a sudden swing of the pendulum ... my view is that possibly we should seek an entirely new role ... we should through our constituency associations seek to promote Liberal policies and principles wherever they are to be found.' This might not mean putting up a Liberal candidate in every case, but giving support to those Liberal-minded people who might get elected. It was, of course, a repetition of my earlier 'radical action' theme.

The party executive stamped on all this at its post-election meeting reasserting 'its determination not to support, under any circumstances whether locally or nationally, candidates of the Labour and Conservative parties'. Russell Johnston in the next issue of *Liberal News* succinctly referred to my views as a nonsense, and the editor said reaction was generally hostile. In advance of the autumn Assembly I developed my theme in an article in the *New Statesman*: the party had to shrug off those on the right who had frustrated Jo Grimond's attempts at realignment. 'The party must continue to declare itself on all the major issues – race, education, defence, constitutional reform, housing, social services, industrial relations – on the left of the dividing line between progress and reaction.' I also appealed for more support for the leader:

The best step the party could take is to let Thorpe, as they never in the end let Jo Grimond, actually lead the party. The legion committees of deposit losers should be told by the assembly to leave the strategy to him and get on with their proper task of providing the ammunition. His task now is to lead a guerilla band rather than a third party of the realm, a band concentrating on a few issues which will strike a response rather than posing as a shadow government with a policy for everything.

And I wrote something I was to repeat in different form in my first speech as leader six years later:

It is worth having another attempt at creating a relevant Liberal party. Those unwilling to risk the discomfort of the journey would do better to get off the train now rather than spend their time pulling the communication cord once it is under way.

The 1970 Liberal Assembly at Eastbourne was the poorest attended for years. The only lively debate was between me and John Pardoe on party strategy where I advanced my well-known arguments and John, buccaneering and bullish, wanted a commitment to fight every seat in sight – a broad-front strategy. He won the cheers, the argument and the vote. In a robust article in the party magazine *New Outlook* the following year he admitted:

... the Party is plainly not now a significant force. It is not an instrument of political change. It is not even intellectually very exciting. What has gone wrong?

But he rebutted arguments – which still rumbled – for a change of leader:

71

Since any discussion of the leadership always brings down on my head accusations that I am after it myself I had better set the record straight. As long as Jeremy Thorpe is leader I am not a candidate for the leadership. As long as the Party imposes the restraints which it does impose on the power of positive leadership I am not a candidate. Nor am I a candidate as long as the Party makes it impossible for someone without substantial private financial resources to be leader. I hope this is enough to show that I do not accept the simplistic solution that a change of leadership would significantly change anything.

The two years after the 1970 election were consistently depressing ones for the Party. I busied myself as Chief Whip trying to maintain a parliamentary presence on everything with only six people. I strongly opposed the 1971 Immigration Bill which sought to entrench some of the 'Kenya Asians' provisions in general legislation, and indeed I served on the Committee of the bill. James Callaghan was leading for the official Opposition and as the bill was highly controversial it was a large committee. Its sittings became so extended that I simply could not cope on my own. I was not just the Home Affairs Spokesman but the Chief Whip and half-a-dozen other things as well. I also served as a delegate on the British Council of Churches from 1972 to 1975. I had resigned the Presidency of the Anti-Apartheid Movement and Scottish chairmanship of Shelter in an effort to concentrate on my parliamentary activities. But I told the Committee both privately and publicly that I could not continue to stay for all-night sittings (when the two big parties were able to supply relay teams with camp beds in the building to keep the debates going) and that I would depart each night at midnight. This led to some good-natured banter.

'Liberals go home at midnight – is that official policy?'

'Yes, it is. I'm Chief Whip and I say so.'

Occasionally, of course, some issue on which I felt strongly would come up after midnight and I would stay on, with other Members pointing at their watches.

The 1971 Assembly at Scarborough was unmemorable, being dominated by rows with the Young Liberals in which as Chief Whip I was supposed to play a pacifying role. Jeremy, who had never much cared for party management, left a lot of the liaison to me. The same accusations that the leader was remote from the party machine came up again in my time.

In October 1971 we had some parliamentary excitement with the votes on entry to the European Community. On the issue of entry, sixty-nine Labour MPs defied the Labour whip and voted in favour. We voted for, as the only party to have argued consistently in favour right from the beginning. (Liberals had divided the House in 1959 and mustered three votes in favour of being a founder member.) But when it came to the guillotine motion on the bill, Labour all voted against as did Tory anti-marketeers. The vote was carried by only eleven, with us in support and a Labour Member thumped Jeremy Thorpe aggressively on the shoulder as the result was announced. We had at last mattered on something. It did our morale good.

In 1971 amid the period of political tedium I had another success in legislation – this time on a much more modest scale than the Abortion Act. A problem on which MPs were deluged by correspondence from their constituents was the amount of unsolicited goods, especially publications such as bogus trade directories, being delivered to homes throughout the country. A Private Member's Bill was going through the House to give consumers greater protection from this form of financial piracy. But the Unsolicited Goods and Services Bill failed to tackle the problem of freely distributed offensive literature which fell short of the kind of obscene publication pro-secutable under the Post Office Acts. When the bill came to its Report Stage on a Friday I sought to introduce a new Clause to create a new offence in the posting of such material to named persons, citing the case of a woman recently widowed in my constituency who had been sent a circular advertising a manual of sex technique.

Re-reading the debate recently I was amused at the tone of reply by Nicholas Ridley, the unfortunate junior minister on duty from the Department of Trade and Industry:

'Having described the existing law and announced my complete sympathy with the hon. Gentleman's intentions – I think that the House is at one on this – I must look at the proposed Clause. The objections to it could to some extent be remedied by drafting ... I am certain that it is the menace of the invasion of privacy that we are really after. A Committee of Inquiry is considering the whole question under the chairmanship of Mr Kenneth Younger. It would be discourteous to the Committee if the House legislated now, prejudging its conclusions and pre-empting the report which will shortly be presented. ... Therefore, I advise the House that the Clause has an excellent and worthy intention but is probably wrongly drafted and moreover, is probably in the wrong Bill. While I am entirely at one with the hon. Gentleman's intentions, I suggest that the House would be wiser to await the publication of Mr Younger's report ...'

These sentiments were endorsed by the shadow spokesman for the Opposition.

I was angry at this front-bench conspiracy to ignore the general feelings of outrage among members, so in my reply I pointed out:

73

'It is interesting that all the speeches to which we have listened this morning have supported the objective of the Clause. No one has said that he disagrees with the intention or the desire to put right the grievance felt by many people at the moment ... I believe that it would be wrong for us collectively to wring our hands this morning and then do nothing about it ... while accepting the weaknesses of the Clause, as a matter of parliamentary tactics we should add it to the Bill. It is, after all, a Bill to make provision for the greater protection of people receiving unsolicited goods. The Clause would then go to the House of Lords where it would receive further discussion and there is nothing like a Clause in a Bill to concentrate the mind of the Government on an issue. Although at the end of the day it might not be possible to pass it into law, that is certainly the course I recommend, and I shall therefore not withdraw the Clause.'

To my astonishment the thinly attended House carried my new Clause by 39 votes to 7 and having been tidied up in the Lords now stands on the statute-book as Clause 4 of the Unsolicited Goods and Services Act, 1971.

In the rounds of local elections in May 1971 and May 1972 the Liberals suffered net losses. Most by-elections showed either no gain or a decline in our vote. At Shoreham in 1971 I nearly caused further by-election problems when I went to speak at a by-election meeting. Not paying sufficient attention because I was reading at the time, I opened my railway carriage door in the dark on the wrong side and fell down between the tracks as the train started off. I lay there as electric sparks flew from the contact between the live rail and the departing engine inches from my face, picked myself up covered in grease and complained to the astonished stationmaster. British Rail sent me a letter threatening to prosecute me for trespassing, which in the circumstances I thought pretty brazen.

Early in 1972 I wrote to our candidate in Rochdale, Cyril Smith, who against the 1970 trend had increased our vote there as a popular and populist former Labour mayor of the town. I warned him that the sitting Labour Member, Jack McCann, was seriously ill and sought to inquire whether, if there was a by-election, he would fight it. At first he declined, but I would not take no for an answer and wrote a second time; still Cyril was not keen to do it. However, when the Labour MP died, Jeremy Thorpe pursued Cyril by telephone and persuaded him to stand. We brought in our best organizer, John Spiller, and Cyril coined the slogan: 'It's a two-horse race, and the carthorse will win.' He did, by just over 5,000 votes. That was in October, and the press tended to write it off as Cyril's victory (which it was) rather than a Liberal victory. We decided on the contrary to bounce off the publicity of the by-election with a determined effort to win the next by-election pending at Sutton and Cheam. Trevor Jones ('Jones the Vote'), who was behind the municipal election successes at Liverpool and had by now been elected President of the Party, undertook to mastermind a community-politics campaign in Sutton and Cheam with a completely unknown young candidate, Graham Tope (who is still playing a major role in that south London borough). We were in the mid-term of an unpopular Conservative Government, ten years on from Orpington. Sutton was similar commuter territory. I took charge as parliamentary minder of the campaign but most of the work and inspiration came from Trevor and his helpers, who included a very young Liverpool councillor, David Alton. They had in fact been travelling up and down to the constituency ever since the appointment of the sitting Tory MP as Governor of Bermuda, well before the Smith victory at Rochdale. They even 'helped' the selection of the candidate. With considerable Tory abstentions, the seat was won in December by over 7,000 votes. I was at the count and rushed back into London to greet Jeremy Thorpe with an exuberant hug on the steps of the Savoy Hotel where he and others were leaving the annual Liberal Christmas Ball.

With two by-election gains we now had a head of steam behind our revival. In March 1973 we came close in the safe Labour Co. Durham seat of Chester-le-Street in a campaign where I was frequently quarrelling with Trevor and others over the style and content of our literature: the Liverpool school of politics is rough and often skates on thin ice – but it was again very effective. They managed to pass off the candidate as a local (he had been born there) when in fact he was an antique dealer in Wiltshire.

We also had a by-election in Lincoln where Dick Taverne was standing as a rebellious independent 'Democratic Labour' candidate against the local Labour Party machine. I was heavily involved in the negotiations to secure the absence of a Liberal candidate, and Jo Grimond spoke in his support. He won, and was the precursor of the bigger realignment to occur ten years later.

This was also our first year of upturn in the May local elections (we won 919 seats), especially in Liverpool where we became the largest single party. In July we went on to score a rather unexpected double in winning two by-elections on the same day: Ripon, with David Austick, a well-known local bookseller; and the Isle of Ely, with the flamboyant Clement ('Clay') Freud. Austick had the bad luck, like Graham Tope, to win on massive Tory abstention, only by 946 votes, and he lost again in the subsequent general election. The Clement Freud campaign was the more hair-raising of the two because of the temperamental nature of the candidate, who is one of those highly intelligent people who suffers from being amusing. The Conservative candidate was unmemorable, and Clay described him as a cardboard cut-out making the same speech time and time again so that he sounded like a Roneo duplicating machine. At the end of the campaign the unfortunate man, having changed his suit, mislaid his speech and was last heard of, according to Clay, plaintively saying: 'Roneo, Roneo, wherefore art thou, Roneo?' Our candidate's answers to questions were unpredictable. At one meeting he told a woman who complained about the new council houses: 'For you, madam, we will build an older one.' But the Cambridgeshire people found him engaging and he became a well-loved and respected constituency Member, fending off four heavy challenges to his slim majority until 1987.

By this time the MP for Berwick-upon-Tweed, Lord Lambton, had resigned. Thirty-year-old Alan Beith, then a lecturer in politics at Newcastle University, had come a creditable third in 1970 in this safe Tory seat which nevertheless had a deep-rooted Liberal tradition – Sir Edward Grey and Sir William Beveridge had in the past been Members for the Borough. It was just across the Border in Northumberland and indeed on two minor roads our constituencies actually joined. I therefore took a special interest. I was expecting Rory's birth over the weekend of the Lambton resignation and Alan could not make the long journey up to see me. So we compromised by meeting practically on the border, at a small petrol-station café on the A68 just south of Carter Bar. He told me he had been offered a post for the next academic year in Scandinavia which he had accepted and was not sure whether he could or would get out of it. I helped him to make up his mind to stay on and fight the campaign. (Years later he was to help me make up my mind also to stay on.) I promised every help. John Spiller was again drafted in as agent and I undertook to 'nurse' the seat, making the long journey to Alnwick every week throughout the summer recess to hold a surgery, thus exploiting the Tories' long delay in moving the writ for the by-election. It was a campaign reminiscent of my own and with gigantic effort we won by just 57 votes after two recounts.

On the same November day, Margo MacDonald won the Govan by-election for the SNP and the Tories resisted a strong challenge from us to hold Hove. The Jones/Alton machine was not allowed near Berwick, where I kept an eye on a traditional campaign, while they were let loose very capably at Hove. I had helped persuade Des Wilson to stand there and they again 'helped' his selection. At one point they phoned to ask if I could confirm that he was a member of the Party. 'Yes,' I replied in terms of which they would approve, 'I signed him up myself only yesterday.'

We ended 1973 in high spirits with the parliamentary Party almost doubled from its six members at the general election to eleven and looked forward

76

eagerly to the next general election, probably in 1974. It was to come sooner than we expected.

In the winter of 1973–74 a clash developed between the National Union of Mineworkers and the Conservative government, with the NUM going on strike to press their pay claim. Electricity had to be rationed, and industry went on to a three-day week. There was the usual straight clash, with the Labour Party supporting the miners and the Tories starting the argument about excessive union power and raising the question of 'Who runs the country?' In all this the Liberal Party kept a low profile, so low that Cyril Smith as employment spokesman complained by the unusual method of a public letter to the Party Leader that we were doing nothing. Relations between Thorpe and Smith were never the same again. Jeremy had, of course, other things on his mind. But we agreed that a mediating initiative should be taken. Jeremy, Cyril and John Pardoe went to meet the miners' leaders at their headquarters and had a well-publicized amicable meeting.

Sensing that the miners were not as obdurate as the Government claimed them to be, the Liberal trio then went to see the CBI, representing industrial employers, who had privately been pressing the Government to reach a settlement. In the middle of that meeting, the news came through that the Prime Minister had called a sudden early election. The Liberal initiative was swept aside as Heath demanded a fresh mandate. The country was uneasy at this classic class confrontation between the two parties representing the two sides of industry, and we were still enjoying popular goodwill nourished by the by-election successes. We stood at 11 per cent in the opinion polls at the start of the election but fielded a record 517 candidates backed by a manifesto which echoed popular concerns: after speaking of 'a crisis of public confidence in the two parties which have ruled this country for the past fifty years', the manifesto said:

Liberals refuse to accept that the present crisis is induced by any one political party, Tory or Labour. It is caused by the type of policies which both parties espouse: policies which employ short-term, instant cures, but which leave behind more problems than they solve; politics which are partisan, dividing and polarizing the nation into confrontation between classes whether they be rich or poor, manager or worker, house-owner or tenant.

This country cannot be ruled from the extremes of right and left which set the people against each other – it must be run by a Government whose neutrality is unquestioned, whose policies are fair-minded, and whose politics is not governed by vested interests.

My own constituency campaign was relatively easy. Defending my 550 majority meant a real squeeze on Labour and SNP voters and I had worked hard in the intervening three years. The new Conservative candidate was likeable and younger than me. In fact Stuart Thom had been below me both at school and university, but the national tide was also running with us this time. The impressive Labour candidate, David Graham, duly lost his deposit and was later to join the SDP and then our united Party, contesting Edinburgh seats in 1983 and 1987.

The national campaign, in which I played a relatively small part, was with limited resources a modest success, Jeremy conducting it brilliantly via closed-circuit television in Devon, such was his own narrow majority. David Butler and Dennis Kavanagh in *The British General Election of February 1974* reported:

In one sense the biggest story of the campaign was the rise of the Liberals and, therefore, the decline of the two main parties. By the final days, the other parties had abandoned their assumption that the Liberals would decline greatly. The newspaper stories began to be about where Liberal support was coming from; which party they were hurting most; how many seats they would get; and what they might do if they held the balance in parliament. The Liberals had an easy ride because almost to the end no one attacked them. But on the whole they made the best of the hand they were dealt. They committed no great errors and they reaped the votes of people who had become disillusioned by the Conservative and Labour performances over the years and were in a mood for change. The Liberal leaders seemed faintly surprised at the sudden upsurge in the polls and the growing interest in their manifesto and policies during the last week.

Jeremy kept acknowledging his willingness to work with others but right at the end stressed his desire to form a Liberal Government, 'going for the jackpot', as he called it, and our support actually fell away right at the end. I felt we were both unconvincing on all the coalition questions and not credible on the outright-victory theme. Nevertheless we finished with 18 per cent of the poll but only fourteen MPs – still, however, the largest number since the war. We lost two of our by-election gains, at Sutton and Ripon, but saw the return of both Richard Wainwright (Colne Valley) and Michael Winstanley (Cheadle), who had lost their seats in the 1970 debacle; and we gained Stephen Ross in the the Isle of Wight, Paul Tyler in Bodmin, and Geraint Howells in Cardigan. My own majority soared to an unnatural 9,017. Our popular vote had risen from 7.4 per cent in 1970, from two million votes to six million. We were once again a substantial power in popular if not parliamentary terms.

But what could we do with that power? The Tories had 296 MPs and Labour 301. We held the balance. Neither party had an overall majority and

78

Edward Heath was the incumbent Prime Minister with 200,000 nationwide total votes than Labour and five fewer seats. My own count – after the shambles of 1970 – had reverted to being held the next day, Friday morning. That evening Judy and I toured the Liberal Clubs to thank our supporters and next morning, Saturday, toured all our committee rooms, ending up with tea with our Peebles supporters in one of the town's hotels.

During our morning travels we heard on the car radio that the Prime Minister had invited Jeremy Thorpe to Downing Street for talks, and he was on his way by the morning express from the West Country to London. The newsreader also said: 'It is believed that David Steel, the Liberal Party Chief Whip, is also on his way to London.

I said to Judy: 'He'd better go there,' handed the two older children over to our mother's help and set off with Rory in his carry-cot.

Neither I as Chief Whip, number two in the parliamentary hierarchy, nor anyone else had been consulted. I was confused and irritated and in the afternoon managed to get hold of Jeremy on the telephone at his house in London. Mr Heath had asked if in the light of the indeterminate election result the Liberals would support him in a coalition with Jeremy having a seat in the Cabinet. Jeremy was obviously attracted to the idea but responded that since Heath was citing his greater popular vote as one justification for remaining, he might also think of the Liberals' six million and the case for electoral reform.

Jeremy and I agreed to meet over Sunday lunch with the Party's elder statesmen, Jo Grimond and Frank Byers (our leader in the Lords). I did not like the sound of all this or the adverse reaction both by telephone from all round the country, and among my constituency supporters. We had left the victory celebration in Peebles with the words ringing in my ears: 'Don't you dare come back here as a minister in Heath's Government.'

I saw Jeremy and argued vehemently against such an arrangement for three reasons: first, Heath had chosen to go to the country himself and had lost his majority; second, the huge Liberal vote was largely a protest against his Government's incapacity to deal with the worsening industrial crisis and it would not seem right now to throw that weight behind him; and third, Tories and Liberals together still did not add up to a majority in the Commons. The new Ulster Unionists were the Ian Paisley variety, not, as before, aligned Conservatives. My views on the folly of our party contemplating propping up a defeated Prime Minister – who by definition had lost public confidence – were formed at this time. I have held them consistently ever since, notably during the 1987 general election campaign.

In spite of all these objections I could see that a cast-iron commitment to change the electoral system might just persuade us all it would be worth joining a short-term coalition. I urged Jeremy to go back and see Ted Heath and clarify that point there and then before our much-publicized Sunday lunch meeting. So late that Saturday night I drove his car round to the side entrance in Downing Street and sat waiting in the dark while he went in for a second – this time secret – meeting, unrecorded in the final exchange of letters between them.

Half an hour later he came out saying that all that was offered was a Speaker's Conference on electoral reform plus a seat in the Cabinet and maybe a couple of lesser ministerial positions. 'In that case,' I said, 'it's not on.' Jim Prior, who was at that time Ted Heath's Parliamentary Private Secretary and confidant, records in his memoirs, *A Balance of Power*:

The weekend was dreadful. We had lost the election and yet there was obviously no great enthusiasm in the country for a Labour government. Although Jeremy himself was quite keen and would have relished the post of Home Secretary, his Parliamentary Party would have split. David Steel and Cyril Smith were not interested in any coalition with the Tories. By the Monday it was clear that only a Government including members of all parties would be acceptable to the Liberals, and neither we nor Labour could stomach that.

Once Ted had reported to us that the talks with the Liberals had broken down, there was no more that he could do other than hand in his resignation to the Queen. For us to hang on longer and perhaps even face the House of Commons was not an alternative, since the miners' strike was still on and we were beginning to give the impression that we were bad losers.

The next day the Sunday papers, radio and television were full of contradictory statements from every section of the party. They had gone bananas, convinced that the Sunday lunch was being set up to sell them down the river. The reaction was understandable, given the total lack of any previous discussion of or preparation for a balance-of-power outcome.

Over lunch we decided to recommend to our colleagues the rejection of Ted Heath's invitation. The MPs duly met on Monday. Early in that discussion it became clear that the almost universal view was that we should not go into a Heath Government. However, in the course of the argument one theme kept recurring on which Jo Grimond, Russell Johnston, MP for Inverness, and I expressed anxiety, namely the proposition that it was quite wrong *ever* to consider collaboration of this kind with any other party. We pointed out that it was nonsense for a party which believed in proportional representation not to be willing in principle to work with others, and that we should be prepared in the right circumstances (which admittedly these were not) to do so in order to secure electoral reform and the processes of realigning and reforming the party political structure; but we were a minority and in any case agreed that this was not that opportunity.

The party endorsed a statement drafted by Jeremy, urging Heath to consider talking to Wilson and himself about the formation of a government of national recovery. If, however, he wished simply to continue with his minority Conservative Government in office we would be prepared to consider giving support from the Opposition benches to an agreed programme in the national interest. This last was in fact precisely the same offer we subsequently made to Prime Minister Callaghan, but it later suited Tory propagandists to pretend crudely that we turned the Tories down but accepted Labour's offer.

After consulting his Cabinet colleagues, Prime Minister Heath decided not to pursue either of these courses but to resign. He drove to Buckingham Palace to surrender the seals of office, to be followed closely by Harold Wilson driving to pick them up.

Over the weekend I had telephoned Roy Jenkins on my own initiative to inquire whether he thought there were any possibility of a Lib-Lab arrangement of the sort we had proposed to Heath to form a more secure government. He said rightly that he thought Wilson would not contemplate this and would simply form a minority Labour Government and, as in 1964–6, look for the earliest chance to turn it into a big majority one.

The whole episode left me with the nagging anxiety that we had been wrong not to prepare for such an eventuality, wrong to pretend at the end of the election we could leap straight from a handful of MPs into forming a government, and wrong to reject coalition in any circumstances at any time. This left us looking like an alternative embryo government in permanent exile.

I therefore determined to try to persuade the party during the minority Parliament to address these questions. The first opportunity came with the vote at the end of the Queen's Speech. The general constitutional view is that a Government which fails to secure endorsement of its programme in the first Queen's Speech cannot continue, nor can it demand a second dissolution of Parliament. This was an opportunity, but the Tories funked pressing the necessary amendment to stop Harold Wilson in his tracks from doing what Roy Jenkins had privately predicted. As Jim Prior put it, they were in danger of looking like bad losers. We *did* table an appropriate amendment but in those days (we have since got the rule changed) the Speaker could not under standing orders call our amendment for division. It would have put the Tories on the spot. Cyril Smith records the episode in his autobiography, *Big Cyril*:

The Speaker, Selwyn Lloyd, refused to take the Liberal amendment, and Harold Wilson's left-wing plans were read unopposed.

I was livid. I wrote an angry letter to the Speaker, accusing him of inexcusable Parliamentary bias. It was another mistake. Selwyn, much to my surprise, simply refused to accept the letter. He handed it to David Steel, who brought it into my office holding it between two fingers like a hot, wet cloth just stripped from a steak-and-kidney pudding.

'You really will have to apologize this time, Cyril,' he said.

'I won't,' I said.

'You will. You see Selwyn had no alternative – Commons procedure forbids the taking of two amendments on the Queen's Speech!'

That time I did apologize. I wrote a letter to Selwyn, completely withdrawing any of the personal criticism.

The Labour Government then proceeded on a short-term course of bribing the electorate with a cynical free-for-all spending spree of pay increases starting with the miners. It was the start of the cycle of runaway inflation.

Meantime inside the Liberal Party the strategy arguments raged between people like me who believed that our way forward was to secure a firmer grip on the next parliament and achieve electoral reform inside a coalition government on which we would also have a useful influence on industrial and economic relations, and those who believed that if we just hung on we could leap through into government ourselves. The latter prevailed. This in fact was a recurrent dilemma in our history from Grimond through to Steel.

In June, as Chief Whip, I was to make a routine party political broadcast on television. I wrote the script and dropped a copy off in Jeremy's office. While he said he agreed with my basic coalition arguments, he demanded some toning-down amendments which of course I agreed.

In the broadcast, I argued that:

the fight against inflation cannot be successfully waged by a government based on one party and narrowly appealing to one sectional interest in the community. In our crisis we surely need a much more broadly based government backed by a real majority of public opinion, and that means all parties must be willing to come together on an agreed programme in the national interest. I find the public demand for a government of national unity is now gaining considerably more force, but it can only come about if we get more Liberals in Parliament. We are ready and willing to participate in such a government if at the next election you give us the power to do so. Naturally, like the other parties, we would prefer you to give us an overall majority of seats, but if you don't, we remain ready to contribute towards the kind of fair government based on partnership which you, the electorate, might be seeking. Any party which refused to consider this would be seeking to put power for their own party before the will of the people . . . . The pattern of the two-party stranglehold on British politics is breaking up. That has not been achieved by politicians: you have done it. You have decided rightly that it must end. And what we Liberals ask of you now is that at the next election, whenever it comes, you give us sufficient Members of Parliament to ensure the end of the system of one-party government, which has failed in recent years to unite the nation, and give our country the kind of reforming government which represents the wishes of a clear majority of our people and which alone will therefore have the capacity to solve our problems.

The broadcast was widely reported in the press, but I was strenuously opposed by many sections of the party and indeed a few days later the National Executive adopted a resolution saying the Liberal Party would 'not join a coalition with the Conservative or Labour parties separately and will make this clear at the next election'. Not for the first or last time I found their response irritating and bluntly responded:

The decision on whether the circumstances and terms are right for Liberal participation in any government will be a matter for the enlarged parliamentary party. That is why the present parliamentary party has not committed us to any firm directions prior to the election and why the Executive decision to rule out options can have no validity.

David Butler and Dennis Kavanagh, in *The British General Election of October 1974*, say of this broadcast that it was 'sprung on an unprepared party', which was true, and that the Executive resolution was 'yet another case of poor party management; no MPs turned up to the meeting', which was also true. I shall deal with these management problems later.

The whole issue stimulated public debate inside and outside the Party. It contributed greatly to the decision of former navy minister Christopher Mayhew, Labour MP for Woolwich, to cross the floor and join us, bringing our ranks to a record fifteen Members. The Liberal poll ratings jumped because we were again both relevant and in tune with public feeling. Tory Party research showed them the public liked these themes stressing unity rather than division. Accordingly, Ted Heath as Conservative Leader started to make noises about bringing non-Conservatives into a future government.

Then unfortunately we let the issue slip from our grasp in the 1974 Liberal Assembly in September.

The Times reported on the eve of the Assembly as follows:

When Liberal MPs and delegates to the annual assembly discussed party strategy yesterday at a pre-conference meeting, Mr David Steel, party chief whip, said it would be illogical for the party to proclaim itself against coalitions with other parties in principle. That would not make sense, he said, coming from a party that believed in electoral and parliamentary reform .... But the party would enter the election untrammelled by any commitment in advance or by talk of alliances with any other party.

Chris Mayhew made a most effective contribution to the debate saying that when he had heard my coalition strategy broadcast: 'I thought that all unknowing, the Liberal MPs were putting down a bridge and helping me across. Is this the time to pull up that bridge because we fear further contamination?'

Although the resolution left the future MPs a free hand, only insisting on a meeting of the party council after an election before options were closed, the issue deeply divided the party. Jeremy was leaned on very heavily before his end-of-Assembly speech, which I found very disappointing. Instead of repeating our summer initiative, he was back to campaigning for an outright Liberal victory, downplaying the coalition strategy to being perhaps a necessity in national emergency.

When Prime Minister Wilson duly called the second election the following month in order to attempt to gain an overall majority, he faced Ted Heath arguing for more broadly based government while we, under the indigestible slogan 'one more heave', ran a stale campaign on all our worthy policies. Jeremy's objective was 'nothing less than total breakthrough'; but the election began badly before the campaign proper started. Jeremy had decided in a stroke of brilliance to tour the south-coast beaches in September by hovercraft, addressing the masses on beaches and in harbours. Unfortunately the weather was atrocious and most of the press and TV coverage was of the repeated deluging of the tiny craft and its political contents. I kept clear of this escapade, in which MPs Cyril Smith, John Pardoe and Paul Tyler had agreed to take part. Jeremy planned the whole operation down to the last detail with great gusto; and had the weather been kind, I've no doubt it would have been a pre-election triumph. As it was, the public image was pretty disastrous. There was one other problem. John Pardoe said to me: 'David, everything was arranged down to the size of our wellingtons. Only no one had given any thought as to what we were supposed to be saying.'

In spite of fielding a hundred more candidates in October than in February our total vote fell 1 per cent and we dropped back to thirteen MPs. Worse still, we were cast out into irrelevance once more as Harold Wilson obtained his overall majority. My own constituency majority settled back a bit to 7,400.

After the election I told Jeremy Thorpe that I wanted to leave the management post of Chief Whip and resume a spokesmanship. I was fed up with the constant balancing act between the party machine and the party leader, and my strategy views had not found enthusiastic favour with either. Eventually he agreed and early in 1975 gave a party at which he presented me on behalf of all my colleagues with a painting of the Palace of Westminster by Nicholas Ridley as thanks for my five years as Chief Whip. In a typically generous personal gesture, he added a pair of gold cufflinks from himself. I was appointed Foreign Affairs spokesman.

My first task was to be the Liberal representative on the 'Britain in Europe' campaign, the all-party group set up to secure a 'yes' vote in the referendum on the entirely unnecessary 'renegotiated terms' of entry to the European Community, which had been Harold Wilson's design for keeping his divided party in one piece on the European issue.

As I have already recounted, the Liberal Party had a uniquely consistent and pioneering attitude to the Community. In the so-called 'great debate', lasting six days in 1971, at the end of which the House had voted to join, after my ritual quotations from Gladstone, *Hansard* records me saying:

I have received a large amount of mail on the Common Market – not necessarily from constituents but from people who feel strongly on it. One letter went roughly as follows: 'Both Mr Heath and Mr Wilson have tried to sell the country down the river at different times. You Liberals are different: you have been consistently honest. You have tried to sell the country down the river all the time.' I admire that back-handed compliment.

In 1975 I was glad to get into a good, going political campaign on an issue on which I felt strongly. The Committee chairman was Roy Jenkins, with Willie Whitelaw, deputy leader of the Conservative Party as vice-chairman, together with ex-party leaders like Ted Heath and Jo Grimond. A great many ex-Tory ministers and current Labour ministers were involved. Each 'side' in the referendum campaign had public funds at its disposal. The chief executive on our side was Sir Con O'Neill from the Foreign Office, backed by an impressive team of Tory Central Office and Transport House mandarins all of whom had experience of running *victorious* election campaigns.

Archy Kirkwood left his employment as my assistant to look after the youth campaign before going back to Scotland to take up his career as a solicitor.

Instead of grubby election rooms, we met over substantial breakfasts in hotel suites to plan the campaign. The all-party public meetings were enormous and I was a regular statutory Liberal opener at these events, such as in the Usher Hall, Edinburgh, with Peter Carrington and Roy Jenkins. It was an exciting and effective campaign, but it gave me an insight into what we as a Party were up against. When I sometimes chafed at our amateur approach, I had to recall the thousands of volunteers who give all the hours God sends to the party, and the hopelessly underpaid officials who toil with inadequate budgets, offices and equipment to keep our show on the road.

This lot, backed as well by substantial industrialists, simply snapped their fingers for what they needed, as clearly they were used to doing in election campaigns. I recall on one occasion, because they insisted I headed a youth press conference, they laid on a private jet complete with stewardess and champagne to get just me and David Hall, my temporary assistant, from London to a meeting in Bonn. On another occasion a helicopter was produced to get me quickly to Norwich, at which meeting I was again to be the warmer-upper. Willie Whitelaw's staff got wind of the fact that the BBC *9 o'clock News* were only going to take the first speech and tried to change the running order. I pretended innocence (since I had been forewarned) and expressed complete satisfaction with my usual lowly role.

In fact the whole campaign was not only stimulating, enjoyable and successful (the vote was more than 2–1 in favour), but it gave me yet more national exposure and increased my working familiarity with leading figures in other parties in a common cause.

In the summer of 1975, following the successful European Referendum, I decided that it was time to return to a new exposition of party policy. The party had a useful 'Strategy 2000' series of pamphlets coming out, looking to the end of the century. I thought this would be a useful vehicle to promote some of my own heresies as well as my version of party orthodoxies in one pamphlet. After all, Jeremy Thorpe would be completing ten years as Leader in that parliament, and while he might go on for many years yet, equally he might not. I had attended for years to the mechanics of politics as Chief Whip and to various single-issue campaigns culminating in Europe. I now wanted to take a broad brush to the canvas.

Under the unexciting title *The Liberal Way Forward* I set out my stall in time for publication at the September Assembly. It received a reasonably favourable welcome. At least it got some attention, even from the *Daily Telegraph* which described it as 'a rich and gaudy miscellany of improbable suggestions'.

I pointed out that while in the October '74 election we had polled 18 per cent of the votes, surveys among the under-35s showed we had 25 per cent of those. I accepted that this was in part a negative reaction to the other two parties. Looking at the Conservative Party after six months under its new leader, Margaret Thatcher, I wrote, with remarkable prescience: 'To them the word "freedom" is not a Liberal concept – theirs is the freedom to exploit others and enrich oneself to a degree which ignores the wider good of the community.'

And of Labour with equal prescience I said: 'Today the short-term interests of powerfully organized better-off sections of the working class can be pressed to a degree which is damaging to the entire community ... socialism as practised elsewhere is seen to be every bit as authoritarian and repressive as old style reactionary capitalism.'

The pamphlet continued with a blast against the politics of size (I had been reading E. F. Schumacher), philosophized about the balance between order and freedom, and went on to outline my views on the need to create an industrial partnership, one of my favourite Liberal themes. The other parties had 'maintained for a quarter of a century an almost wholly arid debate between public and private enterprise whilst virtually ignoring questions of size and industrial democracy in both'.

In one section I addressed some of the issues which were to occupy us in legislation nearly ten years later:

A free postal ballot for trade union elections would be a step forward. To discourage irresponsible industrial disputes social security payments to strikers' families should be limited to those stoppages called in a secret ballot by at least 50 per cent of those entitled to vote. Similarly the Inland Revenue should be required to limit the practice of giving instant tax rebates to those on strike, instead leaving any PAYE remissions to be calculated at the end of the financial year.

These may sound harsh measures, but they are in fact reasonable ones in the interests of the wider community. Power is a constantly shifting commodity. While past governments of all parties were right to advance the powers of the organized trade union movement in the interest of an underprivileged section of society, the time has come to reassess and adjust their power in relation to everybody else's.

I also advocated the phasing out of mortage-interest tax relief, describing it as 'producing the biggest benefit for those with the largest incomes and most expensive houses'; the ending of forty different social-security means tests in favour of a tax-credit scheme; long-term controls over prices and incomes via our inflation tax proposals; larger student grants in return for one year's national service, civil or military; the conversion of council tenancies into home ownership with mortgages; and the maximum of self-government for Scotland and Wales consistent with common sense. I ended with a call to recognize that a commitment to Liberal Democracy might exist in some people outside the Liberal Party, giving as an example:

Many of the self-styled social democrats would be happier company in combination with Liberals than Socialists. Should such an opportunity for an effective regrouping of the left come about it is important that the Liberal Party should not behave like a more rigid sect of the exclusive brethren, but be ready to join with others in the more effective promotion of liberalism.

I happily touted this pamphlet round not just the Liberal Assembly at Scarborough but also the Labour Conference in Blackpool, which I enjoyed attending as a visiting commentator for BBC television.

The Glorious summer 1975 was a period of celebration and the autumn one of fulfilment. Yet the storm clouds were gathering. Down in the West Country, a man shot a dog.

5

JEREMY THORPE
A Tangled Web

Four entire books have already been written on the 'Thorpe affair'. It is therefore difficult to know where to begin to deal with it in one chapter. But the episode was a traumatic one – for Jeremy obviously, but also for me, and indeed for the entire Liberal Party. Only one 'inside' story has been told, written by former MP Peter Bessell and published in America. It is couched in such terms that it could not possibly be published or sold here; and since he died a few years ago he cannot be challenged on his account. It is a hair-raising and eminently readable – at times entertaining – book, written when he felt the need at last to be frank about his own conduct. I see no point in going back over detail well covered (with varying degrees of inaccuracy) in all these accounts. What I intend to record are the events as I saw them and the effect they had on the participants.

I first met the man who was to cause Jeremy Thorpe's downfall in 1971, a whole five years before he became a figure of public controversy. In May of that year he was living in the Welsh village of Talybont and had been befriended by a widow, Mrs Parry-Jones, who was an active Liberal worker. So distressed was she by his story that she wrote to Emlyn Hooson, her nearest Liberal MP in Montgomeryshire, saying that a young man's life had been ruined by 'a leading member of your Party', and that he 'had been promised expenses to settle in Wales'. She sought Emlyn's help to 'influence them to keep to their word and to keep the honour of your Party'. Emlyn replied saying he would need to know who 'they' were and suggested she either come to his constituency surgery or write further in confidence. In her second letter she asked him to 'please tell Mr Peter Bessell that Mr Norman Scott is in a grave situation and if he has any decency he will fulfil his promise made to him immediately'. Emlyn again suggested she should come to see him and arrangements were made for her to bring Norman Scott to see him in Westminster.

The day before he was due to come, Emlyn, a QC, was called away for a murder trial in court and he hurriedly told me the little he knew, suggesting that as Chief Whip I should see them, accompanied by his secretary who had been making the arrangements and would take a shorthand note. At this point we both assumed that the complaint was against Peter Bessell, who had suddenly retired from the House in 1970 after being Member for Bodmin for less than six years. He was in constant financial difficulties and had been bailed out by at least two Liberal benefactors. He had also had a string of ill-concealed affairs with his secretaries, and was then living in America, having abandoned his wife. (He admitted his promiscuous nature in his book.) Nothing, Emlyn and I agreed, would surprise us.

But the story Norman Scott told me in the Liberal Whip's office on the afternoon of 26 May was more shattering than anything I had been expecting. I took a few handwritten notes which I still have and Emlyn's secretary, Helen Roberts, kept a full record.

Briefly, he alleged that he had first met Jeremy Thorpe some years before when a stable boy at the home of one of Jeremy's friends, Van de Vater. Somehow his National Insurance card had not been fully paid up and Jeremy had offered to help sort this out. Scott accused him of 'stealing' his National Insurance card. Jeremy in fact did write to ministers at the Social Security Department, trying to solve this problem. One day Scott turned up at the Central Lobby at the House of Commons and put in the routine green card to see Jeremy, who then offered him a bed at his mother's house in Oxted, Surrey, that evening. Scott alleged that Jeremy committed sodomy with him that night (a graphic account is given in Bessell's book) and that thereafter for a period of four years they had conducted a homosexual liaison at various places he named, including hotels in the West Country, Jeremy's tiny flat in Marsham Court, London and even in his car.

His main obsession was the non-return of his National Insurance card, without which obtaining employment was difficult. The story was – on the face of it – implausible. All MPs are used to dealing with nutcases of varying degrees and this story was none the easier to follow when it was laced with the assertion that he had been arrested with a gun at the House of Commons in 1962 and indeed had been a patient in a mental hospital. Sexual fixations with public figures are not uncommon.

What made this story alarming was the fact that he produced out of a bag a whole series of letters signed by Peter Bessell, and some by his secretary, mainly on House of Commons notepaper, referring to sums of money enclosed. These ranged from £3 to £10 and occurred almost weekly for a time in 1967-8. I took copies of these. He further alleged that Bessell had promised him £5,000 to settle in Wales, and the village garage proprietor would certify overhearing a telephone conversation to that effect. The £5,000 had not materialized and hence his current predicament and Mrs Jones's letter to Emlyn.

Bessell asserts that Jeremy had found Norman Scott at first meeting 'simply heaven'. That is not how he appeared to me, though he obviously had been good-looking and was not yet the gaunt figure that appeared in the public eye five years later. He had a limp, clammy handshake, seemed to perspire profusely and spoke softly and hesitatingly, giving the clear impression of having had some kind of nervous breakdown.

Among other pieces of the narrative, he had two different names, Josiffe and Scott, his luggage had been burgled by Jeremy, he had been sent to Ireland, had married a girl he had got pregnant, but was now divorcing his wife for adultery – this too was somehow Jeremy's fault – and he had been accused by the police of stealing a coat. In short, he gave me the impression of being one of those rather inadequate drifters through life one meets from time to time who are always ready to blame their misfortunes on somebody else.

But there were these letters. He explained that the money had started being paid to help him out over the insurance card problem, then to keep him quiet. They looked surprisingly like the result of blackmail. Having taken all the necessary notes, we suggested they leave. The widow was returning to Wales leaving Scott in London. I undertook to relay the conversation to Emlyn. When he returned to the House that evening, I called him into my room and unveiled the story. Emlyn said I looked as white as a sheet. 'It's not about Bessell,' I said, 'it's about Jeremy.'

Emlyn arranged to see Scott himself and listened to the whole story. Then he suggested the two of us should see Jeremy as soon as he returned from a visit to Zambia. We were now entering the Whitsun recess and I was off on a short caravan tour of Fife with Judy and our two young children. Over the next few days I had sleepless nights and – since this was before the advent of radiophones – kept contact with Emlyn through various wayside public telephone kiosks. The *Secret Life* book, written by three *Sunday Times* journalists, says Jeremy found me 'hard to track down'. Emlyn reached Bessell on the telephone in Cornwall – he was back on a rare visit from the States. Asked out of the blue about Norman Scott, he admitted that he had been making the payments to keep Scott from causing trouble. He seemed to verify the main elements of Scott's story. According to his own account, he then caught the train to London to meet Jeremy on his return from Africa. By the time I got hold of him on the telephone, he declared that Emlyn had misunderstood his conversation and that he had merely been helping Scott over his National Insurance card problem. According to his own account, after speaking to Emlyn he blatantly lied to me.

Emlyn went to see Jeremy himself before I returned to London and repeated Bessell's telephone conversation. Jeremy denied that Bessell had ever acted on his behalf and said moreover that Bessell denied the alleged substance of his conversation with Emlyn. Emlyn told Jeremy that if the allegations were true, then he was a combination of Horatio Bottomley and Oscar Wilde; that if so, he should resign the leadership, stay on the sidelines and take steps to ensure that the matter did not become public nor be allowed to harm the Liberal party. Jeremy gave a very spirited response.

Emlyn and I went to see Jeremy in his room to report on Scott's allegations. Jeremy tried to be calm, putting all the blame on Bessell, who had handled the insurance card question clumsily, but solemnly denying the rest of Scott's allegations. He asserted that Scott could well have been blackmailing Bessell over some aspect of his personal and financial life. At one point the exchange became confused and heated as Emlyn asked him whether, if all this became public and was shown to be true, he would resign as leader. Jeremy replied: 'Of course, but it isn't and I won't.' Emlyn and I wished to inform the parliamentary Party that, having discussed it with Jeremy, we agreed that we ought to conduct a private inquiry into Scott's claims, and involve a senior figure in the party. Frank Byers, leader of the Liberal peers, was an obvious and agreed choice.

We arranged for Norman Scott to come and meet the three of us in Frank Byers's room in the Lords. I introduced him to Frank, and we sat round a large oval oak table. With only minor variations, Scott rehearsed the whole story he had told me a few days before – he was obviously used to telling it. There was one comic addition to his story. He claimed to have been in Jeremy's flat on one occasion when Frank Byers had come to see him. Jeremy, he said, had shoved him into a cupboard. Emlyn and Frank cross-examined him. Did he have any letters from Jeremy? Yes, but he couldn't produce any: they were with a Major Shute in Gloucestershire. The only letter he had produced from Jeremy was one signed by his personal assistant, Tom Dale, to the aforementioned garage proprietor in the Welsh village, who had written direct to Jeremy on his behalf. That letter stated simply and oddly: 'As far as he is aware he does not know Mr Norman Scott. However, he believes that Mr Van de Brecht de Vater knew a Mr Norman Josiffe who may be the same person. Mr Thorpe asks me to say he is under no obligation to this gentleman.'

When Emlyn asked Scott why he was pursuing a vendetta when he himself claimed that his relationship with Jeremy had ended in 1964, he again stressed the importance of his National Insurance card. Emlyn asked if he was after money. Scott broke down and declared that he still loved Jeremy and felt he had been rejected and badly treated. At this point Frank Byers, who was notoriously short on suffering fools, exploded and told Scott he was nothing but a dirty little blackmailer or words to that effect.

Scott burst into tears and fled from both the room and the building. 'He's like a jilted girl,' said Emlyn. I felt the exchange had been less than useful. Scott had given us the name of the police officer – now Detective-Inspector Smith – to whom he claimed he had given a full statement of his complaints against Jeremy some years earlier. We contacted him and he came to see the three of us, together with a colleague. Yes, the police had taken statements from Scott, and there was nothing on which any action could be taken. Penrose and Courtiour in their book incorrectly record that the police officers were actually present when we interviewed Scott. They were not, but Bessell repeats this version, no doubt taken from their *Pencourt File*.

Scott himself went back to the police after our interview and gave them a further lengthy statement going back over the same ground.

Frank then got Jeremy to set out his account of his dealings with Scott in a letter to him. This he duly did, describing him as a 'nutcase' and sending a copy to the Home Secretary, Reginald Maudling. Maudling replied in a brief note, a copy of which I still have in my file: 'Dear Jeremy, Thank you for showing me your letter to Frank Byers. I have shown it to the Commissioner. Neither of us see any reason to disagree. Yours, Reggie.'

That seemed to be that. No one in the party outside the three of us knew about either the Scott allegations or Bessell's activities until the story blew up in the press five years later, following Scott's outburst in that West-Country court. There has been speculation as to why we did not proceed further in our inquiries. *The Pencourt File*, enamoured of conspiracy theories, even suggests an enormous establishment cover-up of which we and Reginald Maudling and everybody else were a part. It asks, for example, why we did not contact Major Shute whom Scott alleged to be holding love letters, when 'we found it easy to locate him'. The answer is very simple: it was up to Scott to produce his letters if they existed. We were not investigative journalists in search of scandal but parliamentary colleagues determined, while seeking the truth, to minimize damage to our Leader and our Party. We could hardly ring up every Shute in the Gloucester telephone directory and say: 'My name is Steel/Hooson. I'm a Liberal MP. I was just wondering if you have any personal compromising letters from my leader to a man called Norman Scott or Josiffe dated about ten years ago.'

We had to consider the evidence before us. Bessell had told two of us contradictory stories and then gone to ground in the States. The police assured us there was no evidence of actual blackmail on Scott's part, nor was there evidence of any criminal offence on Jeremy's or Peter Bessell's part. (Here I ought to mention that in 1967, under the Sexual Offences Act, homosexual conduct between consenting adults over twenty-one in private was decri-minalized. However, if Scott's allegations were substantiated he had been only twenty at the start of the liaison; but it was inconceivable that the DPP would prosecute on such a technicality, dating over ten years before, even if there were any evidence, which there wasn't.) Nothing was going to come to light via the authorities, but might it via the press? We considered that, but took the view that no newspaper could risk publishing any of this. Some years later I discovered that we were correct. Scott had indeed touted his story round Fleet Street. The *Daily Mirror* invited me in great secrecy, once the story became public, to see a most confidential file on Thorpe which they kept at their offices. They were crestfallen when I told them: 'I've seen all these papers – about five years ago.'

Lord Byers never indicated what his personal reaction was to the whole story. He clearly saw it as his duty to ensure that if possible the Party leader should be protected from the scandal, bearing in mind all the inevitable adverse effects it would have on the Party, while testing the possible destructive fall-out from the episode. His gruff manner towards Scott was unfortunate, but it was obviously Scott's fault that he did not produce any of the evidence which subsequently emerged in court about which we could have questioned Jeremy. He failed to co-operate sufficiently to convince us of his story. As to Emlyn, he was in a particularly difficult position. As a QC he of course accepted that there was nothing on which we could act, but he was more deeply suspicious of Jeremy than either Frank or I. His problem was that he would almost certainly at that point have been the main contender for the leadership if it were vacated by Jeremy, a point on which Bessell played (and records vehemently in his book).

As for me, some commentators later suggested a Scottish naïveté on the homosexual aspect. It is of course true that Scottish public opinion has always been more hostile to such conduct than English, and indeed as I've mentioned the law in Scotland was not changed until several years after that in England. While the memoirs of most men who went to English public schools seem to be laced with some such episodes at school, I have to say that life at George Watson's College, Edinburgh, beyond the usual changing room mild hanky-panky and platonic schoolboy crush, was free from such activity. When I was talking recently to some of my friends who were university contemporaries, we agreed that we had genuine difficulty recalling anyone who was homosexual among our thousands of fellow students, whereas no university is complete nowadays without its gay society. It is a moot point as to which experience is the healthier or happier. As a student I recall being impressed by a sermon on the subject in St Giles' Cathedral, Edinburgh, from Sir John Wolfenden, whose Report in 1957 recommended the change in the law for which I subsequently voted as an MP ten years later. Indeed when the Scottish Homosexual Rights Group was set up I was one of the MPs from each party to become an honorary vice-President, especially motivated by what the parents of a young constituent who had committed suicide told me of their sad experience.

If all this sounds a bit prissy and remote, I have to add that in my nearly twenty-five years of politics I have worked with many people including MPs of different parties who are either openly or privately homosexual. Indeed David Penhaligon, MP, used to argue that while he personally disliked homo-sexuals, they made very good politicians and political activists because they could spend so much more time on politics, most being free of domestic obligations. It has never bothered me. I had known Jeremy quite closely, I thought, for six years and had no inkling of any such tendencies. I had seen him suffer the tragic loss of his wife the previous year. In any case what he did and with whom a decade before seemed to me entirely his own business. Mine was a classically Liberal attitude.

In the end we were left to choose between the word of a neurotic stranger and the explanation of our parliamentary colleague. We unanimously agreed that the matter was closed. Less than a year later the Welsh widow committed suicide. At the inquest on Mrs Parry-Jones, Scott told of her approach to Emlyn and me and her disappointment that we had not in some way 'rescued' Scott to whom she had obviously become emotionally attached. He started to blurt out his full story, but the coroner shut him up as being irrelevant. Reporters filed to their newsdesks and we responded to inquiries that we were well aware of these ancient allegations. Nothing appeared in print.

So, I believe, it would have remained but for the extraordinary subsequent conduct of some of Jeremy's friends and associates, fuelled by Jeremy's own unbridled loathing and dread of Scott.

On 29 January 1976 the British public at large first became aware of the existence of Norman Scott and his allegations, and the unfolding of attempts to silence him which would end Jeremy Thorpe's career. Again, since these events and the subsequent trial are fully detailed in so many other accounts, I shall repeat only those aspects relevant to the political disaster which occurred. The police had been questioning a man called Andrew Newton about his shooting of Norman Scott's Great Dane, Rinka, and late-night frightening of Scott with a gun in the middle of Exmoor. He was charged with illegal possession of a firearm with intent to endanger life. Stories about Scott and the shot dog had appeared intermittently in coded fashion in *Private Eye* for some time, and the press were taking fresh interest in Scott's story. Scott made it clear he was going to 'reveal all' when he himself appeared in Barnstaple Magistrates Court, charged with defrauding the Post Office of £58. As part of his defence he started to blurt out all his old allegations against Jeremy. Under the privilege of the Court, the press were at last free to publish the allegations and embarrass the party leader without fear of libel actions.

Jeremy had been aware that both cases were coming up and had prepared his ground. He took Cyril Smith, who was by now Chief Whip, into his confidence, told him to expect some wild tales in West Country courts, revealed the existence of the 'unstable lunatic' Norman Scott, and the holding of the 1971 party inquiry. He also showed him Reginald Maudling's letter and another astonishing private letter from Peter Bessell (still in America) to Jeremy's solicitor, confirming that Norman Scott had been blackmailing him over one of his extramarital affairs. This letter – it later emerged – was obtained by David Holmes (Jeremy's long-term friend and best man at his wedding to Caroline), who went to America and persuaded Bessell to write it in order to protect Jeremy if the existence of any of the letters came out in the Newton shot-dog case. Earlier Jeremy had shown me the same letter. Bessell, in his evidence and in his book, recounted how David Holmes had arrived in California to persuade him to write the false private letter to Jeremy's solicitor. He had typed it and put it in a sealed envelope. On the way to the airport he had second thoughts. Holmes said he would return the letter, but as Bessell was parking the car he hopped it through the airport and on to the plane. Learning of this account, I suddenly recalled that when Jeremy had shown *me* the typed letter, another handwritten one had fallen out of the envelope, beginning 'Dear Jeremy, I was glad to see David again ...' I said, 'Is this for me?' He snatched it away. Much later I realized that it was obviously referring to Holmes. Cyril was dumbfounded by all this but accepted the nature of what he had been shown, confirmed by conversations with me and Emlyn relating to 1971.

Unfortunately, a second thunderbolt – by a truly Shakespearian tragic coincidence – was to hit Jeremy the very same day: the publication of the Department of Trade Inspectors' report into the affairs of London and

Counties Bank, of which Jeremy had until recently been a non-executive director. The report referred to the 'inherent deviousness' of Gerald Caplan, the chairman who had recruited Jeremy and who, the report said, 'had less regard for the truth and a lower standard of integrity than is reasonably to be demanded of a chairman and managing director of a public company'. Not for the first or last time, Jeremy was unfortunate in his choice of associates. The bank had crashed, owing £50 million pounds. He had been paid £5,000 a year and the bank bought his car and gave him a share-option. The fact that he had been on the board of such a dubious outfit was described in the report as a 'cautionary tale for any leading politician'.

Oddly enough, what could have been a devastating blow to his position as leader was actually cushioned by Scott's outburst in court the very same day. Inside and outside the Party there was general outrage that a court could be used to provide cover for such sensational allegations against a public figure. For a few days the sympathy for Jeremy on that score overlaid the criticism of his judgement in being with the failed bank.

In fact the parliamentary Party at its weekly meeting the following Wednesday was intending to question Jeremy about the London and Counties collapse. Instead the general reaction to the press coverage of Scott's outburst plus daily additions of details such as the Bessell letters and payments to Scott completely distracted his colleagues from such a course.

Cyril Smith divulged his having seen in Jeremy's office the letter from Bessell about Scott's blackmail of him, not knowing that Bessell had written this for strictly private use as an affidavit to show to police, prosecution or anyone else inclined to take Scott's allegations against Jeremy seriously. Bessell then told the *Daily Mail* that Scott had never blackmailed him. The newspapers produced titbits day by day. A Dr Gleadle had paid Scott £2,500 for his file of letters, not realizing that copies existed in a number of places, including my own files. There was endless speculation as to who had hired Newton to shoot Scott's dog or possibly even murder Scott. Over these few weeks Harold Wilson as Prime Minister threw in what eventually turned out to be a large red herring by suggesting that South African agencies might be behind the attempt to smear the Liberal leader, on the flimsy basis that one South African journalist – among many – had seen Scott and had been trying to sell the story. The endless press speculation had a devastating effect on Party morale. No one could go canvassing because no satisfactory explanation could be given of anything which kept appearing in the newspapers. The Liberals in general and Jeremy in particular were the subject of jokes in every pub and club in the land. Our children (as Graeme and Billy years later told me) were taunted in the school playgrounds.

As an example of the mood, I recall giving a reception in my hotel suite in Strasbourg for the members of the Liberal group in the Council of Europe Assembly, to which I had naturally invited my British Conservative and Labour colleagues. It has usually been my habit to share a twin-bedded room with my assistant on foreign visits, largely to save money. By this time Andrew Gifford had replaced Archy Kirkwood. He was busy ferrying coats into the bedroom when one rather obnoxious Tory MP, noting through the door the fact that in this hotel the beds were placed together, roared: 'Ho, ho, we know what Liberals get up to.' Andrew looked embarrassed and I took the MP aside: 'You can make crude jokes about me but you have no right to insult my assistant. I expect you to apologise to him.' He did, but that was the flavour of what we were all living through.

Most of us continued to defend Jeremy, recognizing the bank matter as serious but believing he had to be given moral support while all these rumours raged and so long as the court cases had still to come to fruition. He was not being helped by the various contradictory interviews Bessell was giving to reporters in America and the unveiling of bits of Bessell's own private life.

On 4 March our vote at a by-election in Coventry slumped and we lost our deposit. Jo Grimond, caught off an early-morning transatlantic flight by an airport reporter who asked 'Could Jeremy's problems have contributed to the poor result?' responded 'Well, it certainly begins to look like it.' Cyril Smith, never in the best of health, was taken to hospital and the press invaded his bedside. 'Somebody is telling bloody lies,' he said with characteristic bluntness, providing yet more headlines.

We were, in truth, in total disarray. Richard Wainwright and Emlyn Hooson had both been in touch with Bessell by letter to persuade him to tell the truth. They undoubtedly thought Jeremy should resign the leadership in the interests of the Party, but most of us believed he should be given the benefit of the doubt. Then on Saturday 6 March most of the daily papers carried the sensational revelation that the man who had given Dr Gleadle the £2,500 to buy Scott's letters from Bessell was David Holmes, Jeremy's old friend, best man and godfather to his son Rupert. Not only Richard Wainwright and Emlyn Hooson but John Pardoe were all quoted in the Sunday papers, expressing varying degrees of incredulity. I too began to change my attitude to the continuance of Jeremy's leadership. It might *just* be believable that Holmes had made the purchase as he said without Jeremy's knowledge; but it seemed to me inconceivable that once the fact of that payment by somebody had become public, he would not have told his old friend that it was he who had done it.

Jeremy, seeing the tide of support among his colleagues ebbing, quickly issued a statement on the Sunday saying that now that a new system in our constitution for electing a leader was in preparation (involving all party members, not just MPs) he proposed to offer himself for re-election after the annual assembly in September so that the Party in the country could 'have the opportunity of making its views known on the leadership of the party'. His own postbag was full of sympathetic letters of support. He telephoned the Chief Whip to tell him of his public announcement, rather than to consult him, which was to contribute to Cyril Smith's indignant resignation. Two days later I received further information not known to any of my colleagues, which made me convinced that Jeremy had to go, namely that David Holmes had been receiving large sums of money out of funds supposedly donated for Liberal election purposes.

I was having dinner that Tuesday evening at the Chesterfield Hotel with my great friend Nadir Dinshaw. He was not his usual relaxed self. I had first met Nadir late in 1968 when he and his wife were lunching with Jeremy and Caroline at the House of Commons. Jeremy insisted that I come to the table to meet him. They had been friends for some months and after Caroline's death, during which period Nadir had been very supportive of Jeremy, Jeremy asked Nadir to be an extra godfather to Rupert. In the months to come I got to know Nadir and rapidly learned to rely on his wisdom whilst depending increasingly on the very high quality of his friendship. It was I who, on the only occasion the two ever met, introduced him fleetingly to Jack Hayward. Jack Hayward I knew only slightly, having met him over lunch with Jeremy and Caroline in their flat and on two or three other occasions in connection with his sponsorship of round-the-world yachtsman Chay Blyth who had been my constituent and supporter. Subsequently, he was knighted for all his public works, which included the purchase of Lundy Island for the nation, his first contact with Jeremy. In 1970 Nadir had been of enormous help to me during the passage of the Immigration Bill and in the years to come he rapidly became a friend and counsellor with whom I could discuss anything. (Nadir comes from a wealthy and very prominent Parsee family in Karachi, though he has lived for many years in Jersey.) Although well before 1976 he was one of my closest friends, the Thorpe disaster brought us still closer together.

I received an unpleasant shock at what Nadir had to tell me that evening, Tuesday, 9 March 1976. First, he swore me to absolute secrecy. I undertook to tell nobody what he now felt obliged to tell me. He had been that afternoon to see his old friend the Dean of Westminster, Edward Carpenter, and was now telling me what he had told Dr Carpenter. Just after the first of the two elections in 1974 (Holmes, it must be remembered, purchased the Scott letters on the very eve of poll in February), Jeremy had asked Nadir if he would be kind enough to receive the sum of £10,000, which he was arranging to accept from property developer Jack Hayward in the Bahamas, into Nadir's account in Jersey and pay it to David Holmes, to settle various election expenses. He explained away this unusual procedure by asserting that Jack Hayward insisted on anonymity (this was later shown to be untrue) and had been upset that his previous donation to the Party had become public. (In fact it was more Jeremy who had been upset and provoked the resignation of Sir Frank Medlicott as treasurer.) Jack wanted both privacy and for Jeremy to have total discretion over the expenditure of funds. Nadir saw no reason not to comply with such a request from his friend and Party leader. To Jack Hayward, it later emerged at the trial, Jeremy described Nadir Dinshaw as an accountant – which he is not – who had agreed to pay any left-over 'ambiguous expenses' from his election campaign, i.e. those which were partly constituency and partly national. Nadir had agreed to nothing of the kind.

On Jeremy's instruction Nadir paid the whole £10,000 to David Holmes's bank account in London in May 1974 (why Jeremy did not ask Jack Hayward to send the money direct to Holmes is one of the unexplained mysteries in this tale). It was admitted later that this money went to pay off Holmes's overdraft. After the October 1974 election, Jeremy approached both Jack Hayward and Nadir Dinshaw with the same reasoning to repeat his request. They agreed. Early in 1975 David Holmes began to request payments from Nadir in a different form – cash, usually in amounts of about £500. Nadir, who had all along considered himself to be merely a nominee of Jeremy's and who had been told by Jeremy to give the money to David Holmes for these election expenses, reluctantly agreed. He gave Holmes such sums throughout 1975 and by March 1976 he had paid out exactly £7,500. He was shaken by the revelation that Holmes had been the purchaser of the letters, just as I was by the discovery of election funds going from Jack Hayward via Nadir to Holmes. I was flabbergasted and I was also exasperated: 'What on earth did you think you were giving Holmes the money for?'

'Election expenses, of course,' replied Nadir.

'But don't you know that under election law all expenses have to be paid within weeks of the election?'

'How am *I* to know that?' retorted Nadir. 'You politicians live in a world of your own – I bet you couldn't name all the Archbishops of Canterbury this century.' I took his point.

My immediate concern and suspicion centred on the forthcoming trial of Andrew Newton. Who had paid him to shoot Scott's dog? An appalling possibility presented itself – was it David Holmes? Nadir and I discussed what to do. He had told me something in total confidence which I was not therefore free to disclose to anyone else, not even to Jeremy. But I had information now which finally convinced me that Jeremy ought not to remain as Leader.

The next day, with Cyril all over the papers declaring 'There are things going on I know nothing about,' Jeremy replaced him with Alan Beith as acting Chief Whip. Cyril formally resigned about ten days later. I went to see Jeremy and told him that the lifeblood was ebbing from the entire Party because of this increasing mess. I told him that in the interests of both the Party and himself he ought now to resign the leadership. He could say he was doing so temporarily until all the matters were satisfactorily cleared up. Jeremy must have been surprised to receive such advice from me, but he was so buffeted by everything that he showed neither surprise nor resentment. He simply refused, saying he was not going to be brought down by a lot of panicky colleagues.

On 14 March the *Sunday Times* ran a defensive story with material provided by Jeremy and one of his legal advisers, Lord Goodman. This appeared to shift the blame for all the Scott letters on to Bessell, which in turn provoked Bessell on the other side of the Atlantic to further outbursts. The *Sunday Times* – only for that week – was convinced that Jeremy was the innocent victim of a smear campaign. For a few days they helped to rally the party behind Jeremy.

Two days later Newton appeared in court. His cover story, that Scott was blackmailing him over a nude photograph, just stood up. Scott as a prosecution witness dragged out all his old allegations against Jeremy, gleefully reported under court privilege in the press, but the police had established no connection between Newton and Jeremy or anyone else in the Liberal Party. On 19 March Newton was sentenced to two years' imprisonment and *Private Eye* continued to allege that there *was* such a connection.

During April Liberal councillors were desperately attempting to run election campaigns to secure re-election on Thursday, 6 May. Not many of them made it. That morning the *Daily Mail* ran a Bessell interview: 'I told lies to protect Thorpe.' The heat was on again. The next day Scotland Yard complied with an application from Norman Scott for the return of two letters from Jeremy to Norman Scott which they had been holding in their files since 1962 when Scott had handed them over. They also gave copies to Lord Goodman, who decided it was best they be published with Jeremy's explanation in the hitherto friendly *Sunday Times* rather than sold by Scott to one of the tabloids. And so they were on 9 May, letters themselves unimportant except that they revealed a closer affectionate relationship with Scott – 'I miss you' – than

Jeremy had ever admitted, including the reference to him as 'Bunny': 'Bunnies can (and will) go to France.'

Meantime the MP for Colne Valley Richard Wainwright, never a fan of Jeremy's and brimming with Methodist outrage, asked on radio when Jeremy was going to issue a writ for defamation against Scott. This too received extensive coverage. Richard had been in contact with Bessell who had written: 'Those of us who worked for the success of his candidature [as leader] in 1967 did not give Jeremy a licence to use the party for his own ends.' He presumably took to the airwaves because all private pressure, including mine, had failed to persuade Jeremy to go. Bessell had told Wainwright way back in 1966 about Norman Scott and had asked him to deal with another young man who turned up at the House that year making allegations against Jeremy. So he had always been wary.

That weekend Jeremy had gone to Clement Freud's constituency and Clement, one of his most loyal supporters, also tried to persuade him to resign. Early that evening he telephoned me: 'He's agreed to go.' The reason for the call to me was that the new Chief Whip, Alan Beith, had gone to fulfil a longstanding engagement in Scandinavia, leaving me as 'acting Whip' for a week to look after the increasing shambles of the Parliamentary Liberal Party. I arranged to catch the night sleeper to London and met up with Jeremy and Clay at Freud's London home next morning. We discussed already drafted exchanges of letters, in a tired and dejected atmosphere. They were duly typed and released to the press from the Commons, Jeremy's whereabouts being kept secret. His letter and my reply were as follows:

My dear David,

In the absence of Alan Beith, I am writing to you in your capacity as acting Chief Whip. You will recall that the Parliamentary Liberal Party having passed a unanimous vote of confidence in the leadership subsequently agreed that the Party would hold a Leadership election in the autumn. This was a course which I myself had suggested to the President. Until such time it was clearly agreed that we act as a united party.

Since then two things have happened: first, sections of the press have turned a series of accusations into a sustained witch hunt and there is no indication that this will not continue; second, a parliamentary colleague has now taken to the air publicly to challenge my credibility.

Although other parliamentary colleagues have come to my support, and agree that nothing has changed since our decision to hold an autumn election, I am convinced that a fixed determination to destroy the Leader could itself result in the destruction of the Party.

I have always felt that the fortunes of the Party are far more important than any individual and accordingly I want to advise you that I am herewith resigning the leadership.

You will appreciate the sadness with which I do this, but I feel I owe the decision to my family, my constituents, and the many loyal Liberals who deserve better of us than the continued spectacle of a Party wrangling with itself with more concern for personality than policy.

You will know that from the very beginning I have strenuously denied the so-called Scott allegations and I categorically repeat those denials today. But I am convinced that the campaign of denigration which has already endured for over three months, should be drawn by me as an individual and not directed at Liberals collectively through their leader. No man can effectively lead a Party if the greater part of his time has to be devoted to answering allegations as they arise and countering continuing plots and intrigues.

To Liberals all over the country, whose loyalty and understanding has been quite superb and a source of great strength to my wife and to me, I ask that they use this period to redouble their efforts to build up the Party and to recreate the unity upon which alone we can build on our substantial and dedicated Liberal support.

Perhaps you would make this decision known to my colleagues and be responsible for making it known to my fellow Liberals in the country.

Yours affectionately,
Jeremy

My dear Jeremy,

You told me this morning that you had decided over the weekend to give up the leadership of the Liberal Party and I thank you for your letter confirming this. Your decision will be received by your colleagues with understanding but great sadness nevertheless. Your contribution to the party has been remarkable, particularly in your nine years as our leader, for more than half of which I had the pleasure and privilege of serving as your Chief Whip. You have raised us from being a sporadic political force to one with candidates in nearly every constituency, and over five million votes in each of two general elections.

Your personal qualities of leadership, charisma and sheer perseverance, and your triumphs over adversity are held in the highest regard by all your colleagues and admired by the public at large. Your selfless decision to stand down now in the interests of the Party is characteristic.

I am glad that you are remaining with us as a parliamentary colleague. You will be greatly sustained in the months ahead by your constituents as well as your family, and we all look forward to the time, when freed of your present troubles you return to a key role in the public life of our country.

Yours affectionately,
David

But the story was not to end there. In April 1977 Newton emerged from his prison sentence and collected his agreed £5,000 pay-off from his contact man, Le Mesurier. Newton realized that he could make more money by telling the true story and revealing his contacts – Miller, who supplied the gun, and Le Mesurier, who had in turn enlisted Miller. He managed to bungle even that, revealing to an *Evening News* reporter a tape of a conversation with David Holmes. The reporter consequently decided to run a story without the substantial payments Newton was demanding, but therefore without all the details he was able to supply. This they did on 17 October 1977 under the heading 'I was hired to kill Scott'.

Newton's story was followed by others from the increasingly talkative Bessell. By now of course Jeremy was no longer Party Leader, but he was still an MP. On 27 October he called a press conference arranged by Clement Freud, accompanied by his second wife, Marion, and one of his lawyers. He read out a long statement denying any knowledge of a plot to kill Scott – for whom he had had 'a close, even affectionate friendship,' though he insisted that 'no sexual activity of any kind took place'. He had known nothing of Holmes's purchase of the Scott letters. 'I have no intention of resigning, nor have I received a single request to do so from my constituency association.'

After a few innocuous questions from among the eighty or so journalists gathered at the National Liberal Club, a BBC reporter, Keith Graves, went for the jugular: 'The whole of this hinges on your private life. It is necessary to ask you if you have ever had a homosexual relationship.'

Marion Thorpe interjected angrily: 'Go on, stand up. Stand up and say that again.'

Graves did so. The lawyer then intervened: 'I cannot allow him to answer the question.'

'But I thought this press conference had been called to clear the air,' protested Graves, 'and that is the major allegation.'

Jeremy was firm: 'That is not the major allegation – it is that there was a Liberal hired to murder a man.'

'Because he was having a homosexual relationship with you,' said another journalist, recklessly ignoring the fact that even Scott's allegations on that score concerned events of some fifteen years ago.

'It may be,' retorted Jeremy calmly, 'that our priorities are different. It has been alleged that a man was hired to murder somebody. That is a very very serious crime.'

After about an hour, Clement Freud closed the proceedings. It was difficult to see what they had achieved other than providing further acres of newsprint.

By this time, police enquiries included not only Newton, Miller, Le

Mesurier and a man called Deakin, but also Peter Bessell, who was visited by them in California in December 1977. From the summer of 1976, when I was elected Party Leader, I had been trying to restore some credibility to our cause. It was a hopeless task, with new press revelations erupting every few weeks. Neither in the House nor the country was anyone interested in our views on anything. The only talk was of Thorpe, Bessell and the continuing mystery of the shot dog, Rinka. We continued to be the butt of general ridicule, and in spite of Jeremy's departure from the leadership we were still in the quagmire.

By April 1978 the police were interviewing both Nadir Dinshaw and Jack Hayward about the sums totalling £20,000 which had been paid to Holmes. Jeremy tried to put pressure on both of them, initially for Nadir to be less than totally frank with the police. He had earlier suggested to Nadir that he should say that he had some business deal with Hayward to account for the £20,000. Nadir was shocked and refused point blank on both counts. Jeremy then suggested that he would be asked 'to move on' – a crude and foolish threat and a poor return for the staunch friendship that Nadir had shown him. Then on the telephone Jeremy tried to persuade Hayward to threaten to sue Bessell for the £35,000 Bessell still owed him if he returned from California to Britain. Hayward likewise refused.

Throughout April and May (during which another round of disastrous local elections passed) the police interviewed Holmes and Le Mesurier, and then in June, Jeremy himself. In July they reported to the DPP. At the end of the month, the Attorney-General, Sam Silkin, called me in to tell me, as Party Leader on Privy Council terms, that charges against Jeremy and the others would be made shortly. At the beginning of August all four were charged with conspiracy to murder, and Thorpe additionally with incitement to murder. All appeared in West Somerset Magistrates Court and were remanded on bail.

At some point – and I cannot be precise as to when – Jeremy had assured me in general that if charged he would step down as an MP and specifically that he would not attend the September annual Party Assembly in Southport. He changed his mind on both counts, the first partly under pressure from his constituency, and both, I suspect, on legal advice. He was pleading 'not guilty' and so he had to portray a normal life to the outside world, regardless of the embarrassment to his party. The MPs and party managers were furious. The annual Assembly is our guaranteed shop window and here was Jeremy going to walk straight through it, against all entreaties.

Sure enough, he didn't just appear, but with his usual showmanship, the doors at the back of the hall were flung open and he marched down the crowded aisle with Marion to a half-standing ovation. When he got to the platform, I greeted him and showed him to his seat. One journalist shrewdly observed: 'Mr Steel shook him warmly by the hand while looking as though he would rather have gripped him warmly by the throat.' No one was in the least interested in all our worthy debates and resolutions. The main coverage was first, of speculation as to whether he would come, and second, of his arrival. He virtually wrecked the conference and the rest of us just had to put up with it.

In the private sessions of the same conference the Party President, Michael Steed, announced an inquiry into the handling of various party funds during Jeremy's leadership.

On 20 November 1978 the magistrates' committal proceedings opened in Minehead court – six miles from where the wretched Rinka had been shot just over the Devon border, three years before. They dragged on till nearly Christmas, providing yet more columns of newspaper coverage. The magistrates found there *was* a prima-facie case to answer on all counts. They would all have to stand trial at the Old Bailey.

On 4 April 1979 Jeremy applied for, and was granted, postponement of the trial until after the general election set for 3 May. Against almost all advice but with the backing of his constituency, he insisted on standing again in North Devon. I was annoyed because this generated more distracting publicity. Auberon Waugh stood in the constituency as a Dog Lovers' candidate. I was having to fight my first general election as Leader of a demoralized Party with slumped opinion-poll ratings. I needed Jeremy as a candidate like I needed a hole in the head. I tried in vain to persuade him to allow a substitute candidate on the basis of returning once he was acquitted. I sent him a typed message of good wishes, while John Pardoe bravely sallied over the county border to speak for him. His 7,000 Liberal majority was turned into an 8,000 Conservative one. His last redoubt had turned against him. I was talking live on the radio to Brian Redhead from Ettrick Bridge when he interrupted to tell me that the latest news was that John Pardoe had also been defeated. The radio audience heard me choking back tears. Our vote was particularly bad throughout the West Country.

The following week the Thorpe trial opened in London at the Old Bailey, Court Number One. It lasted twenty-eight days. There is no need for me to repeat details recorded elsewhere of all the evidence given, the most sensational being by Scott and Bessell. The prosecution case was that there had been a conspiracy to murder Scott by the four people accused, Jeremy, David Holmes, George Deakin and John Le Mesurier (*not* the actor, of course), the motive being the pressure put on Jeremy by Scott over the alleged relationship between them. Bessell testified that at first the idea of killing Scott was Jeremy's alone, but then later on, with the continued pressure being applied by Scott, David Holmes became convinced that this was the only possible course of action.

Peter Taylor, the Counsel for the Prosecution, then took the court through the various links in the chain. David Holmes had been giving financial advice to George Deakin, a friend of a carpet-dealer, John Le Mesurier, with whom he (Holmes) had business. During one of their meetings, Le Mesurier had mentioned to Deakin that Holmes was having a problem with a blackmailer and had asked Deakin if he could find somebody to 'frighten the fellow off'. Deakin agreed to help and mentioned it to a friend called David Miller who then introduced him to Andrew Newton. In his evidence, Newton said that he accepted the contract, but later his nerve failed him and after shooting the dog, he pretended that his gun had jammed and so avoided shooting Scott.

In his summing-up Mr Justice Cantley was scathing about Newton, Scott and Bessell. In particular what little credibility Bessell might have mustered as he led the court though his many changed stories was wrecked by the revelation that he had a contract with the *Sunday Telegraph* to write his story following the trial. Naturally the story would be worth more if Thorpe and Co were found guilty. He had a vested interest in securing that, having been offered £25,000 more for the story if the verdict was guilty. It had been admitted on Thorpe's behalf that he had had homosexual tendencies. If the jury believed Bessell, then Scott's story would be adjudged true. The judge implied that he should not be believed. He wasn't. The verdict of 'not guilty' was passed on all four. With typical flourish Jeremy then appeared on the balcony of his London house with Marion, waving to the assembled crowd of journalists, photographers, well-wishers and passers-by.

The nightmare for him was over and the rest of us could return to politics which had been blighted for four years by Jeremy's problems. Meanwhile the Party inquiry into Jeremy's handling of funds continued. I insisted that this should be wrapped up speedily and it was. However unorthodox Jeremy's handling of funds, especially Hayward's substantial donations, all was accounted for except the £20,000 which never came near the Party, and which I believe Jeremy later repaid to Hayward. The report was severely critical. I at least understood some of Jeremy's actions. He himself had raised most of the money and he wanted to direct it to help where most effective. Also in those days, there was very little available funding for the Leader's office. He often had to scrape round to raise the salaries for his staff of four. To me this explained both the London and Counties involvement and the special bank accounts outside the control of the treasurer. The Party officers were unsympathetic to these pleas in mitigation. Taking all this into account, together with the misuse of the £20,000 and repeated embarrassments to the Party over the Southport Assembly and 1979 election, it was universally felt in the Party hierarchy that he had no further role in that body. Party members – not knowing of all these ramifications – continued to assert that as he had been found 'not guilty' there was surely still a place for him; but no one who had lived through the four years felt inclined to offer him one.

There had been a further episode in 1976–7 when he had introduced another rum character to save the financially straitened National Liberal Club. This was a Canadian businessman called George de Chabris, later exposed as another rogue who dabbled in troubled financial waters. He had also called himself Baron de Mornay and even Prince de Chabris. His real name was in fact George Marks. For nine months, at Jeremy's instigation, he took over control of the Club. The manager brought in by de Chabris had many accusations of violence and homosexuality made against him. Much of the library, the paintings and the furniture of the Club was asset-stripped. On the day he was finally run out of the Club, he helped himself to the day's takings from the till of several hundred pounds. This treatment of one of our most venerable institutions did not exactly enhance Jeremy's reputation for judgement of character. (In the *Secret Life* book, the authors quote Thorpe's endorsement of de Chabris at a dinner in his honour: 'Throughout history there have been entire families who have devoted themselves to the cause of liberalism; the Gladstones, the Lloyd Georges, the Asquiths and now the de Chabris.' The Club was eventually rescued and restored by the skill and generosity of two stalwart Liberals, Lawrence Robson and his wife Stina, Baroness Robson.

Two years later David Holmes wrote *his* account of his now-past friendship with Jeremy in another Sunday paper: 'I spent ten years trying to help Jeremy Thorpe. My whole thought was to save him. That was exactly what I had in mind when I decided not to give evidence in my own defence.... Under oath, from now until eternity I deny the charge of conspiracy to murder. But the incitement charge, which Jeremy faced, was true and if I'd gone into the witness box I'd have had to tell the truth.' Holmes claimed that Thorpe was the inspiration behind a criminal conspiracy aimed at Scott; and that Thorpe tried to engineer a plot to kill Scott in 1968 and later in 1974 incited him (Holmes) to do so.

The misery through which all of us at the top of the Liberal Party and close to Jeremy lived from 1975 to 1979 is difficult to describe. At moments it was acute. As so often with Liberals we tended to relieve our minds with humour. Thus when it emerged in court that Newton had first gone looking for Scott in Dunstable by mistake instead of Barnstaple, David Penhaligon had us reduced to helpless tears at the Liberal Members' dining table by chortling: 'That's when I realized there must be something in it. It had all the hallmarks of a truly Liberal cock-up.' I responded that my moment of doubt occurred when Scott had told me that the morning after his alleged first night at Jeremy's mother's house, Jeremy had put his head round the bedroom door and asked how long he liked his eggs boiled. That rang true of Jeremy's usual concerns and courtesies. Liberal Assembly revues and Glee Clubs often sang the song 'Exmoor Baht 'at' (to the tune of 'Ilkla Moor Baht 'at') with various scurrilous lines, including 'Then we will all get off scot-free'.

For Jeremy it was a colossally tragic ending to a promising political career. I don't claim that he ever displayed any great original political thought, but he had enormous flair, charisma, showmanship and boundless energy. His wit was devastating. On the night of the long knives when Macmillan sacked half his Cabinet, Jeremy said: 'Greater love hath no man than this, that he lay down his friends for his life.' On occasion in the House and usually in town halls up and down the land, he was a powerful speaker and a totally dedicated Liberal. He was completely devoted to his North Devon constituency, in which he was courageous on liberal issues as well as being a first-class caring Member. His commitment to human rights and racial justice is absolute. He was capable of great acts of thoughtfulness and generosity as well as ones of total misjudgement or profound folly.

The remarkable feature of these years was his capacity to maintain normal public duties while the net was closing in around him, even to fight an election campaign a few days before a murder trial. His greatest asset has been his wife Marion, formerly Countess of Harewood, whom he married in 1973. Since his acquittal and disappearance from public life they have derived much comfort from their shared enjoyment of music. I still see him from time to time. He is now afflicted with Parkinson's Disease which affects his speech. Marion, together with his grown-up son Rupert, training to be a photographer, and his long-time secretary, Judy Young, ensure that he is well looked after.

I find it difficult to sum up his career. Others have made their own comments using old-fashioned and appropriate-sounding words like 'knave' and 'bounder'. He certainly treated some of his colleagues and friends inexcusably badly. In spite of those dreadful years he put us through I cannot forget his personal kindness, and his help in getting me elected to Parliament in the first place.

I wrote a piece for *The Times* two months after his resignation and believe that my reflections still stand:
At the beginning of the publicity on Mr Thorpe's troubles, my constituency

President, an erudite yet down-to-earth septuagenarian, wrote to me saying: 'If ever anything like this happens to you, David, admit it whether it's true or not, and then say it's nobody's business!' He had a point. The criticism of Jeremy Thorpe must remain that from the very beginning he treated Noman Scott's allegations with an importance they did not deserve. All of us by nature would be more outraged by insinuations which were not true than by those which were. The pre-marital, pre-leadership sex life of a Parliamentary colleague is surely of no concern to anybody. Yet to say 'Even if it were true, so what?' is much easier in retrospect than it must have been at the time. For such an utterance would surely have provoked the public response: 'Aha, so it may be true!'

The no doubt well-intentioned but clumsy attempt of his friends Messrs Bessell and Holmes to suppress the allegations merely added substance to them. Jeremy Thorpe himself must ruefully admit that he was less than totally frank with his colleagues, and it was sadly on that score that in the end his only correct and honourable course was to resign – a point overlooked by the righteous letter-writers to this paper.

The poignant feature of the whole episode is that the Liberal Party with its distinguished record of concern to reduce legal and social discrimination against homosexuals has in a fit of embarrassment drawn back from an internal campaign on this topic. Parliament if it is to be the representative mirror of the people must contain its due proportion of homosexuals, lesbians, womanizers, habitual drunkards, card-sharpers, chain-smokers, drug takers and any other cross-section of society you care to mention.

Of course the major figures in public life should be an example of rectitude to us all. But if in addition it is to be demanded that every seeker after public office has to lay bare his private behaviour from adolescence onwards, we shall indeed reduce the scope of recruitment. The finger of suspicion has a dangerous reach. A couple of weeks ago I took my secretary, Tessa Horton, to the première of *All the President's Men*, since I had a second ticket and it seemed a minor reward for all the hours spent in churning out effusions such as this. Amid the flashbulbs in the foyer, she was pecked gently on both cheeks by one of my favourite peeresses of the realm, who absentmindedly assumed her to be my wife. We laughed about it afterwards, but out of such incidents apparently is public scandal easily developed. And are we henceforth to assume that we are not allowed to have friends of either sex towards whom we can use words like 'love' and 'affection' without sexual connotation?

In the downfall of the Liberal leader, among those rightly blamed are himself, his friends, we his Parliamentary colleagues, the press, and possibly alien forces. Is it not true that a further element was the hypocritical nature of public opinion itself?

6

LEADERSHIP
A Bumpy Road

E ven before the actual resignation of Jeremy Thorpe as leader, some of us in the parliamentary Party had been pressing Jo Grimond to consider at least a temporary return to the helm. Indeed six weeks before, John Pardoe hosted a cabal supper at his house consisting of himself, Jo, Emlyn and me, the object of which was to secure Jo's agreement to be drafted, to present that to Jeremy and thereby secure his resignation. But Jo refused to play, making jokes about his age, deafness and other alleged deficiencies: 'I cannot read a teleprompter, which is what gives my broadcasts that air of unmistakable sincerity.' He seemed also reluctant to be part of any move to persuade Jeremy to relinquish the leadership.

We had other considerations on our minds. The Party was – partly out of general dissatisfaction and partly because yet again we were in the van of constitutional progress – in the midst of preparing and debating a new constitution giving votes on the choice of Leader to the Party members in the country, not just the MPs. For a small party, such a step seemed sensible; otherwise, as on the previous occasion, the electoral college could be a mere dozen. The last thing a demoralized party would tolerate was a new Leader slipping in under the net of the old system because its replacement was not yet ready. So when the fateful day came and Jeremy at last let go of the leadership, we were unanimous in the parliamentary Party in demanding that Jo should (a) unite the party and raise our spirits, and (b) see us through the constitutional change due in September.

After some argument he agreed to become temporary leader and entered into the job with relish. But it was decided to hold a Special Assembly (Liberals love assemblies) in June to change the constitution, thus enabling the leadership election to proceed swiftly that summer. Finding a place to hold it at short notice was a problem. One suggestion was Bellevue Zoo, Manchester.

'We cannot,' I protested to Jo, 'possibly hold our Assembly in a zoo. We shall be held up to ultimate ridicule.'

'On the contrary,' declared Jo mischievously, 'I can think of no more suitable venue for such an event.' In the end it was held in another hall in Manchester.

The extension of the franchise beyond the MPs meant that I could not assume that I was heir-apparent. While wholly approving of the extension in principle even though it was against my own interests, I argued that we must build in safeguards against an unacceptable person being foisted in the future on a parliamentary Party by the Party outside. The compromise agreement was that each nomination had to be supported by at least one-fifth of the parliamentary Party. This turned out to be crucial since at that time at least two MP backers had to be found for each candidate.

Within a day or two of Jeremy's resignation John Pardoe declared himself a candidate for the leadership, throwing his hat in the ring first. His campaign was to be headed by Tim, Lord Beaumont, former President of the Party, and Cyril Smith, supported by Richard Wainwright and David Penhaligon. I took longer, not because I was in real doubt that I should stand but because I needed to go home that weekend to consult my family and friends and a special meeting of my constituency office-bearers. John already lived in London; I did not and the implications of becoming leader had to be understood and accepted in my political base, the Borders. I was given full encouragement, as I always have been.

The following week I was due to speak to the Annual General Meeting of the Hampstead Liberals. Not for the first time in that campaign, I could not resist a tease at John's expense. He lived in that constituency and they knew him well. That was where I chose to announce my candidacy, in a well-reported speech setting out my view of how the party should be led:

The role of the Liberal Party is not that of a shadow third government with a detailed policy on every single issue of the day, ready and waiting in the wings for a shift in electoral opinion to sweep us into power. That is the role of Her Majesty's Opposition, and we are nowhere near that position yet. Our task is a very different one. It is to spell out a clear vision of the society we want to achieve; to provide long-term goals to a people weary of the politics of pragmatism, expediency and compromise.

We must concentrate less on giving day-to-day commentary on the policies of others, and far more on setting out our own programme. And we should combine our long-term programme with a readiness to work with others wherever we see what Jo Grimond has called the break in the clouds – the chance to implement Liberal policies. In my political lifetime I have worked closely with those of other parties to promote certain causes: Europe, anti-apartheid, legislation on social reforms, housing, devolution and electoral reform. The experience has not made me less of a Liberal, not compromised the independence of Liberalism. There are occasionally small-'l' liberals to be found on particular issues outside the Liberal Party, and we should never fear to co-operate with them effectively to promote some part of our cause. As Edmund Burke said: 'When bad men combine, the good must associate, else they will fall one by one, an unpitied sacrifice in a contemptible struggle' ... Our role is to renew hope that a more tolerant, a more fair, a more caring, a more open society is within our capacity to create. Let us appeal to those outside our party to come and join us. Let us proclaim with conviction that it is only within the Liberal Party that the aspirations of millions who have long since abandoned all hope and faith in representative politics can be met.

It is by now a well-worn political saying that if you can't stand the heat you should get out of the kitchen. In these days it has been put to me bluntly that if you find yourself in the kitchen anyway you might as well take charge of the menu. And so, bearing in mind that the rules for the nomination of candidates are not yet finalized, I feel I ought to make it clear that in the coming weeks it is my intention to seek candidature for the leadership of our Party.

Emlyn Hooson had indicated that he might stand, but in due course decided that he probably would not have enough support and came to see me to offer to back me, for which I was naturally grateful since, with Geraint Howells in Cardigan, I then had both our Welsh MPs.

Russell Johnston also expressed a wish to stand but could not get the necessary nominees from among the MPs, yet he had considerable backing outside in the party, especially of course in Scotland. At the last minute John Pardoe hit on a jolly wheeze. He would nominate Russell and invite me to second the nomination. There was nothing in the rules to prevent candidates being nominators. If Russell stood, Scottish support would be divided. If I refused, it would alienate Russell's Scottish support which might then go to John. Either way it was a shrewd tactical move. I told him bluntly that I would have nothing to do with the ploy, because I considered it a dodgy way to get round a provision in the constitution for which I had fought. Russell and many of my fellow-Scots were less than pleased, but it was not to be the last time I would have to be hard-hearted in taking a political decision.

There were no ground rules in British political history for such a 'primary' (in US terms) election. So we made it up as we went along. We made a few joint appearances, mainly on television, but by and large we simply tore round the country addressing the faithful in gatherings large and small, pressing the flesh and generally exhausting ourselves for three weeks or so. The party enjoyed it hugely, especially after months of retreat and inactivity. For John and me it was a miserable experience. The truth was that there was not much on policy to separate us and therefore to debate. As Stuart Mole has written:

it was about style and strategy. Pardoe seemed to be the clear favourite of the party activists. They liked his aggressive and abrasive style, his intellectual dynamism and his clear analysis of the Party's future. If Pardoe appealed to the heart, excited by his rumbustious claim to be 'an effective bastard', Steel's appeal was to the head: his solid record, his clear ability as a publicist, his shrewd toughness, his calm pragmatism and his obvious electoral appeal, through television in particular, to a wider electorate.

The press, reluctant to quote our earnest speeches, stirred up any possible disagreement or insult. Cyril Smith said I couldn't make a bang with a firework in both hands. John called me 'traffic-cop Steel', and my response was to provoke him. It is often alleged that I claimed he wore a hairpiece and it became known as the toupee election. In fact, Gordon Greig, the political editor of the *Daily Mail*, correctly recorded what happened in an article headed: 'The art of the political insult – and how to use it to become party leader':

David Steel leaned back in the chairspace of his 6ft by 6ft white sauna cell he calls an office and coolly – mischievously – flipped the question across the desk at his two perspiring visitors.
He purred: 'Something very strange is happening to the Pardoe hairline. Those bald patches round his topknot have somehow been filled in. It's very curious. Do you think he is trying to cultivate the Kennedy look?'
Within minutes the target of that giggle had been contacted. Pardoe's indignation almost melted the telephone line.

The Times reported: 'Mr Steel's reference to the possibility that Mr Pardoe wore a hairpiece appears to have been genuinely meant as a joke, unlike much of the Pardoe-baiting, but it put Mr Pardoe in a towering rage,' and concluded, 'If Mr Steel wins, he may be able to thank Mr Pardoe's campaign.'
'Towering rage' was no exaggeration. John and I had a blazing row in the Liberal Whip's office which must have been heard through into the Members' Lobby. I don't think we fully recovered from it for weeks. His over-reaction at it, coupled with his other almost bombastic claims, left him vulnerable and at a crowded meeting in Brighton, addressed on John's behalf in a witty and well-received speech by David Penhaligon, I quoted part of A. A. Milne's *The House at Pooh Corner* which Judy had dug out and wondered if anyone

recognized the similarity between Tigger and any candidate in the present contest:

with one loud Worraworraworraworraworra he jumped at the end of the tablecloth, pulled it to the ground, wrapped himself up in it three times, rolled to the other end of the room, and, after a terrible struggle, got his head into the daylight again, and said cheerfully: 'Have I won?'

DAVID AND...

It brought the house down.

That night David Penhaligon drove me back to London in his TR6 sports car and admitted that I looked like winning. We were all somewhat chastened by the poor-quality coverage of the campaign. Clement Freud issued a circular on my behalf to party branches:

It now seems to us that so little good is being done to the Liberal cause by public and publicized protestations that one candidate is the bigger (or smaller) bastard; the louder (or quieter) campaigner; the tougher, or even-tougher-than-that leader of men ... that I will simply state that we, whose names appear below, genuinely feel that David Steel would command the greater following in the country and has the deeper respect of Parliament both within and outside our political party.

As you will have read, the majority of newspapers and periodicals, from the *Daily Mail* to the *New Statesman*, agree with this assessment.

By this time, to the chagrin of the opposition camp, I had indeed secured almost universal editorial support in the press, including the Party's own *Radical Bulletin,* edited by Tony Greaves:

David Steel can be rather remote, somewhat arrogant, and may not behave like a cross between Mussolini and Billy Graham (i.e. he is a bit 'quiet'). But he is unquestionably a liberal, he is a moderate radical, and he is universally respected – by ordinary people most of all. He is our choice.

The party magazine, *New Outlook,* remained sensibly neutral:

Either of Messrs Pardoe and Steel would be a perfectly adequate Leader of the Liberal Party. A publicized election to choose one of them can only benefit the Party, and bring a welcome change of emphasis in the publicity it has recently obtained. The debate at the moment inevitably centres around the choice between their personalities – the forceful Pardoe and the quieter Steel. A sufficiently long period for discussion will hopefully bring into the lists their respective ideas for the future policy and strategy of the Liberal Party.

The truth is that debate about the nature and policy of our Party did not advance beyond our opening speeches and manifestos. Bernard Levin said in *The Times*:

Mr Steel looks so boyish that I am sure many people do not take him seriously, which is certainly a mistake on their part, for he has real political stature and understanding, and if the Promised Land is ever to be reached at all by the Liberals, he is the only man to lead them there ... there is a smack of political originality about him.

I quote this because only two years later he was to write of me, referring to what he termed my 'weasel words' about Jeremy Thorpe: 'Steel? Say rather, in the words of the old song, "It must be jelly, 'cos jam don't shake like that."'

An unbelievably Liberal and complicated system of voting and counting took place. Every party member had a vote, but each constituency was given a quota of votes depending on the size of the Liberal vote at the previous election, in theory giving the stronger constituencies greater weight than the weaker. So if a constituency had 1,000 members who voted 600–400 and its quota were 50, the votes were added in as 30–20. A whole day was set aside for this tedious process in the unattractive setting of the Poplar Civic Hall in London. The entire event was rendered almost unnecessary by the habit of each constituency proudly announcing its own result in the days after the ballot closed and before the count. There was therefore none of the drama, tension, excitement or even publicity the devisers had envisaged. Only one constituency, Liverpool Edge Hill, produced a 100 per cent quota result for one of the candidates – John Pardoe. In both John's seat and my own a tiny but respectable minority voted for the other candidate. Apart from Devon and Cornwall, I won all other regions of the country.

To a weary and less than ecstatic mini-throng I was eventually declared Leader of the party by 12,541 quota votes to John's 7,032. The date was 7 July 1976.

Norman Shrapnel, the veteran political columnist of the *Guardian*, in his *The Performers* contrasted my leadership election with Jeremy's – 'a comparatively gentlemanly affair showing the Conservatives the decorous manner in which God intended one Old Etonian to succeed another' with this description:

Ten years later the scene was very different. Yet another Liberal leader had taken over from Thorpe, this time with a conspicuous lack of decorum. David Steel was a quiet and promising young fellow enough, emerging discreetly through the shambles like Fortinbras at the end of *Hamlet*. But the excitements that led up to his modest crowning were almost more than the nerves could stand – and not just Liberal nerves. The theatre was littered with the debris of what they had been going through – brilliant revivals and heart-rending flops, rows between contenders for star parts, abandoned programmes and torn up scripts, scandals and follies and feuds, blood all over the stage.

Among the many notes and letters of congratulation I received was this one from local scholar, poet and historian Walter Elliot, a man of strong Scottish Nationalist sympathies:

A wee note o' congratulation
Ah send upon yer rise in station
And hope ye hav'nae made a slip
In takin on the Leadership

Wi Liberals divided sair
Ye'll shoulder monie a weary care
And next election ye might be
Hard pressed bie Border S.N.P.

The future we will leave the now
Wi laurel wreath fresh on yer brow.

117

This letter, ah have sent
Tae pey an honest compliment.

Tae you, we owe oor sincere thanks
For aa yer thought an deeds and pranks
And aa the ploys ye've had in hand
Tae benefit the Borderland.

We wadnae think it awfae sinister
If ye were Scotland's first Prime Minister
That is a wee deliberation
And no tae be ta'en as invitation

Altho the honest truth tae tell
Ah've voted twice for ye masel'
(A fact, that tho Ah'll no deny it,
Ye'll understand, Ah keep it quiet).

An now, Ah find ma Muse is spent,
Ma best respects tae you, Ah've sent
But lest ye think that ye're perfection,
Ah'll see ye at the next election.

Of greater political significance was the short handwritten note I received during the leadership election from the Home Secretary. It read:

Dear David,

I greatly hope that you win, not only out of friendship and respect, but because I believe that it is very much in the interests of the country.

Yours ever,
Roy

Immediately after the election I had to deal with some little local difficulties. John Pardoe, while observing all the public courtesies, told me that he wanted to think over his political future during the imminent summer recess. Meantime he would continue temporarily as Treasury spokesman.

Cyril Smith, in spite of restraining pressure from John Pardoe, announced that he would not accept a spokesmanship under my leadership and would not campaign in any constituency which had voted for me. Five days later he did in fact accept after some persuasion the post of spokesman on Social Services.

Over the summer I read avidly and pondered on my first speech as Leader to the Liberal Assembly in September. At the end of August I prepared the way for what I wished to say by giving an interview to the *Guardian* in which I firmed up my views on our missed opportunities in 1974: 'I believe that we have to start by getting a toe-hold on power which *must* mean some form of coalition.' I followed this up with an interview on Radio 4's *The World This Weekend* at Sunday lunchtime before the Assembly opened (I have always found this one of the best current-affairs programmes for getting a view across, especially since the opening of the BBC Radio Tweed studio in Selkirk, ten minutes' drive from my home). I said the party must be 'prepared psychologically for coalition' – a clear reference to our lack of such preparation in 1974. Throughout I emphasized the importance of this method of securing electoral reform.

On the Thursday evening of the Assembly I attended a meeting with the Young Liberals and in a mainly friendly discussion argued the need to be ready to join in government if the conditions were right. Next day's papers carried threats to disrupt my Saturday speech if I referred to the matter.

I had arrived at Llandudno with the draft of my speech already typed and showed it to one or two people who were alarmed at its tone. One of these was John Pardoe, who came to see me in my suite, having spent the summer as he had publicly promised ruminating in Cornwall. He told me quietly that he accepted that the party could only have one leader and one strategy. I had been elected, and he committed himself to work with me. All the summer's taunts disappeared – including his accusations that I was 'never out of a dinner jacket' or 'too fond of breakfast with Roy Jenkins' – and from that moment on we formed an effective partnership. He became described by the press as 'deputy leader'. In fact there was no such post, but I was happy for him to have it by assumption. I came to rely on him heavily. He advised me to go right ahead with what I wanted to say to the Party.

Others were more nervous. On the very eve of the speech Archy Kirkwood, Richard Holme, William Wallace and Clement Freud were all advising against provoking a row with my very first speech as Leader. They urged me to think again. Late at night we went out for a walk along the sea front to get some fresh air and reconsider what they thought to be the offending passage. When we returned I said: 'I've decided. It stays in.'

It was an overlong speech, and after forty-five minutes I came to the troublesome part:

We are in being as a political party to form a government so as to introduce the policies for which we stand. That is our clear aim and objective. But I as leader

have a clear obvious duty to assess how most speedily we can reach that objective.
I do not expect to lead just a nice debating society.

If we argue that we alone can be the means of transforming the sterility of British
political life, if we tell the public that only by voting Liberal in sufficient numbers
to prevent one other party gaining a majority, will we achieve electoral reform, and
break the Tory/Labour stranglehold, then equally we must be clear in our own
minds that if the political conditions are right (which of course they were not in
February 1974), and if our own values are retained, we shall probably have – at
least temporarily – to share power with somebody else to bring about the changes
we seek.

The result was uproar. Parts of the speech had leaked to delegates during
the night. Only recently I discovered how. The discarded Gestetner stencils
were retrieved from waste bins and private copies run off on other duplicating
machines. Not only were there shouted protests but about a hundred prepared
placards with the single word 'NO' were raised from the floor of the hall and
in the balconies. They were mainly held by Young Liberals, including
Councillor David Alton from Liverpool. The bulk of the assembly coun-
terapplauded and for what seemed ages (it could only have been a minute or
two) my speech came to a complete halt. After the hubbub died down I
pressed on with my argument:

Of course neither of the other parties will want to relinquish their exclusive
alternating hold on power, but if the people won't let them have it then they will
both have to lump it – Tory and Labour.

I want the Liberal Party to be the fulcrum and centre of the next election
argument – not something peripheral to it. If that is to happen we must not give the
impression of being afraid to soil our hands with the responsibilities of sharing
power.

We must be bold enough to deploy our coalition case positively. We must go all
out to attack other parties for wanting power exclusively to themselves, no matter on
how small a percentage of public support.

If people want a more broadly based government they must vote Liberal to get
it. And if they vote Liberal we must be ready to help provide it.

What I am saying is that I want the Liberals to be an altogether tougher and more
determined force. I want us to be a crusading and campaigning movement, not an
academic think-tank nor minority influence nor occasional safety valve in the political
system. The road I intend to travel may be a bumpy one, and I recognize therefore
the risk that in the course of it we may lose some of the passengers, but I don't mind
so long as we arrive at the end of it reasonably intact and ready to achieve our goals.

None of us in this party is interested in office for office's sake. If we were we
would never have joined the Liberal Party. But we are fighting to achieve those

things in which we believe, for which the party stands, and we must be prepared to do that in the most effective way possible.

I then went on to a rather emotional peroration:

There are some issues on which there can never under any circumstances be the slightest compromise. We cannot, for example, ever do anything which would take away from our absolute commitment to fight the obscenity of racialism, whether at home or abroad. I am tired of the well-meaning politicians who go around apologizing for the variety of communities in these islands, as though this was not always part of our evolving nation.

Freedom is indivisible. If one man or nation lacks it, we ourselves are less free. There will be some who say – in the Liberal Party as well as outside it – that Britain alone must come first, and if others starve or suffer from repression that is their problem, and none of our concern. That is not and never can be a Liberal attitude.

This has been for Liberals an anxious year, a rough year, at times a miserable year.

Many people looking in on this conference must have been wondering: why do these Liberals go on? They throw themselves into battle only to suffer defeat after defeat, with the occasional false dawn.

This year many of you may have wondered whether you should give it all up. You could have had more time with your families, dug your garden, or still with a sense of social responsibility devoted your time to any one of a number of good causes. And if you have felt so tempted, there is no need to feel ashamed. For so have I, and so at one time or another have most of us on this platform.

But we are here because we are heirs to a great tradition. We have been meeting this week in Llandudno, in Lloyd George's old constituency. Had it not been for those who have more recently gone before us to preserve and maintain the Liberal Party when many doubted the need, then the condition of the country today would demand that men and women come together to conspire to invent it.

Progress in politics is in a strange way like mountaineering. You rope a team together, you prepare a base camp and higher camps, only to be beaten back again and again by adverse circumstances, or falter in your advance because some have lost their foothold and we all slip back a little.

You have chosen me to be the lead man; not the entire expedition, but the one who searches for the fingerholds and determines the precise route which we should take.

It's time to start the next assault. The clouds are moving away and the summit is coming again into view.

Together we can reach that summit.

A few months ago I stood at the grave of Robert Kennedy on the hillside at Arlington Cemetery. . . . There on the stark white wall are carved a few sentences of that memorable speech he delivered just ten years ago in South Africa:

> Each time a man stands for an ideal, or acts to improve the lot of others, or strikes out against injustice, he sends forth a tiny ripple of hope.

> What I ask you to do now is to go out from this great Assembly, back to your constituencies to send out ripples of hope – that they swell and join together to form across our land an irresistible floodtide of reform.

The speech hopelessly overran, disappearing abruptly after one hour's allotted live coverage from the ITV screens in favour of *World of Sport*; but it was well received, even most of the critics joining in a genuine standing ovation. When I came off the platform and was swept back to the hotel, I had to lie down on the sofa. The strain and tension of the previous days and the lengthy delivery of the speech itself had made my back go rigid. It had a generally good press and the 'coalition strategy' became established in the Party's mind, though none of us realized how soon it would be put into action.

On Armistice Sunday I assembled for the first time with others to lay wreaths on the Cenotaph in Whitehall. The order was clearly: Callaghan, Thatcher, Steel, followed by ex-prime ministers, of whom only Ted Heath regularly turns up. In the interminable waiting in the corridors of the Home Office beforehand, I therefore acted as an uncomfortable buffer between the Tory leader and her predecessor, who did not appear to be on the chummiest of terms. I had arranged to have lunch with Ted Heath after the ceremonies. When he was Prime Minister I scarcely knew him and such little conversation as we had ever had consisted of stilted pleasantries. But since his demotion I had got to know him slightly in the European campaign, and in the Commons his traditional seat was immediately in front of mine. Therefore I had exchanged words with him from time to time and expressed my approval of his increasingly wise and independent speeches on devolution, foreign affairs and the economy. 'Let's talk some time,' he had said, and so I suggested Sunday lunch that day since I was at a loose end, having no real home base in London.

We left by separate routes in separate cars, and I arrived at his house in Wilton Street with its bombproof windows. I was none the less spotted by someone, presumably paid by the *Daily Mail* gossip column, who thought the event noteworthy. It is one of the more ridiculous features of our political system that MPs of different parties may chat in the Commons (though the Members' dining-room tables are segregated politically) but are regarded with acute suspicion if seen outside in each other's company across the party divides. I have regularly entertained visiting Labour, Tory and Nationalist

MPs at my home in Scotland, but it always has to be hush-hush. I recall one particularly ludicrous occasion when I had been having a private lunch at Roy Jenkins's London house. We sped to the Commons in the back of the Home Secretary's official Rover with its crack police driver and detective in the front. I was unceremoniously dumped at St James's Park lest we be seen driving in together through the gates of the Palace of Westminster. It is all utterly absurd and quite unlike political and social life in America or Europe.

Anyway, Ted Heath was very relaxed and welcoming. We lunched and talked mainly about politics and he surprised me by suddenly asking: 'Has Callaghan talked to you yet?'

'No,' I replied, 'why should he?'

'He will,' was the terse response. I had no reason to think any such thing would happen in the near future, though much later Ted reminded me of his forecast.

Margaret Thatcher had succeeded Ted Heath as Conservative leader the previous year, 1975. In April 1976 James Callaghan had been elected Labour leader in succession to Harold Wilson. Thus in the space of eighteen months the old party leadership triumvirate of Wilson-Heath-Thorpe had been replaced by Callaghan-Thatcher-Steel. By the winter of 1976–7 the Labour Government was running into economic difficulties and political ones at the same time. The leadership election highlighted their internal divisions. Roy Jenkins had left the Cabinet and Parliament to become President of the European Commission. The moderate 'Campaign for Labour Victory' was formed to counter the leftward drift, and the party had lost several by-elections to the Conservatives, thus whittling away the majority obtained by the second 1974 election. The new Conservative Opposition leader was waiting in the wings for her chance to become Prime Minister.

In January 1977 I was admitted to the Privy Council, of which I then became the youngest member. The Council meets rarely; the value of its membership is that intangible attribute, status: it carries the title 'Right Honourable', helps in catching the Speaker's eye in the House, and permits the PC to attend discussions 'on Privy Council terms' on issues of state. The ceremony of admission involves kneeling on a red velvet stool, swearing the oath of loyalty to the Crown and kissing the Queen's hand, followed by a jolly drinks party. Later the same year I was summoned again for the swearing-in of Prince Charles. When I told him I was not very pleased at his arrival, he said, 'Because you *were* the youngest? But you're not much older than me,' which was a comforting if inaccurate thought.

Just before Christmas, the abstentions of John Mackintosh and Brian

Walden in a crucial vote had lost the Government a closure in the Dock Work Regulation Bill, which would have given the dockers a monopoly of cargo-handling for five miles round any port. In March the Government was threatened with a revolt on its public-expenditure plans and determined to meet it by dodging the vote and withdrawing the resolution at the end of the debate. Mrs Thatcher decided it was time to strike. Without any attempt to consult the leaders of other parties – an attitude she has consistently stuck to throughout her time as Tory leader – she tabled a motion of 'no confidence' in the Government.

Throughout the autumn and winter I had continued to argue for both realignment of political forces and greater cross-party co-operation in coping with our economic problems. I wrote an open letter (accurately described as tongue-in-cheek) to Shirley Williams, who was then Secretary of State for Education and Science and who had been defeated by Michael Foot in the election for Labour's deputy leadership, urging her to join in a realignment of the moderate Left. She declined the invitation. This was unsurprising and I have to stress that at this time there was little private cross-party conversation. In this period we were doing appallingly badly in by-elections, twice being pushed into fourth place by the National Front. Party morale and organization were still at low levels. Indeed I had to complain publicly that at one by-election, in spite of months of notice, no one had remembered to order envelopes for the election address.

It was against that background that on Friday, 18 March 1977, Mrs Thatcher announced she was tabling the motion of no confidence which would be debated the following Wednesday. With by-election losses, vacant seats following the death of Tony Crosland and resignation of Roy Jenkins and defection of two Labour MPs to form the independent Scottish Labour Party, the Government now had only 310 voting members.

The economic outlook was gloomy. Unemployment had risen to over 1.5 million. The TUC the previous summer had agreed to a 5 per cent limit on pay increases which was holding temporarily, but the anti-inflation strategy was being undermined by the collapse of sterling. The Government borrowed heavily from American and European banks. In the autumn Labour conference Jim Callaghan had declared they could 'no longer spend their way out of a recession'. The Cabinet had already accepted the need for public expenditure cuts and a hefty loan from the International Monetary Fund. It was at this point that Mrs Thatcher struck.

The month before, the Government had lost its vote on a guillotine motion for the Scotland and Wales Bill which was proceeding at a snail's pace in its Committee Stage on the floor of the House, clogging the entire parliamenatry timetable. After seven days we had reached Clause 3 out of 115 clauses. It was a profoundly unsatisfactory bill combining two different schemes of devolution for Scotland and Wales, making the debates hopelessly unwieldy. As a party with a proud and consistent record on the subject, we were annoyed at not being consulted either on the bill itself or on the now-suggested imposed timetable which would have left acres of the bill undebated and unscrutinized. I urged my colleagues to stand firm and oppose the Government in spite of the wrath this might bring down on our heads from Home-Rulers in Scotland and Wales. The Nationalists, both Welsh and Scottish, supported the time-table, but we were the deciding factor, along with Labour dissenters, and the Government lost. We had already shown what we could do if the Government ignored us and we flexed our muscles.

That experience must have concentrated the minds of the Government that weekend as they faced the prospect of defeat on the 'no confidence' motion. The March Gallup poll showed a Tory lead over Labour at 16.5 per cent. I also saw the chance of putting my coalition strategy at least into first gear. Following the guillotine defeat, there had been some conversation between me and Cledwyn Hughes, the chairman of the parliamentary Labour Party, whom I knew and liked. I had already made it clear to him that we did not fear an early election and that the only way we would consider support for the Government was not on an *ad hoc* basis but in return for consultation on the programme of government.

On that Friday morning, while Mrs Thatcher was telling the Commons of her intended 'no confidence' motion, I was at my constituency surgery at my Galashiels office. I received a telephone call from Cledwyn Hughes, asking what we intended to do. I told him I would have to consult my colleagues, and he warned me that Callaghan was ready to go to the country if he had to. 'So am I,' I told him.

I dictated a short press statement down the phone to my office in the Commons, saying that there would be an extra meeting of the Liberal MPs on Tuesday to discuss our vote:

Either the Labour Party now proceeds on the basis of agreed measures in the national interest for the next two years, in which case we would be willing to consider supporting such a programme, or else we have a general election in which the people can return a new House of Commons. The one thing we cannot do is stagger on like last night with a lame-duck Labour programme which has neither public nor parliamentary support. The political decision as to which course to take therefore rests squarely with the Prime Minister and the Labour Party.

I then asked the Party chairman, Geoff Tordoff, to take soundings throughout the Party and warn them at the same time to prepare for an election. That evening in his own Cardiff constituency James Callaghan gave the impression of business as usual. Asked if he would do a deal with another party, he gave the delphic response: 'I don't think "deal" is quite the word one should use.' I motored down over the Border to Nelson, Lancashire, for the BBC Radio 4 *Any Questions* programme.

On Saturday morning I was displeased by the tone of newspaper speculation that the Liberals were bluffing and actually feared an election. Accordingly I decided to increase pressure on the Labour Party by issuing a further statement:

The confidence vote next Wednesday should wonderfully concentrate the minds of Labour MPs over this weekend and I hope they will convey their views to the party leadership. They must grasp that people in this country will not understand if they insist on committing suicide. They will do this if they refuse to compromise and seek a broader understanding in parliament.

It would be in the best interests of this country if it now begins to be governed on the basis of enjoying the widest public and parliamentary support for a programme of national recovery. If the Labour Party does not respond and acknowledge the political reality – that it cannot continue to push on with full-blooded socialist government because there is no mandate for it, then the thirteen Liberal votes will be bound to be cast against the Government in favour of a general election at which we would put our case for an end to the domination of Parliament by any one extreme – Socialist or Thatcherite.

This led the BBC's one o'clock news programmes, and effectively most of the Sunday papers. On Saturday afternoon I had a call at home from Bill Rodgers, the first official approach via a member of the cabinet, who undertook to convey my views to the Prime Minister at Chequers. Bill and I had got to know each other in the European campaign and could speak freely and frankly.

That evening I had the wonderful distraction of watching our foster son in a song-and dance-part in the Selkirk Amateur Operatic Society's production of *My Fair Lady*. My mind was not wholly focused on the rain in Spain falling mainly on the plain, because I had arranged to call together the Liberal MPs for a private discussion on Monday evening without pressure from the press.

On Sunday, having digested the papers, I did a live interview on ITV's *Weekend World* with the Prime Minister's son-in-law, Peter Jay, down the line from Edinburgh. Afterwards Judy and I went to lunch with Una and John Mackintosh at their house in Edinburgh: John was as usual full of excitement and lectured me with encouraging advice. Phone calls with

Cledwyn Hughes and Bill Rodgers that evening fixed a meeting with James Callaghan for Monday evening.

On Monday I had to travel by train from Carlisle to Birmingham, where I was to support our hapless candidate in the Stechford by-election, whose campaign was now thrown into utter confusion. On my way to Carlisle at some speed, I struck a wandering pheasant and saw in my mirror that it had knocked off my front number plate, which now lay in the roadway beside the fluttering corpse. I put both in the boot, but on entering Carlisle was stopped by a motorcycle police patrol, whether on account of the anonymous car front or excessive speed I was not clear. I explained and apologized that I was racing for the station, having been delayed by the offending bird. He replied, waving me on: 'I quite understand, I know you are rushing to see the Prime Minister.' The publicity was working.

After a near-shambles of a by-election press conference in the afternoon, I made my way by train to London with my personal assistant, Andrew Gifford, and a retinue of press and television, augmented by dozens more at the London station. By six p.m. I was with the Prime Minister in his room at the House.

I had little experience of him as an individual. We had quarrelled over the Kenya Asians, yet worked reasonably together in opposition to the 1971 Immigration Bill. Just after he had been appointed Shadow Foreign Secretary by Harold Wilson, we happened to share a taxi on the way to some event in London. I had asked after his health following his prostate operation. The press had written him off and he admitted to feeling physically frail and wondered if he could cope with his new post. In 1975–6 I had at most two or three meetings with him as Foreign Secretary.

He began by repeating that a defeat on Wednesday would mean an election and I told him that was not a prime consideration for us. I said we were not interested in any covert arrangement to stave off defeat for Wednesday, but only in an open longer-term agreement which would involve consultation with us on the Government's programme with particular emphasis on control of inflation through incomes policy, devolution and direct elections to Europe. The mood was sombre but amicable and we talked for over an hour, at the end of which he gave me some encouragement to think that such an arrangement could be possible; this was sufficient for me to be able to put it to my colleagues that evening and for him to discuss it with some of his team.

After that meeting I got the report I had asked for from Party chairman Geoff Tordoff, which was to the effect that the Party was prepared to fight an election if no clear and public concessions were forthcoming from the Government. Tordoff, with my agreement, expressed the feelings of the Party publicly to the Government: 'Bend or be broken.' This strengthened the hand of the Liberal MPs when they met late at night in my overcrowded room. They agreed to try my strategy of securing realignment by co-operating with the Government and authorized me to see what terms I could get. I drafted these next morning and sent them round, followed by a second meeting with the Prime Minister together with his political adviser, Tom McNally, and the Leader of the House, Michael Foot. They agreed to propose a draft agreement based on my letter and discussion. It arrived at 4.15 p.m. and I discussed it with John Pardoe; we concluded that it was not in a form we could recommend to our colleagues.

At five o'clock I returned it to the Prime Minister's private secretary, Ken Stowe, with suggested improvements and at 5.45 was called round to see Callaghan and Foot again. At 6.45 p.m. I put the further revised draft to my colleagues at a lengthy meeting. They made several changes I thought should prove acceptable, but we wanted a firmer line on the European elections. At 9.00 p.m. I sent round our further redraft and at 9.30 began my fourth meeting with Callaghan, this time with Michael Foot and John Pardoe present. Since we ran into disagreement on European elections, I suggested trying all the other paragraphs, a tactic which worked because it emphasized how near we were to agreement but for obstinacy on that one point. After 11.00 p.m. we formally agreed on a paragraph I was prepared to recommend to colleagues, which I did around midnight. Jo Grimond and David Penhaligon doubted the wisdom of the whole experiment but were prepared to go along with it for party unity.

The Cabinet had the document at ten o'clock the next morning, the Wednesday of the no-confidence debate. At 1.25 p.m. Ken Stowe phoned to say that after some robust discussion the Cabinet had agreed.

Michie and Hoggart, in *The Pact,* say of these events in a not inaccurate piece of exaggeration:

One important point to make about Steel is that he is not at all like the ineffectual boy scout he sometimes appears in the popular image. In a party more noted for its agreeable dottiness and amiable straightforwardness, Steel stands out as a tough, hard political operator with a clear idea of what he wants and a determination to get it. At this stage in events Steel had decided that he wanted a pact with Callaghan, that he wanted consultations between his party and the Government about all details of the legislative programme, and he was going to get it. The other twelve Liberal MPs would have to be jollied, pushed along and almost forced if necessary to provide the votes which would make the pact possible.

Inside the Cabinet, the opposition to the agreement was led by Peter Shore, one of the fiercely anti-EEC section of the Labour Party. The pro-Europe stance was enough to antagonize him without adding both direct elections to Strasbourg and the possibility of proportional representation. He was joined in opposition by Tony Benn, Stan Orme and Bruce Millan, but there was a clear majority in favour.

I had asked Callaghan to postpone any announcement until his own speech following Thatcher's in the House. When she began her opening speech, her own isolationist tendencies had let her down. She had no idea that the agreement had been reached. Her speech, in the words of the report in the *Daily Telegraph*, 'hovered uncertainly between disaster and tragedy and finally settled on catastrophe'. The vote of no confidence failed by 298 votes to 322.

Since I have written a whole book on the Lib-Lab pact, as it came to be known – it was not a pact in any electoral sense – I do not propose to go over the same ground again. The text of the agreement was as follows:

JOINT STATEMENT BY THE PRIME MINISTER AND THE LEADER OF THE LIBERAL PARTY:

We agreed today the basis on which the Liberal Party would work with the Government in the pursuit of economic recovery.

We will set up a joint consultative Committee under the Chairmanship of the Leader of the House, which will meet regularly. The Committee will examine Government policy and other issues prior to their coming before the House, and Liberal policy proposals.

The existence of this Committee will not commit the Government to accepting the views of the Liberal Party, or the Liberal Party to supporting the Government on any issue.

We agree to initiate regular meetings between the Chancellor and the Liberal Party economic spokesman, such meetings to begin at once. In addition, the Prime Minister and the Leader of the Liberal Party will meet as necessary.

We agree that legislation for Direct Elections to the European Assembly in 1978 will be presented to Parliament in this Session. The Liberal Party re-affirm their strong conviction that a proportional system should be used as the method of election. The Government is publishing next week a White Paper on Direct Elections to the European Assembly which sets out the choices among different electoral systems, but which makes no recommendation. There will now be consultation between us on the method to be adopted and the Government's final recommendation will take full account of the Liberal Party's commitment. The recommendation will be subject to a free vote of both Houses.

We agree that progress must be made on legislation for devolution, and to this end consultations will begin on the detailed memorandum submitted by the Liberal

129

Party today. In any future debate on proportional representation for the devolved Assemblies there will be a free vote.

We agree that the Government will provide the extra time necessary to secure the passage of the Housing (Homeless Persons) Bill, and that the Local Authorities (Works) Bill will now be confined to provisions to protect the existing activities of Direct Labour Organizations in the light of local government reorganization.

We agree that this arrangement between us should last until the end of the present Parliamentary Session, when both Parties would consider whether the experiment has been of sufficient benefit to the country to be continued.

We also agree that this understanding should be made public.

10 Downing Street
23 March 1977

The first priority was the setting up of the Consultative Committee, the others being the pursuit of economic recovery, direct elections to Europe and devolution. It was on the surface a thin list and correctly seen as such; but it was part of the wider strategy to depict the Liberal Party as again a serious participant with responsibility for the course of government.

I can best illustrate the success or failure of the Pact by following through four topics. First, economic recovery.

Inflation had started on its sharp upward trend in the last year of the Heath Government, 1973, and continued spiralling through the period of Labour Government from 1974, reaching an alarming annual rate of nearly 20 per cent at the time the Lib-Lab agreement was made. In the eighteen-month duration of our agreement it came down to under 9 per cent. It started upwards again in the last months of the pactless Labour Government, returning to 19 per cent in the first year of the Thatcher Government.

Why was this period so successful? First, there was the creation of a period of political and parliamentary stability unknown since early 1974. The share index and the pound both rallied within hours of the news of the formation of the agreement. The IMF–Government agreement could be successfully pursued against this background. Jim Callaghan had told me how valuable his friend, the German Chancellor Helmut Schmidt, had found his dependence on the minority FDP (Liberal) party in keeping his Left under control. So too did Callaghan remind his Left and the trade unions of the need to keep the Liberals aboard. The pay-restraint deals were adhered to. House-owners saw their mortgage interest rates come down from 12.25 per cent to 8.5 per cent during the pact, only to head then towards 15 per cent under the following Conservative Government.

It was a period when the House of Commons genuinely controlled the

Executive. The Dock Work scheme was not the only casualty of plans based on old Labour dogma. Tony Benn's scheme to centralize electricity was vetoed by us, for example.

"SUN" 29 JUNE 1977

" COME ON, BOY, TIME FOR WALKIES "

Such restraints, and John Pardoe's capacity to milk every source of credit for the Party out of them, did not endear him to Denis Healey, the Chancellor of the Exchequer, with whom he was supposed to be co-operating. Their relations were poor, in contrast to the Callaghan/Steel partnership. This was in part because both are intelligent, strong-minded extrovert characters, and lovers of opera. They relished their dramas. At one point the Prime Minister insisted I should join one of their meetings to try to smooth things along over the Finance Bill. Joel Barnett, as Chief Secretary to the Treasury, was similarly dragooned as the second member of the Treasury in the Cabinet. As we met in the lobby Joel whispered to me: 'I think you and I are only there to hold the coats.' When we got inside the temperature gradually rose, with Healey and Pardoe squaring up to each other.

At one point Healey looked across his desk at me and said: 'I suppose, David, you think I'm a heartless bastard.'

131

'Oh no, Denis,' I replied, 'not heartless.'

Afterwards when I went to dinner with John and Joy Pardoe at their house, John said there would have been another row had I not been present.

The negative restraining hand on the Labour Government worked well, but I was very determined to secure at least one piece of positive Liberal input into the legislative programme. Towards the end of the summer of 1977 I had a lengthy and relaxed meeting with the Prime Minister in Number 10, reviewing the prospects for our party conferences, and the new session of Parliament. At one point he summoned Tom McNally to bring in some opinion-poll details which we discussed, including the fact that profit-sharing was overwhelmingly popular with Labour voters. I retorted: 'I've been trying to tell you that.' The Government had already 'agreed to consider ways of encouraging profit-sharing' in the renewal of the agreement in July. The previous day I had stressed to Michael Foot that I needed to have something new to tell the Liberal Assembly, and that the best hope lay in this topic.

The following week I had a letter from Joel Barnett, in Denis Healey's absence abroad, watering down the section on profit-sharing of my draft assembly speech which I had sent to him. I told him it was now unacceptably feeble, and in referring to changes in the next Finance Bill he agreed to alter 'could' to 'will', thus making the commitment to legislate definite. This was the trump card for my difficult opening speech to the Assembly, justifying continuance of the pact before the delegates themselves debated it. Unfortunately, as was brilliantly captured by James Fenton, political columnist in the *New Statesman,* I did not entirely succeed with the point:

The fact was that, although Steel was appreciatively heard, nobody was actually listening to a word he was saying. They were listening to the cadences. They were waiting for the emphases. They were enjoying the climaxes. They were not thinking about the content, largely because, in all the years they have been Liberals, they have never expected to hear a speech with any content. Content is not really what they're interested in. If they were, they wouldn't be Liberals. Steel has managed to extract from the Government a promise that they would put something about profit-sharing in the next Finance Bill. And not only that, he had gone to great lengths to get permission to announce this himself, so that no one would be in any doubt that this was a Liberal measure. The whole of his speech was conducted in such a way as to lead up to this announcement – look boys, here we are, we've actually got something. Pause. Did you hear? It's really true, after all these years we've done something towards profit-sharing – for crying out loud it's going to be in the next Finance Bill. Applause.

Old habits of thought die hard, and the old habit of Liberal thought is abstract hope, a hope that, like Hamlet's chameleon, eats the air, promise-crammed. Liberal thought is not used to discussions of tactics or deals. It finds it difficult to concentrate, period. That is why Steel, in addressing the party, has the air of a teacher, but a teacher whose points are continually being missed. What was that he said, for instance about a coalition? 'Now we have to demonstrate that if this much can be done by a tiny band of Liberals outside the Government, how much more could be done by a larger group inside the next Government ...' 'Did he really say that? What does it mean?'

The commitment to legislate on profit-sharing was, however, included in the Queen's Speech that November, the draft of which I discussed with the Prime Minister before it reached the Queen. The Government's first intention was to produce a Green Paper on the subject but the official minute records that I insisted the matter be dealt with in the Finance Bill itself, in spite of Government concern at the parliamentary time involved. I said that if necessary other measures would have to be dropped to accommodate this.

The week after the Queen's Speech, I went to Congress House to see the TUC general secretary, Len Murray, to lobby him on our proposals. This I did at the request of Jim Callaghan and it illustrated the extent to which the Labour Government did not move without the sanction of the trade unions. He assured me that trade-union reaction would be limited to unenthusiasm rather than hostility, and said he would prefer trade-union machinery involved in setting up profit-sharing schemes, a proposal I resisted. In the end the Government accepted a simple scheme put forward by John Pardoe, drafted by a Party group under solicitor and candidate Philip Goldenberg.

The scheme, which introduced special tax treatment for certain types of profit-sharing, was introduced in 1979, following the 1978 Finance Act. Employees could have up to £500-worth of shares allocated to them at the prevailing market price, incurring no income-tax liability on the value of the shares. This scheme paved the way for future share-incentive schemes which can also qualify for similar tax relief. The basic scheme, from its humble beginnings, has greatly prospered and was expanded by Chancellors Howe and Lawson. And by spring 1989, 1,600 schemes were in operation, benefiting some one and three-quarter million employees.

The lasting benefits which this modest scheme has brought showed what might be achieved by Liberals in government, taking our industrial-partnership philosophy right into the heart of financial and employment legislation. Although there were lots of minor achievements recorded elsewhere, this was the biggest single positive impact we made into legislation; but it was not the one on which the Party at large had set its heart.

As I've indicated, the greatest difficulty in securing the original pact centred on the commitment to press ahead with legislation on direct elections to the European Parliament and to secure, if possible, proportional representation. I quite understood that the party attached enormous importance to this measure; but I equally understood that it was a point of arcane unimportance to the general public. It was on this issue that the pact almost came to grief twice.

In July 1977 we had 'renegotiated' the agreement with ten points for the coming session. The Party was by now extremely restless because we were still suffering in the polls under the weight of Tory press onslaughts against us. The party magazine was critical of the continuance of the agreement and there were complaints about the flow of votes away from the Party. David Penhaligon put it well when one day the *Evening Standard* ran a headline 'Steel loses 1 million a day' (referring to British Steel's losses). Flourishing a copy, he asked colleagues mischievously: 'Is that pounds or votes?'

I decided to face the September Assembly with an opening speech defending the pact and announcing the profit-sharing legislation I have just described. Referring to the forthcoming Government recommendation of PR for Europe and the free vote I said:

We shall be watching the division lists most carefully. We have a right to expect the substantial majority of Labour members – and especially Ministers whose continuance in office depends on us – to support the Government's recommendation.

And I concluded by arguing the long-term case for the pact:

The task of the Liberal Party is to convince people we need not be governed in a way which divides our people against each other. We need to face an election in which we argue that the voters don't have to choose between a government dedicated to making us all subservient to the state and one anxious to create a society in which you grab what you can for yourself and clobber anyone who gets in the way. Don't let anyone tell you that being moderate means being in favour of timidity or appeasement of the aggressive. I want our party to become the militants for the reasonable man. We need to create a nobler concept of the family that should be Britain.

The Assembly debated the Lib-Lab agreement, and an amendment to renegotiate it was defeated by 716 to 385. Cyril Smith, who had backed the move, resigned his spokesmanship on employment. But there was no way we could stop the Assembly passing an amendment stating that a 'substantial majority' of Labour MPs for a PR system should be regarded as a 'crucial indicator' of Labour support for the pact. We therefore accepted it without a vote. We had survived. I had argued that if we pulled out of the agreement because of loss of nerve, the Liberal Party would 'acquire and deserve a reputation as purposeless incompetents'.

But I had reckoned without the destructive capacity of the Liberal Party Council. This was a vaguely large body of perhaps two hundred or so which met quarterly and whose power to act in between assemblies was now total, to the dismay of successive leaders and Party officers. It was alarmingly easy to become a member of the Party Council and I had long taken the view that the best way of dealing with it was never to attend or give it any importance. On the rare occasions I did so, I almost invariably regretted it.

Its proceedings were often disorderly and the brave souls who soldiered to their meetings were often shouted down by almost juvenile antics and points of order from people who held little responsibility in the Party. This body met in November in Derby, following yet another poor by-election result. I was on one of my regular regional tours, which I felt to be a more constructive use of a Saturday. They passed a resolution saying that if the PR system did not pass through the Commons as a result of the failure of a substantial number of Labour MPs to support it, a Special Assembly should be called to consider the future of the Lib-Lab agreement. It was a direct threat to the authority not just of the leader but of the parliamentary Party, and went further than the Assembly's expression of view.

I had already let it be known that the pact could not and should not be broken *on this issue*; and that if it were, I could not continue as leader. The *Observer* next day led with a much stronger version of my views, namely that I would resign if an Assembly were even held. Much as I loathed the prospect, I could hardly prevent it or adopt such a high-handed attitude towards it; but trouble was certainly brewing.

Jim Callaghan, who has similar problems with the Labour Party Executive, told them of his own intention to support PR (which he had promised me privately months earlier). He had to remind them in a rough meeting that he wouldn't be sitting with Labour colleagues round the Cabinet table but for the Lib-Lab pact.

He was troubled by the Party Council resolution and over a cup of tea I despairingly suggested that perhaps his Executive and my Party Council could have a joint conference somewhere while we took the weekend off, a suggestion which tickled him considerably.

I told him that if PR failed and I lost the argument in a Special Assembly, I would have to resign as leader. He said he had had to threaten to resign at his Executive meeting, but that I should not do so at my age. I said I wasn't threatening. I could not possibly lead the Party in a direction I didn't believe in. If they couldn't follow me, they had better find another leader.

On the Sunday before the fateful Commons vote, I followed the same line on Brian Walden's interview on ITV's *Weekend World*. The efforts the Government were making to secure a majority for PR were illustrated over lunch with John Mackintosh when he told me he had been approached by the Government Chief Whip and told of the 'need to keep David Steel happy'. John had replied that he had long regarded that as one of his chief objects in life and his co-operation could therefore be relied on.

On the day of the actual vote the SNP decided to abstain, so we were down eleven. The Tories then applied a three-line whip on what was to have been a free vote. I had not bargained on this, reckoning that since about 100 Tories had voted for PR for the Scottish Assembly, we could count on that number. We lost by 87 votes. Only 61 Tories, including Ted Heath, Ian Gilmour and Jim Prior, had stuck out against the Thatcher line. Labour MPs had voted in favour by 146 to 115, not the 'substantial majority' demanded by their Party Council. I knew the Government had done what it could. Membership of the EEC was still a sore issue in the Labour Party, direct elections even more so, and PR for those elections was positively abhorrent to most of its members.

The Liberal MPs gathered immediately in the Whip's office in angry mood. They were more upset than I expected, with some justification since four cabinet members – Benn, Shore, Orme and Booth – were among those against. I should have insisted at least on the payroll vote. The Prime Minister telephoned personally three times to ask me to come round and see him. 'Tell him to bloody wait,' shouted Stephen Ross at Andrea Hertz, the Whips' assistant, who put her head round the door to relay the message.

At about 11 p.m. I went round to see him and he gave me the figures. Unusually, he was alone. I warned him of the mood of the Party, and said the Special Assembly was now inevitable. I left disconsolate and returned to the MPs' meeting. I had better leave the description of what happened then to others. Michie and Hoggart speculated on the scene thus:

He returned looking worried and saying nothing. Finally Pardoe asked, 'Well, what did he say?' Steel paused for a moment then said softly: 'He's going to see the Queen in the morning.' Someone said 'Oh Christ, he's not,' and Steel replied, 'Yes, he is. I told him what you all feel and he said it means an election. So we'd better start getting ready.' There was silence for a few moments, and one MP claimed later that some had felt physically sick at the thought of an election. Then Steel revealed that he had been joking, and said they would meet the following day. But it was rather more than a joke; he wanted his colleagues to have a real vision of the dreadful prospect of fighting a general election on the platform of proportional representation for direct elections to the European assembly. However important it might be to the party – and it was important to an almost lunatic extent – it meant little or nothing to the voters.

Cyril Smith recently reminded me: 'You kept your face deadpan. It shook us and finished the meeting.' All I had done was buy time. The serious meeting took place next morning and lasted two and a half hours.

I had an almost sleepless night and the discussion was pretty aimless, acrimonious and badly chaired by me. In the afternoon John Pardoe came in to see me and express his frustration that Healey's pay-policy figures were wrong and Healey had fobbed him off with a meeting on the subject after Christmas. John had been offered a couple of high-salaried jobs in the City and his morale was low. I had to telephone Healey and fix an earlier meeting for them.

Then I asked Jo Grimond to come and see me. He had not been at the morning meeting and although he was also very fed up with the whole pact he resolutely agreed with my line that the Party would be mad to break it off on the PR-for-Europe issue. Alan Beith as Chief Whip and I persuaded him to come to the resumed Party meeting at 6 p.m. and say so.

At 4 p.m. Jim Callaghan came over from Downing Street to see me with Michael Foot and his deputy private secretary, Philip Wood, in attendance. He had been ruffled by the tone of the Smith/Pardoe interviews on the lunchtime news, and stressed he had kept to his side of the bargain with even people like Michael voting for PR and direct elections. I said that I certainly was aware of all this and I was going to have one more try at rallying my colleagues at 6 p.m. He asked me to come back and tell him if it was all off. I said I would do so by 7.30 p.m.

At 6 p.m. the MPs met again. By this time I had recovered my composure. I told them firmly but quietly that my clear view was that we should press on with the agreement and fight for it in the Special Assembly, unless they wished to break it off and fight a general election under a new strategy and a new leader. Jo duly backed me up. The argument raged for an hour and a half. Cyril pressed his proposal to break off and – unusually – we took a vote on it. Four of my colleagues voted to end the pact (Cyril, Richard Wainwright, David Penhaligon and Emlyn Hooson). Five voted to continue (Jo, Alan, Russell Johnston, Geraint Howells and Stephen Ross) plus myself. Two (John Pardoe and Jeremy Thorpe) abstained. Clement Freud was away. The pact continued, and we announced that without revealing the vote, but I now presided over a hopelessly split parliamentary Party and had a potentially hostile Assembly to face. It was a bleak moment.

I returned to see the Prime Minister, who was surprised and relieved at the decision. I told him I could not see the pact lasting beyond next July when the Finance Bill with its profit-sharing measure would become law.

I also warned him that it might end with the Special Assembly next month. He asked what I proposed to do and I said that if the Special Assembly did not back the agreement I would definitely resign as leader. There would presumably be an early election and we would fight under a new leader.

At this point he asked Philip Wood to leave us alone in his room. (I omitted this episode from my book, published in 1980, because Jim Callaghan was still leader of the Labour Party and I wished to create no additional problems for him – but it is clearly written in my diary of that day.) He told me that if the worst came to the worst and I did have to resign, he would like me to join the Cabinet. I thanked him warmly but said that was quite out of the question. Infuriating though I sometimes found them, I simply could not desert my fellow Liberals and I would stay loyal to whatever the party decided.

Thinking it over that night, I thought it could have been just a cynical offer designed to bolster his government if the Lib-Lab pact collapsed. But I don't believe it was, because he went on to say that whatever happened I must come and talk to him about my future. I told him I intended to stay if I could and as I left he said how much he valued 'our friendship' and shook hands as we wished each other a Happy Christmas.

I revealed the conversation to no one except Judy. I believe that my interpretation was correct. He is first and foremost a patriot and he took a much broader view than his successor of his sense of duty to the country. I grew both to like him and to appreciate his qualities. In his own memoirs *Time and Chance* he has written about me:

I had been predisposed to like him from the start for the not very logical reason that thirty years earlier on a visit to West Africa I had stayed with his wife Judy's parents in Sierra Leone. Her father had been a member of the Colonial Civil Service and it is sometimes because of such irrelevant personal contacts that first impressions are formed in politics. In this case first impressions were lasting. Beneath his quiet exterior, David Steel is a determined man, but one whom I found scrupulous in his dealings with me and always considerate in his understanding of the Government's problems, not least with some of its own supporters. ... I trusted David Steel's discretion and frequently took him into my confidence as a fellow Privy Councillor on a wide range of Government activities going well beyond the clauses of our Agreement. I wanted him to have as complete a picture as possible of the Government's overall situation so that he would have a better understanding of our limitations.

A few days later came the crucial meeting of the Party's standing Policy

Committee which had to table the resolution for the Special Assembly. Alan Beith and Richard Wainwright, accompanied by Archy Kirkwood, went off to it armed with an acceptable draft resolution. When Archy reported back to me later that evening, it was to tell me that only by eight votes to six had they prevented a 'break the pact now' resolution being put forward for the Assembly on 21 January. What they proposed was not the draft I had approved.

On Christmas Eve John Pardoe phoned to tell me of his mutually aggressive meeting (the official note records: 'the meeting ended abruptly') with Denis Healey on pay policy. John stormed out and described Healey on radio as 'the second worst Chancellor since the war'.

I spent the Christmas recess on the telephone to John, Jeremy, David and Emlyn persuading them with varying degrees of enthusiasm to fall into line for the Assembly.

I wrote to Richard Wainwright, who was holidaying abroad, that the more I thought about the Standing Committee's draft resolution, the more I found unacceptable their proposed options, the best of which was to give notice now of the ending of the pact in July. I argued that this would give public notice to our election opponents of our intentions, kill the pact without burying it, and make it more difficult to negotiate other items from ministers.

On 3 January 1978 the Party chairman, Geoff Tordoff, and president, Gruyff Evans, came to lunch at Ettrick Bridge. I told them unambiguously that the options proposed were unacceptable to me as leader and we hammered out a draft compromise which allowed the Assembly to hope the thing would be over by July but allowed it to continue until such time as the parliamentary Party decided.

One development that was to prove important in lancing potential opposition at the Special Assembly came from a statement issued by John Pardoe on 6 January, saying: 'No one should assume that if David Steel resigns I shall pick up the pieces; my aim is to ensure that David will not resign.'

The following week I took the unusual step of attending the Standing Committee and putting my case. They agreed that my proposal against ending the pact now could be put to the Assembly. That was a step forward. The next day the MPs (Cyril being absent) agreed to back my line without dissent.

Two days later – Friday, 13 January – I attended my worst meeting with the Party Executive ever. I wrote in my diary:

An appalling meeting with the Executive which at one point is a shouting match. Several say the party is disintegrating, and I listen to worthy verbal essays about 'participating democracy' etc. Towards the end one member actually mentioned inflation. I leave angry and depressed for a quick curry with Evans, Tordoff, and Michael Steed before Archy and I join the night train.

The next morning my morale was restored by a well-conducted debate at the special conference in Glasgow of the Scottish Liberal Party led by Russell Johnston and George Mackie. They voted 210 to 12 to support continuance of the pact. So did the Welsh Party Council. I took a relieved day off on the Monday and went riding with Judy.

On Friday, 20 January, I was driven by Archy Kirkwood and Andrew Gifford to Blackpool where I had a meeting in the evening with Cyril Smith and Gruyff Evans. I outlined to Cyril the support of all the other MPs and suggested that if, as I now expected, he lost the 'end the pact' vote he should make a second, conciliatory speech afterwards. Cyril is his own man but he is also loyal to a cause and he could see the risk of a major Party split. He agreed to do it.

On Saturday morning the Opera House was full to the brim and a very good debate began. I was joined by Judy and Graeme for a filthy picnic lunch in the bleak dressing room behind the stage. I had decided to wind up the debate in the afternoon, not from a prepared text but – as I prefer to speak – from scribbled notes, and not from the platform but from the delegates' rostrum. The last move was deliberate, not just to enter into the debate but to emphasize that my leadership was itself at stake without having to say so explicitly. I had already spelt that out in a letter to candidates which Alan Beith had me tone down, and made my position clear in countless television and radio interviews.

Michie and Hoggart describe the event in ironically purple prose:

In the end, the party climbed down and the special assembly at Blackpool turned into a kind of huge jamboree, an affirmation of the party's love for itself and confidence in its future. With nearly 2,500 delegates it was the biggest Liberal assembly in memory. Hundreds of the delegates came up from London by special train, and as the train was late they actually ran from the station to catch every golden moment of the debate on direct elections to Europe. By the time Steel spoke, gleaming in the lights with an air of confident self-vindication, the issue was a foregone conclusion. He won by 1,727 votes to 520, and the Pact had been saved again. On the other side of the Blackpool Winter Gardens, the annual pigeon-fanciers' show continued in blissful avian ignorance of the momentous events a few yards away.

It was another extraordinary victory for Steel, who had used his own personality and authority to the utmost. He had managed it by persuading the party to hold the assembly as late as possible after the PR vote in the Commons, so that tempers had cooled. He had done it by threatening his own resignation – a perfectly fair ploy, and one which worked. He helped himself with a good, fighting speech, in which he even dared to hint that he would like to continue the Pact for a third session. But most of all he won because the activists, the people who give their energies, their enthusiasm and even their whole lives to the Liberal Party, are still in a minority. When the assembly meets, when the workers and the voters pour in from their constituencies, this silent majority in the end wanted to reaffirm their loyalty by voting for David Steel, their tiny Caledonian superstar.

The following week when I bumped into Jim Callaghan in the division lobby he was congratulating me on the success of Blackpool, a media success which confounded all my forebodings, by saying, 'Ah well, it just goes to show that what our parties need is firmness – it always pays.'

Another main theme of the Pact was devolution for Scotland and Wales. The Liberal Party had since Gladstone's day advocated 'Home Rule all round' and more recently regarded the failure to provide it as the main reason for the upsurge in the SNP, who advocated not internal self-government but total independence as a sovereign state. As I have frequently pointed out, the Scottish electorate from time to time use the SNP as a battering-ram to get attention to their grievances rather than because they support the policy of independence.

But the Conservatives, under Heath, and Labour, under Callaghan, had promised some degree of devolution; and indeed the report of the Royal Commission on the constitution under the chairmanship of the Scottish judge, Lord Kilbrandon, recommended it for Scotland and Wales. The Labour Party, though having some early commitment to the subject among its founding fathers, came somewhat fresh to the subject and was divided – among the outright opponents was Neil Kinnock. The Minister put in charge of the subject was John Smith, whom I knew, liked and respected from the days when he was President of the Glasgow University Labour Club and we used to meet at inter-university occasions.

The Scotland and Wales Bill was drafted with little consultation and was a very bad bill. As I've already described, it looked like making little headway when the guillotine was introduced, and failed. In his memoirs, Jim Callaghan records:

It was only the agreement we reached with the Liberals a month after the Devolution guillotine debacle that enabled the Government to pull back from the precipice. Although the Liberals had contributed to our defeat by voting against the guillotine, as soon as discussions began about an Agreement, I found that David Steel was

141

anxious that the Devolution Bill should be put to the House once more, subject to certain changes which the Liberals would propose and which I undertook to consider. They were extremely keen on testing the views of Members about proportional representation, and as part of the Agreement, Michael Foot and I undertook to offer the House a free vote on whether the members of the new Assemblies should be elected by this means or not.

Part of the pact was to resurrect the proposals in more acceptable and manageable form. This was done with the production of much-improved separate Scotland and Wales Bills, of which the former was the more complete and far-reaching.

As James Naughtie said in the *Scottish Government Yearbook for 1979*: 'The new bill which emerged in November 1977 could scarcely be said to be bristling with Liberal fire, but it was cheerfully admitted in Government circles later that they had won "more than 50 per cent of their battles, quite enough to keep them happy".'

The main negotiation was carried out on our side by Russell Johnston, Geraint Howells and George Mackie, though on one day, to my irritation, John Smith told them he had no authority to negotiate any further on a particular point and that they would have to refer it to Messrs Steel and Foot. At the same time, Denis Healey told John Pardoe that certain points on the budget could only be discussed with me because I was a Privy Councillor. My colleagues and I were united in detesting this concentration of responsibility.

The bill however proceeded with an early timetable introduced smoothly, until a Labour rebellion forced a qualifying '40 per cent of the registered electorate' amendment to the requirement of a majority in the referenda to be held in Scotland and Wales.

The reason why Scots feel so strongly in favour of self-government were well set out in a speech in the 1976 Commons debate by Malcolm Rifkind, MP, from the Conservative Opposition back benches. He had resigned his junior portfolio, along with the Shadow Secretary of State Alick Buchanan-Smith, when the new Tory leader, Mrs Thatcher, did a U-turn and committed her party against the proposals. Since Malcolm (at the time of writing) is now Secretary of State for Scotland and resisting fresh demands for Home Rule, I quote his views with particular relish and approval:

Throughout the 270 years of Union, Scotland has required – and here it is very different from Wales – separate legislation throughout the whole sphere of domestic matters. This is a major anomaly, which the British Parliament has accepted because it has no alternative. It is an anomaly which has not always worked entirely to the advantage of Scotland because as a result of the requirements of a separate legal system, the British Parliament was unable to meet fully the need for modernizing, reforming and improving that legal system. Scotland is the only territory on the face of the earth which has a legal system without a legislature to improve, modernize and amend it . . .

There are other distinctive Scottish characteristics as well. Throughout the 18th and 19th centuries Scotland was governed in a different way from the rest of Britain, with different administrative powers, different local government and a different structure of education. In 1885 a Scottish Secretary was appointed, and in the 1920s he was elevated to Secretary of State. In the 1930s the Scottish Office was sent lock, stock and barrel to Edinburgh. All this administrative devolution was done by Conservative Governments, and it was not done out of a feeling of national sentiment, but because of the administrative requirements needed to achieve good government for the Scottish people.

It may be asked why, if we have had this enormous devolution and if Parliament, with a unitary system, is able to respond to the distinct needs of Scotland, this should not continue. It may be asked why, with a separate legal system and a separate Scottish Office, it is necessary to go any farther and establish a directly elected Assembly. That is a fair question, and it deserves a serious answer. The answer is that throughout the last 270 years a dynamic change has taken place. This is not because the people have changed their minds but because of the increasing complexity of government, requiring more and more administrative devolution, and more powers to be given to the Scottish Office.

We have now a Secretary of State for Scotland who is for all practical purposes a Scottish Prime Minister. He covers a Department the equivalent of which in England and Wales is served by eight or nine Ministries. He has one Department, and Scottish Members are expected to scrutinize his actions. The Scottish Office has more civil servants than the European Commission . . . . There has been a qualitative change in the call for devolution. In the early 20th century the demand for a separate Scottish legislature was the result of national sentiment. That national sentiment still exists, but added to it is the need for good government, good administration and a better deal for Scottish people within the United Kingdom.

The Devolution Bills achieved their royal assent before the ending of the Pact in July 1978. There remained the referenda. Here the Government made many mistakes. The first was delaying them to the following March; the second was the failure to follow the European Referendum precedent and set up with finance two all-party organizations to campaign on each side. Instead the 'pro' side was dominated by Labour, the propaganda including posters of the by-now more unpopular Callaghan inviting the electorate to say 'yes' to him. We were by now well into the 'winter of discontent' with industrial strife over a broken pay policy, rubbish in the streets and the dead unburied.

In addition, the bill contained three fatal flaws: no proportional representation (contrary to Kilbrandon's recommendations – we had lost on a free vote); no tax-raising powers (we had lost our arguments on this); and no commitment to reduce local government from two tiers to one (thus raising the cry of 'extra layer of government' from the opponents). Lord Home in particular was influential in citing these as his reason for voting 'no' although he had been one of the early promoters inside the Conservative Party.

For all these reasons I played a rather small role in the 'pro' campaign. In Scotland a narrow majority, 1,230,937 to 1,153,502, voted for the Scottish Assembly but that represented only 33 per cent of those entitled to vote. Thus the 40 per cent hurdle was not passed and all our months of work failed to produce any change in the 1707 Act of Union.

This was, of course, after the end of the Pact. To hark back to its ending: on a Sunday in February, after the Special Assembly, there was an all-day strategy meeting of the Party Executive and the MPs, the Standing Committee and the General Election Committee; we considered a useful paper by Party President-elect Michael Steed and the meeting endorsed it, setting out my strategy of playing positively the balance of power and expressing a readiness to work with either party after the election to secure electoral reform.

Jim Callaghan and I had started to discuss election prospects, and I told him of my perception that we needed a quarantine period between the formal ending of the Pact and an election. He said he would not decide on an October election until July.

In early March I told him we would probably seek to end the agreement in July. He said he might wish to offer a package for 1978–9 and get a straight 'yes' or 'no' on Liberal support but generally seemed to favour an October election. Later in March I recorded one meeting in my diary:

We went on to discuss election dates. He still wants the option of going on to '79. He doesn't think inflation will necessarily go back to double figures as some forecast, and that in any case people will feel better off over a longer period. There is also the possibility of favourable action from the July economic world summit which could help another budget before the election. He agrees an election desirable after the Devolution Bills are on the statute-book but before referenda, which I argue points to October. He is against the suggestion of my 'giving notice' in April.

In April he expressed the view to me that there could be a minority Labour Government after the election – which was why the pact should not end in a row, but in an orderly way in July as I had suggested. In early May he begged me not to announce the forthcoming ending of the agreement, as I planned to do to the Party Council, because all the advice he was getting was to go on to 1979. Would I please wait until at least the Whitsun recess? He again said we might consider a new Queen's Speech on its merits but I said I thought this course undesirable. On 26 May he told me he would be abroad in the Whitsun recess and he would prefer me to wait until he got back. I told him that after all our upsets on the Finance Bill and our increasing anxiety about pay policy not holding, the Party was pressing daily for an announcement and I could delay no longer. John Pardoe and I would have to inform our MPs quickly. At one point he turned to Michael Foot and, referring to a weekend broadcast of mine, said that next time they would have to involve their parliamentary Party apparently. I laughed and asked him what made him think it was him we would be talking to. He smiled and said: 'I can't quite imagine you crawling into bed with Mrs Thatcher.'

John and Alan helped me draft the necessary letter for the Prime Minister's agreement. The next day, 25 May, in the middle of Cabinet, I had a phone call pleading for an extra couple of hours' delay – until the Stock Exchange closed. At 4.30 p.m. we made the announcement. I gave endless television interviews and flew to Edinburgh for dinner at Holyrood Palace.

The next day's papers led with the announcement. The *Daily Mail* called the pact 'a squalid little affair', while *The Times* described it as 'a brave attempt to establish the conditions in which minority government can be made to work. ... the Pact may be dying but another one may be born again.'

Ten days later at a meeting with the Speaker, George Thomas, he said he thought an autumn general election inevitable and a hung Parliament probable. We therefore began intensive planning for an autumn election. I was conscious of what the editorial in the party magazine *New Outlook* had said:

The Liberal Special Assembly in Blackpool was an interesting exercise in democracy. Called to end the pact with the Government, it ended up not only confirming the agreement but approving by acclaim a broader package which included the possible extension of the pact and an explicit election strategy aimed at securing the balance of power for the Liberal Party. This is the residual power of the directly-elected Leader – to appeal over the heads of the Party's national activists to his electorate. In this case, it paid off. David Steel, who opposed the idea of the Assembly and who successfully opposed the idea that the Asembly should take decisions about strategy, came away from Blackpool with not only a virtually free hand on the pact but also with an endorsement of his broad strategy.

The decision is taken. David Steel has placed himself in a very exposed position: if his strategy fails to deliver the goods, the Party will be looking for a scapegoat and will find one ready-made. The process will not necessarily be a fair one – there are many factors over which the Leader has no control that can make it fail – but the process of sacrificing a lamb has never been a particularly fair one. There are other ex-Party leaders in the Commons who can testify to that – from the lamb's point of view.

After the announcement of the ending of the pact, Denis Healey as Chancellor behaved in a rather cavalier manner and nearly came to grief over sections of the Finance Bill in June on which he had not consulted us. The pay policy in June and July was increasingly held together with *ad hoc* pieces of sticky tape and we were sure an autumn election was both necessary and certain. At the Scottish Liberal Conference I positively called for such an election to be held.

In July came the unexpected news of the death of John Mackintosh, the Labour MP, my friend and constituency neighbour. I was extremely upset. John had been a mentor, confidant and friend all through these events and had been a major influence on my political life ever since my schooldays. His loss was, I believe, to prove crucial in the absence of his advocacy during the Scottish referendum. He had a brilliant mind and sparkling personality, which was perhaps less appreciated south of the border. His failure to secure office was in large part because of his indiscreet nature and love of gossip.

John was one of the few spellbinding speakers in the Commons, a talent he used sparingly. He also had an enormous sense of fun, being both a great party giver and party goer. On one occasion the Mayor of Berwick-upon-Tweed – who that year was the proprietor of the Tweeddale Press, which published our local papers – was being installed in a church service in the town. He invited the local MPs – John and me and our wives – among hundreds of others to this event, which was followed by a splendid marquee lunch in his garden. John and Una, Judy and I settled at a table for four. I pretended outrage that John had come for the lunch but, unlike me, had failed duty attendance at the service. He retorted: 'David, the last time I was in a church was for my first marriage – and that was a mistake.'

He was also an ardent European and loved to tell the tale – suitably embroidered – of how on the same day he had addressed trade-union meetings in Frankfurt and Glasgow on the same theme of brotherhood in Europe. In Frankfurt he had been met by a chauffeur-driven car and taken to the union headquarters, where the glass doors had automatically slid open, and he gave his talk in a warm, carpeted lecture room, complete with visual aids. Catching a direct flight to Glasgow, he had to take a bus ride from the airport, make his way to the Keir Hardie Hall, climb the stone stairs with chipped dark-brown wall paint and settle in a room with rickety wooden chairs and a bare light bulb. At the end of his persuasive address, a voice said: 'But John, ye dinna understand. We're no goin' tae be dragged doon to their standards.' More than ten years after his death I still feel the gap he left in both personal and political life.

John's death and the arrest of Jeremy Thorpe both cast a shadow over my spirits that summer as I stayed at home planning for the election. In early September, following the TUC congress, the Prime Minister booked a national television broadcast following a Cabinet meeting. My diary reads:

The Cabinet were all filmed and photographed emerging from Number Ten in the middle of the day, tight-lipped. The BBC and ITV arrived at my house in Ettrick Bridge ready to record my reaction to the PM's expected announcement of the election that evening. I was telephoned at lunchtime by Michael Foot who said JC had asked him to warn me in confidence in advance that far from making an election announcement he would be indicating his intention to press on for another session. My reaction was one of complete astonishment. I simply thanked him for the call, indicated my surprise and disagreement at the proposed line and sat down to prepare my public reaction. The waiting broadcasters outside realized I would have foreknowledge and wanted to record my reaction in advance to get the tapes back to the studios in time to broadcast in the early bulletins. In view of the surprise nature of the content I thought it best to decline.

Why he decided to broadcast at all was a mystery. Everyone was led to the wrong conclusion including his own party and indeed most of the Cabinet. The TUC were also annoyed that he had successfully played their congress as a pre-election platform. I felt it was all a great mistake and said so.

In my response to the announcement I said:

If, as Liberals have argued, there were ever an argument for a fixed term of parliament and removing this decision from the individual hands of the Prime Minister, this is it.

As it is, the government expects to stagger on through a difficult winter with no majority in the Commons. This will not inspire confidence.

The country had expected an election and will be disappointed. The sooner the government goes to the country the better. We shall act accordingly.

When I next met him three weeks later, I registered my annoyance directly. He had postponed the election because he thought – correctly in my view – that the best they could do was come back to a hung Parliament. I said, 'What's wrong with that?' He argued that the Tories would then have harried them as in 1950–51 into another election. I disagreed on two counts: first, if Mrs Thatcher did not win outright, the Tories' morale and unity would be destroyed. Second, unlike 1950 we had now accepted that Parliament could work and – with a future Lib-Lab coalition, stronger than the Agreement –

the Government could be effective in a hung Commons.

Our forebodings proved correct. The pay policy did not hold. Industrial unrest followed; and without the Pact, the Government lost the confidence of the House and fell not on a date of its own choosing, 28 March 1979.

In the no-confidence debate that finally defeated the Labour Government, Michael Foot made a witty speech castigating all who would not support the Government. I did not escape his barbs when he said:

Which brings me to the Leader of the Liberal Party. He knows that I would not like to miss him out. I am sure that I shall elicit the support and sympathy of the Right Hon. Lady [Mrs Thatcher] when I say that she and I have always shared a common interest in this young man [a phrase she had used about me earlier in the Commons] . . .

She can look after herself. But the Leader of the Liberal Party – and I say this with the utmost affection – has passed from rising hope to elder statesman without any intervening period whatsoever.

In his own memoirs, Jim Callaghan admits that he made a mistake in allowing election speculation to build up so much before his September broadcast, whereas I have never forgiven him the mistake of failing to go to the country at that moment.

We began the 1979 general election with two resultant handicaps. First, although the Pact had finished the previous autumn, the Tories cleverly attached blame to us for everything that had gone wrong in the latter stages of the Labour-only government – the pay rises, the industrial stoppages, the referendum fiasco. Second, the Tories had gone well ahead of Labour in the polls while we had sunk to 6 per cent, once actually to 5 per cent, about the level we had seen in the last days of Jeremy's leadership. The electoral outlook was bleak. Ian Mikardo, the Commons expert bookie, gave me enormous odds against there being more than ten Liberal MPs after the election, which I took with a tenner. The *Sunday Express* said only Jo Grimond might survive. When we left the Liberal dining table for the last time we suspected that few of the fourteen would be back.

Then, having had nothing but bad luck dogging my leadership for its first nearly three years, there was suddenly a stroke of good luck turned into good management. A by-election following the death of the Labour MP was being held in the Edge Hill division of Liverpool. It was a seat where we held the local wards on the City Council and our candidate was the young and talented councillor, David Alton, backed by the formidable election strategist, Trevor Jones. We threw everything into the campaign and I must have gone at least three times. On the very day after the fall of the Government in the Commons, we won the seat handsomely from Labour. Alton and his team had to start all over again with their general election campaign; but it was a terrific morale boost to the Party and, to be frank, a badly needed one for its leader. It meant we began the election showing the capacity to win seats. It made my balance-of-power strategy not so hopelessly incredible after all.

Moreover the Liberal election plans, such as they were, having been put into cold storage in September, were now further advanced than normal. We spent only £135,000 compared with about £1,000,000 by Labour and £1,300,000 by the Tories. I had invented the idea of a battlebus both on cost grounds and as a distinctive way of campaigning round the country. I also used planes, helicopters and night sleepers to be able to address eleven of the seventeen national press conferences in London.

One of the limitations was my three-county constituency, in which I normally addressed over fifty meetings. This was riskily cut down to about twenty, and further reduced by the demands of television. This caused a rumpus between Judy and my agent, Riddle Dumble, on the one hand and my campaign strategists on the other. I decided to back the national campaign as against my local one, with Judy becoming almost a substitute candidate, to her and everybody else's anxiety in the Borders. She was loyally assisted by George Mackie.

My Conservative opponent was the able Gerry Malone, later defeated by Roy Jenkins in Hillhead and eventually (temporarily) MP for South Aberdeen. In fact, my absence seemed to make Border hearts grow fonder because my majority soared to an almost indecent 10,000, in spite of a very part-time candidature.

The object of the battlebus was to tour our existing and winnable seats at minimum cost. Journalists were carried on board for a fee. At the back I had a private lounge. Next to it was an office with radio telephone, photocopier and electric typewriter and two television sets. The battlebus was a brilliant idea with severe drawbacks. Radio telephones were in their infancy and many potential Liberal gains were in areas not served by radio masts at all. Links with HQ in London were somewhat spasmodic. The power supply was inadequate for all the gadgetry, so that on one occasion my hard-pressed secretaries, Tessa Horton and Nali Dinshaw, had to announce to the assembled hacks that they could have a choice either of coffee or press releases of my lunchtime speech, since we could not operate both machines at the same time. They opted for coffee.

We all worked incredible hours. Pratap Chitnis, the heroic agent of the Orpington by-election, later director of our Party organization, whom I had persuaded Jim Callaghan to elevate to a cross-bench peerage because of his work on the Community Relations Commission, took charge of the itinerary and the bus management. Looking back on my daily timetable, I marvel at what we achieved. Taking one day at random: I addressed the morning press conference at the National Liberal Club; went by car to Battersea Heliport, from there by helicopter, accompanied by two TV helicopters, to Newtown, Montgomeryshire, where I addressed a huge crowd in the marketplace, with Emlyn Hooson, and gave two television interviews; on to Aberystwyth to support Geraint Howells; then to Colwyn Bay and Holyhead. From there we flew by plane to Leeds, where we rejoined the battlebus and drove, preceded by sirens and flashing blue lights, at breakneck speed to Yorkshire Television Studios to appear live on their six o'clock regional programme. Then on to a city cinema where I spoke to a packed audience, followed by a late-night drive down the motorway to London, fish and chips having been taken on board in Leeds. The bus was tolerably comfortable on motorways; but on the country roads of Cornwall or the Borders the private lounge, situated behind the rear wheels, swayed like a small yacht in heavy seas, threatening the same physiological result.

While they were exhausting, the effect of these visits was dramatic at each location. The excitement of the battlebus, with all its attendant cameras, boosted local campaigns and candidates, and left behind valuable publicity. The planning of this rushing round the country was greatly assisted by the police. Sadly, their presence had been made necessary by the car-bomb assassination of Airey Neave on the eve of the dissolution of Parliament. I had a permanent team of three armed Special Branch officers. While there was no reason to believe my life was particularly at risk (the only bomb addressed to me was found in the Commons screening procedure, whereas one the same day injured a clerk who opened it at Number 10 Downing Street), any prominent person accompanied by television is a potential target. Plunging into crowds to 'press the flesh', in the vulgar Americanism, is always hazardous, as much from cranks as opponents. The reassuring presence of the Special Branch greatly helped. So much so that a huge rooftop picture on the front of the *Western Morning News* showing the battlebus surrounded by a sea of faces, with me somewhere in the middle, led to a 'spot the members of the public' competition aboard the bus. The crush of Special Branch, local police, party aides, accompanying journalists, television crews, local candidate and aides, local journalists, made it difficult to reach real people. But the greatest value of the police was their radio contact with local forces as we sped round the country, thus maximizing our efficiency and minimizing inconvenience to the public.

The manifesto had been well prepared and written. The *Guardian* gave it

ABOVE Five Steel children (from left to right), Michael, Jill, Ian, me and Felicity.

LEFT In Moscow, 1960, part of the first post-war delegation of Scottish students to go to the Soviet Union.

As President of Edinburgh University Students Representative Council, with Jo Grimond at his installation as Rector of Edinburgh University, 1961.

Speaking for the Scottish Union of Students
Delegation at Klosters in 1961, with its
President, John Hill.

Marriage to Judy MacGregor, October 1962.

'It's Boy David.' Being carried down Jedburgh High Street after winning the Borders by-election in 1965.

Right Arriving at the Commons (with Judy) in March 1965, bringing the number of Liberal MPs into double figures.

Four generations of Steels: Graeme's christening at Caddonfoot Church outside Galashiels, October 1967.

Jeremy Thorpe at
Cherrydene meeting
Graeme.

Judy and I crossing the
River Ettrick at Selkirk
Common Riding.

With mother and
father on my
Moderatorial visit to
parliament, 1974.

Elected Leader, 7 July 1976.

The election campaign on the move, 1979.

THE REAL FIGHT IS FOR BRITAIN

GO LIBERAL

AND THEY'LL HAVE TO LISTEN

Published by Liberal Publication Department, 9 Poland St, London W1V 3DG and printed by T. H. Brickell & Son Ltd., Shaftesbury, Dorset

Liberal Party poster, General Election, 1979.

At the Liberal Party Conference in Margate, 26 September 1979.

Below Remembrance Sunday, 1979. David Steel, James Callaghan and the Prime Minister, Margaret Thatcher. Behind are Francis Pym, Keith Joseph and Geoffrey Howe.

The Leader's office at Westminster.

With coal miners in South Wales, April 1980.

The Steel family, 1981. (From left to right: Catriona, Billy, me, Judy, Graeme, and Rory in front.)

42 points for new ideas against 11 for Labour and 9 for the Conservatives, while *The Economist* declared simply that we had produced strikingly the best manifesto. In my preface I made the appeal:

Of course we want in time to see Britain led by a Liberal Government, implementing a coherent radical programme with the support of a clear majority of voters. But meanwhile we are prepared to co-operate with whichever party will go with us some way along the same road. It would, after all, be a profound and radical change for Britain to benefit from stability in economic policy, to gain a new consensus in pay policy and industrial relations, to achieve a wider agreement on the structure of taxation, or to open up a searching debate on the best use of Britain's limited resources. It would be a radical change in itself for the next government to have to base its policies upon the support of the representatives of a genuine majority of the electorate. With your support, and the support of millions of voters like you, we can ensure that those changes take place.

The title of our manifesto was *The Real Fight is for Britain*; it was accompanied by a brilliant series of posters designed by Adrian Slade, showing me above the slogan against photographs of Callaghan and Thatcher, back to back with pistols in their hands.

The other part of the campaign was of course that conducted on television. We had three party broadcasts, skilfully directed by Justin Cartwright, who had volunteered his services soon after I became leader and has worked as my television adviser ever since.

My final appearance on the last Sunday evening of the election consisted of a face-to-camera appeal from a fireside armchair, while Rory played with his toys in the background. This was of course a replica set in the basement of Broadcasting House, but it created the right atmosphere. I spoke slowly, directly and persuasively, with Justin arranging one of his famous eyeball close-ups at the end. Michael Pilsworth, in his review of the broadcasting in the 1979 election, described it as 'a masterpiece of political broadcasting' while Butler and Kavanagh in *The British General Election of 1979* called it 'one of the most powerful heard in an election'.

In my view very little can be taught in television technique. It is the most revealing and testing of all the media, outstripping platform speeches, Commons performances or press conferences in its ability to expose the good and bad in every politician and especially the phoney. My only advantage is that, having worked briefly in television, I am relaxed amid the technology. I recall Ed Murrow's praise of Jo Grimond in the 1959 election: 'There is nothing to replace the person in front of the camera with something to say and saying it well.'

Margaret Thatcher, on the other hand, who has been known to dismiss me as 'just a television personality', is heavily overtutored and artificial in this medium. She frequently refuses to be interviewed by certain people, and in that election had vetoed Llew Gardner in one of the four major interviews with the party leaders. I was able to turn this to advantage when it came to my interview, as the transcript shows:

GARDNER: Let's take proportional representation. Ah, when you took me on a round tour of Europe a minute ago, you conveniently left out Italy . . .
STEEL: Yes.
GARDNER: which is not a shining example of ah – I would have thought (Steel tries to interrupt). . . . May I finish the question, Mr Steel – of stable government. And surely, in addition, one result of proportional representation is that you open a parliamentary door to minorities such as the Communists and the National Front.
STEEL: I was going to be able to answer your question before you'd finished . . .
GARDNER: Well, I, I didn't doubt it for a minute.
STEEL: I, I – (PAUSE) I, I now see why Mrs Thatcher doesn't let you interview her.

My direct style throughout the campaign on television helped to lift our personal ratings. The popular Tory press did their best to counteract this. 'Disaster looms for Libs' was one headline. The *Daily Mail* was – and is – consistently hostile, becoming more or less a Tory free-sheet. On polling day itself, the *Daily Express* screamed in a last-minute headline: 'A LIBERAL VOTE IS A WASTED VOTE', one of the most unoriginal in history, while the *Sun* mustered all its intellectual force to conclude: 'Anyone who votes Liberal next Thursday is nuts.'

On Thursday 14 per cent duly did so. The Conservatives obtained an overall majority of 43. Jeremy, Emlyn and John Pardoe, as I've already recorded, lost their seats. Eleven of us were returned to the House. A forecast catastrophic disaster had been turned into a slight setback – not nearly as bad as the 1970 result – and therefore seemed almost like a triumph in comparison. We had survived, but the Thatcher era had begun.

7

THE BORDERS

Still Point of a Turning World

N o one can fully understand my political life without a proper comprehension of life in the Borders. Those journalists who have come on
one-off safaris to inspect what they imagine to be some peculiar hideaway
have never grasped what it is all about, whereas those who are regular visitors
have come to appreciate the quality and purpose of existence here.

The area ranges from the village of Carlops in Peeblesshire (now Tweeddale) just outside Edinburgh to the north, to Newcastleton in the south,
whence many people commute to Carlisle. It spreads to Broughton and
Skirling in the west, whose nearest city is Glasgow, to Kelso in the east, not
far from the town of Berwick. Through it flows the River Tweed and its many
tributaries: the Teviot, Jed, Ettrick, Yarrow, Gala, Leader and Leithen. The
old parliamentary seat extended to 1,700 square miles. There were eight
burghs – towns which, under the old system of local government, had their
own town councils – ranging in size from Hawick with an electorate of about
16,000 to Innerleithen with about 3,000. In 1983, three of these – Hawick,
Kelso and Jedburgh – became part of the new Roxburgh and Berwick
constituency, while Lauder joined the remainder to form Tweeddale, Ettrick
and Lauderdale; a network of villages covers the countryside between.

The economy of the Borders depends largely on agriculture and the woollen
textile and knitwear industries, now using mainly imported rather than local
wool. In the last two decades, as employment in the textile industry has
declined, electronics and microcircuit manufacturing companies have moved
into the area, as well as a proliferation of small businesses involved in light
industry. Tourism also accounts for a growing sector of the economy as more
and more people discover the delights of the Border countryside, so often
bypassed in the race northwards to the Scottish capital and the Highlands.

The landscape here is one of gently rolling hills of great natural beauty, and the area is rich not only in scenic attractions but also in great houses with an amazing store of literary, legendary and historic associations.

This was the front line of the centuries-old struggle between two warring nations, one comparatively rich and aggressive, the other poor and struggling to maintain her independence. It was the source of a great heritage of ballads, telling stories of feats of valour, of love and betrayal, and of supernatural forces. And it was the home and inspiration of such literary figures as Sir Walter Scott, James Hogg, John Buchan and Andrew Lang.

At times there has been obvious conflict between the demands and expectations of the national stage and my own wish to pursue a normal life in the locality. That is especially true of election campaigns. One political columnist makes repeated reference to me as a poor public speaker on the basis of having had to listen on one miserable occasion where I had to inflict on a constituency audience the reading out of a written press release, produced by somebody else in London, for the sole purpose of securing a ninety-second slot on the national television news. On another occasion, one of the daily tabloids reported that I had 'flopped' in my own constituency because only thirty-five people came to hear me at a public meeting. In fact that was the first of my evening meetings in the village of Broughton at the far end of my constituency, where an audience in double figures would be normally respectable and where thirty-five exceeded the seating capacity of the school classroom by five. 'Standing room only' would have been an equally justifiable, equally misleading report. National press and television reporters were always out of place at my village meetings and I tried to discourage their attendance. These meetings are normally lively and inquisitorial with a mixture of local, national and international questions and a strong dose of down-to-earth humour.

The day I was first elected in March 1965, we were still living in the rented cottage outside Galashiels on the banks of the River Tweed. The branch line to Selkirk ran past our door with the occasional goods trains but it was closed in 1964. As they took up the track, they removed the metal rails and wooden sleepers but left behind the small wooden wedges used to connect the two. In the winter of 1964-5 these creosote-impregnated pieces of wood in their hundreds kept our fire going and provided hot water. We enjoyed life in that little cottage but clearly we now had to start looking for a house of our own. This was not as easy as it sounds. There were eight burghs in the constituency, each with its own town council, rugby team and annual festival or Common Riding. The rivalry between them is friendly but historic and sometimes intense. A glance at some of the local songs and sayings gives the flavour: 'Hawick's queen o' all the border'; 'Melrose, gem of Scotland'; 'A day oot o'

Selkirk's a day wasted'; or 'I'd rather be a lamp post in Hawick than provost of Galashiels'.

It would be politically unwise to live in and be identified with any one of these towns. My predecessor had lived in London; and successive members of the Buccleuch family as previous MPs had their country houses, thus equally effectively avoiding this problem. I was pledged to live in the Borders; and we therefore had to find a house in one of the villages, and one reasonably central to the only constituency in the United Kingdom which covered three counties. That greatly reduced the scope of what came on our market. Twice we put in offers for houses in Denholm, near Hawick, and twice we were beaten by offers from other purchasers under the Scottish system of house sales.

We looked at a couple of other houses, one in Lilliesleaf which entered straight off the roadway without even a pavement in front. As we were intending to raise a family this we found unsuitable. So a year later we were still in our cottage. By this time we were expecting our first child and really needed somewhere bigger; but an election was being called by Harold Wilson to secure a bigger majority and house-hunting would have to stop. Just at that time we had heard of a house in Yarrow valley, about ten miles from Selkirk, which sounded suitable. As Parliament was about to be dissolved, I agreed with Judy on our nightly telephone call that her first day's canvassing for the election should take place in the parallel Ettrick and Yarrow valleys and that she would look in and see the house, more out of curiosity than genuine intent to purchase.

That evening when I telephoned she was in a state of real excitement. She had seen the ideal house. No, not the one in Yarrow, which was rather large, rambling and remote, but in the village of Ettrick Bridge, the only village in the twenty miles of the Ettrick valley, about seven miles from Selkirk. I tried to reason with her: 'We can't possibly look at a house now. We've got no money and I'm officially unemployed in three days' time. We can't be certain to hold on to the seat. We must concentrate on the election.'

But, not for the first time, she got her way. She had indeed been canvassing in the valley. As she passed Cherrydene, she recalled from the by-election that the people in this distinctive house with its attractive garden were Tories, but decided to call all the same. She was told that they had not changed their mind, but they weren't really interested because they were moving to a flat in Edinburgh.

'Moving?' said Judy. 'You mean you're selling this house. Never mind politics, would you show me round?'

They, being English and not knowing the ropes, had not advertised their house in the *Scotsman*, the main marketplace for local properties, but only in the property page of the now-defunct *Scottish Daily Mail*, which we did not read. There were one or two other people interested in it, and Judy fell for it right away. It had about eight rooms and two bathrooms, being a conversion of three small cottages. She insisted that as soon as I returned from London I should go with her to see it. This I did and agreed with her enthusiasm. The house was originally (about 1725) a row of three two-roomed cottages with a byre, or stable, and hay loft at the end. Over the years it had been converted to one substantial yet compact house. The stable was still there and the hay loft was a sitting-room. In the 1920s a porch had been added at the front door to permit the installation of a bathroom above. Electricity had come as recently as 1946. The house lay at right angles to, and below the level of, the village street as it rose up the hill out of the village. It had been finished in white roughcast and faced on to a beautifully maintained garden, designed we were told by someone from the Royal Botanic Gardens in Edinburgh.

The occupants were a retired merchant-navy captain and his wife. I felt very sorry for them. They had been in the house just over a year. He had dreamed of retiring to the country. His brass telescope hung above one of the doors. But his wife hadn't settled and missed city life. He had even bought her two dachshunds who yelped round our feet, but it was no good. They were off to Edinburgh. The house was in generally good repair but definitely 'in need of modernization'. They wanted £4,500 for it, plus something for the carpets and fittings.

I was advised to see Miss Lowe, a prominent CA who came from the Borders and ran the Bradford and Bingley Building Society office in Charlotte Square, Edinburgh. We had saved the necessary few hundred pounds from my by-election 'winnings' and broadcasting and journalism to raise the modest deposit required, but we had literally no income, MPs not being salaried of course during dissolution, when we cease to be MPs. Miss Lowe was very understanding and approved the mortgage application. We put in an offer of £4,000.

Towards the end of the 1966 election campaign I had to address a public meeting in the village school. I recognized the sellers sitting in the back row of the classroom and hoped my speech would not provoke *too* much of their disapproval. Judy and I always went to the door at our meetings to shake hands with the audience as they left. Our supporters liked the habit and it discomfited the Tories. On this occasion the Cherrydene owners came out at Judy's side. As they shook hands, she heard them whisper, 'We've instructed our solicitors to accept your offer.' We went home in high elation, almost forgetting we had still to win the election.

After that had been accomplished and before Parliament was recalled, we went up to have a closer look at our new house. I had spent only twenty minutes looking through it and could scarcely recall the layout. We sat and had tea. The couple had decided that, given two offers roughly the same, they wanted their house to go to 'that nice young couple expecting their first baby'.

'But what about our political differences?'

'Oh, we voted for you as well to make sure you had a job.' They were my most expensive but worthwhile two votes ever recorded.

We did not care for the name of the house, which stemmed from its original cherry grove of which only two enormous trees remain on our lawn. 'But,' we were told in the village, 'it's aye been Cherrydene.' And so it has remained. The village itself was known to the post office as Ettrick Bridge but to the locals as Ettrickbridgend or Brigend, it being the village just over the bridge carrying the valley road across the Ettrick Water.

The village, of less than a hundred inhabitants, has changed little in physical terms since the beginning of the century, and it turned out to be an idyllic place to bring up a young family – which began to arrive after our move – for it provided a freedom that is rare in the experience of children in Britain today. James Hogg's classic evocation of an unsullied boyhood is still pertinent:

> Where the pools are bright and deep,
> Where the grey trout lies asleep,
> Up the river and o'er the lea,
> That's the way for Billy and me.

Through this natural paradise runs the Ettrick Water. J. B. Selkirk, a popular poet of the early part of this century, lovingly traces the course of the river from its source to its confluence with the Tweed in 'Epistle to Tammas', an imaginary letter from a Border émigré to a friend in Ettrick. This is how he describes the river at Ettrick Bridge:

> And then is there a bonnier bit
> On ony water, head to fit,
> Where, tumblin' doon the rugged streams,
> The lashing water froths and creams,
> Till o'er the salmon-loup it spins
> 'Tween green Helmburn and Kirkhope Linns,
> Where Ettrick rins?

Up the river from the village is the manse pool, hemmed in between tumbling falls at either end, while to right and left rise the rocky cliffs known as the Linns, whose formation gives the area special geological and scientific interest. In summer its dark surface is never rippled except by the rings of a rising trout. Downstream the Ettrick falls in a fan-shaped cascade to the Glebe pool, and on the adjoining rocky outcrop, bog-myrtle, marsh marigold, and tiny, pallid violets grow. In the lower cliffs, dogroses, hawthorn and rowan saplings insinuate their roots into crevices, while the summits are crowned with birch, pine, holly and elm.

Our first problem was how to carry out limited work with hardly any cash. We had the two huge white porcelain sinks in the kitchen removed and bought a do-it-yourself kitchen unit kit which Judy in an advanced state of pregnancy put together with some help from me. An ancient but effective Rayburn served as cooker, water heater and room heater all in one.

There were tiny fireplaces in almost every room which we just left; the only one regularly lit was in our small study. The bathrooms were rudimentary and we decided at least to have the cast-iron baths boxed in before we decorated. We invited the village joiner, Thomas Mitchell, to call. He arrived with his younger brother Jim.

'Before I come in, Mr Steel,' said Tom, 'I just want you to know that I've always been a Conservative and always will be.'

'I couldn't care less about your politics,' I said. 'I just want you to do some joinery.'

'Just let there be no misunderstanding,' was his reply. That taught me a precept which I have followed ever since. I do not politick in the village. There was at that time a strong local branch of 'The Unionists' (long since disbanded, I am glad to say) and they were worried lest I would spend my time proselytizing.

To this day, beyond the handful of committed Liberal activists, I do not know how my neighbours vote, nor do I ever ask. On this basis we have been accepted over the years as just another village family whose head of household happens to earn his daily bread in London.

Over the years we have greatly improved Cherrydene. A garage and carport were built; the field next to the house was at first rented and then acquired when the church sold the manse glebe next door to us. We broke through a door direct from the house into the stable, creating a drawing-room which faces south across the field to the river. The hay loft then became our bedroom. Upstairs we built a passage with our own hands, taking a slice off two bedrooms, so enabling us to get from one end of the house to the other without going through two rooms. Central heating came in 1980, at first solid fuel (coal and logs) which was a mistake, and later Calor gas.

Finally in 1986 we added a conservatory on the south gable wall. Meantime the garden was made more manageable for semi-absentee control by liberal extensions of grass, gravel and concrete paving where formerly were intricate shapes and flower beds.

In the summer of 1966, just as we were moving to Ettrick Bridge, Judy passed her driving test at the fourth attempt. I suspect that the examiner, listening to the tale of how this obviously very pregnant lady was going to live up Ettrick with one bus a week, did not dare to fail her. We could afford only one car, which meant she had usually to come with me to the airport or night sleeper and come back to collect me at the end of the parliamentary week. We decided we definitely wished to bring up our family in the Borders, not in London, where I took a room at the National Liberal Club in Whitehall Place. By using the night sleeper I saved one night's hire of the room; but in those days there was also a late-night mail flight from London to Edinburgh which could get me home in the small hours of the morning. After a couple of years I moved to the basement of Michael Shea's house.

Our first child was born in August, in Galashiels Cottage Hospital because we had not yet got round to registering with a doctor in Selkirk. It was a difficult birth and ended as a forceps delivery.

We called him Graeme (because we liked the name) Scott (my family name) MacGregor (Judy's family name). I recall vividly the excitement of seeing his purple and lopsided face over the first couple of days of his life and driving him ever so gingerly home from the hospital, cradled in Judy's arms in the back of the car. Judy was a determined breastfeeder and so Graeme came everywhere with us. Judy became adept at breastfeeding him discreetly under a coat or shawl at the back of meetings. Sometimes it was not so discreet. We were visiting Norman Hackett's landlady in Edinburgh on one occasion where her dining-room contained at least half a dozen students, somewhat shy in the presence of an MP. Judy made to retire as Graeme demanded feeding. 'Jist you stay there,' bade our hostess, 'mother nature's dairies, I always say.' 'Mother nature's dairies' were to become a regular usage in our family as the babies were taken to meetings, conferences and even the Council of Europe in Strasbourg. Catriona Judith followed in December 1967, this time at Selkirk Cottage Hospital where Judy had another prolonged labour. Then Rory David was born in the same hospital in June 1973. Neither of these maternity units now exists. Indeed the Selkirk one was very small and short-staffed, there being only two other mothers there at the same time. We had asked if I could be present at Catriona's birth but this was not encouraged.

By 1973 we tried more insistently and I became the first father ever to attend a birth of his own child at that hospital.

Mind you, it nearly did not happen, because at about 4 a.m., as yet another prolonged labour seemed to abate, I had gone home to bed. When things started up again around 6 a.m., Judy suggested I be telephoned. 'But,' said the midwife, 'the poor man has been up most of the night.'

'And what do you think I've been doing all night,' retorted Judy. 'I want him back here.'

I wouldn't have missed it for anything. I was gowned and masked, helping the sole midwife as an assistant passing instruments and holding Judy as and where required. Rory emerged about noon looking like a skinned rabbit. It was a magical experience.

Having two toddlers we decided to start a valley playgroup. This was in the infancy of the playgroup movement. The children's room in the house was used. Judy bought all sorts of equipment, including a climbing frame for summer days in the garden, and arranged a rota of about twelve children and mothers three mornings a week. As it grew larger it transferred to the village hall, where the playgroup still meets to this day. It is a great boon, especially to house-tied mothers, as well as being useful in the social development of children.

Our children all went on to the local primary school, about 200 yards away at the other end of the village. School began early at 8.30 a.m. because of the problems of rural transport. It has two classrooms and two teachers, each teaching a span of several primary years. The total pupil numbers fluctuates between thirty and forty. It was a good basic education.

Our regional councillor, John McKerchar, was the moving spirit in starting a community bus unique in Scotland. The vehicle, a second-hand minibus, was bought by the regional council. And a team of volunteers drives it and collects fares. Judy is a regular, and I an occasional, member of this rota.

The village is a wonderful place for young children. They wandered about in and out of each other's houses with a freedom rarely available in cities. In the summer they would learn to swim in the deep pools of the Ettrick just across the field from our house, where on warm evenings we can have a bonfire supper.

Animals were an important and natural part of their childhood. My parents had usually had Siamese cats and early in our married life we acquired Suki, who came with us to Cherrydene, had a fine life catching field mice and baby rabbits, producing litters and dying of old age. Then we were advised on security grounds to get a dog. The children wanted one anyway. Catriona had fallen for a young black Labrador which the owner, next door to Judy's parents, wanted rid of. She was fully grown and trained. Jill entered our lives and became an excellent guard dog, family pet, mother of many pups and good-nosed retriever – a splendidly popular all-rounder and companion. She died in May this year aged thirteen. Two of her offspring have gone overseas. One I gave to President Ceauşescu of Romania as a thank-you after an official visit. By all reports it still lives in the presidential palace and is a favourite of the elderly autocrat. The Romanian embassy in London has to dispatch tins of its favourite food and biscuits in the diplomatic bag. Another went to the German ambassador in London, Dr Jürgen Ruhfus, whose wife proudly showed him off to me as a fine-looking dog a couple of years ago in Bonn. He is (at the time of writing) now with his master in Washington. Another pup went to the deputy editor of the *Guardian*. Jill had always been popular with visiting journalists, photographers and television crews because she was so biddable. We even used her in a couple of party political broadcasts.

During the 1987 election the Cornish Liberals asked if I would accept a black retriever pup as a presentation during a battlebus stop at Bodmin. It would make wonderful pictures, they argued. Jill was listed in the Kennel Club as a 'Labrador retriever' and they assured me this was what they had in mind. A black bundle was indeed handed to me and its attractive face beamed at millions on the television news that night as planned. I realized on sight that it was not a Labrador and sure enough when I opened the accompanying documents it was a flat-coated retriever. Because Jill was getting old, I agreed to have another dog; but Judy was opposed to starting another younger animal needing exercise just as the children were leaving the nest. We compromised. Lucy comes to Cherrydene when I'm at home. Otherwise she lives with Graeme at his flat in Galashiels, where he has a kennel and enclosed run in his garden. She is already proving a good working replacement for Jill, having adopted all her characteristics.

Ponies were the other main part of our animal husbandry – and certainly the largest expense. A few bantams and ducks came and went, even a goose and a peacock, but ponies became a permanent part of our lives. The Borders has possibly the highest level of horse ownership of any part of the country. This is mainly due to the large number of Border festivals or Common Ridings to which I've made passing reference. Most of these involve mass participation in following the year's chosen town standard bearer, cornet, braw lad or callant (depending on which Border burgh you are in) on rideouts from the town.

The origin of each festival varies, the Common Ridings at Lauder, Selkirk and Hawick being the most steeped in history, commemorating events of the sixteenth century. The riding of marches is undertaken to assure the townspeople of no encroachment on their lands. Selkirk has the highest turnout, now regularly over 400 people of all ages as mounted followers, the largest annual gathering on horseback anywhere in Britain.

Hiring horses can be expensive – yet everybody does it. Unlike in many parts of Britain, it is not an upper-class occupation. Examining damp on a council estate some years ago, I was struck by the number of riding hats to be seen on top of wardrobes, not a common sight in many towns. When I first came to the Borders, I made a point of joining in these festivities, though I was far from an accomplished horseman. It was an easy, informal way of meeting people and the local press reported my completion of those longer rides (twenty-five miles) securing the coveted Mosstrooper, Redeswire and Kelso-Yetholm badges.

We always hired horses from Will Boyle's stables at Galashiels. He would try to find each year a suitably quiet yet sufficiently impressive mount for the MP to get through the Common Riding season (virtually every weekend through June and July). One of the lads he had hanging round his stable at that time – always a popular pastime with boys and girls in the town – was Ian Stark. After he won his silver medal at the 1988 Seoul Olympics, I happened to sit next to him at a dinner and asked if he remembered our meetings, because I had to admit I didn't recall him among all the others.

In 1970 I hired a horse which had just come over from Ireland, a polished black beast. At the first canter across the river out of Selkirk on only our second outing, I fell off, the only time I did so in all our years of Common Ridings. The greatest danger is being trampled underfoot by some of the 1,600 hooves clattering by. I've seen it happen often, and unfortunately there are one or two broken limbs and even the occasional death at such events. I made for the nearby stone dyke. Normally the riderless horses career on over the next couple of hills while disconsolate riders tramp after them. In this case the horse turned into the field and waited for me to remount. That settled it. This was the horse I would buy. We had cancelled our summer holiday in Denmark because of the June election and so we used the money saved to buy the horse which we therefore named Hamlet. Graeme and Catriona already had a pony called Prince, but kept calling the horse 'Omelette', being unaware of the Shakespearian allusion.

Hamlet is still with us, now retired and aged about twenty-seven. He becomes very shaggy each winter and looks like a black teddy bear while in the summer his smooth black coat glistens in the sun. We had him trained to pull a governess cart which we used locally when the children were smaller. Judy caused some hilarity by taking it once all the way to Selkirk for shopping, and tying Hamlet and trap to the town well where she and the traffic warden agreed after disputation that the double-yellow-line rules could not be applied. Hamlet has been lent for occasional film and TV work quite apart from appearing with us. His greatest moment was in 1982 when the standard-bearer was a friend and neighbour in the village, David Mitchell, and he chose to ride Hamlet, carrying the burgh standard round the marches at the head of the cavalcade.

In 1985 when I was out riding with Rory I had a bad fall and decided it was time for both me and Hamlet to retire together from this activity. Hamlet has been the permanent occupier of our field as other ponies have come and gone. Starting with bad-tempered small Thelwell-type ponies and ending with large competitive beasts, all our children with varying enthusiasm have indulged in riding, Billy and Catriona to rather higher standards. At one time we were up to four residents. Horse boxes, hayshed, extra fencing, another field, a trailer, then a lorry were all added to the complex. But it was fantastic family fun and I look back on those days with fond nostalgia.

Our only modest extravagance, other than horses, was holidaying abroad. We bought a second-hand Dormobile as a second car, Judy and I sleeping in a bed below, Graeme and Catriona in canvas stretchers above. For three or four summers we toured all over Europe, sometimes treating ourselves to *dîner à deux* in restaurants where we could park the vehicle outside the window, thus easily keeping an eye on supposedly sleeping children. We also used it in this country, saving on hotel bills. Our last trip was to Scandinavia when Rory was a baby and could sleep in his carrycot on the floor. Five became too many for this kind of holiday, and we took to package tours where I would wear sunglasses all the time, avoiding conversation with other Brits, and the children ran daily competitions awarding imaginary fivers to the first tourist who saw through the disguise.

At the time I became leader, our family expanded in an unexpected and unplanned way. In 1970 Judy had found a part-time job which suited both her qualifications and our lifestyle down to the ground. She was appointed as one of the first Reporters to the Children's Hearing under the Social Work (Scotland) Act of 1968. This did away with juvenile courts in Scotland and brought children 'in need of compulsory measures of care' – for parental neglect or ill-treatment, for offences they themselves had committed, for truancy, for being beyond general control – before the informal tribunals known as Hearings. The decision on whether to remit a child to the Hearing, plus the administration of the system, was in the hands of an official to be known, a bit inappropriately, as the Reporter.

Naturally a small county like Selkirk only merited a part-time appointment. There was not a tremendous caseload; but at that time, when the system was being set up, there was a great deal of hammering out amongst the first generation of Reporters (who included Donald Dewar) of the direction the whole system would take. For once, it was possible to be creative in shaping a new area of law. She continued in this very happily until the reorganization of local government in 1975 transformed three part-time jobs into a full-time one.

Amongst the most regular attenders at the Children's Panel in Selkirk were a family of four boys. By 1974 their situation had become so acute that they were put into care – the elder two into 'approved' schools and the younger two into foster-care. By coincidence, the foster-family were neighbours of ours, and the boys became regular visitors at Cherrydene. At the end of the year, the younger boy returned, temporarily, to his mother: Billy, given the choice, elected to stay in Ettrick Bridge with Mr and Mrs Elmitt, where his sporting and musical activities flourished. In his first term at Selkirk High School, he was given the lead part in the school production of *Oliver!* Selkirk being the kind of place it is, many of the audience knew Billy's circumstances. His performance was memorable for the emotional response he wrung from them. Judy was in the audience.

Within a few months Billy's own fate was as poignant as that of the part he had played. His foster-mother suffered a recurrence of cancer: she and her husband knew they would need all their resources for the gallant attempt to conquer the disease. Regretfully, they informed the social workers that they could not continue to care for him. He went into a temporary placement, again locally, but it didn't work out. At the beginning of July 1976, as the Liberal leadership election entered its final phase, he came to Judy, telling her that he was due to go back to a Hearing where another move would be decided. There were two alternatives: either a return to his mother, which would almost certainly be short-term, ending probably in more offences and a spell at a special school with its typical progression through other institutions; or else Billy would be put into the care of the local authority Children's Home. At that point there were no potential foster-parents.

Judy was angry. She felt that Billy, a child of whom she was not only fond, but whom she respected for the difficult decisions he had clearly made, deserved better. Furthermore, she felt that his individual talents were being ignored in a welter of socialese. There was only one practical course: because she had been Reporter, she knew the system. She knew that a child was entitled to his or her own representative at a Hearing, and offered to go with Billy.

Ultimately, though, there were still only the two alternatives. To give the child time, she said, 'In that case, I'll take him for the summer, and the department can surely come up with an alternative.' The next day she came down to London for the leadership count; within a couple of days of her return home, the newest member of our family arrived on the doorstep with half a dozen cardboard boxes.

By the end of the holidays, Billy wanted the arrangement to become permanent. So did Judy. I was more doubtful: I felt I was leaving her enough to cope with each week with three young children of our own. On the other hand, surely we, whose lives had been so lucky, should be prepared to share? The social worker was strongly opposed: maybe over the difficult years ahead, her opposition strengthened our determination. At any event, what began as an *ad hoc* temporary arrangement has continued from then on. He remained fostered by us from age thirteen to sixteen, at which time he was released from compulsory care. He opted to remain and so we turned the fostering into adoption with his adopting our name. On leaving school he attended the Arts Educational School in London, at which college he did a course in music and drama; since then he has become a talented young actor with all the ups and downs that involves. During college he shared my rented flat in London, a pattern Catriona has since followed while studying hotel management at Westminster College.

I am often asked to give advice on adoption and fostering, and I hesitate to do so because our experience was so untypical. Certainly the older the child, self-evidently, the more difficult the adjustment. Billy had a deeply disturbed background and this continued to show up through his teens in many traumatic ways, exacerbated by intrusive press interest. I would not advise anyone to enter into such an arrangement lightly, though we all look back on it now as a most enriching and rewarding experience.

I mention the intrusive press in passing because this is something my family has had to live with. To some extent it is inevitable, but I do resent the way in which politicians' children are exploited by the more sensational media. Some members of the present Cabinet have suffered far more than I from this repugnant tendency. The village itself is very protective. On one occasion when a couple of reporters were pursuing a line of questioning in the pub opposite our house, the proprietor said: 'If you're looking for gossip about the Steel family, you've come to the wrong place.'

'Would it make any difference if we showed you our cheque book?'

'Yes,' was the response, 'you can leave now.'

My children have all hated being singled out, whether at school or in newspapers, though they do admit to having enjoyed some of the privileges of leadership, especially being taken on trips in helicopters or on foreign travel or enjoying VIP lounges at airports. One aspect of the downside was the invasion of our privacy at Cherrydene. The Instamatic cameras or autograph hunters were just tolerable, but a tour bus began treating us as a regular stop. From the height of the coach windows the passengers could see over the fence and down into the garden. We got used to the timings and I used to hide inside when I heard it coming up the village for its two-minute stop. I was at first horrified and then amused when I noticed the children and their friends dancing up and down in the garden, making gestures towards the tourists which could scarcely be described as ones of welcome.

My other hobbies beyond family are few, though now with the children off our hands I increasingly share Judy's interest in the theatre as well as indulging my own fondness for orchestral concerts. We are both regular supporters of the Edinburgh Festival and its Fringe, and last year bought a one-roomed studio flat in a conversion of an old primary school in the city to enable us to enjoy the cultural life of Edinburgh more regularly.

I also fish, mainly for trout, though now and then for salmon. In the last few years I have taken a boat each week on Bowhill Loch, six minutes' drive from my house, in a syndicate with my father, my doctor Lindsay Neil, and an old friend and now colleague as well, Menzies Campbell. On average over the summer I suppose I get there once a fortnight, if only for a couple of hours. The relaxation and meditation is as important as the actual fishing. I am also an irregular and not very good shot, again enjoying the fresh air and exercise and working the dog, rather than counting the numbers of pheasant or grouse. I managed to keep this activity out of the public eye during the twelve years in leadership because it is always controversial both within and outside the party. I neither wished to offend supporters' feelings nor stir up the inevitable *paparazzi* who pursue politicians on such occasions.

My attitude to bloodsports is straightforward: I do not indulge in those I dislike, such as fox-hunting; but since I do not want anyone to outlaw my fishing, I am reluctant to join in legislating against other people's pastimes. Man has always hunted for the pot and my days of greatest enjoyment in shooting are usually just wandering round the nearby farm doing my neighbour a favour by shooting rabbits. The only argument I accept as valid against all bloodsports is that put forward by vegetarians; but I notice that in the countryside even vegetarians are more tolerant of such activities than their counterparts in town and city.

My rural pursuits were successfully kept from the press, although I had two narrow shaves: once in the 1987 election at a large and televised 'Ask the Alliance' meeting in Glasgow where Roy Jenkins and I were appearing. The questionmaster, Magnus Magnusson, took a fairly standard question from the audience on legislation on bloodsports. Magnus first asked Roy, who ruminated over his first few sentences that he did not indulge in any himself, 'but David, of course, shoots'. I could have shot him. I never denied doing so, but always illustrated my own answers by admitting to fishing, which is a much more popular sport. The other occasion was when Robert Maclennan became leader of the SDP at the end of the summer recess in 1987. We checked diaries on the phone and agreed the easiest place for an early meeting was over lunch at the Tanlaws at Eskdalemuir, where I was having a weekend's grouse shooting. Bob's office unwittingly released the venue to the press, and we had hurriedly to switch the much-photographed meeting to the local hostelry in mid-afternoon.

My colleagues who knew that most years I went grouse shooting at Lord Tanlaw's estate and pheasant shooting at Lord Mackie's farm used to tease that the only way to get nominated by Steel for a peerage was to have the kind of gracious living to which he could be invited, quite a good joke but in singularly bad taste if one looks at the list of those I have actually recommended for appointment to the upper house over the years.

Another long-term pastime has been my love of old cars. As already mentioned, my first car had served time as a hen-coop: in my last year at school during a summer job on a Perthshire estate a friend and I invested our joint week's wages – £15 – in a 1931 Morris 8. It had no remaining side windows, thus affording the hens easy access. We covered the gaps with cellophane, and used to travel the seven miles to the nearest village, to the danger of the lieges.

I was still a learner in 1956 and my fellow pupil had only recently acquired a licence. The accelerator was situated between the clutch and brake, and in those days before MOT tests the brakes operated on only one of the four wheels. We ran the car all summer to our great enjoyment and mechanical education.

After a short-lived motorbike experience (my brother broke his leg on his identical BSA Bantam), I bought my first real car with my holiday earnings at University — a 1938 Morris 8 on which everything functioned reasonably well. So it should at £75! That lasted about three years, during which I did all my own servicing and most running repairs.

I then moved up to a 1939 Rover 10 with magnificent woodwork and leather, and a freewheel mechanism which I suppose nowadays would be illegal. When I was about to marry in 1962, I spent most of my remaining assets – £60 – in having it resprayed to go on honeymoon to Skye. My bride was therefore forewarned. (She currently drives a seven-year-old MG Metro after a series of Morris Minors.)

During my first job I acquired an even grander machine, a 1949 Daimler Consort, a huge barouche with a modest two-litre engine but a delightful pre-selector gearbox.

The day after my victory in the Roxburgh, Selkirk and Peebles by-election in 1965 the enterprising salesman at my local garage turned up at the door with a rather smart-looking two-tone grey Humber Hawk, six years old, which had belonged to a deceased local doctor. He argued that as local MP I could no longer be seen in the decaying sixteen-year-old Daimler. I bought it for £400 and have kept its JKS 900 registration on my cars ever since for good luck and because it's easy to remember.

It was the first of three Humbers – a Super-Snipe and another Hawk followed – which I owned in succession. Buying a low-mileage, large, second-hand car has always been my value-for-money policy, each lasting about two years with the huge mileage I drive annually. I reverted for a short time to a Daimler Barker Special Sports three-seater drophead which I foolishly sold for £100 for a return to more practical family motoring.

This took the form of a Triumph 2000 estate car and later a 2500 PI estate whose tailgate lock was faulty, so that on one memorable family trip down the M6 it flew open depositing sleeping bags – but fortunately no young Steels – all over the outer lane. My family greatly enjoyed my successful retrieving efforts. A Rover 2000 TC was succeeded by a sizzling 3500 S as the shortest-owned car I ever had. My then assistant, Archy Kirkwood, drove me skidding head-on into a lorry during a general-election campaign in the constituency in 1974, writing off the car, but leaving its occupants saved by crumple zones and seatbelts.

My next pride and joy was a Triumph Stag which ran well until the engine inevitably blew up and I moved on to a couple of Rover 2600s, sound machines for heavy work. An automatic version of this in black served as the Party Leader's car, based in Westminster.

My only new car ever in thirty years of motoring I bought three years ago. It was a Ford Escort XR3i cabriolet, a truly magnificent design in body, suspension and engine with which I enjoyed the fresh air, scenery and twisting roads of the Borders.

My interest in 'collecting' old cars had led me to two successive Austin 7s. The current 1936 Opel two-seater convertible lives in Melrose Motor Museum and is exercised only occasionally. I found it while on holiday in Jersey where it had, I was told, been hidden under hay bales during the German occupation and was therefore in good condition. A lovely but impractical Alvis TD Graber convertible, now beautifully restored, made way for a Mark IX Jaguar (bought with the local Peeblesshire registration DS 5121) then a Mark II and currently a six-year old XJ6 bought for less than the price of the cheapest new Sierra. The smell of leather and sight of polished wood as well as the silky-smooth power and comfort of the machine makes it a luxury hobby worth paying for.

Returning to politics, I had mounted three specific campaigns in the Borders at the time of my election: 1) to secure some Government assistance to revive the local economy; 2) to save the Border railway; and 3) to obtain a new district general hospital. Of the three, the first was a swift and long-lasting success, the second a glorious failure and the third a long-drawn-out and much delayed achievement.

In my maiden speech as 'baby of the House' in April 1965 I referred to the characteristic of babies to cry when they needed something and I said I would often be heard crying the needs of the Borders. Throughout 1965 in the House and the Scottish Grand Committee I pressed forward the arguments in my pre-election pamphlet, *Boost for the Borders*. Why were industrial grants limited to areas of unemployment? When Border folk were unemployed because of the decline in jobs in farming and wool textiles they left the area. In the ten years from 1951 to 1961 the population of the region in the 20–45 age group had dropped by 21 per cent. The attraction of jobs in England or in the new Government-inspired developments in Central Scotland drew them away. The local papers printed regular lists of families emigrating, mainly to Australia, New Zealand or Canada. The Conservative Government had produced no answers. The new Labour Government should pay attention to the plight of this area as they had done in the Highlands.

In 1966 the Government's Economic White Paper accepted the argument. Depopulation would be included in the criteria for determining development-area status and thus we became a development area, with useful cash incentives for industrial building and new machinery. The effect over the next fifteen years was dramatic. The woollen industry could afford to modernize and secure its place in a highly competitive world market, even though total numbers employed continued to decline. More important, new small local businesses flourished to become substantial employers while outside invest-ment was attracted from other parts of Britain and abroad. The 'all eggs in one basket' feature of the Borders woollen economy was changed for good, with electronics providing some of the largest industrial units.

At the same time the Government's public housing agency, which had no parallel in England or Wales, the Scottish Special Housing Agency, started to build large numbers of new houses to attract people in, notably at the Tweedbank development alongside advance factories. Depopulation was halted and indeed slightly reversed. Although the present Government abandoned the 1966 criteria and we lost the advantages of development-area status in 1980, the strength of the local modernized economy remains for all to see.

Contemporary with that campaign was the one to save the ninety-seven-mile railway line from Edinburgh to Carlisle via the Borders which still carried one sleeper train to and from London St Pancras each night. I have mentioned the prominence of the Beeching Report's recommending closure in the by-election campaign. Barbara Castle had included a social clause in her Transport Act and I cited our line as a good example of its application. I thought our case was strengthened by becoming a development area. I raised the issue repeatedly in the House, petitioned Number 10 Downing Street alongside the Earl of Dalkeith, then Tory MP for Edinburgh North, who at that time lived near the railway village of Newton St Boswells. We got support from our several Border peers in the Lords and we had a public inquiry for which the local authorities hired a rising young QC to present our case – James Mackay, now Lord Chancellor. All to no avail. I went to see the head of the Scottish division of British Rail in Glasgow to demand a breakdown of the alleged £350,000 annual deficit on running the line.

He began, 'Well, there is for a start the £25,000 allocated cost of the upkeep of Waverley Station in Edinburgh.'

'Excuse me,' I interrupted, 'will you explain how closing our line will save you that £25,000. You still have to run the Edinburgh station and the costs will be the same.'

'I suppose so,' he said, knocking the £25,000 off his arithmetic. Barbara Castle was succeeded as Minister of Transport by Richard Marsh, who never showed any sympathy for our case, asking me at one interview, 'How do you pronounce Hawick?' – the largest town on the route. In desperation, recognizing that the tunnel on the southern section was a major cost problem, I persuaded the local authorities to hire a consultant who produced an excellent report recommending retention of just a branch line Edinburgh to Hawick, with unmanned halts, single-track working, and fares collected on the train. That too was rejected, to our collective fury.

The last train was due to run on a freezing cold night in January 1969, the sleeper to St Pancras. I booked a berth. At Galashiels I was photographed and filmed shaking hands with the engine driver along with the Provost. We repeated the procedure at Melrose. At Hawick an enormous crowd filled the platform and the local people loaded a black coffin on to the guard's van addressed to Mr Marsh. After some delay the train left the station preceded by an engine to clear the line of fireworks and railway alarms placed on the line by sympathetic railway workers. The press went to file their stories and I went to my berth.

About half an hour later the train halted and after another quarter of an hour I was aware of my name being called. I opened the top window, looked out, and there was a railway inspector standing with a swaying lamp looking for me. 'We're just outside Newcastleton. The people are blocking the line and you're the only one that will persuade them to move.' I dressed hurriedly, clambered on to the line and was escorted alongside the carriages in the freezing darkness.

There in front stood the pilot engine at the level crossing whose gates were firmly open – across the line – with what looked like half the population of the village, at least two or three hundred people. Newcastleton is a village largely created by the building of the railway and they felt more strongly than most about the closure because of the loss of employment as well as transport. I was met by the parish minister, the Rev. Brydon Maben. 'They'll expect you to make a speech,' he said. 'It's midnight and the temperature is about ten below freezing,' I replied, 'so it will be a short one.'

We climbed on to the footbridge and both addressed the congregation below with the diesel engine chuntering in the background. I thanked them for their demonstration, regretting that the press and television were not there to record their feelings. I said it was the saddest day of my parliamentary career so far and then urged them after listening to their minister to disperse peacefully to their homes. The minister made a similar speech denouncing the Ministry of Transport in no uncertain terms but omitting my appeal. By this time reinforcements for the solitary local bobby, in the shape of sixteen policemen, had arrived from Hawick, twenty-one miles away over a twisty icy road. They attempted to close the gates by pushing, but they were hopelessly outnumbered by the crowd who pushed back. Tempers began to fray and Brydon Maben was arrested and taken away to the police station. 'We want our minister' became the war cry and an impasse had clearly been reached.

I went round to the station and suggested to the officer in charge of the Hawick band that the only hope of getting people off the line and closing the crossing was to offer to release their minister without charges if they moved. He agreed. I went back and climbed on to the bridge again and put the proposed bargain to the crowd. With some reluctance they also agreed. The line was cleared. I got back into the train and we moved on to St Pancras two hours late. As far as I know it is the only case ever of an inter-city train being stopped by an angry crowd, but the media missed it. Meantime the police went back to the manse for coffee and sandwiches, one of the sixteen being the minister's son. That is the temper of the Border folk: hard fights but no hard feelings. Nowadays I expect that at least the branch-line proposal would have been given a try. It makes no sense to shut down railway lines, resulting in more traffic congesting our roads and cities.

My third fight was for a new Borders hospital. Peel Hospital, which served the district as a general hospital (but lacked several services such as a maternity and gynaecological department), was a wartime wooden-hutted emergency building which had a suggested life of ten years. It had survived twenty but was hopelessly and cheerfully out of date. I was an in-patient only once, for the removal of a kidney stone. There were long thirty-bedded wards with glass cubicles at the end. I was put into one of these cubicles under protest but, I was told, for the peace of the rest of the ward. Next to me was a young man recovering slowly from a serious motorcycle accident. He was mainly unconscious and connected to a breathing machine. His relations had brought in a portable TV which he was unable yet to sit up and watch. The nurses suggested they moved it to the foot of my bed. I wasn't really ill, just in acute intermittent pain relieved by increasing doses of painkilling drugs. (I can at least understand how people can become addicts, as I lay floating on a warm cloud after each injection.)

As they disconnected the set, somehow the life-giving machine stopped. The nurse called another and a feverish discussion took place as they wrestled with a maze of cables and plugs, all of which emanated via two multi-socketed adaptors from the only electric socket. It served, among other things, the electric floor polisher. I got out of bed to help and was appalled at the muddle – the sort of thing you see advertised in public safety campaigns on TV. At this point purple headlines raced through my drug-befuddled brain: 'Youth dies as MP grabs TV set'. Somehow the right plug was found and connected to the power supply, the machine resumed its work and the boy slept on, blissfully unaware.

The incident accelerated what had already been a persistent campaign to commit successive governments not to the principle of a new hospital but to money and a timetable for it. Eventually in December 1973 it was announced that it would be ready for opening in 1979. It was in fact opened by the Queen in 1988. A more frustrating example of bureaucratic and ministerial delay I have never come across. At one point early in the Thatcher Government, the whole project was set back six months by being redesigned on cost-cutting grounds, the costs saved being overrun by inflation in the meantime. The result is not the attractive, low, slate-roofed building it should have been, but in the circumstances I was relieved to see its creation at all. In the course of my campaign I came up against Professor Hugh Trevor-Roper (Lord

Dacre), whose vacation house was next door to the site and who objected strenuously to it. I went to see him at his house, Chiefswood, and pointed out that he would see the new building only from his driveway and by standing up to look out of an upstairs window at the back of his house. I think he felt I was less than sympathetic to his complaint.

Two other features of my life in Scotland I ought to mention. In 1982 I was elected Rector of Edinburgh University, an honour which I especially appreciated as we were about to celebrate our quatercentenary in 1985. Chairing the University Court at a time of financial constraints was not easy, as I was always a target for special pleading by those affected (party politics are a sea of calm compared to university politics); but it was a real privilege, made all the more pleasant by the special quatercentenary celebrations of our 1585 creation. I ran weekly 'surgeries' for the students as general ombuds-man, greatly helped by a student contemporary, constituent and friend, Bill Goodburn, whom I appointed to the Court as my assessor. I declined suggestions of standing for a second three-year term of office because the time demands were too great an addition to those of constituency and party.

At the time of writing, I am also engaged in another wholly unrelated activity, the possibility of restoring Aikwood (Oakwood) Tower, a derelict peel tower built around 1600, situated about three miles below our house in the Ettrick Valley. At present it is owned by the Duke of Buccleuch; but following my recent successful libel action against Murdoch newspapers, we are in discussion about its acquisition and restoration with the historic build-ings authorities in the Scottish Office. It would be good to have a hand in rescuing an actual part of Scotland's architectural and historic heritage, having written with Judy two coffee-table books on the subject. But that is another story and possibly another book.

In 1990 I celebrate twenty-five years as MP for the Borders. In 1988 in a colourful ceremony I was given the freedom of the District of Tweeddale, the citation reading making me 'an Honorary Freeman of the District of Tweeddale with all rights, privileges and immunities pertaining thereto in recognition of his outstanding service as a Member of Parliament for the area for over twenty years and as a national and international statesman and of the distinction which he has thereby brought to Tweeddale'. And Ettrick and Lauderdale District Council has decided to mark my twenty-fifth anniversary next spring.

That's as may be and of course I appreciate it greatly, but I can truthfully say that what has given me the greatest pleasure, happiness and satisfaction in my political life has been my good fortune in representing, working for and living in this unique part of Britain.

173

8

THE WIDER WORLD

Foreign Affairs

I suppose it is partly because of my early years overseas that I have always had an intense interest in foreign affairs. My years as Party leader gave me an unrivalled access to world leaders both in their own countries and on visits here. The sceptical onlooker may wonder why this should be. There are several answers. First, successive British governments have always been eager to parade the virtues of Westminster-style democracy. Therefore on state occasions, both at home and overseas, the leader of the Liberal Party was always on parade alongside the Prime Minister and Leader of the Opposition as living demonstration of these. Second, because of its ex-imperial role, Britain still enjoys a genuine influence and affection round the globe. The Liberal Party was part of that history and its leader was a Privy Councillor, frequently quoted in the international press and world service of the BBC, and seen on television by visiting statesmen to this country. Third, I played an active role as Vice-President both of Liberal International and of the Federation of European Liberals and Democrats.

Rather than confuse the reader by dropping foreign visits into my narrative, I have brought them all together in this chapter, recognizing that I run the risk of it sounding like a Cook's tour. I start with my first love, Africa.

I must have paid a dozen or so visits to sub-Saharan Africa in my time as an MP. My first was to my old stamping-ground of Kenya where I took Judy in 1968, mainly for a holiday, though I was heavily involved in meetings with the Asian community in the backwash of the immigration restrictions I've described in Chapter Three. It was amazing to see the city of Nairobi transformed from the colonial settlement it still was when I left as a schoolboy in 1953 into a bustling international city. We looked up my old friends such as the O'Mearas and Archers, and visited my father's church, my school, and our friends George and Helen Inglis, who were teaching in Nakuru. We made new friends among the Asian community, some of whom I had met during the lobbying in London, and we attended a Hindu arranged marriage wedding ceremony. I paid a short visit to the Kenya parliament and met Charles Njonjo, the Attorney-General and a friend of my father's, together with Vice-President (later President) Daniel Arap Moi.

I then went on to Zambia, at the invitation of the Zambian government, for a short visit, which included a meeting with President Kenneth Kaunda, whom I had met briefly in London. The most memorable part of my stay there was a visit to the copperbelt and a tour through one of the mines.

On my return I stopped off for a weekend with the Inglises and some of their friends. We hired two single-engined aeroplanes and flew to the idyllic island of Lamu where eight of us, including George's brother Ian, spent our time swimming, drinking beer and water-skiing. Unfortunately on the last day I was skiing across some choppy water where we were not supposed to be and took a fast fall, tearing a muscle in my thigh. It was extremely painful and I had to cut a rough walking stick and hobble on and off planes all the way back to London and Scotland.

While on Lamu we had a close brush with the forces of law and order. Out in the creek lay a rusting deserted cargo ship of indeterminate nationality which was being held by the authorities for non-payment of harbour dues. Ian Inglis decided to swim out to it while the rest of us watched. He climbed up the side and danced about on the deck, at which point an askari (policeman) appeared beside us armed with a rifle. He was there to guard the ship and was coldly angry, saying simply: 'I will have to shoot your friend. These are my orders.' Others were contemplating knocking the rifle out of his hands, which would have landed us all in jail, when I declared that I was a British MP, and a friend of his Attorney-General, that the person on board meant no harm and if he would kindly desist from his 'shoot to kill' policy I would swim out and ensure that he came ashore and gave himself up immediately for cross-examination. The askari looked doubtful at first, but agreed. Ian, totally unaware of the drama on the distant shore, had disappeared below deck and rummaged in the flag locker. Finding a Red Ensign he decided to take it as a souvenir, stuffed it down his trunks and returned to the sea.

I swam a short distance out to meet him, explained that I had just saved his life (for which he seemed remarkably ungrateful at the time) and that he would be under arrest as soon as he got ashore. He then told me about the flag concealed about his person, transferred it to my custody, and swam ahead to meet the askari. I paddled ashore a little later, while the askari was fully engaged in questioning Ian. A few beers with the man and all was soon forgotten and forgiven. Last year, attempting to find the Inglis house in northern Italy, we saw it marked clearly with the Red Ensign flying in welcome.

In 1971 I returned to Kenya for a very brief visit en route to Somalia. This time I attended a moving demonstration outside the British High Commission by sixty-five Asians who were British citizens and were being kept waiting for entry vouchers under the 1968 system. This imposed terrible hardships on families deprived of their livelihood and waiting to enter Britain. I also visited Attorney-General Charles Njonjo in his office.

The Somali visit was arranged by veteran Labour MP James Johnson, who was one of those involved with African politicians in the decolonization debates. He had been asked to assemble a parliamentary team to visit the country to see what was going on under alleged Soviet influence and try to lobby for greater British involvement in aid programmes. He got an impressive group of five, which included Arthur Bottomley, the former Labour Commonwealth Secretary, Bill Deedes, a former member of the Macmillan Cabinet, later editor of the *Daily Telegraph*, and Christopher Brocklebank-Fowler, the only Tory MP later to join the SDP.

Christopher was also spending a day or two in Nairobi *en route* and he telephoned me with a proposition that I should join him on a private plane to Somalia. He had met a representative of British-Norman Islanders who was showing off the plane in Kenya but could not get entry-clearance to go to Somalia. A couple of MPs would give him that entrée. I thought simply of doing our best for British exports and agreed. I was familiar with the aeroplane which has short take-off and landing characteristics ideal for rural Africa.

The three elder statesmen arrived on their scheduled flight in Mogadishu without us. We flew brightly in a couple of hours later to a distinctly frosty reception from them: the Russian MIGs had been scrambled to intercept us. Johnson was livid: 'Don't you two young pups realize you've upset the protocol.' Members of the Cabinet had been on hand to receive the five of us and had to turn out a second time to meet us. Our patriotic explanations about British exports were not well received.

Somalia is the poorest country I have ever been to, with nomadic families scratching a bare subsistence from the desert on the Ethiopian border. We were impressed by the small team of British vets helping their agriculture and pleaded for more on our return. We also saw the most remarkable piece of Soviet aid in the form of a modern meat factory where live cattle walked in at one end and little tins of stew and onions emerged at the other.

One of my closest brushes with death came on this visit. We were flying from the capital, Mogadishu, to Hargeisa, the largest town in the old British-protected northern part of the country, aboard a Soviet-built twenty-four seat, high-winged air-force plane with two members of the Somali Cabinet and the British Ambassador. As we came in to land, the entire British community of about fifteen were lining the small runway. We appeared to fly past them while attempting to land. Almost halfway down the runway the front wheel of the plane hit the ground with an almighty bang and we flew on till, about three-quarters of the way along, the main wheels struck the runway very heavily – at which point the pilot decided he had no room left to land and attempted to take off on the bounce. For a moment, according to the horrified onlookers, the plane seemed to hang in the air about to stall, but the take-off was successfully achieved. It turned out that we had been trying to land with the wind behind us instead of into the wind, an error for which the ground controller was summarily dismissed by the military member of the Cabinet accompanying us. Meantime we had to circle the airstrip for twenty minutes while radioed argument raged over what had gone wrong. The co-pilot came back to peer out of the windows at the state of the main wheels which could be seen suspended from the high wings. The front wheel – which had burst its tyre – could not be seen but damage was suspected. We sat in silence while a second landing was successfully attempted from the other direction.

More than a little shaken, we dutifully met those waiting on the ground before being driven off to recuperate over a breakfast of large brandies. During that interlude we exchanged our 'last thoughts' as they occurred during those awful moments. Christopher Brocklebank-Fowler led off the discussion with the reflection that as he was sitting near the emergency exit alongside Arthur Bottomley, it would be all right for him to leave if he saved Arthur first. Bill Deedes said he was deep in prayer throughout and decided that only a promise to be nice to James Johnson through the rest of the entire trip would be a sufficient atonement for past sins. The others gave equally high-minded reflections: then it came to my turn.

'Well actually,' I admitted shamefacedly, 'I was thinking of the extra temporary insurance policy I had taken out at London airport which guaranteed my widow £50,000 if I were killed on my travels, but it only covered scheduled flights and this wasn't a scheduled flight.'

'Typical bloody Scotsman,' they all roared.

Later that same year, 1971, on my way back from Rhodesia and after a brief stopover in Nairobi I went to see for myself what was going on in Uganda. The Foreign and Commonwealth Office, through our High Commissioner in Nairobi, made it clear that I went at my own risk. A British official met us at Entebbe airport and our car, in spite of its diplomatic number plates, was stopped twice at roadblocks by President Idi Amin's forces. The

Asian community were being expelled and, as I had predicted in the 1968 debates, Britain had to take them. The scenes outside our High Commission in Kampala were of chaos bordering on panic. I talked with senior consultants at the hospital later to become famous as the scene of Mrs Bloch's abduction and murder after the successful Israeli raid on Entebbe. I also had a rather sad meeting, in a large tourist hotel in which we were the only customers, with Semei Nyanzi, who had been President of the Labour Club when I was at Edinburgh University and later a member of President Obote's Cabinet. He somehow survived the Amin purges. The British High Commission insisted on our returning to the airport in daylight by 6 p.m. even though our plane did not leave till midnight.

Archy Kirkwood and I waited a miserable six hours at the airport, watching the departing Asians having their baggage looted, watches and jewellery removed, by Amin's soldiers and airport officials. I have never witnessed such scenes of unbridled abuse of power and virtual anarchy.

In 1974 I spent a fortnight in Tanzania with a five-man parliamentary delegation of the Commonwealth Parliamentary Association, two Conservatives, two Labour and me. I was actually reserve on the delegation and only went because one of the chosen members – John Stonehouse – was missing, then presumed drowned in his famous fake accident off Miami beach. This led to one cruelly witty remark. Granted a free hour, Caerwyn Roderick, the Labour MP for Brecon, and I opted to go swimming in the Indian Ocean just north of Dar-es-Salaam. I was lying flat on my back in the warm salty sea when I heard his unmistakable Welsh lilt saying, 'Oh David, isn't this marvellous – and just think that John Stonehouse has been floating about like this for three weeks.'

It had been twenty years since I had travelled in Tanzania. The physical change was not as striking as in Kenya. In fact the Socialist policies pursued by President Julius Nyerere, while having a tonic effect on the moral climate of government as against the freebooting one of Kenya, had a depressing effect on the economy, especially inward investment. The 'ujamaa' (community) villages, run on co-operative lines, were fine in theory but destroyed individual initiative. Nevertheless there was something admirable about the tone of government and (for Africa) its relative freedom from graft and corruption. Nyerere of course took his degree at Edinburgh University some years ahead of me, so he had a good and principled education. We enjoyed our meeting with him, as well as travels to projects in different parts of the country.

As part of our itinerary we spent a couple of days in Zanzibar, which was still recovering from the previous regime. We enjoyed an evening with the colourful Wolf Dourado, former Attorney-General, and visited an imaginative housing project which involved the island's government giving plots of land with drainage and water on which people could build and own their houses. My left-wing colleague David Lambie, MP for Cunninghame South, was deeply shocked. As we stood in the blazing sun on the white sand amid the palm trees, discussing the development with government ministers in flowing Arab robes, he uttered a solemn warning: 'Give people their own houses and you'll turn them into Tories.' It seemed improbable in that situation, yet Mrs Thatcher must have heard him.

In 1977 I paid my only visit to Nigeria to attend the UN conference on apartheid along with Frank Judd, then Minister of State at the Foreign and Commonwealth Office. I had not realized until then just how different West Africa was from East in so many ways, apart from climate. I did not take to Lagos with its endless traffic jams, chaotic management and aggressive lower-level officials.

I did very much appreciate the role played then and now by General Obasanjo, who was then President, and Brigadier Garba, then Foreign Minister, who were the main conference organizers and whom I've enjoyed meeting since in their international roles. The conference itself was painful for Frank Judd, who looked at the text of my speech and wished he could deliver its more forthright terms in place of the blue-paper draft he had from the Foreign Office.

In 1983 I spent my third family holiday in Kenya and made the mistake of agreeing to take the last day doing the political rounds in Nairobi, including giving a press conference before I departed. I called on the Foreign Minister, Robert Ouko, whom I already knew; and Sir Len Allinson, our High Commissioner, was particularly pleased to have got the Vice-President Mwai Kibake, whom I also knew, to lunch with us at the High Commissioner's residence, the first time he had been able to entice Kibake across the doorstep. We had a wide-ranging political discussion à trois. In the afternoon, Judy and I called on Charles Njonjo at his house for tea and an amiable chat. That evening before leaving for the airport I gave my ill-fated press conference in the relaxed atmosphere of the garden of Fitz de Souza's house. It was arranged by the British press attaché.

Casually conversing over cold fruit juices, I was in expansive mood, extolling the virtues of Kenya, describing our discussions, reminiscing on my schooldays etc. when one of the African journalists slipped in a question about the style of government in Kenya. I blethered on about visible social and economic progress and then said that Kenya was not very good at dealing with dissent, that it was less open than in the past and many countries still had to learn the difference between opposition and treachery. These fairly mild remarks were made with such things in mind as the banning in exile of Kenyan writer Ngũgĩ wa Thiong'o, whom at that time I had never even met, and the closure of the university after disturbances by students.

Unfortunately, partly because of the translation of 'dissent' into Swahili, partly because of the arrest that very day of Oginga Odinga's son, and partly because a handful of air-force officers were awaiting trial for their part in an abortive coup the previous year, much more serious criticism was read into my remarks, which had nothing to do with these events. Kenya too has its tabloid press, most of whose representatives were not actually present. I left on the plane and over the weekend they led with vivid headlines and colourful accounts of my 'attack' on the Kenyan government. One paper pointed out that a British official had been in attendance (the hapless press attaché) and that Oginga Odinga had visited Britain just before the attempted coup. I was accused in an editorial of 'abusing the country's hospitality'.

In vain the unfortunate Sir Len pointed out the gross distortion of my remarks and the fact that in any case I did not represent the British Government. He threw in mention of our £25 million aid as well, but was summoned to the Foreign Office to receive an official protest from Ouko.

The Kenya parliament went into emergency debate accusing Charles Njonjo of being a friend, which he admitted but added correctly that we had never even discussed the failed coup. Within a short time he was relieved of his Cabinet post. A British visitor who was present complained in a statement of 'shabby journalism'. It was all extremely unpleasant. I will never know whether I was set up by the press as part of a deliberate campaign to get rid of Njonjo. Through intermediaries to the Vice-President it was made clear eventually that all was forgiven, and in January 1988 I made a return visit to my favourite African country for a charity aid project to which I will refer later.

In 1972 I made my first visit to South Africa and Rhodesia. Having been so critical of Ian Smith's UDI in 1966, I realized I would not be welcome in Rhodesia. In fact Sir Alec Douglas-Home, as Foreign and Commonwealth Secretary, had received messages that neither I nor Denis Healey, then the Opposition Spokesman, would be welcome visitors. Yet I was determined to see for myself. I got the Foreign and Commonwealth Office to issue me with a new passport which made no reference to my being an MP. Armed with this I travelled in through the back door on a local flight from South Africa via Botswana to the southern town of Bulawayo.

There my assistant, Archy Kirkwood, and I passed unnoticed through immigration control, my passport being stamped not on one of its pages but on a loose piece of brown paper inserted for the purpose. This was clearly one of the sanction-busting measures, since the paper could be thrown away on leaving the country, thus removing any evidence of a visit. Continuing to avoid detection, we hired a car to drive to Salisbury, stopping only to telephone the former Liberal Prime Minister, Garfield Todd, at his remote farm – with his daughter Judy I had addressed several anti-UDI meetings in Edinburgh (when her father was prevented from attending) and London.

Salisbury as a city struck me very much like Nairobi a quarter of a century before. It looked the same. Europeans dressed and spoke and thought the same way. More than half of them were postwar immigrants, not bush pioneers, wanting to hang on to a privileged style of living. Ian Smith was their hero. In Salisbury we had a couple of days of talks, staying in an unfashionable hotel, again to avoid easy detection. We also went to a students' meeting at the university being held by one of Smith's opponents. Either there or by tapping the Todds' telephone my presence was discovered by the regime.

As we went through the exit passport controls, Archy Kirkwood and I were arrested and taken to separate rooms for questioning. That experience makes me understand the psychology of solitary detention, though mine can have lasted only half an hour. The inner terror of being alone and in the grip of dictatorial power has to be experienced to be believed. Outwardly I remained calm while I answered their questions. I had nothing to hide about where I had been and whom I had met.

They took papers from my briefcase and photocopied documents belonging to the black trade-union movement in South Africa about which I was rather troubled, but they missed some letters I was carrying to exiles in Britain. I was handed a certificate declaring me a 'Prohibited Immigrant' which I have kept proudly to this day. They stamped my passport which thus testified to my exit but not to my entry and bade me leave, as I was due on the waiting flight to Zambia via Malawi. I rather pompously told them I recognized neither their certificate, their legislation nor their government and looked forward to returning to the country 'when legality and loyalty to the Crown is restored'. I'm sure they wanted to kick my backside.

On rejoining Archy, who seemed genuinely relieved to see me as he had been shoved out through a different route, we then had another nasty moment. As we were sitting on an ancient Air Malawi Dakota, the engines suddenly stopped and we were all ordered out. 'This is it,' we thought, not being sure what 'it' was. (Archy subsequently found that they had removed the country's telephone book from the bottom of his bag in the hold. Perhaps it ranked as a secret document.) But in fact it turned out there was a technical fault in the vintage aeroplane. In the transit waiting room was a public telephone. I rang

Reuters to tell them of the outrageous conduct of the Rhodesian authorities. The story was well covered in the British media, but more important we arrived to headlines in the Zambian and Kenyan press which hailed us as heroes. Doors magically opened and indeed we went straight to talk to President Kaunda at State House.

In 1976 I received a visit from a Rhodesian tobacco farmer, Jack Kay, with whom I had corresponded since he had emigrated from my constituency after the war; he still had family in Kelso whom he visited every few years. He sought my support for an all-party mission to Rhodesia to try to reach a settlement. He thought we in Britain were too hard on Ian Smith, though he was not himself a political supporter. I floated the idea in an article in *The Times* but with the conditions attached which I thought Smith should accept.

In March 1978 Smith had capitulated to the extent of involving three black leaders – Bishop Muzorewa, Chief Chirau and the Rev. Ndabaningi Sithole – in an internal settlment. He installed Bishop Muzorewa as acting Prime Minister, but the main guerrilla war by the Patriotic Front of ZAPU and ZANU, the two nationalist parties, led by Joshua Nkomo and Robert Mugabe, continued. Smith and Muzorewa both made strenuous international efforts to have this settlement recognized and sanctions lifted, but the international community refused and continued to demand a negotiated solution which commanded the full and free consent of the people.

In January 1979 it seemed timely to return to the country. I did so travelling via Nairobi, where I met Vice-President Kibake; Dar-es-Salaam, for talks with President Nyerere; and Lusaka, where I met, in Joshua Nkomo's absence, with Josiah Chinamano, Vice-President of ZAPU, and again with President Kaunda. After a stopover in Johannesburg I went direct to Salisbury, having had assurances from Bishop Muzorewa, whom I had met several times, that my P.I. certificate had been withdrawn. (He told me it had taken a Cabinet decision to get it revoked.) Apart from meeting Muzorewa and the other two black leaders as well as General Walls, commander-in-chief of the government forces, I went out to visit Jack Kay at his farm.

I was shocked at his situation. The farmhouse, some twenty-five miles from the capital, was surrounded by a tall fortress wall and the area patrolled by anti-mine vehicles. He took me to a typical white settlers' country club where there was a local festivity. With me, acting as aide on this visit, was Tim Sheehy of the Catholic Institute for International Relations, who knew southern Africa well and fortunately took copious notes. One elderly club member was heard querying the large police presence. He was told that it was because David Steel was visiting. 'What!' he thundered, 'David Steel? Fella's worse than Nkomo. Knew his father in Kenya.' One of the characteristics of Africa was the migration of the white 'last-ditchers' from Kenya to Rhodesia and now to South Africa.

Jack Kay and most of the whites were fairly certain that Muzorewa would win the election. He invited me to go into his kitchen where I would meet Muzorewa's local area chairman. He would leave us alone. I did, and asked the party local boss who he thought would win in his area. 'Mr Mugabe,' he confided. As far as I was able to judge African opinion, this seemed to be the general view. Four black MPs told me that the rural areas where 89 per cent of the people lived were wholly behind the guerrilla forces.

Meanwhile I also met the smooth and arrogant P. K. van der Byl, Ian Smith's Foreign Minister, and one of the hard-line instigators of UDI, who told me that he thought France and many Francophone African states would in due course, together with the USA, recognize the internal settlement. In all I had twenty-one meetings with different groups in Rhodesia and found no one who supported the 'government's' electoral optimism.

From Salisbury we flew via Johannesburg to Maputo, the capital of Mozambique. Here I had a meeting with the Foreign Minister (later President) Joaquim Chissano. The Mozambique Government eventually played a key role in getting Robert Mugabe into serious negotiation. I had a lengthy discussion with the latter and the leading figures in ZANU, including Edgar Tekere and Didymus Mustasa, at their headquarters in exile. Maputo was a sad, broken-down place suffering the legacy of the belated but precipitate Portuguese withdrawal from the country.

I had met Robert Mugabe only once before at the conference in Nigeria. He was quiet, intelligent, well-spoken and not at all like his partner in the Patriotic Front, the flamboyant Joshua Nkomo of ZAPU. He was relatively unknown to the British and regarded as a Marxist terrorist. He accused Britain of flirting with the internal settlement and of giving it moral support. I explained the domestic situation, with the Labour Government under constant harassment on the Rhodesia issue from the Conservatives in a monstrously unfair – and in a true sense unpatriotic – manner. (Indeed I had come to the conclusion, which turned out to be correct, that it would take a Conservative Government to bring the Smith regime to an end, because Smith's intransigence was bolstered behind the back of a Labour Government by the Conservatives.) He was suspicious – not without justification – of attempts by the British Government to install Nkomo as President, a course favoured by Kenneth Kaunda as an old friend of Nkomo's. He would only come to a constitutional conference which would guarantee the actual democratic transfer of power.

As to the future of the Europeans he explained that 'those who cannot adjust [to a black government] had better leave – those who can adjust should stay.' At the end of our meeting he gave me an interview on Tim Sheehy's tape recorder, later used by the BBC.

When I got back to Britain I wrote a private report on my visit and conclusions for the Prime Minister (sending a copy to Francis Pym as Opposition foreign affairs spokesman), who was having a difficult time trying to restrain the far right of the Conservative Party. (Peter Carrington in his memoirs records: 'For some reason Margaret Thatcher had not bent her mind to Africa. Her instincts were in line with those of the right wing of the party.') I reported on the private assessment of the security situation given me by General Walls and gave my own conclusions on the political future. I estimated 80 per cent support for the external leaders against the internal-settlement ones, and pointed out that Mugabe, not Nkomo, was the leader with most undisputed support. British policy of covertly favouring Nkomo should be abandoned and our future policy 'based on attempting to secure conditions in which fair elections can take place under external supervision'. David Owen, writing of this period as Foreign Secretary, says that 'right up to 1980 white Rhodesians and the Foreign Office believed that Robert Mugabe would be outnumbered and that a coalition government would be formed by Nkomo and Muzorewa'. I did my best to dispel this illusion.

I recorded a 'sad change' in Bishop Muzorewa since I had last seen him and reported that in Tanzania President Nyerere, in a relaxed conversation at his own private house, had told me he was prepared to 'help rescue the bishop' and use his influence to that end with the Patriotic Front. Indeed he had asked me to pass on his warm regards to Muzorewa, who expressed great surprise when I conveyed them.

Among my specific recommendations I suggested 'the appointment of a special representative, not a diplomat, in Salisbury, but an acceptable political animal of authority able to do the rounds ceaselessly and look for openings. Cledwyn Hughes or George Thomson are the kind of people who could do this, though there may be someone more identified with the Conservative Party who could do it.' (This was a role which Christopher Soames eventually performed with great distinction during the transition to independence.) I concluded: 'We must alter the impression that the Anglo-Americans are sitting on their hands waiting for something to turn up.'

Among those to whom I sent a copy was Robin Renwick, the very able official in the Foreign Office who handled the Lancaster House conference and became Soames's political aide when Governor. I had known him since we sold ice-cream together in our student vacations. Sir Robin is now our Ambassador in South Africa.

The general election in Britain overtook these events and, as I had suspected, the new Conservative Government with Lord Carrington as Foreign and Commonwealth Secretary succeeded in bringing the UDI rebellion to an end and securing peaceful transition to democratic independence for Zimbabwe with Robert Mugabe as Prime Minister (now executive President).

My advocacy of his case has led to our continuing good relations. In 1986 I flew into Harare for a few hours by private plane simply to call on him as Prime Minister and discuss my visit to South Africa. He welcomed me mischievously: 'How is your Patriotic Front getting on? We are about to merge.'

'I wish we were,' I replied, 'but I expect David Owen is more difficult than Joshua Nkomo.'

'I don't know if you're right,' he laughed.

On another occasion when he was visiting London, Mrs Thatcher gave a dinner for him at No. 10 Downing Street to which I was invited. The two Prime Ministers welcomed guests at the top of the stairs. As I entered, Margaret Thatcher in her best unctuous tones turned to Mugabe and said, 'Do you know the leader of our Liberal Party, Mr David Steel?' At which point he simply embraced me round the shoulders and said 'Hullo, David.'

In April 1980 I was invited to join the official British delegation for the Zimbabwe independence celebrations. I leapt at the chance. Prince Charles was heading our delegation, and we would all travel on the Royal Flight – Lord Carrington, Peter Shore as Shadow Foreign Secretary, and me. It was a most joyous occasion both on the flight itself and in Zimbabwe.

The VC 10 is an elderly but magnificent British airliner now only in service with the RAF. A couple of these, specially fitted out, are used on all the long-haul VIP trips. The layout is intriguing. Up front is a lounge with a bed for whatever royal personage is aboard. Next to it is a slightly lesser lounge for Prime Minister, Foreign Secretary or whoever is next in the travelling pecking order. Then comes a still lesser one – with no bed but very comfortable – for the likes of me and Peter Shore. Then there is a well-equipped office for Foreign Office officials and secretaries, then what looks like an ordinary first-class lounge for other VIPs and finally a pretty squalid economy-class cabin for policemen, security, catering staff etc., followed by the toilets in the tail. Only the British could achieve such regulated class distinctions.

By this time I suppose I had flown in the plane a couple of times. We flew overnight to Nairobi where we were to stop for refuelling. After a pleasant dinner together we retreated to our allotted places in the scheme of things and Peter Shore saw me pacing out the space between our lounge chairs.

'What on earth are you doing?' he asked.

'Wait and see,' I said.

I worked out that there was just enough space on the floor to make up a bed, using cushions from the chairs. The attendants agreed and brought blankets. Then I decided I might as well be fully comfortable. I always travel light, and had my suitcase on board, not in the hold, containing just essentials and my safari suit. I went through all the compartments to the rear lavatory and changed into my pyjamas, walking back through the disbelieving sections of humanity.

As I got into my bed an RAF sergeant handed me a large tumbler of malt whisky as a nightcap. 'Now this,' I said to Peter Shore, 'is the way to travel.' I expect I had as good a night's sleep as HRH and Peter Carrington. In the morning we duly stopped over at the VIP lounge in Nairobi, where I knew both Kenyan and British officials. 'Is there anything we can do for you,' they politely inquired. Well, as a matter of fact there was. We were due back to refuel in a couple of days, so I asked them to get me a basket of fresh fruit and avocados from the Nairobi market to take back to Judy. The word quickly spread: 'Do you hear what David Steel's arranged?' Soon everybody was ordering similar goods to be put aboard on the return journey.

In Zimbabwe itself the celebrations included a private dinner for Prince Charles with the Mugabes and others, given by Governor Soames at his best in the splendid colonial dining-room of Government House, a most relaxed and amusing occasion over which Christopher and Mary Soames presided with great warmth and style. Next day the enthusiasm of the ceremony in the stadium got slightly out of hand during the arrival of Kenneth Kaunda, Indira Gandhi and other international guests and we all collected a fair whiff of tear gas in the VIP stand.

Afterwards I had a meeting with David Smith, the Scots-born Finance Minister, whom I had met only briefly at Lancaster House and who had no reason to relish my politics. He was the one member of the illegal regime that Mugabe kept on in his cabinet. He leaned forward at his desk and said, 'We've had many disagreements over the years, but I have to tell you I have served in Cabinets in this country under four prime ministers, and Mr Mugabe is not only the most able, but also the most courteous.'

I went back to Wedza to visit Jack Kay and his wife at their farmhouse. The fortified walls had gone and we looked out over the farm. He later stood for one of the reserved seats in parliament and is currently a minister in the Mugabe government.

In 1972 I spent ten days in South Africa, staying partly with Sheena Duncan (whose sister was a constituent of mine) and partly with her mother, Jean Sinclair, both of whom in turn chaired the Black Sash organization. It was my great delight to hand over to Sheena the Liberal International prize for freedom at our congress in Hamburg in 1986. The Black Sash was originally an organization of courageous white women who demonstrated in public places, wearing black sashes in mourning for the constitutional changes which expunged the remaining political rights of the coloured community. They had become a major group dedicated to mitigating the worst social effects of apartheid on families, housing and employment. Through sitting in their casework office I understood the harshness of the Pass Laws and was deeply moved by both the plight of the people and the efforts of the Black Sash workers.

There were talks with the black trade unions and in Lusaka, Zambia, with the ANC about the future for South Africa, and many arguments with white citizens about the current sports boycott, which they knew I supported and they hated. Helen Suzman was at that time the only member of the Liberal opposition in parliament and was a regular visitor to London. I also had encountered 'banned' anti-apartheid campaigner Helen Joseph in the pews of the Anglican Cathedral after morning worship – the only place where banned persons were allowed to meet more than two people.

In the intervening years I shared anti-apartheid platforms in London with many South African leaders such as Oliver Tambo and Desmond Tutu. In 1986 I returned to the country as Party leader to give a lecture at the University of Capetown on 'The road to a Liberal revolution'. I was determined to meet as many different viewpoints as I could, visiting Archbishop Tutu at his home in Capetown, Chief Gatsha Buthelezi (whom I met for the first time but have seen since) at his parliament building in Kwazulu, the Rev. Allan Boesak, and lots of industrialists, academics and pressmen in Johannesburg, Pretoria, Durban and Capetown. In particular I enjoyed talking with the veteran Liberal writer Alan Paton. I also saw for myself the conditions in Crossroads, Khayelitsha and Soweto.

I had an hour, early in my visit, with the Foreign Minister Pik Botha. I found him unexpectedly engaging and – by South African government standards – liberal. He kept talking about 'these right-wingers' of whom he seemed afraid. He craved commendation for the political restoration of rights which should never have been taken away in the first place. Certainly I saw a visible improvement with the abolition of petty apartheid. He blamed everyone from the ANC to Communist agitators for the discontent in the country but never questioned the moral basis of the regime nor its role in creating discontent. On that there was no meeting of minds. During the meeting he complained that there was too much discussion of the merits of the imprisoned black nationalist leader Nelson Mandela. 'The chap's got no

experience of government. He's hardly made a speech, held a press conference,' he said, pausing for thought. 'Mind you, I suppose it's not entirely his
fault.'

Winnie Mandela declined to see me on the grounds that I had talked to
Botha and Buthelezi, the kind of attitude which makes me despair; and of
course the government refused me permission to visit her husband Nelson in
jail. Later I met ANC leaders Oliver Tambo and Tabo Mbeki in Lusaka at
our High Commissioner's residence. I also dined with Kenneth Kaunda and
some of his Cabinet colleagues at State House when he was very gloomy and
said memorably: 'I tell you David that the Third World War will break out
over South Africa.'

My visit was hosted by our sister Progressive Liberal Party, with MPs Colin
Eglin and Peter Soal joining Helen Suzman in making the hospitable and
worthwhile arrangements. As usual I insisted on being taken where others
usually declined to go, right into one of the tough, riot-torn areas of Soweto
with a couple of local African journalists as guides. In addition to my personal
assistant, Graham Watson, I had as aide and adviser Justin Cartwright, who
was born in South Africa and who did a masterly job arranging for the
attendant TV film crews to get good coverage.

At one point I stopped our convoy totally at random and asked to see some
of the housing and the communal lavatory blocks which had been described
in the Commonwealth Eminent Persons Group report. They were appalling
and included a dead dog which the cameras avidly filmed. To judge from the
outraged government press reaction to my visit one would have thought that I
had not only set the whole episode up but personally throttled the unfortunate
animal.

In my report on the visit, which included brief stopovers to see Mr Mugabe
in Harare and President Masire in Botswana, I wrote:

The only real fear South Africans should have is fear of their own government's
blindness which is leading them on the path to a long-drawn-out agony of civil war.

I am also disturbed by the nature of the sometimes bitter antagonisms among the
different sections of the opposition. It seems to me that this is only playing into the
hands of those who wish to represent the opposition to apartheid as fragmented and
anti-democratic.

My own view is that the international community has to make its aversion to
apartheid known to Pretoria in an unmistakable fashion. The western nations in
particular must make it abundantly clear, both at home and in Africa, that they will
no longer tolerate normal relations with the South African government. At the same
time it seems to me that the front-line states must make a concerted effort, in
conjunction with the West, both to apply effective pressure and to deal with the

inevitable consequences of sanctions. I would also like to see these sanctions more clearly agreed and focused effectively on political targets.

In contrast to my familiarity with the African continent, the long-standing problems of the Middle East were a closed book to me, and when I became leader, it was suggested that I head an extensive party delegation to tour that troubled region. This we eventually did in a fortnight during September/October 1980. My only knowledge of the complicated politics of the area stemmed from a most useful visit I had paid to the General Assembly of the United Nations Organization in New York in 1967 as a member of the annual five-strong parliamentary delegation. At that time our distinguished UN representative, elevated in status from Ambassador to Minister of State at the Foreign and Commonwealth Office, was Lord Caradon (formerly Sir Hugh Foot, brother of John, Dingle and Michael). Under his wise guidance the UN had just adopted the famous Resolution 242, agreeing the basis of an international settlement guaranteeing Israel's security in return for restoration of seized land.

The purpose of the visit was to hear the widest possible range of opinion from all the countries, organizations and people involved in the Middle East conflict, and to try to reach agreement among the delegation on a report which might form the basis of the development of Party policy on the Middle East. Hitherto, to be candid, the Party was thought of as being uninterested in the Arab side of the problem, and heavily identified as an uncritical supporter of the state of Israel. After that visit, while we reiterated our support for the right of Israel to exist within internationally recognized and secure borders, we took a more balanced view of some of its policies, and measured these against Palestinian claims for a just solution which involved the establishment of a Palestinian homeland. Indeed the Report we published in 1980 was ahead of its time and is still remarkably relevant today.

I took an able and carefully balanced team: Russell Johnston MP, our foreign affairs spokesman; Stephen Ross MP, our defence spokesman and President of the Liberal Friends of Israel; David Alton MP, chairman of our Standing (Policy) Committee; Roger Sibley, chairman of both our Defence Panel and Middle East subcommittee; and Stuart Mole, my personal assistant, now a member of the Commonwealth Secretariat.

We travelled first to Syria, and experienced an amusing incident on our arrival. I had been invited by the captain of the Boeing 747 to be on the flight deck for the landing at Damascus. Being thus absorbed, I was unaware of the minor panic which gripped my delegation once the aeroplane had taxied to a halt. From the window, my colleagues could see an impressive welcoming party, complete with military guard of honour, television crews, and a small band. The Vice-Minister for Foreign Affairs, the British Ambaassador, Sir Patrick Wright, now PUS at the FCO, and other dignitaries were lined up in welcome. All this was too much for my five colleagues, who were not expecting to be participants in so much pomp and protocol. A desperate and confused struggle took place for hand luggage and duty free cartons. Below the upper deck, however, the cabin staff were having increasing difficulty holding off the great press of passengers, anxious to disembark. With the delegation disorganized and the Liberal Leader still missing, the airline felt they had at least to disembark an extremely frail and rather ill old gentleman. Assisted by a nurse, the man tottered to the door of the aeroplane and proceeded to stagger down the steps, whereupon the band struck up, the honour guard presented arms and the television cameras rolled. As the Vice-Minister, hand outstretched in greeting, stepped forward, the British Ambassador murmured in his ear, 'I think you will find, Minister, that that is not the Leader of the Liberal Party.'

Outside Damascus we visited the small city of Kineitra, systematically destroyed during Israeli occupation, and travelled right up to the strategically important Golan Heights. We could see how easily, prior to the 1967 war, Syrian artillery on this position had threatened Israel. We were in no doubt that any peace settlement must secure the demilitarization of this zone. The Soviet Union's military expenditure was obvious and we felt that Britain should be doing more to develop trade and cultural links with Syria.

The delegation was received by President Assad in a large state room in his palace and had a lengthy discussion. An austere figure, he gave us the standard Syrian line on Israel's withdrawal to 1967 boundaries and the creation of a Palestinian state. He also gave us a first-hand experience of the hostility towards the Camp David process and especially towards Egypt for breaking Arab unity and solidarity: 'Weak Arabs cannot achieve peace,' he commented cryptically.

While in Damascus we had an opportunity to meet Yasser Arafat, leader of the Palestine Liberation Organization (PLO). As far as recorded history is concerned, I was the first British Party leader to meet him; but this is not strictly correct, because I was present in a crowded palace anteroom earlier that year in Belgrade during the Yugoslav President Tito's funeral when our relatively new Prime Minister, Mrs Thatcher, was glad-handing those present ('I'm Margaret Thatcher, *so* pleased to meet you'). Being without any aides in this distinguished gathering, she gave the distinct and understandable impression of not knowing who everybody was – she had not dealt much with foreign affairs in her political career. Among those she greeted with happy incomprehension was Yasser Arafat. The distinguished American statesman Averell Harriman was being ushered into the same room when he backed out hurriedly on spotting Arafat.

Nevertheless I was the first to hold substantial talks with him, something which gives me amused satisfaction when I see nearly a decade later Conservative and Labour politicans rushing to have audience with the PLO leader. It was not a popular move, either internationally or domestically. Indeed a few party members resigned and I was given a regular going-over by the influential *Jewish Chronicle*.

The prelude to the meeting bordered on farce. Such is the tight security surrounding Arafat that he never stays in the same place for more than a few hours. Our meeting was held in security and secrecy so elaborate that the time and place were not disclosed, even to those taking us to meet him. At around midnight we were speeding through Damascus in circles in a small convoy like something out of a Keystone Cops film. Eventually we met in the basement of an anonymous-looking house. In a small room our delegations sat on either side of a dining table. Arafat was of course hostile to the Camp David agreement, rejecting an apparent choice of federation of the West Bank and Gaza strip with either Israel or Jordan; 'We insist on living as human beings and not as slaves – in a sovereign state.' We pressed him on the recognition of Israel: 'I cannot do that at present – this is a card for the Security Council.'

Questioned about the PLO's oft-quoted commitment to destroy the state of Israel, he denied this and argued that it was to misinterpret the PLO charter to say that the Israelis would be driven into the sea: 'That does not represent our position.' He was hostile to President Sadat – a traitor who would have to go before Egypt could be welcomed back into the Arab world.

The Palestinians had few cards to play, but their right of veto was their strength. He added: 'We are stateless and homeless. We have suffered too much. None of us want other generations to live as we have suffered. ... We will never accept a solution without a Sovereign State. There will never be a solution, never stability, no security unless and until the Palestinians regain their rights.'

I have met Yasser Arafat on two or three brief occasions since then, and known his representatives in London, one of whom was assassinated for his too-moderate views. I have always regarded Arafat himself as a moderate presiding over a very loose organization which includes some unpleasant fanatics. Watching him over the years, he has struck me as a genuine seeker after rights for his people and peace in the Middle East which he is increasingly desperate to see established as he gets older. His recent speeches and willingness to enter dialogue came as no surprise to me.

We then travelled to the Lebanon, spending the first day visiting the United Nations peace-keeping force, UNIFIL, then under the command of the Ghanaian Major-General Emmanuel Erskine. I have the highest opinion of these forces, who received the Nobel Peace Prize this year. In the case of UNIFIL they had lost forty-five men in twelve years, acting as buffer between Palestinian groups in the north and Israeli-backed forces in the south. Erskine put it well when he said: 'We are the peace-keepers, but you have to make the peace before we have any chance of keeping it.'

We then flew by UN helicopter from UNIFIL's headquarters to visit the Fijian contingent in the field. FIJIBAT, of around 4,000 men, actually constituted a sizeable proportion of the total Fijian army strength. Its officers were thoroughly amiable, but in the briefing held in the Officers' Mess, soon ran out of anything to say. In one of the awkward silences which followed, I nudged Russell Johnston, with the clear message that as foreign affairs spokesman he should find something to talk about. His eyes searched for inspiration and rested upon a picture of the Duke of Edinburgh. 'Is there any reason why you have a picture of Prince Philip on the wall?' he asked. 'No particular reason,' came the laconic reply, 'he just happens to be the husband of our Queen.'

Among the Fijian officers serving with UNIFIL at that time was the now Brigadier Sitiveni Rabuka, the leader of two military coups in Fiji and the person most responsible for taking his country out of the Commonwealth and turning it into a Republic. I hope it was not Russell who first began to undermine the Fijian army's hitherto intense loyalty to the Crown.

Later – against Foreign Office advice – we travelled back into South Lebanon from Israel with Major Haddad and his forces.

In Beirut itself we went to a series of meetings escorted by a dangerous scale of armed guard. Apart from the usual police escort and flashing lights to which we had got used in Syria, the car in which I was travelling was immediately preceded by a large American estate car with the tailgate open. It swung closed whenever we encountered a pothole – a regular occurrence and inside the back lounged two khaki-clad militia, each brandishing enormous machine-guns which seemed to be pointing in my direction. We toured bomb-torn Beirut for two days in this manner. The tragedy of that country was well put to us by President Sarkis: 'There will never be a lasting solution to the Lebanese problem without a lasting and global solution to the problems of the Middle East.'

From there we flew to Jordan, where we were received with great courtesy.

At the airport to welcome us, apart from British and Jordanian foreign-office officials, was a figure in resplendent military uniform who was introduced as the aide-de-camp. How kind, I thought, of His Majesty to send his ADC to greet me. It soon turned out that he was to be *my* ADC. In addition to the now familiar police escort clearing the public out of the way for the leader of the Liberal Party, I had this officer travelling in the front of the limousine, opening and shutting my door and saluting at every entrance and exit. Insubordinate hysteria gripped the rest of the delegation: 'He'll be impossible when he gets home – he'll expect the Queen to lend him a detachment of the Household Cavalry.'

'There's nothing wrong with a dash of old-fashioned courtesy,' I retorted, though I was a little discomforted by King Hussein's Sandhurst habit of calling me 'sir' throughout our meeting. On later occasions when I met him and his brother, Crown Prince Hassan, both in London and Amman, they were more relaxed. I consider that these two brave men have a firmer grasp and fairer perspective of the issues in the Middle East than any of the other participants. In 1984 Crown Prince Hassan and I organized a joint Liberal International Arab thought forum in Amman.

In addition to our many meetings in Jordan, I paid my first visit to a UN refugee camp. UNRWA is a sadly underfunded, overstretched organization. In that one camp alone, for twelve years nearly 60,000 people had been living in 8,000 huts. Sadly the Middle East is dotted with such camps, perhaps the most iniquitous consequence of our collective failure to settle the Middle East conflict.

From Jordan we drove into Israel via the Allenby Bridge and the West Bank. Here our reception was, though friendly on a personal basis, officially much colder. Prime Minister Begin was the only head of government not to receive us. They thoroughly disapproved of the Arafat meeting. But we were impressed by the intellectual vigour of those we did see: General Chaim Herzog (not yet President of Israel); David Kimche, director-general of the Foreign Ministry; Professor Moshe Arens (now Foreign Minister but then Chairman of the Knesset's Defence and Foreign Affairs committee); and also Shimon Peres and several of his Labour Party colleagues, including Abba Eban. We had lengthy talks on both the military and the political position of Israel.

The British Consul-General in Jerusalem hosted a meeting for us with important leaders of Arab opinion from the occupied West Bank. We also had an agreeable breakfast with our colleagues in the Independent Liberal Party, led by Moshe Kol, and a thoroughly disagreeable dinner with our other colleagues in the official Liberal Party, led by Yitzhak Modai, at which tempers were roused. Our relations with them have always been strained even when they hosted the Liberal International Congress in Tel Aviv a few years later. The so-called Liberal Party is in fact part and parcel of the Likud, whose leader and current Prime Minister, Yitzhak Shamir, when I met him in London struck me as the most intransigent and difficult of men.

My admiration for what the Israelis have achieved for their country surpasses my criticism from time to time of the policies of their government. To stand at the narrowest point – seven miles – of the country is to recognize its vulnerability. To visit the holy places of Jerusalem, Nazareth and the sea of Galilee, and Bethlehem and the Holocaust museum of Yad Vashem where we laid wreaths are unforgettably emotional experiences. My contact has been maintained over the years through friendship with two superb Israeli ambassadors in London, Shlomo Argov, sadly struck by a would-be assassin's bullet, and Yehuda Avner.

From Tel Aviv we flew to Cairo, a flight itself only made possible through the Sadat/Begin *rapprochement*, and again launched into two days of intensive meetings. By this time we were all pretty exhausted. In the absence of our Ambassador, the British chargé d'affaires helpfully gave us the run of the embassy garden and swimming pool, round which our delegation began to discuss its report. He bade us to dinner at which we had to chat to the usual embassy list of important locals and British businessmen. We stood for more than two hours over cocktails and eventually I sent Stuart Mole to inquire of our host when we were going to be able to sit down to eat. 'Not till ten' was the message back – they eat late in Egypt. Drink and fatigue took over. 'Tell him,' I told Stuart, 'that since I am the guest of honour whom these people have been brought here to meet I either want food now or I'm leaving.' Dinner was served.

We arrived on a Tuesday and were due to leave the country on the Thursday. President Sadat was at his party conference and sent a message to the effect that if we could extend our stay to Saturday as guests of the Egyptian government, he would be keen to meet us. Two of our number had to leave on schedule but four of us decided it was worth staying on. We split into two groups for the interval, one going up the Nile to visit temples and the other – David Alton and I – going to visit Alexandria.

We travelled across the desert on a train crowded with passengers, including large numbers of soldiers accommodated on the roofs of the carriages. On arrival we were met by our Consul-General, who gave us an informative briefing on the history of the area and took us to an elegant beach hotel to be left alone. That evening we set off for a Greek restaurant in the old city, at which Eisenhower, Churchill and Montgomery had dined to plan the battle of Alamein. We were escorted to the same corner table.

According to Alton I then proceeded to draw charts all over the paper tablecloth, mapping out the future battleground of British politics and outlining my war strategy. He claims that what I portrayed largely came to pass over the next three years with the birth of the SDP and the creation of the Alliance.

What I do recall clearly is that on returning to our hotel he wished to sample the local nightlife in the basement disco while I decided to get some sleep. Ever the Scot, I was of course sharing the bedroom. I took the only key and said I would leave the door off the latch for him. On arriving at the bedroom I was taken aback at finding a man in uniform armed with an automatic weapon of some kind sitting on a chair outside the door. He leapt to attention and gave a passable salute as I vanished inside. I went to sleep.

In the morning the Mediterranean sun streamed in and I woke to see David standing on the balcony gazing out to sea. He came in and declared: 'This is the last time I travel anywhere with you.' As I struggled to consciousness he explained that at some later hour he had arrived at the door to find the man asleep in his chair outside with the vicious-looking gun across his knees. He had to make a quick decision to try to slip into the room without waking the guard, fearful that in so doing he might be riddled in the back with a hail of bullets.

I thought the episode very funny until I emerged for breakfast. I was approached by a man in a crisp white uniform who introduced himself as a colonel in the Egyptian security service. He had been sent from Cairo to take charge of my security. After so many days in different countries being closely guarded I had deliberately not said where I was spending my forty-eight hours' free time, but I suppose the British embassy had to tell them. 'What is your programme?' asked the colonel.

'I haven't got one,' I pleaded, 'I'm just taking a couple of days off. No one knows I'm here and I feel perfectly safe. There really is no need for you to trouble.'

He was insistent. When we took deckchairs down to the hotel beach, stripped off to swim and to read books in the sun, the colonel still in full uniform drew up a deckchair two yards behind us and sweated in the heat. When I went to the lavatory he followed me into the next stall. David could take no more. 'This is ridiculous,' he announced. 'I'm off to walk in the park by myself.' So saying he disappeared in a sulk which lasted several hours, leaving me with my melting colonel.

We returned to Cairo as advised across the desert in an American air-conditioned bus. The straight road through the desert was punctuated only by the debris of crashed vehicles, sticking out of the sand on either side like rusty cans on a badly kept sea shore. We even passed one on the road on fire about to join the graveyard. Egyptian driving both in the desert and in Cairo has to be experienced to be believed.

We were received by President Sadat in his domestic palace for a long talk. A strikingly tall man, his imagination and bravery (critics would say foodhardiness) in going to Jerusalem to address the Knesset was fresh in our minds. He was an eloquent and intelligent realist, recognizing that no further progress was possible on a Middle-East peace until 1981 when both Israeli and American elections were out of the way. He expected the Americans then to bring further pressure to bear on Israel. 'Ninety-nine per cent of the cards are in the hands of the USA,' he said. As for his portrayal as a betrayer of the Palestinians, he was forthright: 'Only the Palestinians can solve their own problem.' He did not seek to speak for them or impose his own solution. He looked forward to a peace conference at which they would represent themselves. A year later he was assassinated on the platform while reviewing the annual national military parade.

With some of my colleagues I have made two visits to the Gulf States, meeting rulers in Saudi Arabia, the United Arab Emirates and Oman.

In Saudi Arabia King Khalid provided a private jet for my gulf tour and we met with Prince Saud, the experienced Foreign Minister. On a second visit we went to the house of one of the younger princes to meet some of his friends. We sat on the floor round a carpet piled high with food, including the legendary sheep's eyes, at the consumption of which I'm afraid I baulked. After the all-male dinner was over, we retired to a drawing room for conversation, the doors slid shut to partition off the dining area and behind them we could hear the merry chatter of the wives eating the left-overs. Later, when I met the Oxford-educated prince in London in a lounge suit rather than elegant, flowing robes, we had a fascinating conversation on his capacity to switch between two such different cultures.

In the United Arab Emirates, where my former researcher, Peter Hellyer, was editing a newspaper and was an invaluable guide, we were invited by the President, Sheikh Zayeed, to travel by helicopter to his country palace where we met him and admired his afforestation programme, reclaiming the desert. He gave each of my colleagues a gold watch and me a magnificent decorated dagger.

Some of the Arab states are stricter than others in the matter of alcohol. In Saudi Arabia it is totally banned. When I met up with my old friends George and Helen Inglis, who were teaching there, they invited several other Scots round to their flat to meet me. I regretted that the hip flask which I carry permanently in my suitcase was empty. They made me produce it and passed it round the assembled company for a good Scotch sniff just to remind them of home.

In one of the other states – it may have been Kuwait – I recall being given a banquet in a hotel where the entire wall of the room was a magnificent wine cellar, but because this was an official function we drank orange juice.

The Oman visit was enlivened by a summons to meet Sultan Qaboos at his summer palace in the south. We were to travel in his private plane, a Boeing 707. As we boarded I realized that in another part of the cabin were six finance ministers of other Gulf States, probably the richest group of ministers ever assembled in one aeroplane. On arrival at the palace we were shown into a suite of comfortable rooms to wait for an uncertain period while His Highness met the finance ministers. An Englishman appeared from a neighbouring suite and seemed glad to see us: 'I've been waiting for an audience for a couple of days and may well have to wait another couple. I hope you're not in a hurry.' This was his Savile Row tailor with a batch of fresh uniform designs.

His benevolent government has wisely used the fruits of the oil boom for the benefit of the people. After some hours we were ushered into his friendly presence – ahead of the tailor – and had an enjoyable and instructive hour or so with him. On return in his plane I went exploring, to discover that it was equipped with two self-contained cabins each with double bed and bathroom. So this was how the other half lived, and travelled. The finance ministers, by now totally relaxed, proceeded to quiz me on the latest British political gossip on which they were all extremely well informed.

The Middle East is a region both rich and tragic. I hope that the European powers may yet use their good offices with the USA and USSR to achieve the long-awaited peace settlement which will both recognize Palestinian rights to self-determination and give solid, international guarantees for the security of Israel. Making vast sums, as all countries do, out of selling arms to both sides in the perpetual conflict has not been an elevating role for the outside world.

My visits to America and Canada began in 1967 with my participation in the UN delegation in New York, after which I went on to meet some of the ruling Liberal caucus in Canada. I have lost count of the number of subsequent visits.

With the Canadian Liberals we have had a perpetually close connection. They are among my favourites. John Turner, recently retired from the leadership, I first met there twenty years ago. Pierre Trudeau I got to know as Prime Minister both in Canada and on his visits to London. At one point when he was temporarily leader of the Opposition I visited him in his home in Ottawa not long after his wife, Margaret, had left him looking after their three boys. Trudeau introduced me to his sons as his 'opposite number in Britain' at which one of them incredulously asked why in that case he had never heard of me.

On another occasion I was asked to join a Liberal Cabinet group at their summer meeting in a remote mountain retreat in Quebec where Alan McEachen as Foreign Minister was conducting a seminar on foreign and defence issues. On yet another I was guest speaker at their special policy conference in Halifax, Nova Scotia, where Judy came with me and we enjoyed the welcome of a large Scottish expatriate community. Senator Al Graham as one-time President of their party has been a good friend and stalwart of Liberal International. I also gave a guest lecture at the law faculty in the University of Toronto. In April 1982 I was on a visit to Washington when I received an invitation to attend the 'patriation of the constitution' ceremonies in Canada over which the Queen was to preside.

Prime Minister Trudeau had asked three representatives from the UK: Lord Chancellor Hailsham, former Prime Minister Callaghan and me. I explained it was going to be difficult, whereupon he sent an executive jet down to Washington to pick me up. On the eve of the ceremonial we attended an intensely patriotic Canadian event in a theatre. I had my son Billy with me and they invited him as well. When we returned to our hotel I found we had each been allocated a splendid, sumptuous room equipped with bar. Billy, having come and given me an excited goodnight hug, retired to his room. Next morning I called him on the telephone. No reply. I knocked at his door in vain. I asked the hotel staff if anyone had seen him. Eventually they used a master key to gain entry only to find him lying in bed semi-conscious, having sampled every drink in the bar, a terrible temptation for someone aged nineteen.

I helped him dress and dragged him off to the ceremony to be held in brilliant sunshine in front of the Canadian House of Commons. We British all sat together near the front with Sonny Ramphal, Secretary-General of the Commonwealth. The Queen and the Governor-General and Trudeau were on a covered platform. Suddenly the heavens opened in the most violent thunderstorm. Quintin Hailsham had a Lords attendant with him equipped with umbrella, and beat a quick retreat behind the rostrum. Jim Callaghan disappeared altogether into the Parliament building. The audience thinned. I said to Billy through clenched teeth, 'We are staying here.' He disappeared once to be sick. Sonny Ramphal, the rain streaming down his face, turned to me and said with pretended seriousness: 'I trust that Her Majesty in her hour of travail will note that the Commonwealth and the Liberal Party stood fast by her.'

Afterwards we were bidden to lunch with the Governor-General. My habit of travelling light had let me down and my only suit was wringing wet. I pleaded with the hotel to do their best to dry it out before the lunch as I paced my room in my underwear, lamenting the disaster of the entire trip.

I have also been a regular visitor to the United States since 1967, having been on the US Information Service guest programme, conducting a coast-to-coast lecture tour, delivering enjoyable guest lectures at the Kennedy School of Government in Harvard. In 1987 I was awarded a visiting fellowship at Timothy Dwight College Yale, which Judy and I enjoyed so much that we stayed on over a weekend instead of going as planned back to New York, which she hated.

In 1976 Judy and I were part of the British delegation for the American Bicentennial celebrations led by George Thomas as Speaker and Lord Elwyn-Jones as Lord Chancellor. The delegation presented a gold copy of Magna Carta to Congress. This was the only occasion on which I have visited the famous Oval Office in the White House, as guest of President Ford. I seem to have bad luck when accompanied by my family. This time Judy found she had left some underwear in a drawer in our hotel room. We were due to go straight from the White House to the airport. On telling the captain in charge of our car in the cavalcade, he ordered a motorcycle police escort to race back to the hotel to retrieve the various items before joining the others at the White House gates.

In 1982 on a visit to the States which included a series of meetings with the *New York Times*, the *Washington Post*, Caspar Weinberger, Secretary of Defense in the Pentagon, Larry Eagleburger, Assistant Secretary in the State Department and many others, I was staying with Annie and Robin Renwick, who were then in the Washington embassy. Renwick persuaded me to meet over breakfast in the Senate an up-and-coming senator called Gary Hart. In spite of my loathing of working breakfasts, I enjoyed our first encounter.

The following year Hart invited me to an international seminar which he was hosting in South Carolina, called grandly 'Leadership in the Next Twenty Years'. Other Brits invited included Kenneth Clarke, Chris Patten and Denzil Davies. Geraldine Ferraro and Chris Dodds were among the Americans. I found this three-day head banging session very stimulating.

In 1984 I attended as a guest the Democratic Convention in San Francisco, listening to speeches from Gary Hart, Governor Mario Cuomo and Jesse Jackson, as well as the presidential nominee, Walter ('Fritz') Mondale, whom at that time I had met only briefly as Carter's Vice-President. I was profoundly impressed by the sheer scale and drama of the whole occasion. At one point I was taken through the floor to a seat on the platform, an honour normally reserved for those giving large donations.

Later I was to get to know Mondale in London over dinner and in Hamburg, where he was addressing a Liberal International Congress and he suggested we should breakfast. Out of deference I agreed. On struggling to the top floor of the hotel to find the appointed private dining-room, I found Fritz standing in the corridor outside the locked door. 'Why are we doing this?' he said, 'Why don't we forget it and go back to bed.' I hastily agreed, at which point a white-coated waiter appeared with a key and we went ahead with our reluctant breakfast. He is a most intelligent and likeable man who somehow managed to come across badly in the presidential campaign.

The Americans and Canadians clearly had exaggerated ideas of both the importance and the expense account of Britain's Liberal leader. I was often having to rescue myself from expensive hotel suites which they arranged. In San Francisco, Richard Holme and Ming and Elspeth Campbell, who were staying somewhere sensible, came to tea with me in the Mark Hopkins hotel on Nob Hill and have never let me forget the look on my face when the bill arrived. I had asked my assistant, Graham Watson, to try and get us out of there; but all he could find was the opposite extreme, a sleazy room above a sex shop.

Before the Convention I had returned to Texas and South Carolina to join Gary Hart on the primary campaign trail. It was a gruelling and illuminating experience. Crisscrossing the States in a large jet, mainly containing journalists and television crews, I was very impressed on first hearing his speech until I realized it was played like a gramophone at every stop. I admired the skill with which he used the same themes to a gathering of two dozen donors in an elegant drawing room and to thousands of students in a baseball stadium. I felt he was right to stick to clear punchy points over and over again. Even if his entourage was bored, it was clear and fresh to each new audience. The punishing schedule of primaries and elections in the USA is absurd. Politicians spend so much time running for office that they must be exhausted when they reach it.

I did not endear myself to the presidential candidates' aides by ridiculing the timetable. In Austin, Texas, one of them hissed at me as we boarded the plane: 'Gary was asking at the Governor's breakfast where you were. He wanted to introduce you.'

'I trust,' I retorted, 'that you told him I was where any sane politician should be at that hour – in bed.'

Later I went through his daily schedule as we sat together on the plane. He literally ran from breakfast through to late-night fundraising parties. 'Snacks' were perpetually provided. I advised him to set a time deadline at night and then settle down with a decent steak, a bottle of wine and just one or two close advisers, which was my own practice. To my embarrassment he eagerly repeated this advice, attributed to me, to his staff on the plane, who were not approving.

In January 1985 I invited Gary Hart to join me at a joint fundraising dinner at the House of Commons for Democrats Abroad and Liberal International which Clement Freud organized with great flair. Neither of our speeches was memorable, but this Hart made up for the following day.

The next day we flew to Edinburgh where as Rector I had invited him to give a public lecture at the University. His wife, Lee, and Judy made a tour of Edinburgh while we did interviews. Then we went across from the Rector's office to the lecture theatre to find we had hopelessly underestimated his appeal. The hall was packed and a further thousand or so stood outside disappointed. He gave a commanding lecture on US–European relations and I introduced him in the manner I was used to at the Convention as 'the next President of the United States'.

It was not to be. The Donna Rice affair and especially his taunting of the press were his downfall. It was not only a tragedy for Gary, it was fatal for the Democratic Party who were left to choose between comparative unknowns. In 1988 when I attended the Democratic Convention in Atlanta – my last overseas visit as party leader – the candidate who emerged, Michael Dukakis, had neither Hart's charisma nor his knowledge of international politics. I continue to see Gary Hart occasionally and through the National Democratic Institute, run by Walter Mondale and Brian Atwood, relations with the American Democrats on the international scene remain close.

In the American sphere of geographic influence I have paid short visits over the years to Jamaica, Nicaragua and Panama. The Caribbean and South and Central America are places I cannot claim to know adequately.

The other superpower, the Soviet Union, I have visited five times, once as already described in my student days, three times for state funerals and once as a leader of a Party delegation in January 1984. At that time relations between our two countries were distinctly cool. There had been no high-level political visit from our side to Moscow by anyone for some time. The Soviet Ambassador in London was anxious that someone should break the ice and I felt it was time to update my own knowledge of the Soviet Union. They invited a delegation and I put one together consisting of me and Judy; Russell Johnston as our foreign affairs spokesman; Christopher (Lord) Mayhew, our defence spokesman, who as Under-Secretary to Bevin in the Foreign Office had the longest and most detailed experience of the country; Anthony Jacobs, the party treasurer (for two reasons: *one*, we wanted to quiz them on treatment of Jews and refuseniks, and *two*, he owned the executive jet which I used in elections and had asked to borrow for this visit – he did *not* make his inclusion a condition of lending it); and Graham Watson my political assistant. We also took Colin Brown of the *Guardian*, though for all they printed of his reports we could have saved the seat for someone else. We had an intensive six days. Judy and I were staying in the grandeur of our embassy with its unique view across the Moskva river to the Kremlin. The rest were billeted in the uninspiring Russiya Hotel.

The artistic highlight was a concert at the Moscow Conservatoire by the renowned pianist Emil Gilels, since sadly deceased, though his recordings are still sought after. I mention this only because it was more memorable than our many dreary political meetings, the highlight of which was the meeting in the Kremlin with an elderly Supreme Soviet delegation led by politburo member B.N. Ponomarev, now thankfully retired. General Secretary Andropov was described as 'indisposed' and died within a fortnight. A couple of top generals in massive scrambled-egged uniforms sat on one side of the table alongside the politicians, who included Leonid Zamyatin, now Soviet Ambassador in London, while we sat down the other side. Simultaneous translation was efficiently supplied. I began with a short statement and series of questions to start the dialogue. The meeting lasted nearly three hours; but Pomonarev took over twenty minutes to read out a prepared statement which showed remarkable knowledge of Liberal policy and assembly decisions, yet did not really answer any of the points I had raised. This stonewalling was characteristic of the entire discussion and most of our other meetings in the Soviet capital.

I stress this only because of the stark contrast with the current regime. When David Owen and I met Mikhail Gorbachev for an hour in the Commons on his visit to London that December, we got more of a genuine discussion than in our entire six days in Russia in January. That difference was underlined by a subsequent meeting in my office in the Commons with Eduard Shevardnadze, the new Foreign Minister. Both men are open to frank discussion in a way totally unknown during the long cold-war era, and this spirit has percolated through to most of the Russians I have met since. No longer are we told the joke in Moscow: 'What is a musical trio? A quartet that has been on a tour of the West.'

We flew also to Leningrad where we sat selfconsciously in the Tsar's box at the ornate Pushkin theatre, visited the magnificent restoration of Queen

Catherine's summer palace outside the city and, most movingly, the museum and memorial of the siege of Leningrad. Perhaps in that city more than in Moscow one can get a sense of the genuine if misplaced fear of western militarism as the Soviets see it, derived from their horrific Second World War experiences.

The visit was passingly covered in the British media – the highlight being the laying of an enormous wreath, which took two people to carry, at the tomb of the unknown warrior; but it was treated with exaggerated importance in the USSR. The Soviet Ambassador was pleased and when later visits by Foreign Secretary Geoffrey Howe, Margaret Thatcher, and the Labour leadership took place used to say, 'You paved the way,' which was flattering but not, I think, entirely accurate in ascribing cause and effect.

As we said our goodbyes little did I realize I would be back so soon for my second Russian state funeral.

It is perhaps time I said something of the importance of the working funeral in international diplomacy – a good subject for someone's Ph.D. My first, as already mentioned, was to President Tito's in Yugoslavia in May 1980. The British delegation was led by the Duke of Edinburgh and included Prime Minister Thatcher, Leader of the Opposition Callaghan and Liberal leader Steel. As I made to leave the VC10 Mrs Thatcher spotted me wearing a bright red tie which I thought entirely appropriate for a Socialist country. 'David,' she scolded, 'we are arriving in a country in mourning.' I changed quickly into my black tie. She tended to fuss round us like a clucking hen, which I found rather endearing. I think in these little ways she is genuinely kind and motherly, brushing people's collars and seeing ties are straight. All manner of heads of state, government and royalty get flung together on these occasions, quite apart from the legion of small formal private meetings hastily arranged. Chancellor Helmut Schmidt of Germany and Foreign Minister Hans Dietrich Genscher greeted us familiarly and wagged their fingers at me and Callaghan, saying: 'We told you you should have kept together.' Vice-President Walter Mondale I met for the first time, while I was able to ask a beaming President Ceaușescu how my dog was getting on.

At one point after the ceremony while we were hanging about in the open air, I noticed Prince Philip brandishing what I thought was a cigarette lighter, but turned out to be a tiny camera with which he snapped the rest of us. He explained to me, 'You can't go to these things with a camera strung round your neck. This I can keep in my pocket.' That did not stop the American delegation at every funeral I attended arriving in grotesque numbers and chattering along like a busload of tourists. I took his advice and invested in a similar camera on my return to London.

Within three months I was able to use it at another funeral, that of Seretse Khama, President of Botswana. On this occasion our delegation was led by the Duke of Kent. The present runway at Gaberone had not been completed and the old one with which I was familiar was still in use. So our travel out by VC10 had to be via Harare, where we had to transfer to a military Hercules flown out for the purpose. It is rather like flying in a corrugated-iron garage, being large, tinny, windowless and noisy, more used for carrying troops and vehicles than VIPs. An attempt had been made to install more comfortable seats at one end and in the middle stood an incongruous portaloo.

Seretse Khama was genuinely loved by his people. I had met him only once, fleetingly; but by a strange coincidence David Finlay, who had been at school with me in Edinburgh, had been on his staff since independence. He had a key role in organizing the simple ceremony in a football stadium, the aftermath of which was utter chaos as none of us could find our cars in the melee.

At the new President's reception afterwards, all my old African chums from every country were there. Robert Ouko, the Kenyan Foreign Minister, looked glum as he had to wait another two days for a flight back to Nairobi. 'But,' I said cheerily, 'we're stopping there to refuel and pick up my order (more fruit and avocados). I'm sure we could give you a lift.'

I suggested it to one of our officials, who reacted stuffily: 'You can't do that. Do remember this is a Royal Flight.'

I have the highest regard for our foreign-service officials as I've seen them operate around the globe; but just occasionally some chinless wonder with the right breeding and no brains gets in among them. They rarely get far.

'Don't be so ridiculous,' I said, 'I'll ask HRH myself.' I then approached the Duke and explained my premature offer.

'Quite all right,' he said without hesitation. 'Glad to help.'

In my now long experience of members of the royal family I have never found them standoffish in any way. They are sometimes badly served by those who think they are protecting them from real life and who thus create the wrong impression, as this man had done.

He got his own back. On the flight back from Harare to Nairobi, a decent dinner was served at which I was to have joined the Duke with Sir Ian Gilmour, the Lord Privy Seal, and Peter Shore at table. Of course, it was explained, the Kenyan minister would have to be invited; and since there were only four places and I was the most junior, I had to eat my meal in my seat on my own. I was in disgrace.

Then came my trilogy of Russian state funerals. Brezhnev in November '82, Andropov in February '84, and Chernenko in March '85.

The three Russian funerals all took place in the grip of Soviet subzero winter. The ceremonies were identical and ponderously impressive. Brezhnev's in 1982 was for me the most striking. It was my first visit to Moscow since the student trip, and the improvement in the ordinary standard of living – notably the dress – of the people was evident. We were whisked everywhere in cumbersome black Russian cars which were entitled to use the special VIP lanes. (In capitalist London, there are special lanes for buses; in communist Moscow, special lanes for high-ranking officials in their limousines.)

We stood for hours in the freezing cold of Red Square beside the famous Lenin mausoleum of russet marble (when I had been inside as a student; Stalin was lying alongside Lenin, each looking like a waxwork; but he had since been removed in disgrace). There was an endless military procession to the repetition of a funeral march, the square itself being filled with soldiers and citizens. The gun carriage arrived bearing the deceased leader in an open coffin, heavily made up. Speeches were made by Politburo members. Then the coffin, followed by the relatives, was carried by pall bearers round the side of the mausoleum where it was buried close to the Kremlin wall to the sound of gunfire.

Then we went to the great gold and glass hall inside the Kremlin where we stood in a long line without refreshment to convey condolences and meet the new leader, Mr Andropov. During all this time we rubbed shoulders with or chatted to people as varied as Mrs Gandhi, Pierre Trudeau, Vice-President Bush, Fidel Castro and Yasser Arafat. On this occasion the British contingent consisted of Francis Pym as Foreign Secretary, Michael Foot as Leader of the Opposition, and me.

After a welcome warming drink and lunch at the embassy, we all went off to separate meetings or telephone chats as was customary at working funerals. Michael Foot and I were given an hour free with a Russian car and driver at our joint disposal. We went sightseeing, Michael also I think having been there only once before and some time previously. He said he had never seen the magnificent Moscow underground stations, built like palaces. I asked the driver if he would stop to let us look at one, which meant he let us out of his sight for the only time that afternoon. We went down the escalator and then like a pair of truanting schoolboys sneaked on to a train, travelled one stop to admire the next sation, and then back again to emerge into the daylight expressing enthusiasm to our minder.

It was about this time that my staff shamefacedly admitted to a classic office 'cock-up'. Before the coming of the word processor, the only way we could cope with the volume of correspondence, especially on controversial issues which generated even greater post bags, was by having a standard letter for general issues, which I would 'top and tail' to instruction. I had come in for some criticism for attending the funeral of the Soviet leader Brezhnev, who very much symbolized the old-style and repressive Soviet system. In response to those critics I had a standard letter. In the aftermath of the Falklands War, also during 1982, I came under fire for not attending the Falklands Victory Parade through the City of London. While I meant no disrespect to our armed forces (and had attended a Thanksgiving Service in St Paul's Cathedral), I found the triumphalism of the parade unappealing. After all, the Services had had to clear up the mess left by the politicians and did so with great professionalism. But the loss of lives on both sides and the huge waste of resources involved as a result of political bungling was not, in my view, a cause for particular celebration. And so I again had a standard letter explaining my position. I am afraid that an irate retired Colonel in Surrey, loudly protesting at my absence from the parade, mistakenly got the Soviet funeral standard letter instead. With mounting apoplexy, the Colonel would have read that my attendance did not 'imply approval', that I found the whole affair 'macabre and grisly', but that I took advantage of the occasion to 'renew my personal contact with those from foreign capitals who were also in attendance'.

The Andropov funeral was in 1984. This time the British contingent was Thatcher, Howe, Denis Healey representing the Opposition, Steel and Owen. Having been through this before I went equipped with Damart underwear and advised the others accordingly. It was so cold I thought my feet were blocks of ice. As the open Andropov casket came by us I saw that the morticians had done a magnificent job. I whispered to David Owen: 'He looks a lot better than the last time I saw him.' We said hello to the new boss, Mr Chernenko.

On our return to the embassy to thaw out for lunch, I realized that Mrs Thatcher was sleeping in the bed Judy and I had been in a fortnight before. I wished I had left a pea under the mattress. David Owen and I were billeted with two of the attachés but meantime were given a room to change out of our winter woollies before lunch. We were in the middle of struggling out of our long johns when Denis Healey blundered in by mistake. His vulgar humour got the better of him: 'Ho, ho, ho, so this is what the Alliance is all about.' After lunch the three of us were shown the various attempts by the Soviets to 'bug' the embassy which included tunnelling extraordinary devices capable of listening to the keys of the typewriters and hence reproducing correspondence. A secret briefing took place in a secure padded cell floating like a submarine in a basement.

A year later we were back again to bid farewell to Mr Chernenko. Neil Kinnock came, but otherwise the same British cast list attended. I was the only one with the dubious distinction of completing the hat trick. For some reason we had to get from the Commons to Heathrow in a hurry and so a military helicopter was standing by at Wellington Barracks, across from St James's Park and Buckingham Palace, to whisk us out to the VC10 at Heathrow. Military versions of helicopters, as I've found the world over, are much noisier than civilian ones. No weight is wasted on sound-proofing or padding the interior. We were each handed a pair of white linen-covered heavy earmuffs. Mrs Thatcher waved them away – they would spoil the coiffure for the cameras at the airport. As we took off in a roar, Kinnock removed my left ear muff and shouted: 'That's her, you see, go deaf for Britain.'

This time, as the freezing veteran of these events, I took not only my extra underwear but my hip flask full to the brim with good malt whisky. After a couple of hours in Red Square, I passed it round the company, including one or two African chums, and all accepted a grateful swig except for Prime Minister Thatcher, who declined the offer politely. This time President Mitterrand and UN Secretary-General Pérez du Cuéllar were with us in the queue to meet the next incumbent, Mikhail Gorbachev. We had of course met him before and he looked like lasting longer than his two predecessors. At the time I wrote about the funeral in the *Scotsman*:

Female privilege still rules in the USSR. When we arrived inside the Kremlin, we were all swept up the grand staircase in the wake of Mrs Thatcher, passing all other visiting Prime Ministers, Presidents, foreign ministers and others dutifully standing in the queue. While doing so, we each shook hands with the different figures each of us recognized, though seeing foreign counterparts out of context makes instant identification rather difficult. It was like shaking hands with people passing on an escalator. To each we muttered apologies for queue breaking and extolled the advantages of having a female head of delegation.

I also referred to Mr Gorbachev, the new Soviet leader:

Gone is the stiff and wooden delivery of texts across the table. Instead he listens to argument, joins in and argues back with remarkable ease, in spite of the need for an interpreter. He is a warm man, unlike the cold fishes I have met in the Kremlin, and this may prove to be of crucial importance, for so also is President Reagan. I have a hunch, therefore, that if a long-overdue summit is now arranged between the two superpower leaders they may hit it off rather well. This could, in turn, provide the much-lacking political motor drive behind the Geneva arms control negotiations.

Indira Gandhi's funeral was very different. For one she had been tragically assassinated. And, secondly, it was held in baking heat and we sat on comfortable white sofas in the sun in front of the funeral pyre. Earlier we had paid our tributes as she lay gracefully in state at her house with rickety air conditioners dripping water round the bier to prevent rapid decomposition. They dripped surplus water into strategically placed tumblers.

Our party was joined by Princess Anne, who was on a Save the Children Fund visit when the assassination took place; by ex-premier Jim Callaghan, who also happened to be in India; and by Denis Thatcher. As we stood in the High Commissioner's elegant drawing room, one of the military was making a fuss about the excessive weight of the wreath the Princess would lay on our behalf. 'Have you ever,' she snorted, 'tried carrying a bale of hay?' – which put him neatly in his place. The directions for attending and leaving the funeral were vague, unlike the Soviet precision. 'I tell you, David,' said Denis Thatcher, glass in hand, 'it will be one big almighty balls-up.' We were shipped to and fro in a series of commandeered street buses lacking some windows. As Jim Callaghan and I grabbed a front seat together, he suggested I give up mine to an elderly oriental gentleman I did not recognize, but whom Jim knew – the Japanese Prime Minister Nakasone.

At another point, in the crush to board the very high-slung vehicles, the one I was trying to get on started to move off, threatening to run over the diminutive woman in front of me. I hoisted her into the vehicle and clamboured in alongside. She turned to thank me. It was Mother Teresa of Calcutta. On the return journey the bus in front of us, which included Mrs Thatcher among its passengers, got stuck in the sand. Denis's prophecy, which I had thought straight out of a *Private Eye* letter, was amply justified.

In the warm sunshine of Delhi, in the spacious enclosure for foreign guests, it was possible, while waiting for the cortege to arrive, simply to wander about talking to anyone you wished. What makes life confusing in these circumstances is trying to recognize people out of their own contexts, and to remember where you last met them. 'Ah David,' said somebody, 'you haven't met our Prime Minister.' I then had what I hoped was a semi-intelligent couple of minutes' conversation with the said Prime Minister, at the end of which I still had no idea which country he governed.

Only at State funerals, coronations, presidential inaugurations and the like is it possible for the world's politicians to meet each other totally informally, without advisers, and without elaborate and stifling preparations. It is a pity that we cannot devise more such opportunities for dialogue, without demanding more funerals.

One hazard of visits to the Soviet Union – especially that in 1984 – was the quantity of vodka expected to be consumed at official functions. When the Supreme Soviet gave us a splendid formal lunch we could not help reflecting on the difference between the magnificence of the caviar and de luxe vodka and the queues in boring food shops on the Moscow streets. One was expected at each toast to gulp a small glass of vodka, to take a delicate sip being regarded both as effete and insulting. Over the years, especially when due to make speeches, I have developed various techniques for getting rid of unwanted alcohol. I rarely drink before a meal, going for non-alcoholic drinks if possible, and if not standing by the nearest flower vase. During meals, glasses can be switched with friendly neighbours or simply left standing full, but this did not work in the Soviet Union. When the British Ambassador gave a 'return' lunch for me, which started very late, it went on until after four o'clock with our Russian guests downing endless glasses. One of the Gorbachev reforms has been to cut out compulsory official alcoholism.

Something of the same problem afflicted us on a visit to China in 1981. Judy and I went as guests of Chairman Hua Guofeng, who had invited us during his state visit to Britain. Unfortunately he had been deposed by the time we got round to arranging the visit, which gave it a somewhat unusual comic aspect that lasted throughout our two weeks' stay. The Chinese ambassador, Ke Hua, had kept pressing for the visit via our friends, Simon and Rina Tanlaw, Lady Tanlaw herself being Malaysian Chinese. They were to accompany us, which meant that we would have our own interpreter as well as good company.

On our first day in Peking, Judy and I kept being ushered in and out of an enormous black limousine laced with chrome outside and curtains inside. It was like being in a mobile ballroom with lots of red velvet seats. Our accompanying Foreign Office official sat up front beyond the glass, next to the driver, while a girl interpreter sat with the Tanlaws in a large, ugly, green saloon following behind.

I suggested that there was plenty of room to spare for us all in the limousine and asked Simon and Rina to join us, at which point the official, whose command of English was rudimentary, went beserk and shouted: 'No, no, no – this car for Right Honourable Steel and wife – other car for "and party".' He bowed, gesticulated and more or less pulled them away from our car and into the inferior one. From then on we addressed the Tanlaws simply as 'and party'.

I suppose I ought to write lyrically about the glories of China. We travelled to Shanghai, the garden city of Hangchow, Canton, the Great Wall of China, and via a steamer on the Yangtse River. We saw the Forbidden City and the

Summer Palace, as well as various Buddhist temples; we visited a hospital to see acupuncture in action, a school, a rural farm and a carpet factory, where we bought a small silk carpet which adorns our bedroom.

At the farm, where we saw ducks waddling in line to a force-feeding machine, we were glad we had had our delicious whole Peking duck dinner the night before.

But the abiding memories are of the endless episodes of near-farce. At one remote place Judy took herself off to one of the public communal lavatories, which were universally disgusting. She came back to recount how it was a social centre with open cubicles. No sooner had she squatted over one of the drains than a group of chattering Chinese arrived to see this white lady joining them. On another occasion, while travelling overnight by train, the same Chinese official sought to give me earnest advice on the use of the 'hole in the floor' loo at the end of the carriage. It seemed to be important whether one faced or was back to the engine. The four of us were reduced to helpless tears, while he hesitated between stony face and artificial laughter.

China was in transition, emerging from the terror of the Cultural Revolution and Red Guard period. Looking out of the hotel windows in the morning, you could see literally thousands of Chinese men and women dressed in identical blue Mao jackets, bicycling to work about ten abreast. From a height they looked like scurrying ants. The Foreign Office had given three important pieces of advice in their briefing: 1) Do not ask after Chairman Hua – do not even mention him (difficult, since he was technically our host); 2) Do not mention the Gang of Four; 3) Do not attempt to make jokes. The first I managed, just.

On the third I fell down hopelessly at a banquet given by the Mayor of Shanghai. There were to be no speeches and so I must have consumed too many of the powerful cups of warm rice wine, known as Mau Tai, which the Chinese treated in the same way that the Russians did their little glasses of vodka. The Mayor spoke no English and even via the interpreter perched behind us seemed to have nothing to say. We were served halfway through the meal with a bean soup. I asked what it was. On being told, I foolishly forgot the Foreign Office advice and merrily asked the interpreter if the Mayor had heard about the exchange in a Chinese restaurant: 'Waiter, waiter, what on earth is this?'

'It's bean soup, sir.'

'I don't wish to know what it's been – I want to know what it is now.'

Fifty minutes later, as the meal came to a close, I was still laboriously trying to explain a pathetic joke based on an English pun via a Chinese interpreter, with all those around joining with increasing curiosity.

The second rule went by the board when I was received with full pomp in the grand hall of the People's Palace in Peking by the senior Vice-President, Li Xiannian, then well into his eighties. As we waited in the anteroom I regaled the others with the incident when, calling on President Ceauşescu in Romania, I had been ushered into the main hall through similar huge gilt doors. I was then so blinded by the unexpected bank of television lights as I walked through the door that I could not see where the President was standing to greet me and the British Ambassador had to guide me by the elbow to the right spot.

There was no such problem here. We went in solemn procession and the two of us sat together in huge armchairs while the others were spread out round the enormous room as virtual spectators at our conversation. I had a discreet note of points I wanted to raise; but before I could do so, the elderly statesman had his list of things he wanted to ask me, among which, curiously, was the founding of the SDP, which had just taken place that month.

'Who is their leader?' he inquired politely.

'They don't have a leader,' I found myself saying before I could stop, 'they have a Gang of Four.' The British Ambassador rolled his eyes stoically to heaven.

The most striking memory of our tour was the visit we paid to an Easter church service. The Christian Church, having been forced underground, was just emerging, and the Ambassador advised that it would indeed be interesting to see how our official hosts would react to a request to include a church service on our programme. We made the request, explaining that Easter was an important occasion for us. After three days our custodian announced proudly that a church had been arranged in our printed programme. (We never got these for more than a day at a time, so it was something of a grand mystery tour, discussion of the day's programme being a regular source of further mirth.)

'What kind of church is it? Is it a Protestant church or a Catholic church?' I asked out of genuine interest.

'A Christian church,' was the pleased reply.

We were driven there but this was the only time we were otherwise unaccompanied. We were met by a white-robed priest. Inside the church was crammed. It looked – and I think was – Methodist. Half the congregation were clutching tape recorders to send the service to relations outside the capital.

A choir which had been rehearsing since it had assembled three months before gave renderings in Chinese from Handel's *Messiah*, one of my favourite choral works, and we joined in singing familiar Easter hymns, in our different languages. Older members of the congregation were openly weeping – it was their first Easter for about twenty years. The minister, he explained afterwards, had been in prison for his faith. It was a profoundly inspirational and uplifting occasion.

I think I would like to see the new China. I have never spent so many days in a country and come away feeling I knew as little about it as before I arrived. Inscrutable was the word.

We then spent a couple of days in the vibrant territory of Hong Kong for a quick round of meetings. I had last been there on my first foreign travel as a very green MP in 1965. This was supposed to have been a three-party delegation but the Labour MP – Shirley Williams – didn't turn up, leaving me travelling with Sir Nigel Fisher, who as Under-Secretary for the Colonies in the previous Tory Government had virtually been in charge of the place. I was simply swept along in his agreeable wake. The Governor took us for a Sunday trip on his palatial yacht, which still had the names of Princess Alexandra and Angus Ogilvy on the doors of two of the cabins from the previous weekend trip. We moored off one of the beautiful islands and a boat was lowered to take us ashore for picnic lunch.

'I'd like to swim ashore,' said I, getting ready to plunge off the deck.

'Hang on,' said the Governor, 'I'll get my ADC to go with you – there are a lot of very poisonous jellyfish around.'

As we swam to the island, the young captain struck one of these and spent the rest of the day in his bunk in agony. I was not a popular member of that afternoon's party.

This time, as Party leader, the Governor, Sir Murray Maclehose, invited me to join him on the steps of Government House at a garden party while the police band played the national anthem. Later they played one of the Selkirk Common Riding songs, which I thought a remarkably intelligent tribute to my presence until I remembered they had performed at the Edinburgh Tattoo, along with a Selkirk contingent, the year before.

I also addressed a lunch of the Hong Kong Reform Club, which is loosely attached to Liberal International. From my connections with the Hong Kong Chinese in 1965 and 1981 I must express some unease at our subsequent settlement with mainland China. Faith and hope more than charity seem to have been the moving spirits behind it.

My main overseas political involvement has been with Liberal International and with the European Liberal and Democrat Federation, of both of which I have been Vice-President. The main value has been the at first easy access to, and then friendship with, senior figures in NATO and EC governments through these organizations. I have mentioned the Canadians, but nearer home our colleagues in the German FDP – Hans Dietrich Genscher, now the longest-serving Foreign Minister in Europe, economic ministers Otto Graf Lambsdorff and Martin Bangemann, foreign-office ministers Helmut Schaefer and Irmgard Adam-Schwaetzer have all been firm associates. Various Dutch and Belgian ministers have come and gone in government, notably Willy de Clercq and Fritz Bolkestein. In Denmark Liberal leader Henning Christopherson became a European Commissioner and was followed by the urbane Uffe Ellemann-Jensen, who is currently Foreign Minister. In Italy Giovanni Spadolini of the Republican Party was Prime Minister and then Minister of Defence, while their sister Liberal Party contains the veteran and wise Senator Giovanni Malagodi, former Finance Minister and President of Liberal International. In France the political map is constantly changing, but Simone Veil, who was President of the European Parliament, is a regular attender at our meetings. Former Luxembourg Prime Minister Gaston Thorn became President of the Commission and was succeeded by Colette Flesch as Party leader. Of the new community members, Anibal Cavaco Silva is Prime Minister in Portugal and leader of the Social Democrats, while in Spain Antonio Garrigues-Walker led a brave Liberal faction now succeeded in a wider grouping by former Prime Minister Adolfo Suárez, the man who headed the first government after Franco. In Greece Liberal leader Nikitas Venizelos has been struggling to revive his party.

We have also had very good contacts with both parts of Ireland. The Alliance Party of Northern Ireland first under John Cushnahan and then John Alderdice as leader became a member of our European federation and therefore formal allies. I have twice been the only British Party leader to address a public meeting in Belfast, where I have been a regular visitor over the years in conditions of very tight protective security. One of those visits was to the King's Own Scottish Borderers' regiment stationed there early in the troubles, another to the Maze prison where we talked with one of the determined hunger strikers who died vainly a few days later.

Garret FitzGerald as Taoiseach we regarded as an honorary Liberal, though his Fine Gael party never linked with us. Instead the new Progressive Democrats under Desmond O'Malley have done so formally, while Charles Haughey and his Fianna Fáil party have always been open and welcoming.

Two of my happiest experiences are walking with O'Malley and Alderdice in the central shopping area of Belfast, unannounced because of security, but being warmly welcomed by an astonished public who are not used to seeing politicians from the UK, the province and the Republic on walkabout together. In the Republic at their Party's annual conference the three of us linked and raised hands together, giving an emotional climax to O'Malley's forceful televised speech. I have not the slightest doubt that however long it takes, such a co-operative cross-border, cross-sectarian approach to politics is the only hope for peace in that strife-torn island.

Outside the Community we have happy relations with the Swedish Liberal Party whose sole postwar Prime Minister, Olla Ullsten, came with me to Central America, while in Iceland our meetings have been hosted by Prime Minister Steingrímur Hermansson, whose moment of international triumph came with the Gorbachev/Reagan summit in Reykjavik.

I mention all of these to emphasize both the close international framework in which we operate and the fact that Liberals with far lesser domestic support than we enjoy in Britain are in coalition government in many countries. Indeed one of the outrages of the British electoral system is that we export a distorted delegation to the European Parliament at Strasbourg and unbalance the political groups there.

At an election meeting in Hamburg a few years ago, Hans Dietrich Genscher greeted me on the platform, saying 'He envies me my power, but I envy him his votes.' This was after we had polled 25 per cent in an election, whereas the FDP hovers in Germany between 5 and 9 per cent. I have never forgotten something Hans Dietrich said to me the first time we met. He was in London for a NATO ministerial meeting and I had just been elected Party leader. He said in his then-broken English, which has since been transformed, 'We German Liberals have so much to be grateful to you British for. After our defeat in the war, as the occupying power you insisted on three things for the new Federal Republic: you gave us one industry, one union and a system of worker participation in companies which have given us good industrial relations; you gave us a decentralized federal system of government so that not too much power is held in Bonn; and you gave us a system of proportional representation which has underpinned our new democracy. And you are so generous, you British: you gave us these three things and you have taken not one of them for yourselves.' That seems a sound thought on which to return to the domestic political scene.

9

THE FORGING OF THE ALLIANCE

Down a Chosen Avenue

I t became apparent early in the Thatcher Government that Britain was destined for a period of unyielding 'conviction' politics allied to monetarism. The search for consensus was over, and the Labour Party reacted with further lurches to the left. Within weeks of the election I was in Brussels with Russell Johnston and found myself bidden to dinner by Roy Jenkins. The arrangements were made on the telephone by our secretaries, and beyond accepting I was a little vague as to the reason for the invitation. I had, after all, on previous visits lunched or dined with British members of the Commission, usually in a small format. I remember Russell asking me if he could come as well. I said it was not my arrangement and that he should just ring up Roy's secretary (Sara Keays) and find out. The answer was clear. David Steel was expected for dinner *à deux* at Roy's house. Only then did I realize the nature of the event.

Jennifer, Roy's wife, was in London, and we settled down to a solitary but pleasant meal while we ruminated over the new political scene. In his *European Diary* Roy records:

David Steel to dinner. A rather gossipy talk with him, more about the election than the current and future political situation. He was pleased with his election campaign, although disappointed with the votes obtained, and went rather out of his way to tell me that as a result of it, he had become a major public figure, possibly the best known after Callaghan, Heath and Mrs Thatcher. In other words, he was, I think, underlining in the nicest possible way that in any future political arrangement he wasn't to be treated as an office boy.

He was, of course, accurate in his assessment. In an unusually quiet interlude during the 1979 campaign itself, I had bumped into both Roy and Peter Carrington at Reginald Maudling's memorial service in Westminster

Abbey. As a former Party Chairman whom I did not know all that well, Carrington was remarkably fulsome about the conduct and impact of our campaign, as was Roy himself. We had snatched survival out of the jaws of utter disaster, and from then on my own personal popularity ratings in the polls started to remain for several years consistently above all the other Party leaders. This was no time for a shrinking violet. I must have seemed rather pleased with myself, because I was.

My own feelings at the time were written at the end of my book *A House Divided*:

I do not see how any new 'centre party' could hope to beat the present system, though Liberals are always of course on the lookout for allies. The small 'l' Tories are at present wholly in the grip of the mad ideologues of the right. The Labour Party's intellectual right has lost Roy Jenkins to Europe, Shirley Williams to defeat, John Mackintosh through death, David Marquand to the academic world, Dick Taverne to new-party failure and Brian Walden to television. What is left is ill-equipped to oppose the strength of the hard left who at least have a credible if repugnant economic credo on offer.

So I was very much on the lookout for allies to break out of the Labour Party and link with us. This coincided with Roy's own mood and his contemplation of return to Britain in eighteen months' time. He had had contact with the same three of the four MPs who had privately seen me at various stages over the previous year or so – Reg Prentice, who had gone over to the Tories; Tom Ellis and Neville Sandelson, both of whom were to become founder members of the SDP; and Dick Crawshaw, a former Deputy Speaker.

At this stage the other major figures, Shirley Williams, Bill Rodgers and David Owen, were scarcely mentioned. I had no discussion with any of them, though Roy knew their moods well. The main interest in this meeting has been the oft-repeated assertions that Roy sought to join the Liberal Party and that I advised against his doing so. That is not so. (It is true, however, that a few months later I advised David Marquand against doing so but to wait instead to see if a new party would emerge.) Roy and I agreed that some new organization founded mainly on a massive exodus from the Labour Party but linking up in alliance with us would stand the best chance of 'breaking the mould' of British politics. The adhesion of two or three figures to the Liberal Party, while welcome, would have nothing like the same cataclysmic effect. Jeremy Josephs, who was my number two assistant in this Parliament, records in *Inside the Alliance* that it was 'an extraordinarily risky strategy for a Liberal leader to pursue; as John Pardoe later commented, only David Steel would have had the sheer effrontery to proceed in this way'.

My interest stemmed from the knowledge that we as a party were still not cracking the Labour strongholds. Something 'extra' was needed to achieve that. Roy and his colleagues, I thought, could provide it. Roy and I were clear as to our strategy. We would both continue our discussions with dissenting Labour MPs in private and maintain contact with a view to encouraging the formation of a new grouping. If, and only if, that failed then Roy on his return to Britain would probably formally join the Liberal Party but did not wish to play an active part in it. There we left it.

Towards the end of 1979 Roy was invited (as President of the European Commission) to give the annual televised Dimbleby lecture, which he entitled *Home Thoughts from Abroad*: he sent me the draft script – though I had no hand in it – and I realized immediately its political impact. It was a polished, elegant historic overview of the current state of British politics, calling for a strengthening of the political centre. In particular he pledged himself to electoral reform:

I am unfrightened by the argument against proportional representation that it would probably mean frequent coalitions – although not across the whole board of politics. I would much rather that it meant overt and compatible coalition than that it locked incompatible people, and still more important, incompatible philosophies, into a loveless, constantly bickering and debilitating marriage, even if consecrated in a common tabernacle.

The speech obtained massive coverage and comment in all the papers over the next four days. I was enthusiastic and stepped up my contacts with Labour figures, while some were remarkably ungracious. Shirley Williams, for example, said: 'I am not interested in a third party. I do not believe it has a future.' Jo Grimond, reviewing the lecture for the *Listener*, wrote bluntly:

If Mr Jenkins agrees, let him come down into the battle. Let him shove with the rest of us. All too many social democrats have gone off into banking, consultancy, TV, academic life etc. It is Mr Steel who has been in the scrum. Will they join him? The opportunity is indeed great ... but time is short.

In 1980 the realignment process really got under way.

In early January I lunched with Roy and Jennifer Jenkins at their home in East Hendred, Oxfordshire. Since by this time I had abandoned keeping my diary, I am happy to repeat his published *Diary* recollection, which is important because it demonstrated just how far our thinking had developed in that three-hour talk:

He perfectly understands that there is no question of me or anybody else joining the Liberal Party. He equally is anxious to work very closely, and possibly, if things went well, to consider an amalgamation after a general election. He would like the closeness at the time of the election itself to take the form not merely of a non-aggression pact, but of working together on policy and indeed sharing broadcasts, etc. He says that for his point of view he has overwhelming support in the Liberal Party.

He agreed with my view that a lot of the calculations were based too much on deciding how much water there was in the kettle, as it were, and how it could be shared out, whereas there was a lot more to be brought in from outside, people uncommitted to and uninvolved in politics. He agreed that it would not be sensible to think purely in terms of Liberals having Tory seats and our having Labour seats: this was too simple an approach. He fully accepted my point that if, which I was not committing myself to in any way, I wanted to fight a by-election during 1981, it would probably be much better to do this in a Tory-held seat than in a Labour-held seat, and indicated that his people would make way for me in those circumstances.

Altogether a thoroughly satisfactory talk.

Afterwards I wrote to thank Roy and Jennifer, drawing his attention to a poll which gave a putative alliance 29 per cent: 'If we can launch a campaign on that figure we can present a serious alternative government to the electorate.'

I also gave a speech to a huge audience at Edinburgh University, expressing the hope that Liberals would provide the core of a new party. An opinion poll in *The Times* declared I was favourite to lead it, but I pointed out I was already doing so. In a television interview I indicated that I had no objection to the name 'Liberal' being incorporated in the title of a new party – I was nearly ten years ahead of that happening.

In April I went one Sunday evening to dinner and to stay overnight with Roy and Jennifer at East Hendred, when we had a further long and mutually reinforcing talk. I am amused to see that Roy records in his *Diary* that I 'had quite a difficult hurdle to clear in the shape of a Liberal gathering at Worcester in May which would be less favourable than the Assembly in some way or other, but was fairly confident that he could get over it' – a clear reference to yet another troublesome meeting of the Party Council.

In April I also decided to enter the Labour Party debate rather cheekily by publishing a pamphlet called *Labour at 80 – time to retire*. I described the state of the Labour Party:

Labour is in a sorry state. No day goes by without the comrades savaging each other publicly about policy, about the constitution or about the leadership. Even the Left which knows what it wants and has a clear, albeit terrifyingly unattractive, alternative, is divided. Yet the only policy comes from the neo-marxists. The social democrats are shell-shocked. The apparatchiks of the know-nothing centre try to hatch up new deals with the trade unions and sink ever deeper in the swamps of political indebtedness. Membership has been declining for fifteen years. With the draining away of popular support more and more constituency associations are ready to fall like rotten apples into the hands of tiny groups of well-organized extremists. The only possible source of unity lies in opposition to the Conservatives, thus emphasizing the negativism of British politics which has already done so much to damage the country. Power, plain and simple, unalloyed by idealism or compassion, is the only fuel that can get the clapped-out machine on the road for another run at government.

And I went on to be very free in my advice to others in my conclusion:

There are other Social Democrats whom I respect, like Shirley Williams and Bill Rodgers, who are nearing the end of their tethers. I cannot judge what their final decision will be nor that of the handful of others who may follow their or Roy Jenkins' lead. If they had the courage of their convictions they could help change British politics. They should recall the example of those who went over from the Liberal Party to Labour fifty years ago or more, putting their commitment to reform and radicalism above party loyalty. What Haldane, Wedgwood-Benn, the Mallalieus and others did then, they should do now, helping to build up a broad-based reform movement rather than patching up a creaking and internally-divided party structure.

If we need a new start and new policies with a complete change in our national priorities, as I believe we do, we must first change our politics. A movement of reform coalescing around a resurgent Liberal Party is the first step. A great national government of reform is where it should lead. There is room in both for socially responsible Conservatives and radical Socialists alike. Indeed their support is essential.

I am convinced that simply to turn from the disaster of Thatcher conservatism back to the moribund Labour Party would be no answer at all. It would delay reform and deepen decline. Britain needs a new solution from its politicians. The Labour Party should take the hint of history and step aside to make way for new ideas and new leadership. It's time to retire.

In June Roy made his second *démarche* into the domestic political scene with an address to the Commons Press Gallery. This came two days after David Owen, Shirley Williams and Bill Rodgers – who were becoming known as the Gang of Three – said they would leave the Labour Party if it committed itself to withdrawal from the European Community. This was their toughest and most specific joint utterance. As spearhead of the Campaign for Labour Victory, they had little to show for their efforts against the drift to the left. David Owen had been shouted at during his courageous speech to the Labour Special Conference.

Roy's speech to the parliamentary press asserted his own wish to get involved on his return in six months' time in the cause of realignment and ended with an appeal for the 'rapid revival of a Liberal and Social Democratic Britain'. It was a good speech but suffered from too much anticipation. The *Economist* said it was all magnificent 'but it is not war'. I had to telephone him in Brussels a couple of days later to reassure him about its beneficial impact. He felt somewhat isolated and without clear collaborators – none of the others had contemplated launching a new Party.

In August I had a further telephone chat with Roy in which he describes me as 'remarkably bouyant'. This was because at the beginning of the month the Gang of Three had written an open letter to their Party colleagues in the *Guardian*:

If the NEC remains committed to pursuing its present course, and if, consequently, fears multiply among the people, then support for a Centre Party will strengthen as disaffected voters move away from Labour. We have already said that we will not support a Centre Party for it would lack roots and a coherent philosophy. But if the Labour Party abandons its democratic and internationalist principles, the argument may grow for a new democratic socialist party to establish itself as a party of conscience and reform committed to those principles.

To this I responded with some vigour and asperity in the same paper. I was getting a little impatient with their running at a different tangent from that which Roy and I were taking. I sent an advance copy with a private letter to Bill Rodgers saying that although it was mainly for public consumption I would 'very much welcome a chance of a serious private talk with you'. I sent copies also to David Owen and Shirley Williams. None of them responded and I suspect they regarded me as a meddler in their private struggle. My open letter led the *Guardian* front page and in its full text, occupying most of an inside page, I wrote:

The first and most vital step is to sort out what principles and policies 'a party of conscience and reform' – your own phrase, which aptly sums up what so many of us are seeking – should accept as its central core. It is of course rhetorical nonsense for Shirley to say that any new party would lack roots or a coherent philosophy. The Liberal Party and the Labour Party have both evolved out of the various strands of the radical tradition in British politics, with its concern for individual liberty, equality, and brotherhood. When the Liberal Party split at the end of the First

World War, the Labour Party became for a while the main standard-bearer of this tradition – though from the outset joined in an uncomfortable coalition with the authoritarian Left and the conservative elements within the trade union movement.

Labour has attempted – and failed – in the past 20 years to sort out its own internal contradictions. It is Labour which now lacks any coherent philosophy, while the intellectual ferment over how we adjust to a world of scarce resources, slow growth and continuing technological changes goes on outside. Your open letter, with its questioning of some of the orthodoxies of postwar socialism, moves the three of you some way towards the redefinition of priorities round which any successful radical government would have to be built. The Liberal Assembly this September will be debating many of the same issues, though happily unhampered by the constraints of the orthodox Labour definition of socialism.

The second step is to sort out the structure of such a radical coalition. Given the limitations of our electoral system, there would be nothing worse than the emergence of two or three competing progressive parties, each with overlapping philosophies and policy proposals, all appealing to the same sections of the electorate. That would guarantee another Conservative victory, even on a reduced proportion of the vote. We are forced therefore to combine if we would succeed.

It's sad but not surprising, that it remains taboo within Labour's internal debate, however bitter it becomes, to mention the term 'Liberal'. . .

It is time surely for you to end your dialogue with the deaf and start talking to us with a view to offering a credible alternative government to the electorate in 1983 or 1984.

I signed it 'Yours fraternally, David Steel'.

In the 1980 Liberal Assembly in Blackpool the following month, I took the chair at a fringe meeting on realignment addressed by David Marquand. In my own speech as leader I openly trawled for a new alliance:

It is *our* Party, the Liberal Party, which holds the key. It is *we* who have to call into being a whole new world of politics to redress the balance of the old. To all those of whatever persuasion who share our analysis we should wish success in their courageous efforts to break up the monoliths of the old parties. But they should also know that without Liberal leadership, a Liberal agenda and Liberal commitment their efforts are doomed. The trail of British politics is littered with the skeletons of well-intentioned breakaway groups who tried to go it alone. With us they could make a formidable contribution. Without us they will perish.

The following Labour Party conference voted for unilateral disarmament, withdrawal from the EEC, and a change in leadership election procedure, including a trade-union block vote. In November Michael Foot was elected by 159 votes to Denis Healey's 129 as the new and unashamedly left leader of the Labour Party. Ten days later David Owen announced that he would not seek re-election to the Shadow Cabinet.

Early in December, Neville Sandelson wrote to me saying that he thought a meeting between me and the various discontented Labour elements would be premature – February, perhaps. Meantime Robert Maclennan took a personal initiative and sought a private meeting with me to discuss the political developments. Tom Ellis circulated to nine Labour colleagues and to me a paper calling for the formation of a Social Democratic Party. He stressed the need for it to be in alliance with the Liberal Party. The pace was hotting up.

There was frenetic activity at the beginning of 1981. On 12 January, a fortnight before yet another Labour special conference, I decided to launch publication of a Liberal ten-point plan for economic recovery which we had been carefully preparing since before the Christmas recess.

I had two objectives: to attract social-democratic approval in terms of policy and to reassert Liberal policy in its own right, since most of our publicity in the previous year had been comments on *Labour*'s policy and organization. This time, unlike my open letter in the *Guardian*, I circulated copies in advance to disaffected Labour members. I accompanied the well-received launch with a party political broadcast – yet another of Justin Cartwright's eyeball confrontations with the public. The whole initiative attracted a lot of favourable attention including public comments from Labour MPs Ellis, Horam, Wrigglesworth and Sandelson.

Roy Jenkins had ended his four-year semi-exile in Brussels on 6 January and in the week following my ten-point plan had two meetings with what now became the Gang of Four, at Shirley's and Bill's homes in London. They issued a pre-Wembley statement.

The fateful Labour conference duly met on 24 January and voted to establish an electoral college for the leadership with 40 per cent of the votes going to the trade unions. David Owen made a trenchant speech in favour of the principle of one man, one vote, and this rather than Europe became the top burning issue.

The next day the Gang of Four met, this time at David Owen's East End house, and in a declaration hence known as the Limehouse Declaration announced the formation of a Council for Social Democracy, still within the Labour Party. Nine Labour MPs gave it support.

In February I wrote a long letter to our candidates which I made public – again chivvying the process along – in which I welcomed this development and noted:

But their first step must be to leave the Labour Party and this they have not yet done. I hope they will soon. If they don't we must press on by ourselves. The public demand as shown in three opinion polls now is for an effective non-Socialist alternative to Thatcherism. If the politicians fail to meet this demand, it must not be the Liberals' fault.

Throughout the entire birth process of the SDP, my approach was publicly to embrace them, smother them with kindness and assume a putative alliance.

A telephone poll in the *Sun* actually gave a putative Liberal-Social Democrat linkup 51 per cent of popular support. A hundred prominent people backed the Council for Social Democracy in an advertisement in the *Guardian*. Shirley Williams resigned from Labour's National Executive while Tom Ellis and Dick Crawshaw both resigned the Labour whip.

In March the intention to form the SDP was made clear. Christopher Brocklebank-Fowler, the only Tory MP to do so, crossed the floor to join it, and amid great razzmatazz it was launched on 26 March. There was colossal public goodwill and some attempts at wrecking ribaldry. Roy Hattersley said it stood for 'the need to build a Britain free for credit-card holders' while Simon Hoggart waspishly described them as 'London intellectuals surveying a declining Britain from the comfort of Holland Park'.

The following weekend in April there occurred one of these seminal events which happen out of the public eye and largely by accident. Hitherto my own involvement had been limited to long-term discussions with Roy Jenkins and some of the other participants plus public declarations and harrying of the Gang of Three. I had not actually had the chance to discuss the situation with them at all, apart from a very public appearance with David Owen on BBC1's *Question Time* shortly after the unveiling of the Limehouse Declaration. Robin Day in the chair encouraged it to become almost a public negotiation and it was the only occasion on which I had at that time any discussion at all with David himself.

But suddenly I found myself with Shirley Williams and Bill Rodgers at the annual Anglo-German conference in the attractive Rhine village of Königswinter, an occasion at which we were all intermittent but faithful attenders. Richard Holme and John Roper were there and the five of us arranged a lunch together in the Rheinhotel restaurant. They were eager for a discussion and excited by the success of their launch, but had clearly given little thought as to the next step – the formation of an alliance. There were doubters in both parties, including Cyril Smith, who had advocated their being strangled at birth.

Now for the first time we got down to brass tacks. On one of the paper napkins Richard drew up what became known to insiders as the Königswinter Compact. We decided there would have to be a joint publication of principles for an agreement – which seemed unlikely to encounter much difficulty – to be followed by an accord to fight alternate by-elections if possible and then to get a mechanism for deciding who fought which seat at the general election. At this time I had in mind that the SDP might fight a hundred constituencies in all, while Bill was insistent that their eventual share-out should be nearer 50 per cent of the total candidatures. I much later discovered that Bill was coming under fire from within the SDP for limiting the SDP's position only to an equal share-out of the seats. Talking to Kenneth Harris, David Owen commented on Bill Rodgers's public declaration on the equal share-out of seats which had 'never been discussed and many of us had a far larger number of seats in sight'.

After lunch we cheerfully went for a walk in the spring sunshine up the hill to the Drachenfels Castle. As we left the hotel Shirley sweetly inquired of Richard: 'Does this mean I'll have to support proportional representation?'

Journalists and other MPs watching at a distance realized something was happening but we all kept quiet. Hugh Stephenson in *Claret and Chips* records: 'That Königswinter lunch and the walk that followed it were the moment at which the leadership of the respective parties became engaged to each other at least in a contract to pursue seriously a pre-election alliance, though not a merger itself. It remained to be seen how their rank and file would take to the idea.' On their return to London Bill and Shirley did not have an easy time in the National Committee of the SDP. This had been a wholly fortuitous and private initiative. David Owen and others were very hostile to what they regarded as premature and unauthorized discussion.

In the May round of local elections we fared extremely well and by 16 June we had our formal declaration of principles ready printed. It was a comprehensive but thinnish seven-paragraph document entitled *A Fresh Start for Britain*. We launched it amid much media hype outside the room in Dean's Yard where we had been meeting as a small working party, ostensibly to draft it. It was in fact written by David Marquand and Richard Holme and touched up by our press officers, Paul Medlicott and John Lyttle. Stephenson unkindly describes Shirley and me as 'sitting on the grass in the middle of the quadrangle behind Westminster Abbey looking like superannuated student lovers'. It certainly made a famous photograph.

In the *Scotsman* a few months earlier James Naughtie had written: 'David Steel is in a curious position these days. Instead of trying, sometimes desperately, to make things happen they are happening all around him. He is at the still point of a turning world.'

The next 'happening' was the by-election at Warrington, a 'safe' Labour seat where the sitting member became a judge and where we did not have any significant record. If the SDP wished to fight with one of their stars – we expected Shirley – the Liberals were happy to support them. To our surprise Shirley declined and the unexpected figure of Roy Jenkins entered the lists instead. An industrial seat in the North did not seem his natural stamping ground. Yet it was here that he gathered the affection of the Liberal Party beyond the leadership. His brave risk in fighting a seat with no obvious track record and his commanding conduct of the campaign with Alec McGivan as agent, and his especial welcome to campaigning Liberals from Merseyside and elsewhere endeared him for the the first time to grass-roots Liberals. 'Week by week,' writes Stephenson, 'David Steel teased his party down his chosen avenue.' Warringon marked the turning point where I no longer had to do this on my own.

I managed to get Roy to woo Cyril Smith into speaking. I addressed a huge eve-of-poll rally with Roy in Warrington Town Hall; and in the course of the campaign I had my wallet stolen (it was found minus the cash) while visiting a funfair with him.

Bill Rodgers had asked for a clear run in the by-election for Shirley. With only 2,873 votes in the constituency at the previous election, we gave it to Roy on the unwritten understanding that the next by-election would be fought by a Liberal. Roy polled 12,521 as 'SDP with Liberal support' and slashed the Labour majority from over 10,000 to 1,700. In a brilliant speech after the count he declared: 'This is my first defeat in thirty years of politics and it is by far the greatest victory that I have ever participated in.' The media certainly treated it as such.

We went into the summer recess in high spirits and started planning the September Liberal Assembly. On the Saturday before the Assembly the Scottish Liberal Party, as so often, set the pace in agreeing the changes in their constitution to allow for the formation of an alliance, backing the SDP in some seats.

The debate at the Assembly itself was overshadowed by a remarkable 'fringe' meeting in the main hall in Llandudno on the eve of the Assembly, at which Roy and Shirley were guests with Jo Grimond and me speaking at a highly emotional packed rally. All of us were in top form. *The Times* led the next day with a story written by four reporters headed 'rapturous welcome for SDP leaders on eve of alliance debate'. The previous day their lead story had all been about how I was marching too far ahead of my troops.

That meeting clinched the debate. It marked 'the historic turning point in the fortunes of the Liberal Party', according to one press report. *The Times* referred to that 'remarkable meeting at which they instilled genuine warmth, even fervour into the proceedings so that the decision of the conference became almost a formality'. We won the vote, at the end of the debate introduced by William Wallace, by about 1,500 to 112. Bill Rodgers attended that debate and said he was sure the SDP would endorse the decision at their conference. The one member of the Gang of Four missing at this euphoric event was David Owen. In his book he reveals his distance from and disapproval of the whole occasion:

At the Liberal Party Conference in Llandudno in September, a packed fringe meeting was addressed by Shirley Williams, Roy Jenkins, Jo Grimond and David Steel. This fringe meeting circumvented the decision taken by the Steering Committee the previous May that no representative of the SDP should speak at any regional or national Liberal conference. In fact, Shirley had only just been given permission by the Steering Committee to speak at any fringe meeting, on condition that she spoke by herself and for herself. The Committee wanted to avoid the SDP becoming too closely associated with the Liberals at this stage. When they agreed that Shirley could speak, there was no question of Roy Jenkins and David Steel being present at this meeting. In short, the SDP Steering Meeting had expected Shirley's fringe meeting to be low key. It was nothing of the sort.

At the end of my own address to the Assembly I used the now oft-quoted words to ringing cheers: 'Go back to your constituencies and prepare for government.' (At a memorably funny fringe revue a couple of years later, this was translated into: 'Go back to your constituencies and bloody well stay there' – which was a measure of the mixed affections held between the party and their leader.)

The SDP at their rolling conference by train duly addressed the concept of an Alliance and by mid-October we had agreed guidelines for dividing up the constituencies, a task which a working party headed by me and Bill Rodgers undertook. Negotiations were to be conducted on a regional basis.

At around this time I held secret talks at their request with a small group of Conservatives who were contemplating leaving their Party and joining the Liberal part of the Alliance. In the event none of the MPs involved actually did so but their confidence in my discretion remains, since their identity never became known.

We had another by-election problem. One arose in Croydon North West which under the tacit agreement was ours to fight. But we had very few members and again a poor track record. Shirley was willing to fight. I had to try to persuade our previous candidate who had polled only 4,000 votes in 1979 to stand aside since I did not believe he could possibly win.

My efforts to dissuade candidates from standing were far from being the most successful feature of my leadership. I had already tried this in Bermondsey, where for a long time we had anticipated a by-election to be caused by Bob Mellish's appointment to the London Dock Development Corporation and to the House of Lords. Knowing this was in the offing, we decided to move in a young barrister, Simon Hughes, who worked in a law centre in the area and who had the obvious capacity to attract and build up a good fighting team of volunteers. The previous candidate was a decent, dozy middle-aged man who had made little impact. Unsuccessful efforts were made to get him to step aside.

Eventually Clement Freud, who was chairman of our by-election unit at the time, came to see me: 'There is only one way to get rid of him. You will have to invite the man and his wife to tea here and persuade him yourself of his duty to the cause.' Under protest I agreed. Tea was duly served in my office and I stressed his great service to the party ... the need to step up fresh activity in anticipation of the by-election ... younger blood ... pressures of by-election campaign as against a general election ... and so on. At the end they left politely.

A week later I asked Freud the outcome. 'Er, well,' he muttered, 'I'm afraid it didn't quite work as I had planned. His wife is going round Bermondsey saying that so highly is her husband regarded by the party nationally, they were actually invited to tea in the leader's office at the House of Commons!' At the selection meeting he beat Simon Hughes, who had failed to collect together a sufficient vote. Fortunately, so long was Mellish's departure delayed that Simon fought the GLC election in the constituency and later won the selection for the by-election itself.

Against this background I came to the problem of Bill Pitt in Croydon. He was a London activist and various feelers were put out to him through the Party to stand aside. (This included one phone call to him by David Alton from my flat. The wires were hot as I sat listening to one side of a fruitless conversation.) Instead he gathered all the members of his association in his house and not surprisingly won their backing. Again the leader's intervention was required. This time a few of us took the candidate to lunch in a private room at L'Amico's. We tried to kill him with flattery, food and drink. He politely discussed every aspect, listened to our arguments in favour of Shirley and said he would consider them with his local members.

In fact he had no intention of doing so. Instead he astutely exploited all the massive publicity surrounding the moves to get Shirley in. He gave endless interviews locally and nationally. Having been a total nonentity, he was transformed by our efforts into a local hero. The by-election writ had not yet been issued and he was not the adopted candidate, so the media could give him extensive coverage. On BBC *Newsnight* he was asked if he would consider standing aside for a national figure. To which he replied: 'but I am one now'. The picture in Croydon of 'our Bill' bravely resisting the machinations of Steel, Williams etc. gave him a headstart in the actual by-election in October. He coasted home with a surprise majority of over 3,000.

He had also got the Liberal Party Council, of which he was a member, to pass an emergency resolution by 10 to 1 backing his candidacy. Now the mood in the Party was going to be more difficult. If Bill Pitt could win Croydon, we could, some argued, win anywhere. In fact, apart from my unwitting local assistance, the significant factor was that he was the first person to stand and be elected under a 'Liberal-SDP Alliance' label, a step taken at our initiative. He had the support on platforms of all the SDP heavyweights.

Jeremy Josephs says in his book:

There was understandable concern in the SDP camp that Steel could not stand up to a local Liberal association in which there were merely some forty members. David Owen was furious. In private he made it clear that in his view Steel ought to be vested with constitutional powers with which he could then deal with troublesome associations not toeing the leader's line. Yet to even contemplate such a notion revealed a profound ignorance about the fiercely autonomous and independent nature of a local Liberal association.

There was a new line-up at the Cenotaph in Whitehall that November of 1981. Michael Foot made his first appearance there as Leader of the Opposition, and there occurred one of those strange episodes which can be so accidentally and disproportionately damaging to political reputation. He appeared for the wreath-laying ceremony alongside all the black overcoats in a short, green, duffle-type coat. I have always worn a morning coat without overcoat and every year received letters complimentary about my appearance. It is a major national occasion of great importance obviously to many people. As we were about to leave the Home Office I said: 'Michael, you're not going to wear that coat, are you?'

'What's wrong with it?' he said. 'My wife just bought it last week.'

'No doubt,' I said, 'but it doesn't seem very suitable for this occasion. On your head be it.' It was. The criticism varied from accusations of being disrespectful to wild cartoons.

No sooner had Bill Pitt been adopted in Croydon than a vacancy occurred in Crosby, Lancashire. Again we started to persuade the previous candidate,

Tony Hill, to stand down, on the grounds that it was the SDP's turn. David Alton as the nearest MP was making good progress on this when suddenly, possibly because of the Croydon experience, Shirley announced from the SDP conference platform her readiness to fight the seat. This annoyed me and the Crosby Liberals. I gently rebuked her in my fraternal speech to the conference next day. Fortunately thanks to the good grace of Tony Hill, who had polled a respectable 9000 votes at the previous election, the upset was overcome and she was selected as the agreed candidate, with Alec McGivan again as at Warrington being drafted in as agent. It was another smashing Alliance campaign and in November she romped home by 5,000 votes in a seat where the previous Tory majority was nearly 20,000.

A week later the *Economist* front cover featured a staged photograph of Roy, Shirley and me under the heading 'Her Majesty's New Opposition'. In December 1981 we reached our highest opinion poll ratings. We ended the year in confident spirits.

Meantime the seat negotiations for the general election had been dragging on round the country. They consumed a vast amount of the time of able people locally and nationally. They were frankly wearisome and debilitating. The SDP tended to regard the high autumn poll ratings as mainly due to them – which was true – while Liberals pointed to our superior numbers on the ground and electoral management. There was an understandable reluctance to hand over well-organized seats to the newcomers.

The essential difference between the parties, however, lay in the nature of their make-up. For us the negotiation guidelines were recommendations which had to be carried by local persuasion. For the SDP they were orders handed down from on high. Any local objections were considered intolerable, even by those with whom we worked well. There was a particular problem in accommodating sitting Labour MPs now in the SDP but against whom Liberals had fought, in seats such as Greenock where the capable and personable former minister Dickson Mabon became their leading Scottish recruit. This was especially so in cases where the MPs had jumped ship in desperation at deselection rather than out of conviction, a trend against which Alan Beith and I had both publicly and privately warned the SDP.

Bill Rodgers was the member of the gang of four with the difficult task of leading his side in the negotiations. At the start of the Christmas recess he blew his top and unilaterally suspended the negotiations.

Later he gave his own explanation, saying that the key question was not if there should be a row, but when it should take place: 'I judged that an early row would clear the air and give an impetus to progress, while a later one, well into 1982, would be profoundly damaging.' With that presumably in mind, he went public in the *Observer* just after Christmas, complaining about the unfairness and difficulties of the allocations. I believe he made a grave error of judgement in doing so, because any public row at any time was bound to damage the successful image of the whole alliance.

I therefore sought to defuse the row as quickly as possible. Adopting the Harold Macmillan technique of 'little local difficulty', I quickly changed into a woolly sweater on learning that an ITN crew was on its way to Ettrick Bridge, sat in my armchair by a roaring log fire and suggested Bill must have had too many mince pies for Christmas. That left the SDP looking like the troublemakers and indeed, though I understood their exasperation – which I sometimes shared – at Liberal procedures, these were rooted in democracy. I began to find dealing with a Gang of Four somewhat frustrating. Bill was successfully upping his profile in the gang while no single person was in leadership authority.

Our poll ratings started to fall immediately. The damage was real and was only contained by the pending by-election at Glasgow Hillhead, which Roy wished to fight, and by the lack of any personal rancour between me and Bill. The tone of our discussions was well reflected in Bill's later comment that he accepted my diagnosis of the problem as a hiccup but he remembered that a Pope had once died of hiccups. We arranged a well-publicized *rapprochement* at an obscure London restaurant. When its identity later became known, the *Spectator* carried a cartoon by Heath of a couple at table looking at the menu and saying to the waiter: 'We'll have whatever Steel and Rodgers had – we're trying to save our marriage.'

David Owen writes critically of that period: 'Too many of us in the SDP were afraid of a crunch and a public row.' So was I, and we were right.

Looking back over this episode, I have no doubt at all that the SDP should have been much more relaxed about seats and numbers. This was where *our* strength lay. Theirs lay in their top leadership. No Liberal in either House had been even a junior minister – except the current Lord Mayhew – and in any potential government they had not only the Gang of Four but a group of experienced parliamentarians. But a Party which relied on a mainly postal membership had no chance whatever on its own of making an electoral breakthrough. We made an ideal alliance so long as we capitalized on and combined our different assets.

An example of that successful combination came to hand in Hillhead. It was now in theory our turn to fight after Crosby, but Roy was most anxious to join the other three in the House, and we all wanted him there. Warrington showed what he could do in an unlikely seat. Yet Glasgow Hillhead was one of our few well-organized Glasgow seats with elected councillors and an able

Middle East tour, September/October 1980.

Left Meeting with Yasser Arafat in the basement of an anonymous house in Damascus, Syria.

Below: With Shimon Peres in Israel.

With the late President Sadat in his domestic palace, Egypt.

'Her Majesty's New Opposition'. With Roy Jenkins and Shirley Williams on the front of *The Economist*, December 1981.

'Superannuated student lovers'? With Shirley Williams, launching the Alliance's formal declaration of principles, *A Fresh Start for Britain*, 16 June 1981.

Tinkering with my pre-war Austin 7.

With President Mugabe in Zimbabwe, 1986.

Below As Rector of Edinburgh University in 1982. From left to right: Lord Provost Morgan, Chancellor Prince Philip, Principal Sir John Burnet.

With George Bush, then Vice-President, in February 1983.

Posing with Billy in a fishing boat for a *Daily Mail* photographer on holiday in Tenerife, October 1983.

'As you may have heard, I took a few days off this Summer. . . .' Rory and Judy join me on the platform after my address to the Assembly in 1983.

A meeting of the kitchen-cabinet at Ettrick
Bridge. Rory, Judy and I having coffee.

Meeting with Mikhail Gorbachev on his visit
to London, December 1984.

Right Alliance press conference, June 1987.

Left With David Owen, General Election campaign, 1987.

Going to vote in Ettrick Bridge with Judy, Catriona and the faithful Jill, polling day, June 1987.

Above With Judy and the new puppy, Lucy, a flat-coat retriever, 1988.

Below Cherrydene: 'the best-known political house in the Borders'.

prospective candidate in Chic Brodie. But our poll ratings had now slipped 10 per cent and it was by no means certain that he would win, though I think he might just have done. In any case both Chic and the local Liberals decided to back Roy. It was a most difficult campaign because it was a three-way fight between Tory, Labour and us with regular opinion polls giving different forecasts. It became clear that Roy's lack of Scottishness was a handicap and I was dragged in more frequently than normal for the campaign, addressing a letter for example to every household. A week before polling day, Roy and I spoke at a successful meeting and went on to dine together afterwards when we received the latest poll putting Roy third. I could see this shook Roy and I left for the night train very depressed. He fought brilliantly on and when I returned for the eve-of-poll meeting it was a highly charged, overflowing event with people pressing at open windows. He won by 2,000 on 25 March. The next day we marched together in televised triumph down the packed hall of the Scottish Liberal Conference in St Andrews.

A week later the political momentum of the Alliance was stopped dead in its tracks by an event over which we had no control. Argentine forces invaded the Falkland Islands. Fate dealt us a cruel blow. With the sending of the task force, British domestic politics were virtually swept aside. We had to back our boys and our Maggie, leader of the War Cabinet.

Thus in May both in the local elections and in the next by-election at Beaconsfield where Paul Tyler had had high hopes of returning to Parliament, we advanced only marginally. These and two other by-elections in June at Mitcham and Coatbridge became almost khaki elections with Paul Tyler complaining that the Tories were 'hiding behind the marines'.

The Falklands War was to alter the entire political scene and crucially affect the general election a year later. There was an emergency debate, of which David Owen claims: 'the occasion gave me a tremendous, unexpected public role which I could not have foreseen'. That is not quite the full picture. As leader of the third party in the House the Speaker always gave me priority, but I decided that this made no sense for this occasion.

After all, David Owen had not only been Foreign Secretary, he had actually dealt with a previous Argentine threat to these islands. If I used my position, he would be called well down the list. Consistent with my view of the Alliance, I decided we should play our best card. He should speak up front with Russell Johnston, our foreign-affairs spokesman, adding a Liberal voice later in the debate. David appreciated the gesture at the time. He is a better speaker in the House than on the public platform and he was right to be pleased with his impact. He had a natural authority on the subject which paid us – but especially him – well. My critics say it was yet another example of my deference to the SDP leaders. I would say it was fully justified, from an Alliance point of view.

The episode deservedly enhanced David's reputation not just in the eyes of press and public but of his own party. He had a good war. The result was that the July leadership election in the SDP was not the walkover for Roy Jenkins which was previously expected. He won by a respectable margin of 26,000 votes to David Owen's 20,000.

Throughout the war David Owen and I together accepted private briefings on Privy Council terms from Margaret Thatcher, Francis Pym, the new Foreign Secretary, and John Nott, the Defence Secretary on the conduct of the war, (an offer refused by Michael Foot as Leader of the Opposition) but in the main I was happy for him to lead in public on this issue.

The war ended in the summer but the political repercussions persisted through the by-elections later that year in Gower, Peckham, Northfield and Queen's Park where we made further but unspectacular progress in adding to our votes. By the time of our autumn Assembly the alliance was smothered by the external effect of the Falklands and internal difficulties over seat allocation.

In my speech I criticized the post-Falklands outlook of the Prime Minister:

Whilst I realize that it does not do to be too fastidious in politics, I have to confess to a real sense of repugnance at the way the Prime Minister has tried to use the heroism of British servicemen in the Falkland Islands campaign to the greater glory of herself and her Party. As one Tory MP wrote candidly on Sunday: 'The party is high on the Falklands factor, the gift of courage and skill of our servicemen, which has served to mask for a time the realities of politics.'

But that it not enough for the Prime Minister. She has presided over a shambles of incompetence in her conduct of foreign policy and defence. Yet she has set out, quite deliberately, to cover up her Administration's nakedness by wrapping herself in the Falklands bunting, by belligerence of language, by a simplistic invocation of the Falklands spirit in the totally different sphere of industrial relations, and by a wish to turn a service of remembrance into a glorification of war. As she plans her parade she should learn there is a difference between patriotism and jingoism.

I had particularly objected to the way in which all the intelligence warnings prior to the Falklands invasion had been ignored, especially with the announcement of the withdrawal of HMS *Endurance*. She also had declared – ridiculously – that the wishes of the islanders would be paramount, a view which has resulted in the expenditure of £2,761 million and a freezing of non-diplomatic relations with the Argentine.

The Franks report of inquiry was in fact highly critical of long-term

Government policy was but packaged and presented in such a way that only the absence of specific blame for invasion that day was highlighted.

In 1980 Mrs Thatcher's Government had been contemplating handing over the islands on a lease-back arrangement to the military junta; yet Britain has failed to capitalize on one of the major benefits of the war – the collapse of that junta and the return to democracy. In 1985 I met President Raúl Alfonsín in the Argentine Ambassador's house in Madrid, just across the road from our own Ambassador's residence which I used as my base. We were both in Spain for the Liberal International Congress. We drew up a joint agreement which could fully restore relations and safeguard the interests of the islanders. The wishes of the British Parliament are paramount on the issue, but personal obstinacy on Mrs Thatcher's part prevents a sensible settlement even being considered.

Elsewhere in my Assembly speech I had to come back to our seat-negotiation problem:

But a great deal of our energy and concentration has been devoted during the year to the cumbersome, complicated and contentious task of allocating the constituencies between Liberal and SDP candidates to make our Alliance effective. It is worth stressing again that the vast majority of these 600 individual decisions were achieved amicably and democratically between our two parties at local level.

In about thirty cases we had real difficulty; the only surprise is that there were so few. At the end we have had to push through agreements with some acute disappointments in both parties, but more of course in ours where already adopted candidates have been asked to withdraw.

I understand the pain which these decisions have caused, but they had to be faced sometime and I want to say something to those candidates and those associations who will not be fighting the next election: when I listened to the outstandingly generous speeches made by some of the candidates personally affected through the week, I was proud to be leader of your Party. The role which you will play in providing the campaigning lead for our local government effort next May and for our SDP allies in the next general election is central to the success of our endeavour and therefore crucial to a liberal future.

Former party president and well-known psephologist Michael Steed had written: 'As the year 1981 had been the year of breakthrough, so 1982 became the year of bickering.' He gave his description of what happened in a pamphlet:

In the spring and summer of 1982, there were several voices from the areas in contention arguing for joint selection. Consideration of this had been promised in the guidelines, and an imaginative Alliance leadership could have set this up before May, and seen most of the dispute *en route* to resolution before the summer recess.

233

... Instead the Alliance leadership went for what was surely about the worst way of resolving the problems. Despite often mounting local pressure for something to happen in early summer 1982 (joint selection, re-negotiation or a final decision), the logjam was left to drift until the eve of the Liberal assembly in Bournemouth in mid-September. Then, despite all assurances about local negotiations and respect for the Liberal Party's constitution, the two party leaders made a much publicized personal deal. A few constituencies were exchanged or decided without arbitration, some to the Liberals and some to the SDP's benefit, but in the majority of disputed areas, David Steel simply agreed to what the SDP wanted (confirmation of provisional agreements).

This would probably have been acceptable to the Bournemouth assembly anyway, since a large majority of local Liberals were happy with the allocation in their own constituencies and there was a widespread will to bring the damaging dispute to an end. But to ensure ratification, the Liberal leadership adopted as their own the SDP's negotiating ploy – the argument that the Liberals had got the better of the deal. Some delegates believed it; some did not. But the media, having now heard that argument from both sides, seized on it, and repeated it as if it were established fact – and went on doing so despite the publication of analysis which showed it was untrue. Bernard Levin, in *The Times* of 24 August 1983, despite the actual June 1983 election results, was still able to say with a supreme arrogance of total ignorance: 'look at the consummate ease with which he (David Steel) diddled the SDP out of anything remotely resembling a fair share of winnable seats.'

... David Steel, who was blamed so much by Liberals for ineffectiveness in this situation, in another sense deserves credit. He sought the interests of the Alliance rather than, as urged on him, the interests of the Liberal party.

But the constant bickering was both damaging and enervating. One local negotiator – a councillor in the Midlands – was so fed up with endless complaining telephone calls that he half-seriously threatened to put on his answering machine: 'Don't blame me, I voted Pardoe.' It is difficult to convey adequately the mixture of anguish and tedium which these procedures involved, which was why I suggested joint selection of candidates; but this was met with no great enthusiasm in either party.

Since so much detail of individual seat problems has been published in various books, I have deliberately avoided mentioning any specific examples. It is perhaps interesting to note one of many letters I had to write – this to the forcibly deselected candidate in the next-door seat to mine, Dumfriesshire.

I promised to write to you formally after our Liberal/SDP meeting and before your Association Executive. I would like you to place this before them:

I am very sorry on both personal and political grounds that we have had to concede Dumfries in the course of our 3–1 deal in the South of Scotland. I am fully aware of the hard work which you and the Association have put in to the building up of our support in the constituency.

I hope however that you do not feel it is wasted effort. Far from it. As I've said generally, those Associations who stand down are making just as great a contribution to the Alliance as those who stand. I hope that your Association will therefore continue its support 1) of the Scottish Liberal Party; 2) of Liberal local election candidates; 3) of an acceptable SDP candidate in Dumfries, and 4) of the Liberal candidate in Galloway for those within reach.

I much admire the way in which you responded to a very disappointing personal setback, and am very appreciative of it. I hope that the Dumfriesshire Liberals will respond in equally far-sighted manner in spite of the understandable anguish the seat allocation causes them.

This particular story had a happy ending. Jim Wallace, the candidate concerned, won the selection in 1983 for Jo Grimond's seat in Orkney and Shetland as an outsider between two locals, where he is now MP and the new Party's excellent Chief Whip. Elsewhere the mood was less cheerful and was well summed up in the 1982 Assembly revue song sheet:

> HYMN 666
> Eternal David for the fight,
> With others thou bidst us unite.
> With prophets odd; with doctrine strange.
> For these we must our seats exchange.
> O hear us when we cry to thee:
> Why must we love the SDP?
>
> Thou tied us to the Gang of Four.
> We shall pure Liberals be no more.
> What help or gain dost thou believe.
> From this surrender, we receive?
> O hear us when we cry to thee:
> Why must we love the SDP?
>
> Accept our prayer in spirit meant.
> We do not question thine intent.
> We share with thee the will to win,
> The Tories out and Liberals in.
> Eternal David, just for thee
> We'll try to love the SDP.

That was a fitting epitaph to 1982.

Once again a by-election came to the rescue of morale. This time it was the long-awaited one at Bermondsey, where Labour was fielding a candidate whose selection Michael Foot had told the Commons back in 1981 had not been endorsed 'and so far as I am concerned never will be'. There was therefore an unofficial 'real Bermondsey Labour' candidate who ran a rough campaign against Peter Tatchell and actually beat the Conservative.

The preparations with Simon Hughes paid off and he led a well-organized campaign to a stunning 9,000 majority victory. It was our first gain from Labour. Since it was just across the river from Westminster, the media circus was ever present. At one point during a market stall scrum, with camera and microphone bearers threatening to trample over babies in pushchairs, I said to one bemused citizen: 'I'm here to support Simon Hughes' – to which I obtained the stunning retort: 'And I'm here to buy some lettuce.'

At the end of February Bermondsey was the spark which relit the flame. It was promptly put out again by the SDP's failure to win Darlington a month later. They started as favourites in the polls, thanks to Bermondsey, and had selected a local TV presenter, Tony Cook, who would have made a perfectly adequate general-election candidate and MP. But he was totally inexperienced and by-elections are very different kettles of fish.

After the first press conference I berated Bill Rodgers, who was his minder, for allowing him to be so exposed. When Richard Holme had minded Bill Pitt at Croydon, he was allowed to speak only on rehearsed licence. Moreover they stupidly agreed to his appearing on all-party televised debates where his inexperience showed. Given his own television recognition, they should have followed the example of my by-election in 1965 and declined to participate, awkward though that always is. We lost by nearly 8,000, beaten into third place, and the effect of the Bermondsey bounce into a general election was thrown away. The SDP had shown that once their stars – Jenkins and Williams – were elected they could not mount a victorious campaign without one. This had a depressing effect on the last of the seat negotiations, but it was the last time the SDP was left to run a by-election on its own.

The leadership of the Alliance had been a rumbling problem right through 1981–3. Should there be an Alliance leader as well as leader of each of the two parties? Before the SDP leadership election, David Owen thought there should. So did I at first, but then thought it impractical. After Roy Jenkins's election as SDP leader in mid-1982, he and I lunched or dined together regularly once a fortnight to catch up. Roy has a public reputation as a gourmet and claret drinker, but as Alan Watkins of the *Observer* was fond of pointing out, it was just that he let it show more than I did. We genuinely enjoyed these occasions, sometimes at his London home and others at watering holes of our alternating choice. They were also essential occasions for keeping the Alliance show on the road.

The personal rapport of the leaders through such stressful vicissitudes as I've described was vital but somewhat resented by colleagues in both parties. At one meeting of the parliamentary Liberal Party I began to report: 'Roy has proposed to me ...' when Clement Freud butted in: 'Congratulations, David, I think you should accept.'

In February 1982 at a weekend meeting of the leadership of both parties at Kiddington Hall, we discussed the leadership problem and agreed that nearer the election we would announce which person would lead us in government. We would not leave it to the lottery of whoever had more seats. In March Roy and I privately agreed that assuming he became SDP leader we would fight the election as joint leaders, with me heading the campaign both because of my experience in that area and because he had marginal Hillhead to defend. We would make it clear that in the event of our forming a government he would be Prime Minister and I would be deputy.

In July we agreed we should form a joint Shadow Cabinet. In September I said that I hoped the party would agree to those dispositions around the turn of the year. By January 1983 I was under severe pressure from colleagues not to make any such announcement. Their argument was that I was far ahead in the opinion polls and that if a premature announcement were made, Roy would be dubbed leader of the Alliance. I made it clear to them and to Roy that I stood by our understanding of what would happen in the election. We had planned the announcement for our Central Hall relaunch rally.

David Penhaligon in particular was against my decision anyway, pointing to a 52 per cent *Sunday Times* poll preference for me as against 14 per cent for Roy as putative leader. Unfortunately he went public with his view on television.

In March 1983 I publicly advised members of our parties to stop damaging speculation on the issue. Shirley Williams, David Penhaligon and David Alton all ignored my exhortation and gave their conflicting views, forcing Roy to say at a press conference: 'Anything (on leadership) that does not come from David Steel and me is not to be taken seriously.' *The Times* reported after one weekly meeting of the Liberal MPs:

Mr Steel was criticized by his colleagues for his autocratic style. They felt that he had not consulted them sufficiently on the issue.

There is a feeling among many Liberals that Mr Steel appears to have come to a private understanding with Mr Jenkins over the prime ministership without talking to them about it.

At the end of the month it was agreed that no announcement should be made until the election was imminent. I told my colleagues I would not stand against Roy and that the arrangement we had made together was therefore the only sensible one. In late April with the election obviously imminent we made the announcement.

Just before that I had a letter from Bob Maclennan, complaining that I was being deliberately dilatory on the matter, and shortly afterwards another from Michael Meadowcroft protesting at my 'persistent and increasing attempts to push Roy Jenkins into the pre-eminent position within the Alliance'. They were both wrong.

My motives were both clear and consistent. I took the view that if by some chance we did find ourselves the largest single grouping, then Roy Jenkins was the right person to be Prime Minister. He had been a widely acclaimed Home Secretary and Chancellor of the Exchequer as well as President of the Commission. He was sixty-two. I was forty-five and had held no office. He had a sweeping command of both political history and political experience and his writings and speeches were of the highest quality. There was absolutely no doubt in my mind that if the unlikely happened, he should head our Cabinet but obviously with more power for the Deputy Prime Minister as leader of his own party than was possessed by Willie Whitelaw. On this we were agreed.

Equally I was aware of the public opinion polls, and the fresh appeal which I brought especially to television, where Roy's ornate gothic constructions fitted less happily. I was also conscious of the greater Liberal campaigning capacity and experience, all of which suggested I should head the actual campaign. We were to remain joint leaders. It all seemed to me at the time – and still does – an eminently sensible arrangement.

The Times next day began its leader pompously:

In putting himself forward as 'Prime Minister Designate' Mr Jenkins, aided by Mr Steel, has anointed himself with a constitutional nonsense.

and it concluded:

That is the window dressing. Behind the counter, however, most members of the Alliance – Mr Jenkins included – will be struggling hard to retain their seats. In those circumstances Mr Steel is right to dominate the centre, secure not only in his hold over his constituency, but also in the knowledge that he is likely to be leading a larger group of MPs in the next Parliament than Mr Jenkins will. It may not be the stuff of dreams, but in his party political management, Mr Steel has never shown himself to be much of a dreamer.

Our first problem was that neither of us had suggested nor used the expression 'Prime Minister Designate' which had a ring of Gilbertian pomposity about it. The description was wished on Roy by some of his supporters and therefore the media. It made our sensible proposal sound faintly absurd and we suffered from that all through the election. Our election campaign opened with the early publication of our impressive manifesto, ahead of the others: *Working Together for Britain – The Alliance Programme for Government*. As in 1979 it was mainly well received. The preface was signed jointly by me and Roy. In it we argued:

The General Election on June 9th 1983 will be seen as a watershed in British politics. It may be recalled as the fateful day when depression became hopelessness and the slide of the postwar years accelerated into the depths of decline. Alternatively it may be remembered as the turning point when the people of this country, at the eleventh hour, decided to turn their backs on dogma and bitterness and chose a new road of partnership and progress.

It is to offer real hope of a fresh start for Britain that the Alliance between our two parties has been created. What we have done is unique in the history of British parliamentary democracy. Two parties, one with a proud history, and one born only two years ago out of a frustration with the old system of politics, have come together to offer an alternative government pledged to bring the country together again.

The Conservative and Labour parties between them have made an industrial wasteland out of a country which was once the workshop of the world. Manufacturing output from Britain is back to the level of nearly 20 years ago. Unemployment is still rising and there are now generations of school-leavers who no longer even hope for work. Mrs Thatcher's government stands idly by, hoping that the blind forces of the marketplace will restore the jobs and factories that its indifference has destroyed. The Labour Party's response is massive further nationalization, a centralized state socialist economy and rigid controls over enterprise. The choice which Tories and Socialists offer at this election is one between neglect and interference. Neither of them understands that it is only by working together in the companies and communities of Britain that we can overcome the economic problems which beset us.

Our press conferences were not brilliant since we ended up mainly reacting to the others, and the campaign organization itself suffered from being split between SDP and Liberal headquarters. Nevertheless the spirit was good. The Campaign team had five a side, the other four Liberals being Lord Evans, Lord Tordoff, Paul Tyler and John Pardoe, whom I had persuaded to cancel his holiday and rejoin the battle.

We had secured a 5–5–4 split of party political broadcasts, which in turn dictated our increased quality of news coverage. Our broadcasts were generally acclaimed the best as we had entrusted them again to Justin Cartwright. According to Butler and Kavanagh's *The British General Election of 1983*:

The first programme tackled the problem [of joint leadership] directly by showing Roy Jenkins and David Steel working together and separately, soliloquizing in voice-over commentary about each other's qualities, in an attempt to show in word and action that they had a close working relationship. Although difficult to achieve – the occasional fulsome presentation led one critic unkindly to liken the programme to a commercial for a gay dating agency – the gamble seemed to succeed, perhaps because the reality of the Alliance was always greatest at the summit.

I took to a battlebus again and the feel of my tours round the country was well encapsulated by Frank Johnson in one of his sketches in *The Times*:

So the opinion polls were showing the first signs of a move in the direction of the Alliance.

This meant the British people, having remained calmly extreme for weeks, were at last being affected by the hysterical moderate propaganda to which they have been subjected in recent days. Many of us had feared that it would come to this.

... So it was time to go in search yesterday of the man who sought to inherit Butskell's evil legacy: Mr David Steel. 'You can catch up with him in Oxford or in Cheltenham,' said one of the always helpful officials at the National Liberal Club in London.

'He will only be ten minutes in Oxford, but at Cheltenham he's making a speech.'
'I'll go to Oxford,' I said.

Along the A40, the news from the car radio was of moderation sweeping the country. No extremist was safe. The polls, it seemed, were the proof.

... Ten minutes was perfectly sufficient to assess a man capable of doing this to Britain. At Cheltenham, he may be making a speech. But I had already heard his speech. I had not seen him over the more difficult distance of ten minutes ...

... Oxford, the Great Royalist city looked more defiant than ever in the glint of the first summer sun. But by the town hall there was a reminder of a darker England. A mob of moderates had gathered.

They were awaiting their leader and his hated Battlebus. It was coming in from the West – from the direction of Thorpe Country.

In due course, a huge, luxuriously appointed coach full of excited photographers turned the corner. A cheer went up. The coach passed by and out of sight. This was principally because it was made up of Japanese tourists.

They thus took home a completely false idea of their popularity with the British.

Eventually, the one and true bus arrived. This time there was silence from the crowd. It might be another Japanese ruse.

But the cameramen aboard appeared to be from the Occident, though not their equipment. Mr Steel followed the cameras into the crowd. The resultant melee bore him away in the direction of The High. I followed. Suddenly, I came face to face with the dangerous man coming the other way. Mr Steel was now moving in the direction of Christ Church.

Surely this was not the best way to test opinion in one of our ancient universities? It could explain much about his policy on higher education. 'What's it all for?' asked an undergraduate-looking youth, presumably – by his question – a philosopher.

Soon Mr Steel found himself back at the coach steps. Mr Evan Luard seized a microphone. As a Labour MP for Oxford some years ago, he was a raving moderate. He seems to be some sort of SDP candidate now.

'Welcome to this great city of Oxford,' he raved. 'Named last night on *Newsnight* as one of the seats the Alliance expected to win.'

He thrust the microphone at Mr Steel. There was a huge cheer. Mr Steel quoted Doubting Thomas, Roosevelt, *Newsnight* and MORI, in ascending order of importance. To another cheer, he disappeared into the Battlebus, which moved off towards that speech in Cheltenham. A man can do a lot of damage in ten minutes.

There was one novelty in the campaign. Knowing that the other party leaders were to be addressing ticket-only rallies of the faithful, I invented an 'Ask-the-Alliance' formula where people would genuinely put questions at random to two leading figures from the Liberals and SDP. This was also to reinforce the Alliance image, and they were a great success with Magnus Magnusson, Ludovic Kennedy, Bamber Gascoigne and Steve Race acting as question masters. By 1987 the formula was possibly a little tired; but then it was fresh and appealing, and we attracted overflow crowds.

Back in the constituency Judy became for the second time the surrogate candidate, canvassing in mills and on doorsteps, addressing the smaller meetings – though I was always back in time for the weekend ones in the towns. The boundary redistribution worked in my favour. Though I regretted losing the towns of Hawick, Kelso and Jedburgh (and perhaps most all, the remote, warmhearted and superbly organized village of Newcastleton), it meant that the smaller constituency of the districts of Tweeddale and Ettrick and Lauderdale was more like one thousand square miles than seventeen hundred. Our candidate in the new constituency of Roxburgh and Berwick-shire was Archy Kirkwood: standing against him was the pompous junior-ministerial figure of Iain Sproat, who was one of the Prime Minister's especial favourites. He did himself little good by abandoning his marginal seat of Aberdeen South in the forlorn belief that Roxburgh and Berwickshire would be more fruitful territory. He had lived in Melrose for many years and his election literature conveyed the impression that he had been born there. It was not so, as Judy could testify: she and he had been pushed out in their prams together many miles to the north.

My own opponent was a likeable, ineffectual, Peeblesshire farmer who had been selected only at the last minute. It was difficult for the local Liberals to get very worked up about his campaign, especially given the more strident and odious challenge in the neighbouring seat. Many of them spent some time helping Archy.

As usual, Peter Hellyer flew in from the United Arab Emirates and stayed at Cherrydene. For Judy, who found the national campaign circus intrusive and at times insensitive to the constituency's needs, he was a support without which she could have faltered badly. He knows both the constituency and the Party and has an abundant store of humour and wisdom and anger – all of which ingredients are necessary for electioneering.

Other arrangements for the domestic front of the election were less happy. For the three weeks of the campaign, both house and family would suffer total parental neglect, and a housekeeper would be needed. A friend volunteered the services of a friend, currently between jobs. The experience was disastrous. It is amazing how, in the midst of a well-running operation, one out-of-place piece of grit in the machinery can take on an irritation out of all proportion. The major drawback to this particular lady was that in the first weekend that the Battlebus and attendant media visited the village, it became clear that she preferred to spend her time being indiscreet to journalists than keeping house. She expected to be thanked as well as paid for every duty she performed and every dish she prepared, and upset Judy's regular and delightful twice-weekly home help so badly that the latter was, we discovered later, on the verge of leaving herself.

On the second weekend of the election Judy insisted that the temporary housekeeper took the weekend off (the very time she was in theory most needed.)

'She is not to come back. She's positively dangerous. You've got to tell her,' I insisted.

'I can't,' protested Judy. 'She's X's friend.'

The opportunity to disentangle ourselves came in an unexpected way. On the Sunday morning of the weekend, in the early June dawn, we were conscious of two of the Special Branch team hunting around our bedroom. 'Go back to sleep,' they urged us, and it wasn't until a few hours later that we discovered what the alarm was.

A tent had been pitched on the hillside across the river from our house. It was, to us, nothing unusual. To the Special Branch it was a vantage point for a sniper. They made their way to the tent, and summoned up the powers of the air to reveal the source of the campers' number plate. Back came the information: it belonged to a Liverpool resident with an Irish name who had been seen in a demonstration, in favour of either hunger strikers or convicted bombers – I forget which. In fact, the owner of the number plate wasn't inside the tent: he had loaned the car to a friend who wanted a secret weekend with a woman friend. Their awakening can hardly have been the idyll they expected: in place of the dawn chorus and the ripple of the Ettrick, it was by a posse of uniformed and armed police.

After all was explained, there was general amusement, but the Special Branch team took more seriously than the rest of us the possible alternative implications of the incident. I can't remember who came up with the bright idea that the tightened security arrangements could include the nonadmission of the housekeeper back to Cherrydene. One of Judy's numerous nieces was prepared to take over her duties: it was she and the inspector in charge of the Special Branch team that broke the news to the housekeeper that henceforth we could be surrounded only by those who were of the family, or had been positively vetted. It was a display of acting that should have earned both of them an Equity card.

Returning to the national campaign I said at the opening press conference:

The two major parties will concentrate on what they fondly believe is their devoted and faithful vote. Their leaders will appear bathed in floodlights at ticket-only rave-ins. We have a different and much more creative task. Our job is not to rouse the faithful but to convince and convert those who are seeking a new politics.

The Labour campaign was divided and ineffective with Michael Foot coming across badly. Splits on defence culminated in Jim Callaghan's distancing himself from the manifesto halfway through. Later Denis Healey described Mrs Thatcher as 'glorying in slaughter'; while Neil Kinnock, responding to a heckler who said she had guts, retorted crudely: 'And it's a pity that people had to leave theirs on Goose Green in order to prove it.'

The Tories had only two sticky moments: when Mrs Thatcher was questioned persistently on *Nationwide* by a Mrs Gould about the sinking of the *Belgrano* and was embarrassingly evasive; and when Kenny Everett at a Tory concert yelled: 'Let's bomb Russia. Let's kick Michael Foot's stick away.'

By contrast our campaign proceeded without incident – that was its problem. We were not getting anywhere. The Conservatives retained a commanding lead in all polls over Labour while we stuck around 18/19/20 per cent. I was not too gloomy, recalling the lift towards the end of the '79 campaign; but when Mrs Thatcher went off to a summit with President Reagan on the last weekend of the campaign, I decided to switch our regular campaign meeting from London to Ettrick Bridge, to treat it cheekily as a rival summit, mainly to provide press and television with some more interesting shots of Alliance VIPs helicoptering in to the picturesque village, but also to emphasize my being in charge.

It all went somewhat awry. For a start there was fog and so helicopters were abandoned. People arrived late in dribs and drabs and bad humour by car. It also nearly led to a break between me and Roy which would have been my fault had it happened.

All through the previous week there were rumblings of discontent about the television coverage of our campaign, and especially its emphasis on Roy as Prime Minister Designate. This was largely accidental. On the day of dissolution I was in my constituency and so he represented us in the three-leader line up of the opening national programmes on both channels. The other four major setpiece interviews we had arranged to split between us; but by chance his two came in the first half of the campaign while mine were due later. The effect was therefore very one-sided, and while Roy never put a foot wrong in any of these interviews they were not the format in which he showed to the best advantage.

On top of this clear imbalance within our ranks we had a further problem which again was not of our making. The TV news editors had decided to give the two of us roughly alternating attention in the regular bulletins with only occasional look-ins for others in the Alliance, a source of great irritation all round. Roy was sticking as arranged to the difficult task of defending Hillhead with only necessary forays outside to the national press conferences and Ask-the-Alliance rallies, at both of which he excelled. Unfortunately he also undertook with typical generosity relatively unplanned personal excursions. One of these was to the Ayr constituency being fought by Chic Brodie, who had nobly stood down in favour of Roy at the Hillhead by-election. It was a short daytime visit to a constituency which was not in any sense among our target or better organized ones. Not unnaturally therefore they took him on a walkabout – as it happened in wind and rain.

On the same day I was in the Welsh border country in brilliant sunshine and drawing large televisual crowds, especially in the marginal seat of Hereford where I must have addressed 2,000 people from the roof of the Battlebus in the market place. I noted with satisfaction the TV crews on the roofs of surrounding buildings obtaining magnificent shots. As we drove back to London on the motorway in high spirits we turned on the nine o'clock BBC and ten o'clock ITN news. The journalists on board shared our surprise that not a foot of all our day's film appeared.

Instead a rather sending-up report appeared of Roy wandering along a rainswept shopping street, accompanied by one or two blowing umbrellas, looking for anyone to meet and ending up giving an incongruous interview standing behind a tiny shop counter. In contrast to the allotted news slots of the other campaigns ours looked amateur and low-key. All the buzz and excitement of the campaign we had been on all exhausting day ended up in the editors' bins. We were all both angry and profoundly depressed.

On top of this – and partly because of it – the daily opinion polls were highlighting the difference in popularity ratings between Steel and Jenkins. Mine had always been high, Roy's not so, and now the problem was accentuated with mischievous questions about how people might vote if Steel rather than Jenkins were Prime Minister Designate. The difference was sufficient to stir up pressure from the ranks.

Those in 'winnable' seats with whom we were in closest contact were the most vocal. They criticized my lack of profile in the campaign – which was entirely understandable – and reopened my decision to play the Alliance leadership with what they saw as Roy in the superior role. As the days went by these calls became more urgent, with demands that in order to secure the seats we were hoping for 'something should be done'. There was no other course but to raise the matter direct with Roy, but somewhat unsatisfactorily via wayside telephone kiosks. It is a sign of our good working relationship that he did not at all resent this discussion and fully recognized the scale of the problem. My argument was that since the Conservatives were clearly heading for re-election we should now be seeking to replace Labour in the popular vote. The whole 'Prime Minister Designate' title had become an irrelevance and should simply be dropped in favour of getting as large a vote and group of MPs as possible, the implication being that I would be spearheading the effort.

The next campaign stage was in Plymouth. I had spent two days in the West Country being bounced around the roads of Devon and Cornwall, and was beginning to feel ill from both the effects of this and a heavy cold. At one point Pratap Chitnis noticed I had fallen asleep on the sofa in my swaying compartment. He ordered the driver to take a bypass instead of proceeding through yet another village as planned where the assembled masses were primed to cheer and wave at the passing coach. The result was a deputation of outraged Cornish arriving at the evening rally at Plymouth Guildhall. At the television studios in Plymouth I made an early evening rendezvous with David Owen as arranged and said: 'You're supposed to be a doctor, what do you recommend I should take?'

'A large brandy,' was the sensible prescription.

We walked outside in the sunshine to talk privately on the lawn away from the inevitable entourage. He was in a highly nervous state. At the previous election in 1979 he had survived as Labour MP for Devonport after a filthy campaign against him from the Conservatives, mainly on the Rhodesian question. Now he faced the problem of fighting the seat against both Tory and Labour parties. he was also very critical of the national organization of the 'Ask-the-Alliance' meeting in Plymouth where he feared a disaster because of lack of adequate advertising. On that last point his fears proved unfounded because we had a crowded audience, and he described that meeting as the turning point in his campaign.

Anyhow, I thought it useful to consult the only other member of the Gang of Four with whom I had contact, and David was fully supportive of the proposition that something had to be done. He agreed that dropping the 'Prime Minister Designate' was worth a try but was doubtful whether Roy would agree. Roy told me on the telephone before coming to Ettrick Bridge that he would not agree, but when he arrived I thought it worth having another try, especially since I had received a *cri de coeur* by telex from our campaign headquarters. Uppermost in my mind were all the candidates I had been visiting, especially those like Richard Holme, Alan Watson, Stuart Mole and Menzies Campbell, with whom I had worked so closely and whose success hung in the balance.

I decided not to take Roy's 'no' for an answer, convinced that he was wrong, and raised the matter at the beginning of our meeting in the dining-room at Cherrydene. It was inevitably somewhat strained and this time Roy did resent my pressure. After a frank discussion it became clear that he would not be budged, and we turned to other routine matters.

Judy had laid on a superb buffet, and Roy and I went across the road to the village where we had a crowded press conference, agreeing simply that the campaign was on course but that I would be taking a higher profile in the remainder. We got away with it, and months afterwards Roy and I reflected that we had been extremely lucky that none of the unpleasant strain of the meeting had percolated outside. The summit itself was a media success rivalling in attention the Thatcher/Reagan meeting in Williamsburg. I read with a wry smile David Owen's retrospective protestations of shock and outrage at my attempted manoeuvre. In the meeting he said little. In the garden privately he commended my efforts.

The second part of the campaign was indeed more successful, and with the continuing slump of Labour a couple of polls on the final Monday put us one per cent ahead of them. I broke this news to a jubilant crowd of several hundred outside the hall in London where Roy and I were appearing at the final Ask-the-Alliance meeting. They were unable to gain entry to the overcrowded hall, so I gave an impromptu speech from the roof of the bus before joining Roy inside.

The only problems over the last days were that my cold had definitely become flu and was turning me into a zombie. On the bus Tessa and Nali plied me with every patent remedy. On the final Saturday I failed to notice the signal from the police car in front as the Battlebus proceeded slowly down Galashiels High Street in my constituency. An overhanging rope struck me across the neck, leaving a nasty burn scar.

We went on to poll 25 per cent on polling day, beaten by only 2 per cent by the Labour Party but with a cruelly disappointing share of seats – 23 out of 650. Labour had 209 seats for their marginally greater showing. This revealed the injustice – fraud would be a better word – of our electoral system more than ever before. But at 25 per cent we were now a mass popular movement, a long way from that 2.5 per cent party I joined as a student. Although acutely disappointed at the parliamentary outcome, I felt we had at last laid a solid foundation for success.

10

JOINT LEADERSHIP

Two Davids

A lthough the '83 election seemed a relative triumph when results ended on Friday, 10 June, events moved turbulently over that weekend. On Sunday, 12 June, Michael Foot announced that he did not propose to seek re-election as Labour leader in the autumn. On the very same day, I subsequently discovered, Roy Jenkins and David Owen were arguing over the future of the SDP and the Alliance. Next day, Monday, 13 June, Bill Rodgers telephoned to let me know that Roy was announcing later that day that he was resigning the leadership of the SDP. He had had enough. This came to me as both a shock and a sadness, but I could understand his frame of mind. The SDP itself had only six MPs compared with twenty-nine before dissolution and we now faced at least a four-year slog to the next election.

David Owen was heir presumptive. We quickly arranged to meet the following weekend at his country house in Wiltshire for a preliminary chat. We discussed the possibility of a merger, for which Russell Johnston had publicly called. David publicly described a merger before the next election as 'extremely unlikely'. Privately he was even more hostile to the idea. I commented to the assembled press that 'we are not ruling out anything but if there were to be a merger of the two parties at some time in the future there would have to be a general consensus in the two parties that they wanted it. Now, frankly, that does not exist.' The SDP leader-in-waiting was the main opponent, but some Liberals also disapproved of the idea. Within three days he was formally elected leader of the SDP, unopposed. It is easy with the benefit of hindsight to see that I should have pressed the matter of a merger more thoroughly at this time and at least opened up the subject for wider debate within the SDP before they chose a new leader. I failed to do so largely because I was anxious to start off the new Alliance partnership on a positive and co-operative footing. I therefore allowed his objections to act as a veto on the subject.

I had dinner with Roy Jenkins following that weekend meeting, mainly to restore our somewhat strained relations – which we did – and also to mull over both the election and the future. David Owen had turned up at Roy's house for the Gang of Four meeting on the Sunday following the election determined to secure Roy's resignation. Bill and Shirley had failed to get elected to the House and there had therefore been only one possible replacement. Roy took the view that a bruising leadership election was not in the SDP's interests, nor was he in the mood for one. He therefore gave way gracefully. Thus within days of the general election and thanks to our joint acquiescence, David Owen had secured both the leadership of the SDP and a veto over merger of the two parties into one. It was a remarkably bloodless coup.

At the same time I was having serious difficulties in my own Party. When the new band of MPs met for the first time on the morning of 15 June during the swearing in of new MPs, the newcomers, Paddy Ashdown (Yeovil), Malcolm Bruce (Gordon), Alex Carlile (Montgomery), Archy Kirkwood (Roxburgh and Berwickshire), Michael Meadowcroft (Leeds West) and Jim Wallace (Orkney and Shetland), were astonished at the tone of the meeting. I did not expect warm congratulations but neither did I expect at our opening meeting to run into a barrage of criticism in support of a proposal that they should elect a deputy leader and the Chief Whip. The main antagonists were David Alton and Cyril Smith, supported by Simon Hughes.

Part of their complaint was on 'we told you so' lines about the dual leadership and Prime Minister Designate formula; but they seemed more outraged by the fact that when all the commentators described the Ettrick Bridge summit as including 'leading Liberals' they were not invited. In fact only Alan Beith as Chief Whip had been added to our usual election team, and he was only an hour's drive away. There had been other difficulties in my visits to the Smith and Alton seats. My visit to Rochdale was the only one in the entire election where the timing went seriously awry. Bank holiday weekend traffic on the motorway had reduced us to a crawl in spite of the assistance of a veritable flotilla of police escorts. Cyril had organized a brass band and heaven knows what else for a proper leader's welcome and we had turned up an hour late to find him not in the best of humour.

As for David's seat, I had refused to address a city rally in Liverpool because of the presence of an Alton-backed Liberal candidate in the Broadgreen constituency against the 'allocated' SDP candidate Dick Crawshaw. This made it impossible for me to go to a citywide meeting as planned, since it would inevitably draw attention to one of only three seats in the entire country where we were in conflict. Instead I would come through Liverpool in daytime and do a pavement visit to his boundary-revised Mossley Hill seat. In fact that visit went pleasantly enough and he held the seat comfortably but he was still offended by my decision against the evening meeting.

All of these resentments spilled out during our first couple of meetings and I was far from being at my best in handling them. I had scarcely recovered from my flu and was generally feeling exhausted and found all this extremely hurtful and disagreeable.

On 14 June – the very day before the first of our meetings – and before my first meeting with David Owen I had said in a radio interview that we should have a short debate about the future of the Alliance hinting at merger as an option: 'If we are going to maintain separate parties, we've got to think about the position of the Liberal Party in those constituencies we gave over to the SDP to fight.' I also said that I was by no means committed to staying on and leading the Party into the next election.

The events of the next two weeks increased my doubts on that score. There were moves in different sections of the party outside Parliament on other issues which I felt directed against me. Roy's decision to leave the leadership clearly cast doubts on the growing union of the two parties. I had been leader for seven years and at that moment did not relish a further four. I sat down over the weekend of 1/2 July and wrote a letter to the then-Party President, John Griffiths, which is so self-explanatory that I reproduce it here in full:

Dear John,

As you know, I told both the party officers and my parliamentary colleagues that I would reflect and decide by the end of July on whether I wished to continue to lead the party through to the next election. I see no virtue in delay and I am writing to you now formally as President to tell you that I have decided not to continue. I do not want to be thought irresponsible in timing and I realize that July is not the easiest month to hold a leadership election. I should be grateful if you would discuss the timing therefore with your fellow officers and my parliamentary colleagues next Wednesday. (I am sending a copy of this to Alan as Chief Whip.) If it is your wish I will remain until the Assembly. In fact I shall be away from Parliament next week – I think it is the first time in seven years that I have missed an entire week – attending to my duties as Rector of Edinburgh University in the quatercentenary week. I have three dinner speeches and a lecture to deliver and I am finding the university life a positive antidote to the rather depressing state of affairs in the party.

Let me set out my reasons in full:

1 The Parliamentary Party.
We returned to Parliament after an election which, in spite of its obvious disappointments, was the most successful the party has enjoyed for 50 years. I expected morale to be high and for a common determination to exist to build on our success in the popular vote. Instead, the first problem is that two of my colleagues are refusing to accept their share of the work in spokesmanships, thus depriving us of the advantage of now having enough MPs to cover each ministry without doubling up or using peers. Until such time as we are large enough to elect a shadow cabinet, each of us in the parliamentary party must carry a fair share of the workload if we are to demonstrate a coherent alternative to the government. The fact that the two concerned are both colleagues for whom I have particular personal regard has made their decision all the more painful for me.

2 The Worthing Declaration
Even more disturbing is the tone of the conference of the Association of Liberal Councillors. It is bad enough that remarks accusing me of being a dictator should be warmly applauded, but even worse that the conference should solemnly adopt a series of proposals which would amount to setting up a party within a party. This was how the militant tendency started. The Association of Liberal Councillors should stick to the job they do superbly well – developing our local government base. Otherwise as individuals they should seek to influence the party though its democratic structures. The threat of 'Association of Liberal Councillors approved candidates' and the rest is most serious and dangerous. It must be stopped.

3 Assembly Resolutions
The proposal to remove the authority of the leader over the manifesto is irritating. (If anything I regret not having so much control over the last one!) But what is quite preposterous is the idea that control over party broadcasts should be transferred from the leader to the Standing Committee. No matter what justified criticisms could be made of my leadership, the broadcasts are one area of triumphant success. This is verified by audience research but has never been understood by some of the party's activists who seem to think that broadcasts should be developed to appeal to *them*, rather than, as I believe, to millions of people largely uninterested in politics. Significantly, the best received broadcast in the election was the one even I thought went a little far beyond normal political presentation.

4 Party units
There is at present an alarming disposition to allow regional parties, city parties and constituency parties to decide strategy at variance with the Assembly and the Executive. I cannot accept that this is a virtuous characteristic of Liberalism, and it gives rise to the present attempt to steamroller strategic resolutions through these various organizations. In my first Assembly speech as Leader I said I did not wish to lead just a nice debating society. I certainly do not intend to lead a nasty one.

The party must come to terms with this habit of allowing parts of its own organization to do what they want even to the damage of the national effort.

None of these four points would individually justify my leaving now, but collectively they add up to a picture of a grave lack of purpose and discipline which has to be put right. What is required is a calm determination to look together at the way the party is run (including of course the leader's role, for as you know from my reaction to your own letters I do not resent *constructive* criticism and really wish to see a wider spread of responsibility). In particular, I now think there is a chance for MPs to play a greater part in the running of the party. But the necessary spirit of determined harmony is lacking. Instead we seem to be heading for a period of backbiting and recrimination.

It has been argued by some in the last few days – not least by Judy – that I have a wider responsibility outside the party to the millions who voted for us. That is a powerful argument, but frankly after the strain of the last two years and especially the last two months I simply cannot find the mental or physical energy to begin to cope with a bout of internal argument. That is itself a good argument for starting with a fresh leader, and I hope the shock of having to do so will persuade the party to truncate the whole process and concentrate as soon as possible on building outwards on our 25 per cent.

I intend to devote more time to my family and to repairing the Steel finances! But I assure you that I do not intend to sulk in my tent. In the autumn I will accept a spokesmanship under the new leader, give him loyal support, and having spent seven years largely on Liberal strategy, devote more time to writing and speaking on Liberal philosophy and policy.

You or others may wish to persuade me to change my mind. Please do not do so, because I wish to carry out my university role next week in peace.

Yours ever,
David

Since I was at Ettrick Bridge over the weekend – and this was before the advent of the Fax machine – I had the letter typed by Archy Kirkwood's wife Rosemary, who worked for me part time. Archy was to take the letter with him to London and deliver it on Monday to the President and Chief Whip. Archy and Judy then organized a private get-together in my kitchen to persuade me to withdraw the letter, after consulting Alan Beith on the telephone, who retrieved the letter from the President the next day. I was, they argued, in poor fettle to make such an irrevocable decision which in their view was a disastrous mistake.

Under this kitchen-cabinet pressure I relented on condition that I would take a three-month sabbatical and that as Chief Whip Alan would become acting leader. The summer recess was imminent in any case and he could use the time with fresh authority devoid of personal antagonisms to sort out the party. The assumption was that I would thereafter resume, starting with the Assembly at the end of September. Meantime I would give neither speeches nor interviews nor attend Party meetings, though I would – contrary to the public impression – continue with my usual constituency work.

This was all agreed. The resignation letter was suppressed and we made an agreed announcement. Philip Webster reported it fairly in *The Times*:

Mr Steel is standing down for two months because he is hurt by backbiting criticism from within his own party, tired by the strains of the general election and being leader for seven years and anxious to spend more time with his family.

He is also unhappy over views about the long-term development of the Alliance expressed by Dr David Owen, the Social Democratic Party leader, since their weekend talks three weeks ago. Although Mr Steel ended those talks with the understanding that Dr Owen shared his belief in the need for greater convergence between parties, he believes that the SDP leader has laid too much emphasis since on their separate identities.

Meantime, with Willie Whitelaw's elevation to the Lords, there was a by-election at Penrith and the Border, just across the English/Scottish border from my constituency. I could hardly ignore it in spite of my sabbatical, and our candidate was the able Michael Young, a recent convert from the Tories who had been an assistant to Edward Heath. I made three visits in the summer recess, but neither the Party nor the press were taking it seriously, exhausted by the general election and regarding it as a remote safe Tory seat. We failed to win by just 500 votes. It was a well-deserved boost, and a missed opportunity at one and the same time.

Instead of my letter of resignation, I circulated to colleagues a letter setting out a number of points which I thought might usefully be cleared up during my absence. I criticized the fact that the Political Secretary of the Association of Liberal Councillors had during the election campaign been unhelpfully attempting to draw distinctions between our agreed election programme and what he maintained to be 'Liberal policies' as passed by Liberal Assemblies. I made it clear that I could not accept removal of the leader's veto over manifesto content from our constitution and spelt out my attitude:

I am certainly willing and indeed keen to continue as leader, but only on the basis that the party itself is gearing its efforts to offering an alternative government to Mrs Thatcher at the next general election.

If it wants to potter about on the sidelines I will be happy to remain a loyal member but not to continue indefinitely as leader.

Although refusing to speak to the press in interviews I was quite happy to give relaxed briefings at home to individual journalists whom I knew and trusted. Early in August, Allan Massie, the distinguished Scottish writer who had recently moved into my constituency but whom I had then met only once, was commissioned by the *Glasgow Herald* to write a profile. It was a perceptive piece from someone who does not share my politics:

First, he [David Steel] has the sort of family that every politician should have to give him security, and incidentally save him from pomposity. Second, he gets an 'enormous kick from being a constituency MP'. Of course he has a marvellous constituency; it wouldn't be as satisfying to be member for a London or 'even Edinburgh' suburb. As it is, his satisfaction in caring for his constituency has given him what is now an absolutely safe seat, where even non-Liberals will concede 'he is the best MP we ever had'.

In return, he has made his rambling cottage in Ettrick Bridge the best known political house in the Borders since Liberal leaders used to congregate at the Tennant House, The Glen, a couple of hill ranges away towards the Tweed, at the end of the last century. And he would probably agree with Margot Tennant [Mrs Asquith] who said: 'Border people are more intelligent than those born in the south and are 100 years in advance of the southern English.'

His attachment to family and constituency enables him to say that 'if the Liberal Party goes off the rails, then I would be under no obligation to lead it'. And it is quite clear just what, at this moment, he means by going off the rails. In such circumstances he would carry on as his mentor Jo Grimond did, after relinquishing the party leadership, as a wide-ranging freelance MP. 'I would give more attention to Scottish affairs and foreign affairs.'

... When he says he would feel under no obligation to lead the Liberals, he really means it. Leading a Liberal Party that is not prepared to make sacrifices of purity and self-indulgence that are necessary if it is seriously aiming at government is, after a few years, no great shakes.

'You go round the circuit making the same sort of speech. Second time round, it's a diminishing pleasure.' Jo Grimond discovered that, and David Steel is very sensitive – always – of Grimond's experience. He quoted Grimond's questioning of the party: whether it could be a credible political instrument. 'When you want to use it,' he recalls Grimond saying, 'it breaks in your hands.'

... The conviction that the world is moving his way, that he represents the future, is strong in Steel. He is too prepared to laugh at himself, to take his work more seriously than he does himself, for the adjective messianic, in its vulgar sense, to be applied. But his grasp of what he sees as the logic of circumstance, as the inexorable moment of history, has something of Calvinist certainty in it.

Steel has often been portrayed, a little dismissively, as the 'good boy' of British politics; but the Scottish tradition of virtue is of something stern. The next few years are likely to show, as Graham Greene said of Stevenson on the eve [of publication] of *Weir of Hermiston,* the trim surface cracking up, the granite coming painfully through.

If that scares the Liberal Party, then he will be left as an isolated rock in a political desert; but if it doesn't and the Alliance holds, he could be the rock on which the house inhabited by British politics for the next quarter century will be founded.

There are fascinating months ahead.

The other piece later in the month came in *The Times* from Geoffrey Smith, whose in-laws were constituents and who is a regular visitor to the Borders:

Mr David Steel's leadership of the Liberals during the past seven years has been characterized both by his remarkable success in guiding the party in the direction he has always intended and by his autocratic methods. His autocracy has, to my mind, had much to do with his success.

... But in exercising his power he has not always paid sufficient regard to the sensitivities of his party. It is essentially a matter of style.

So beneath all the flurry over reports of resignation threats and constitutional changes, the test for the Liberals this autumn is clear: can harmony be restored without diminishing the substance of Mr Steel's authority?

A group of senior Liberals in and out of Parliament – including Mr Alan Beith, Lord Evans of Claughton, Lord Tordoff, Mr Richard Holme, Dr William Wallace, Mr Stuart Mole and Mr John Roberts – are coming together to try to smooth feelings within the party and to strengthen the partnership with the SDP. The two purposes go hand in hand. Neither the Liberals nor the Alliance can afford to weaken Mr Steel's position, and he cannot afford to lose the reputation for calm reasonableness which accounts for so much of the respect he has acquired over the years.

These writers both correctly assessed my mood in August. At this point I was about to take off with Judy for a pre-Assembly September week in the sun of Tenerife to think further and write my Assembly speech. I made a stopover in London where I had lunch with Richard Holme, Tessa, Paul Medlicott and Graham Watson, who was taking over from Stuart Mole as my political assistant. He records that I looked tired and drawn and was 'acting like a spaceship' talking of my 're-entry' at the Assembly.

Unfortunately Judy's father was terminally ill (he died the following month) and Judy felt she could not leave. We had paid for the tickets and I did not wish to go on my own. We agreed that Billy would come instead. He was good company as I baked in the sun during the day and in the evening while he toured the discothèques I got on with writing my speech in the apartment we had hired. One morning when I had gone out for some provisions I came back to the flat to find him looking glum: 'You're not going to like this. The *Daily Mail* has been at the door.' I was amazed. What were they after? Sure enough, when I looked over the balcony there was a photographer with an enormous telephoto lens. Billy had tried unsuccessfully to persuade them I wasn't there. He told me that the reporter was from the parliamentary lobby – it was John Harrison, now of the BBC's political staff, whom I knew well. John had apparently assured his editor that if they sent out a sleuth they would get nothing. He was right and after I had overcome my initial irritation at their tracking me down, I talked to him, posing with Billy in a fishing boat for the photographer. What the *Daily Mail* readers made of this expensive exclusive I do not know. If ever there was a non-story this was it. I was alive, sane and writing my conference speech.

Meantime the SDP was meeting in their annual conference. On the eve of the conference the Joint Leaders Advisory Committee with Alan Beith standing in for me agreed that 'in exceptional circumstances' there could be joint selection of candidates for the 1984 Euro-elections. In an interview David Owen had stated: 'I can see no case for joint selection, unless we had agreed to merge the parties.' So the limited agreement was seen as a concession by him.

The conference itself held a vigorous debate on both joint selection and merger in which David Owen's cautious views prevailed, to the disappointment of many Social Democrats who spoke in the debate and of David Penhaligon who, speaking at a fringe meeting, warned that the two parties would either have to move seriously towards becoming one in the next four years or tragically they would begin fighting one another. His accurate prophecy went unheeded. Roy Jenkins warned that no relationship in human affairs could remain static and they must be prepared for an advance and, he believed, a substantial advance.

David Owen successfully persuaded the conference that the time was not right for a merger but that they should continue to forge the partnership. According to *The Times* report, he added that (my italics) *it would be an extremely foolish person who took the view that there would never be a merger. No one could know what the position would be after the next general election.* On joint selection, on which he was 'not wild', he said that a party which gave up the right to select its own candidates surrendered its claim to an independent existence.

On the eve of the Liberal Assembly at Harrogate there was still much press speculation about whether I was any longer interested in politics. Peter Jenkins, for example, writing in the *Guardian* said: 'Mr David Steel is no longer clear master of his own party after a long run.'

I returned to the political fray by making a speech to the Scottish Liberals' special conference at Perth, where as usual they were both sensible and supportive: 'I think I should tell you straight that assuming the membership so wishes, it is my intention to lead the party through the entire parliament and at the next election.' On the same day the party's National Executive meeting at Harrogate regretted that joint selection of candidates was to be only 'in exceptional circumstances' and warned the SDP that party members could not be expected to work for the election of candidates whom they had not formally helped to select.

The big internal issue dominating the press at Harrogate was the attempt to remove the provision in our constitution that 'the leader of the party shall have final authority over the contents of the manifesto'. This was easily beaten off by a majority of two to one.

My parliamentary colleagues, while genuinely welcoming me back, were fearful that I would offend too many in the Party with my criticisms. At a cordial meeting they urged me to have private discussions with the Councillors' organization, whose activities I had criticized as getting out of hand. The Assembly also voted by a large majority not to have a deputy leader of the Party. It did however, even more strongly, carry a resolution expressing a desire for future joint selection of candidates.

The Assembly went well but was far too dominated in publicity terms by all three internal considerations. Geoffrey Smith wrote in his *Times* column: 'Mr David Steel will have to deliver a pretty poor speech this afternoon if he is not to receive a rapturous reception from this Assembly.' Actually it was a jolly good speech but since it has been published elsewhere I will not dwell on the details except to say that it began with a passable joke:

As you may have heard I took a few days off this summer. But I'm back now and I must say you're all looking a good deal better for it. I did notice that during my absence my own rating in the Gallup poll reached record levels. There must be a moral in this somewhere.

The rather long address ended thus:

If I try to sum up my five themes, they amount to a plea for us to listen to what people are telling us in Britain today. To listen to the cry of men and women who feel themselves the victims of blind economic and political forces beyond their control. To recognize the frustration of people excluded from the process of making decisions even over their own lives, the feeling of hopelessness and powerlessness to shape their own destinies.

The duty of our political movement is to display such conviction, imagination and responsibility that we establish ourselves as the mainstream reformers in touch with the feelings and aspirations of ordinary folk. We have to restore faith in democratic politics, and invite new recruits in to help us.

In my first speech to you as leader in 1976 I said that the road I intended us to travel back to power would be a bumpy one. And indeed we have climbed some rough terrain together. But look where we've got to. We have established for the first time in fifty years a really secure base camp. We are ready to begin the final assault on that summit.

Frank Johnson in his sketch the following day began: 'Mr David Steel took a complete rest from politics during quite a long part of his speech to the Liberal Assembly yesterday', but added grudgingly: 'Mr Steel's speech, as professionally delivered and polished as ever, received the compulsory standing ovation.' Judy and Rory joined me on the platform.

In October Neil Kinnock was elected leader of the Labour Party and in December the SDP's national committee voted by 14 to 10 to allow two Euro-seats to engage in joint selection of their candidates. It was like getting blood out of a stone. After a meeting with David Owen, Graham Watson records that I expressed alarm that he was becoming both more Thatcherite and at odds with so many in his own party in frustrating joint selections. My own advisers urged me to press for a full merger, but I decided that this would be neither fruitful nor therefore useful.

In a perceptive end-of-year column Geoffrey Smith wrote that 'the Alliance needs the two Davids. . . . the Alliance has benefited from David Steel's strong leadership in the past. Sometimes a leader needs to receive as well as give encouragement. Dr Owen cannot give the Alliance all the leadership it requires so long as he has a slightly semi-detached attitude towards it.'

The new year, 1984, got off to a bad start with the sudden death of our leader in the House of Lords, Frank Byers, who had forged with Chief Whip Geoff Tordoff and SDP leader Jack Diamond an effective Alliance partnership in the House of Lords, continued by his elected successor, Nancy Seear. The broadcasting authorities agreed for the first time that the Alliance, as well as the Labour Opposition, should have a formal right of reply on television to the budget in March. David Penhaligon was very cross when I agreed that Roy Jenkins, as a former Chancellor, should give the first one.

In May we had some unsubstantial local election gains and we had also polled well in parliamentary by-elections in Chesterfield and Stafford, and even better at South-West Surrey where Gavin Scott reduced a huge Tory majority to 2,500. In the June Euro-elections, in spite of all our agonizing over selections, we again failed to get a single candidate elected, although polling 20 per cent of the vote, something not one of our European allies can understand or forgive. However, rather contrary to expectations including our own, we won the Portsmouth South by-election after a strong campaign led by local councillor Mike Hancock of the SDP.

We were doing well but not outstandingly so as we approached the autumn conference season in 1984. In one of his thoughtful pieces at the time in the *Listener* John Cole described the two Alliance leaders thus: 'The conscience of a Scottish Presbyterian makes Steel more vulnerable than most to anxiety. David Owen worries more about not being macho than any politician ought to.' This supposed difference certainly showed itself on the issue of the role of nuclear weapons in our defence policies.

Although Liberal assemblies were sometimes inaccurately caricatured as unilateralist, we never were so; but of course there has always been a unilateralist and indeed pacifist minority in a party which was so much imbued with the Quaker tradition.

The issue before us in 1984 was the growing presence of Cruise missiles in Britain. The leadership supported the nuclear-freeze concept (as did Roy Jenkins) and a negotiated removal of Cruise missiles – which is what eventually happened.

The Assembly, however, voted by the narrow margin of 55 votes out of 1,200 for the removal of Cruise missiles 'forthwith'. I took to the Conference floor to argue that this would destroy the credibility of our defence policy. I lost, as the new MP for Yeovil, Paddy Ashdown, backed the winning side to the considerable annoyance of his parliamentary colleagues. Afterwards on television I said: 'I took a risk. It did not come off but it isn't the end of the world. We are not going into an election on this policy. There is a lot more to be done.' But the damage, especially in alienation from David Owen's somewhat gung-ho approach to the same issue, was considerable.

The episode meant even longer 'reassuring' cheers than usual at the end of my leader's speech, possibly also because earlier that week in one interview I went on record saying that I would step down from the Liberal leadership unless I had some role in government after the next election.

In the speech I was strongly critical of the Government's handling of the coal dispute:

During the mining dispute we have seen the Thatcher way at its very worst. She appointed as Chairman of the National Coal Board an elderly American company doctor whose reputation at British Steel had been made by cutting back rather than building up. She has effectively torn up the Plan for Coal and replaced it with nothing except a general sense of hostility to what is one of this country's major assets. She has set up a confrontation which suits her Marxist opponent Arthur Scargill very well. She has allowed attitudes to harden on both sides.

Then this week she has the nerve to talk about the strike going on for a year and demands 'victory' over the 'enemy'. It may be the Thatcher way but it is not the way to conduct industrial relations – and it is deeply damaging to the national economy.

Three weeks later fate again cruelly intervened, this time in the shape of an IRA bomb at the Tory conference hotel in Brighton. Five people were killed and several severely injured in the attempt to assassinate Mrs Thatcher. Public sympathy naturally rallied to her side. On a visit to the town a few weeks later I visited in hospital the Government Chief Whip John Wakeham, whose wife was among those killed and whose legs were badly injured in the blast.

Over the next few months the violent pictures of the militant pickets clashing with police overlaid the arguments about the rights and wrongs of the mining dispute itself or the methods used to promote and suppress it, all to the glory of the Government. In March 1985 the strike at long last ended. In May we had a great boost with over 300 Alliance gains in the County elections in England and Wales, leading to the creation of a number of Alliance administrations. In fact the local-government groups were doing more to cement the Alliance than the two parties nationally.

In July we had the hard-fought and well-deserved triumph of Richard Livsey in the Brecon and Radnor by-election with a majority of 500; and in the middle of our Party Assembly at Dundee, the Gallup Poll gave us a commanding lead over the other parties of 39 per cent with 29 per cent each to them. The Assembly was valiantly opened by our Scottish President, George Mackie, though his wife Lindsay was dying of leukaemia in a hospital in the city. David Owen in his fraternal address was loudly applauded when he assured the Assembly that he did not aim to hold the balance of power though he had spoken of it in the past. More and more people had begun, he observed, to feel the Alliance could form the next government.

This was a brave and resolute approach, coming after his own SDP conference at Torquay where a confidential memo from one of my regular advisers was somehow leaked to the press. In it William Wallace claimed that the Alliance was totally unprepared for government, hindered by divisions within the SDP, and that their ministerial experience was a wasting asset. Such home truths were not drafted in a form intended to see the light of day. At Torquay I had made light of it, reminding my audience of the fate of an earlier William Wallace – being hanged, drawn and quartered in London for sedition. The paper contained a lot of good sense as always from William but he had allowed it to have too dangerously wide a circulation.

In my Dundee speech I referred back to his report:

So we must very seriously prepare ourselves for government – and incidentally, I wouldn't say that Liberals are not ready for government. It is government that isn't ready for the Liberals. Whitehall is going to have to come to terms with a different style of working – from a reforming Alliance, with a more open style.

In contrasting the record of Thatcherism which we would find on coming to office with our own intentions, I said:

Yes, the rich will be richer – but this is the only respect in which the Thatcher revolution will have succeeded. The next government – and I believe it will be the Alliance next – will face the grim reality of the post oil era with a weakened economy, a more divided society and widespread pessimism about the future. The legacy we inherit will be a heavy mortgage on Britain's future.

So what will we do about it?

We must embark on a revolution of our own, a revolutionary shift in values and attitudes.

First we must rekindle the British genius. We must junk all this monetarist and socialist ideology and get back to basics. And for any Liberal the basics are very simple – they are the potential of each individual. We must liberate all the wasted energy of the people of this country by finding new ways to work together rather than against each other. We must create a new partnership in every company, in every community and in the nation as a whole.

The role of government is not to command – as Conservatives and Socialists both believe – it is to enable: to enable each individual to use his or her talents to the full – and incidentally what sort of country is it that fails to use all the talents of half its people, its women – to enable industry and commerce to thrive; to enable the arts and learning to flourish; and to enable political decisions to be made at the level of the people most affected by them.

And don't undersell one of the greatest virtues of the joint leadership of our Alliance. A Prime Minister with a deputy PM who is leader of his own party will bring to an end the quasi-Presidential system of government where one person's views, prejudices and constant meddling interfere with the judgement and collective responsibility of a strong Cabinet team.

When we win power you will have to go back to 1906 to find a parallel occasion when the Cabinet consisted of so many people who had not held office before. Yet what was the verdict on that government? 'There has not been throughout British history a more talented team of men in government' – wrote one historian, adding: 'four became Prime Ministers' – that should be enough to keep everybody happy.

There should be no confusion about the Alliance aim: we want to take power, to share power, and to use power:

● to take power away from those who have misused it for so long and put it back in the hands of the majority of the British people;

● to share power in every community, throughout the nation and with those in Parliament who seek the common good;

● to use power to help the helpless and to give new hope to the hopeless, both within and beyond these shores.

That is our aim.

... Our task is to enable every individual to flourish, to grow tall, to join us in achieving great things. We have to redouble our efforts. I say to those who've been watching over these last two weeks at home – don't just sit on the sidelines and cheer us on. Come in and join us now because

> There is a tide in the affairs of men,
> Which, taken at the flood, leads on to fortune.

On such a full sea we are now afloat.

The tide has been out – for Liberalism and for Britain – for too long. Our nation has been beached, strewn with the rocks of class conflict, our economy left high and dry by our competitors, our institutions stagnant and our people stranded. But now we can all sense the change and take heart. Our message to Britain is:

> Here comes the turn
> Here comes the turn of the tide.

We ended 1985 feeling that it really had.

The year 1986 began with turmoil in the Thatcher Cabinet and the resignation of Michael Heseltine as Secretary of State for Defence over his treatment by the Prime Minister and her acolytes, especially in the leaking of a letter from the Solicitor-General to his colleague, Leon Brittan, Secretary of State for Trade and Industry, critical of some of Heseltine's proposals concerning the future of helicopter manufacturing by the Westland Company. The Prime Minister chose to institute an inquiry into the leaking of the letter which it turned out to no one's surprise had been done by officials at the DTI and Number 10 with Leon Brittan's authority. He subsequently resigned as well. The loss of two Cabinet ministers in such murky circumstances certainly put the Prime Minister's future at risk.

In the emergency debate she was saved by an unbelievably incompetent and windy speech from the Leader of the Opposition, Neil Kinnock, who failed to concentrate on the key issue on which I had focused four days earlier when the PM had reported the outcome of the inquiry to the House. The Prime Minister read out her prepared defence amid noisy interruptions from a frustrated Labour Party seeing their quarry escape. The press gallery began to empty, sensing it was all over as David Owen rose to speak on our behalf, I having spoken in the earlier Westland debate. By then it was too late.

In February 1986, in a routine Sunday morning recorded TV-AM interview with Jonathan Dimbleby, I was asked about a possible merger of the Liberal Party and the SDP after the next election; TV-AM issued the text and it was prominently reported on the Monday that I said 'on balance it is a good idea. I think there will be desire in both parties to have an open discussion on that and I would certainly encourage that.' To this the lobby reporter of *The Times* added: 'It was said by close aides that Dr Owen has always accepted the fact that the two parties would legitimately wish to debate the question of a merger after the next election.' This of course was over a year before I formally suggested that we should do just that.

On the same day Channel 4 broadcast the hour-long documentary in the *My Britain* series which I had filmed under Justin Cartwright's direction the previous summer in the Borders and Liverpool. The Tories made a last-minute effort to persuade the IBA to stop the programme, but were told Jim Prior also had one in the series. It was an effective testimony, lost in the Sunday-night Channel 4 ratings.

In April 1986 the Labour Party won their only by-election from the Government that Parliament – at Fulham – where in spite of fielding a high-quality candidate, Roger Liddle, the SDP came third, a victim of the old two-party squeeze in a marginal seat.

A month later, however, we Liberals almost scored a remarkable double for the Alliance. Elizabeth Shields took the safe Yorkshire Tory seat of Ryedale and Chris Walmsley almost grabbed West Derbyshire, failing by only 100 votes after a campaign in which the Tories, including the resigned Member, Matthew Parris, deliberately exaggerated prospects of a Labour victory after Fulham and thus hindered an effective squeeze on the Labour vote. We also on the same day made spectacular Alliance gains in the annual round of local council elections. We predicted 250 seats for the Alliance in the next House of Commons on the Ryedale/West Derbyshire swings.

A week later, in high spirits, David Owen and I more realistically addressed a joint circular to our candidates setting out our agreed position on the process of consultation and negotiation which would take place in the event of a 'balanced' (our preferred word to 'hung') Parliament after the next election. In the very same week, things began to go wrong in the Alliance on the crucial issue of nuclear defence.

We had been troubled by divisions within and between our parties on nuclear weapon development, both Cruise missiles and Polaris with its possible replacement, Trident. We had therefore appointed a high-powered Commission of both experts and politicians to draft recommendations for our two parties. It had been beavering away for two years under the chairmanship of John Edmonds, former leader of the UK delegation to the Comprehensive Test Ban Treaty Negotiations, who together with General Sir Hugh Beach, whom I appointed to the Commission, was part of that growing part of the electorate which belonged to neither of our parties but supported the objectives of the Alliance. It was about to publish its unanimous report dealing, I thought effectively, with those contentious issues.

One day I had accepted a routine invitation to lunch with two of the *Scotman*'s lobby correspondents. I was naturally in rather relaxed good humour because of the election results and because the *Scotsman* is the most influential daily paper in my part of the world. Also the two journalists concerned, Martin Dowle (now of the BBC) and Andrew Marr, were both men I like and respect.

Other politicians (Michael Havers, Paul Channon and others) have fallen foul of the lobby-lunch syndrome in this last year. It is a hazard of our mutual operations. They never take place, and everything said is off the record and unattributable. It is a system which suits both journalists and politicians nicely until it goes wrong, as it did on this occasion. In my experience when it does go wrong, it is better, as I did, to admit it.

What happened was very straightforward. One of them casually asked how the Defence Commission was coming along and I said that its report would be published in the next couple of weeks or so. It was all very satisfactory. Did it commit us to a replacement for Polaris? At this point I should have changed the subject or told them to wait and see. Instead I foolishly, but accurately, replied: 'No, it doesn't.' Martin Dowle then wrote a story only slightly, but yet significantly, misinterpreting my response saying that the Report would come out *against* replacing Polaris and that this would be hailed as a victory for the Liberals over the SDP. A further nightmare was that the duty sub-editor that night decided to run this story as the *Scotsman*'s front page lead under the glaring headline: 'Alliance Report rejects UK deterrent – Owen's nuclear hopes dashed'.

I did not see the paper at first because that morning I was attending a meeting of the Privy Council with the Queen at Buckingham Palace (about a dozen of us were summoned) to approve the marriage of Prince Andrew to Sarah Ferguson, a time-consuming piece of harmless nonsense, and then flying and driving in the afternoon to my constituency for two evening engagements. David Owen was at his SDP Council in Southport. Not for the first time the geographical separation over that weekend was to prove crucial.

I was appalled when I saw the *Scotsman* front page and naturally felt guilty about it. However, I thought damage limitation was possible, given that no Fleet Street paper had carried the story, and I thought there was therefore plenty of opportunity to put it right. Unfortunately David Owen, in whose reading I had assumed the *Scotsman* did not regularly feature, was about to address his Party Council when someone either showed him or told him of the story. Perhaps because of his upbringing in the Labour Party, he tends to subscribe to the conspiracy theory of politics and felt that he was being deliberately done down. Without checking or contacting me, he blasted off not just by inference against that story but against the Report of the Defence Commission itself: 'I must tell you bluntly that I believe we should remain a nuclear weapon state.' He rejected the Commission's sensible conclusion as 'deserving a belly laugh from the British electorate'. This of course gave the general press a much bigger story about new splits in the Alliance.

Bill Rodgers in a letter to *The Times* defended the Commission's conclusion on the Polaris replacement point:

When the Polaris missile system comes to the end of its life in the late 1990s, should it be replaced? This is not a question of principle and ought not to be a test of political virility. It is a matter of cost and opportunity – set against the changing international scene.

He continued that the decision should be taken only in the light of a thorough and up-to-date review of alternatives and the international situation.

It is surely sensible to postpone a final decision on Polaris replacement while these matters remain in the balance. This is not a fudge. There's no deceit or humbug in admitting an open mind until a review has been completed. The real fudge is to say unequivocally that Trident should be cancelled but that Britain should remain a nuclear weapons state.

He concluded:

Certainty is not always a virtue. Nor is conviction itself evidence of truth. The Commission's Report is not an exercise in evasion and compromise. It sets out a credible policy that both Social Democrats and Liberals should support.

Meanwhile in the *Daily Mail* Shirley Williams wrote:

It does not follow that what the leader said is the same and identical with the policy of the party. . . . The present policy of the SDP is that the Party is willing to replace Polaris under certain circumstances but not irrevocably so. . . . It would be excellent if he's prepared to listen to other points of view and possibly even consider whether there is room for some movement on his part as well as on the part of the rest of us.

When he learnt that Owen's outburst had been because of the *Scotsman* report, Roy Jenkins said: 'In that case the man's totally unfit to hold public office.'

Once again the Alliance was being damaged by itself, not by its enemies. My own view is that in spite of our best subsequent endeavours, that weekend marked the beginning of a worrying lack of trust at the heart of the Alliance between David Owen on the one hand and me with Roy, Shirley and Bill on the other.

As far as David and I were concerned, we tried to repair the damage as best we could. Whether I ever convinced him of the series of errors leading to the *Scotsman* story I do not know. I accepted my share of the blame for giving them a partial account in advance of seeing the actual text from the Commission.

One sad effect of the Owen outburst was to obscure the value of the whole of the Commission's report. At one point he even suggested that we could fight the election as Alliance partners with each having its own defence policy, a lunatic proposal which I had to rebut clearly. On ITV's *Weekend World* I responded to questions on this: 'He [Owen] is right to say it is not the end of the world if that happens, but in my view it is pretty close to it'; and at yet another pretty dreadful meeting of the Liberal Party Council in Wigan I was more specific:

In his first Conference speech as SDP Leader, David Owen invited people to tell him when he was talking nonsense. On defence matters I would never say that, but there is one question on which I feel bound to take up his invitation. The suggestion that we could live with SDP and Liberal candidates saying different things at the next election on defence is profoundly misplaced ... to be blunt, to have Liberal candidates saying one thing and SDP another would be unacceptable to me and incredible to the electorate.

I know that he was annoyed at press reports before publication. He had every reason to be. There is no reason for party triumphalism in our Alliance. But as I have pointed out to him from rather longer experience of the bed of nails which party leadership sometimes is, we must both expect to be angered by many press reports we don't like before we get to polling day at the next election. Precisely because we are two parties, we are obliged to continue – paradoxically – to have a closer unity between us than exists within either the Tory or Labour Parties.

About this time too we were both giving frank interviews. I went on record as saying that he was 'not the easiest person in the world to work with. He never has been in any post he has held'; while he correctly described us as 'not bosom pals' for which he unleashed a good deal of undeserved criticism. We never pretended otherwise, while maintaining throughout a perfectly civilized and mainly friendly political partnership. I always thought he was at his best and most relaxed when I saw him with Debbie over supper in their kitchen at Limehouse. We knew we had to make the partnership work.

David Penhaligon challenged me at one meeting of the Liberal MPs: 'When you wake up in the morning, do you think of the Alliance or the Liberal Party first?'

'The Alliance, of course,' I said.

'I thought you'd say that. Now I'll ask the other fellow the same question when he comes.'

He did, and the other fellow waffled. 'That's my point, you see,' said David.

I was also celebrating that summer my ten years as leader and gave a series of reflective interviews and speeches. At the National Liberal Club celebratory lunch I said: 'I make no secret of the fact that I believe it almost inevitable that this unity will grow before long into a formal union between our parties.' In a perceptive leader at the start of the summer 1986 recess *The Times* declared:

In a sense it does not matter when – whether – there is some final act of marriage; for it is already being consummated by joint manifestos and the growth of an Alliance identity which, however vague and amorphous in ideological terms, will inevitably gain from common experience of powerholding or opposition locally. It is noteworthy that Mr Steel has in the past few weeks permitted himself to raise the issue of merger, albeit in a gentle and rather dreamy way.

... The question for the autumn must be: has Dr Owen been educated about joint leadership of the only political vehicle he has got? The public, evidently, had doubts about the way he exposed his convictions. He, too, will have to bend and accommodate. The two-headed party is a stranger in the British political bestiary, and the animal appears the odder when the heads are snapping at each other. It may well be incapable of surviving beyond an election.

11

MERGER

Back from the Brink

During the summer of 1986, in spite of the public rupture, the Alliance reduced the safe Labour majority at the Newcastle-under-Lyme by-election to 799. Our opinion-poll ratings had started to drop. We might have won otherwise. We started to explore together one other area of the Commission's recommendations, that the European pillar of NATO should be strengthened. Did there lie here a possible alternative to purchasing Trident from the Americans? We set off on a much publicized tour of Europe, seeing among others President Mitterrand in Paris and the NATO European commanders in Brussels. It was a wholly useful and constructive exercise in which we found a genuine welcome for our views on European defence co-operation. The French Prime Minister, Jacques Chirac, told us: 'But I've never heard British politicians talking like this.'

To which we responded almost in unison: 'That's because you talk to Margaret Thatcher.'

David Watt, the Director of the Royal Institute of International Affairs, wrote:

The journey made together by David Owen and David Steel to Paris, Bonn and Brussels last week has turned out to be much more interesting than most people have realized – or perhaps even than the voyagers expected. Conceived as a device for helping the Alliance parties to get safely through their dangerous party conference debates on defence, the trip has opened up intriguing vistas in the field of European defence. In particular it has revealed a remarkable new readiness on the part of the French government to discuss Anglo-French co-operation on nuclear weapons.

... Also significant was the Steel-Owen discovery that General Bernard Rogers, the Supreme Allied Commander, welcomed the prospect of closer Anglo-French nuclear co-operation.

These were early and tentative approaches, though significantly even the present Government has now pursued the path at least as far as co-ordinated deployment of the submarine deterrents is concerned and on arms procurement.

We were both quite pleased with the outcome, and it enabled us all to pull David Owen back into the area of the Commission's recommendations, i.e. no specific commitments until we could examine all the options at the right time in government, a formula which, though open to misinterpretation, held together perfectly well through the following election.

Unfortunately, while reuniting with the Doctor I failed to notice growing unease within the Liberal Party itself. Des Wilson – correctly I think – judges in his book, *Battle for Power*, that I had been so busy trying to heal the breach between the Commission and David Owen that I had too readily assumed the Commission's recommendations to be acceptable to the Party. ('Were it not for the suspicions engendered by Owen they probably would have been,' assessed Des.) The Commission had produced the basis for a new Alliance policy, which made it anathema alike to the SDP separatists and the Liberal purists.

Some in the party, including MPs Meadowcroft, Hughes and Kirkwood, thought that some new statement of *Liberal* policy should be made and, while lacking the expertise of the Commission, set about producing an unhelpful pamphlet, telling no one about it until too late.

'To Steel,' according to Des Wilson, 'a gathering of two policy committees was in fact one gathering to determine one policy. To many Liberals, and to many Social Democrats, probably including Owen, it was an on-going negotiating process from two clear positions.' Des is correct in his perception – which applied also to the later merger negotiations. I simply assert that my approach was right and theirs wrong. Des complained, for example, that I early on abandoned separate pre-meetings of the Liberal side of the Joint Strategy Committee, wholly consistent with my view of how we should be proceeding. Some Liberals gathering at the Assembly at Eastbourne saw this as the last chance to establish a powerful *Liberal* position for the final negotiations with the SDP on the joint policy programme. Of this tendency I was, I'm afraid, wholly unaware.

I had had another good reception from the SDP Conference and they had produced a reasonable defence resolution along the lines of the Commission's recommendations. I expected us to do likewise and put the unfortunate episode behind us.

As often happened, the anarchic nature of our constitution and practical arrangements then let us down. I have touched on this point so often that I had better digress to explain. The Liberal Party was intensely democratic, but in a disordered way. Thus it was very easy for anyone determined to do so to become an Assembly delegate. It was not all that difficult to get elected by one of various routes to the Party Council, a small minority of which regularly treated it as a form of political entertainment three or four times a year. Some two hundred people were often crammed into wholly unsuitable venues round the country. Successive Presidents were driven to despair at trying to control proceedings.

The Agenda Committee had no power to control the agenda. So anything scribbled on the back of an envelope could get on to the Council's agenda and, if passed, purported to become policy in between Assemblies. The Executive was a smaller body of about thirty who could be overruled by the Council and affected by decisions of the quite separate Finance and Administration Board, and were spectators on policy matters which were handled by the Standing (Policy) Committee. As if this were not complicated enough, the Executives and Councils were normally held on Saturdays when the leader and other MPs were usually engaged in their constituencies or on flag-raising expeditions for the Party around the country. It was this disorderly way of making policy which largely caused the need in the Party's constitution for the leader's veto over the policy content of the manifesto. The new Party's constitution is a great deal more rational and the key committees meet – as those of the other parties all do – on weekday evenings so that there is now greater parliamentary input.

If all that were not difficult enough, when it came to the annual Assembly real power lay in the Assembly Committee, which was elected to run a decent conference – which I must say it usually did. To this Committee fell the choice, and indeed rewriting, of amendments to the resolution on Defence, thus overriding the policy committee, the parliamentary party, the Defence Commission and everybody else, even though they might not have been appointed for their expertise on the subject.

On the opening Monday of the 1986 Assembly, that Committee happened to meet at the same time as the MPs. We were therefore unaware of their decision until too late, and no MP was present. Their amendment wished to add to the 'European co-operation' section the proviso 'provided that such a defence capacity is non-nuclear'. This they had concocted from those submitted.

I can best quote Des Wilson's critical account of what then happened:

There was no consideration of persuading the movers to withdraw the amendment, or of tactics to rally support for the platform the following day.

This is crucial – *no attempt was made at that meeting to set about managing the Party to achieve the result the Leadership wanted*. Of course this can be interpreted positively. It could be said that, unlike other parties, the Liberal Party is genuinely democratic, that there is no attempt at manipulation of, or dictatorship to, the Party on policy. This would be more convincing if the Leader did not have a veto on the Party manifesto, and if on other occasions he had not made it clear that he would simply take no notice of an Assembly resolution. No, it was not for these idealistic reasons that no plans were made by the MPs to manage the debate and achieve the required result. The real reason was lack of contact with their party. Those responsible for party management, for leadership, were not in touch with what was happening in the hotel bars and the fringe meetings, where resistence to the unamended main resolution was being developed. By their failure to sense the mood of the party, their failure to be represented at the Assembly Committee meeting and try to influence the choice of amendments, their failure to organize a vote-collecting initiative the following day, their failure to consider the nature of the speeches that would need to be made, they had made themselves vulnerable to defeat.

On Tuesday Jim Wallace as defence spokesman competently moved the resolution, backed by Paddy Ashdown, the rebel from yesteryear, who was equally competent. Simon Hughes then made a highly emotional speech for the amendment referring to 'a Euro nuclear bomb mountain with twelve fingers on the button'. This was rubbish but it was glorious rubbish and the Assembly loved it. Alan Beith made an incisive counterattack for the motion but by this time it was greatly damaged. At this point I wondered whether to seek to speak myself on the politics of the situation we faced. I thought that to do so might smack of panic and lack of confidence in my colleagues who had done well on the issue itself, but I also recalled the 1984 Assembly voting against my recommendation and decided that this might only exacerbate the difficulty we were now in.

The amendment won by the narrow margin of 652 to 625. I tried immediately to play it down to the press as 'a minor irritant rather than a setback'; but I was, correctly, fearful that this was not how it would be portrayed.

That evening we had a bitter meeting of the parliamentary Party, not helped by the fact that Simon Hughes was addressing yet another fringe meeting and arrived late, while Archy Kirkwood and Michael Meadowcroft arrived even later from one of their successful musical engagements on the fringe. In their absence the mood was angry. I opened quietly enough, saying that I believed we now had a dangerous political problem on our hands, that a defence policy would still have to be hammered out but that the three

MPs who had broken ranks had been naïve in not recognizing the likely consequences of their actions or the way the outcome would be misused by our opponents.

Elizabeth Shields, normally mild-mannered, was rougher, saying she felt betrayed and that the MPs had not followed the spirit of the Alliance which had won her Ryedale. David Alton as Chief Whip was furious about the publication of their pamphlet without consulting the defence spokesman. Alex Carlile and Russell Johnston were virulent in their criticism while George Mackie regarded their conduct as little short of treachery. When Simon arrived he was at least contrite, and expressed sorrow at the upset but said he had a right to put his views. He accepted that a greater sense of collective responsibility should be introduced, at which Stephen Ross exploded, 'It's a bit late now, Simon.' When Archy and Michael arrived, Michael was more defensive. He condemned the way the defence policy had been arrived at, made familiar points about party democracy, and gave the mirror image of the Owen 'separate identity' argument. He was not well received. Archy very wisely kept quiet.

I wound up one of our unhappiest meetings by saying that we were stuck with the issue for the rest of the conference and that I would have to jettison my prepared leader's speech which had been majoring on housing and education and return to the defence issue with a new speech. I went to bed feeling that the world was about to fall in.

Next morning, Wednesday, we had the worst headlines in the entire history of the Alliance. It was worse than I feared. Our tabloid enemies led their front pages: 'No nuke Libs beat Steel in big vote' (*Daily Mirror*); 'Ban the bomb vote shatters the Alliance' (*Daily Express*). Even our often friendly *Guardian* ran 'Liberals rebuff Steel over nuclear policy'. *The Times* lead headline was 'Steel defeat puts Alliance in disarray'. We had a uniformly appalling press.

As delegates munched their cornflakes in their hotels and boarding houses, the full enormity of what they had done in a reasonable debating atmosphere must have dawned on them. Supporters round the country were outraged, and blamed those at the Assembly.

On Thursday I was scheduled to helicopter to London to appear with David Owen jointly on ITV's *This Week*. We were in a hell of a mess for such a long-planned programme. I arranged to meet David privately beforehand. He was instantly supportive, saying that we were both in this together and that anything which damaged me and my Party damaged the whole Alliance. It was genuine and I was equally genuinely grateful. I had been working on my new speech and told him the gist of it. We could not accept the Assembly decision as manifesto policy and I would have to rescue the situation by being necessarily hard-line in my Friday speech.

I was, and the speech led the news bulletins and the heavy Sunday newspapers, though the hostile tabloids failed to give it equal treatment to their earlier coverage. I publicly went a little over the top (but it was essential) when I described the amendment passed as no better than the placards on Lambeth lamp posts proclaiming a nuclear-free zone.

I referred to the completely misguided belief that it was the Assembly's task to accentuate the few remaining points of difference with the SDP so as to 'strengthen my hand' in manifesto discussions with David Owen: 'That is a breathtaking misjudgement. We are either in alliance or we are not. We must live and breathe the Alliance. It is unthinkable that we enter the election with two defence and disarmament policies.'

The speech settled the press, the SDP, and the party rank and file. The editorial and broadcast comment was as uniformly good as the earlier coverage had been bad, but I'm afraid I offended many of those present who were not used to being spoken to in those terms. 'Without power,' I reminded them, 'all our resolution, all our idealism, all our compassion, will remain mere intention, mere hope, mere dream.' Jo Grimond had helped by writing an article from which I quoted: 'For Britain alone to abandon nuclear weapons would be to retreat from those doctrines of international collaboration and collective security which have been the main aim in Liberalism.' I neared the end on a positive note:

Neither of us subscribes to the doctrine of infallibility of party leaders, at least I don't, but nor does he. No one should be worried by differences in style or even occasionally in opinion between David Owen and myself. The reality is that this relationship will work and the two leaders are growing steadily closer together.

Robin Oakley, in a lengthy piece as political editor of *The Times*, concluded: '... and another more fundamental problem is revived: are the Liberals seriously interested in winning power?' Another *Times* leader, noting that I had been booed in parts of the speech, concluded bluntly: 'The Liberals may lose some candidates altogether; they may lose some MPs. But there is no alternative if the smell of failure is not to become the smell of death.'

In October 1986, I asked Des Wilson as Party President, Jim Wallace as Defence Spokesman and Simon Hughes to Ettrick Bridge over the weekend to hammer out a solution to our problem. The location provided the right atmosphere conductive to agreement. We succeeded in drafting a new agreement to put to the Party's Policy Committee under which we would agree to maintain the nuclear deterrent until it could be negotiated away in world arms-reduction talks, any necessary modernization being no greater than the capacity of the existing Polaris force. Equally we were not forecasting what precisely that modernization would be, which required a shift by David Owen back into the area agreed by our Defence Commission, and which, I repeat, caused us no difficulty in the 1987 election. Both the parliamentary Party and the policy committee and then indeed the Party Council, in the new calmer atmosphere brought about by recognition of the damage caused at Eastbourne, accepted it. This was the gist of what entered our joint policy document, *Partnership for Progress*. It would have been a lot simpler if we had all accepted the Defence Commission report in the first place.

In November, battling Rosie Cooper raised our spirits by polling 35 per cent at the by-election in the safe Labour seat of Knowsley North, when our national poll rating had declined to 17 per cent. We headed for the Christmas recess in a mixture of relief and exhaustion only to be struck by a fresh and cruel blow. Early in the morning of 22 December Ro Kirkwood came rushing up to our house in tears to tell us that David Penhaligon had been killed in a car crash. I phoned his wife Annette immediately. It was true – he had been paying a pre-dawn visit to Christmas postal workers when his car was struck on black ice by a van. He had been killed instantly. We were all devastated. As Neil Kinnock so aptly described him, he was 'a decent sweet man with a wonderful sense of humour and independence'. David had driven me and Judy and Annette back to our block of flats after the annual Alliance Ball – he being teetotal – just four days before. That was the last time I saw him. A few weeks before, I had half-teased him about his year as President preparing him for leadership. 'No,' he said, 'I saw enough of your kind of life in that year to know I couldn't do it.' Besides, he argued, he had his handicapped daughter Anna to think of.

'But you're the obvious successor if I give up after the next election.'

'Well, maybe,' he replied, 'but I don't like to think about it.'

That day I too was out on my Christmas duties. As I visited one old folks' home a helicopter descended in the grounds bringing a TV crew. I made my tributes and I'm afraid my mind was neither on Christmas nor on my aged constituents as I continued my rounds.

December 1986 ended with what was supposedly a private family occasion. The parish church just outside Truro where David and Annette had married and attended was packed. Afterwards Judy and I joined the family for the private interment, feeling utterly miserable at the loss of such a vital colleague and even more at his family's loss as husband and father.

The next day we left with two of our children – Graeme and Rory – a day late for a week's cheap holiday over the New Year in Tenerife. I was poor company for them, brooding over the tragedy at Truro. But the few days in the sun reinvigorated me, and my sorrow turned to determination that David's death meant the rest of us having to try harder.

On 31 January 1987 we 'relaunched' the Alliance at a great rally in the Barbican Centre in the City of London amid a barrage of media publicity from *Wogan* to *Weekend World*. In a pre-Barbican article in *The Times*, the political editor, Robin Oakley, speculated:

What of Steel's own future? If the Alliance does not make the breakthrough this time, will he really have the will to continue, having nearly quit after the 1983 election? Steel says he has assured his MPs that he would not 'walk out of the door' immediately after the election, even if the results are disappointing. But he says: 'If it is just a modest advance, but nothing dramatically different, then I think the party would want to say thank you and goodbye, or maybe no thank you and goodbye' ... The way Steel intends to go is clear: 'The SDP policymaking structures have a logic and cohesion which ours lack.' Is that a subtle hint to Owen that maybe merger might not be a bad thing after all?

For weeks we had been building up to a pre-election event which would mark the culmination of seat negotiations between the two parties, the publication of a new book by David Owen and me, largely drafted by a team of researchers, setting out our policies under the slogan *The Time Has Come*, and the presentation of our new prime-gold livery. The Rothwell Temperance brass band was there to proclaim our new theme, Purcell's trumpet tune. The election spokesmen were to be unveiled and Jo Grimond launched the whole event in a typically amusing and uplifting ten minutes, declaring: 'No other party could persuade two and a half thousand people to pay £7 to hear eighteen speeches. It must strike terror into the hearts of our opponents.'

We had a professionally designed stage-set with all the MPs and election spokesmen sitting on display on one side, while video films, illustrating the various subjects being presented, were shown on huge screens above the stage. The whole event was brilliantly stage-managed and well presented for that night's TV news bulletins. It was an enthusiastic Alliance occasion at which David Owen, whose House of Commons mastery never seems to translate to the public platform, made rather a lame speech. My own I had carefully prepared over several days; and I decided to use an autocue, making the delivery much more relaxed. I included some good jokes – old ones are the best on these occasions – and the audience particularly enjoyed my presentation of our Alliance team compared with the qualities of the Government: 'What is it,' I asked, 'that we are supposedly unable to match? The charisma of Geoffrey Howe? The humanity and charm of Nigel Lawson? The judgement of Jeffrey Archer? The common sense and common touch of Nicholas Ridley? Or is it just the quiet dignity of Edwina Currie?'

But it was not all fun. Referring to David Penhaligon's death, with great emotional difficulty, I quoted the words of the hymn by Archbishop Darbyshire:

> Not names engraved in marble make
> The best memorials of the dead,
> But burdens shouldered for their sake
> And tasks completed in their stead.

It was one of my better speeches, because I had spent a lot of time drafting and redrafting it myself. Judy and Debbie Owen were sitting in the front row. Immediately afterwards David Owen and I filmed pieces in the hall for a party political broadcast, David being in slightly tetchy mood as he always seemed to be with television crews. Afterwards Judy and I went to an unlikely fund-raising event in a wine cellar near Blackfriars where we sat with Bill and Sylvia Rodgers, who seemed not to be on speaking terms with David and Debbie Owen. The Owens sat with their children, while the Rodgers sat at the opposite end of the long table.

From the Barbican we were propelled in high spirits into the Greenwich by-election. At first sight this Labour seat was not a likely prospect for us, but two things helped. First, Labour chose a standard London 'loony Left' candidate who was – unfortunately for her and her party – quite well known. Second, we were in the borough shared by John Cartwright's Woolwich West constituency, with his own considerable expertise and his local party machine available. The Tory press attacked the Labour candidate mercilessly, but Greenwich was not the sort of place likely to vote Conservative. Our next good fortune was that our unknown and inexperienced candidate, Rosie Barnes, who was a new member of the SDP, turned out to be competent, with an attractive personality which conveyed her sound common sense in an appealing manner to the electorate. Alec McGivan, the SDP's national organizer, was the agent once more, and several experienced professionals and volunteers from both parties provided a really crack by-election team. This was the first actual Alliance by-election contest, all other by-elections having been organized by one or other party on behalf of both (a fact which made Rosie's subsequent desertion of the Alliance particularly painful). A victory from Labour was of special importance as we had to demonstrate we could take seats not only from the Tories.

The result was a triumph for the Alliance and our opinion-poll rating rose as a result from 21 per cent to 29 per cent. The subsequent by-election at

Truro on 12 March 1987 was another triumph, won by David Penhaligon's research assistant, Matthew Taylor, with a majority which was a real tribute both to David and to the Alliance steamroller. We therefore entered the general election in a mood of some confidence, bolstered by good opinion polls and local election gains of over 450 seats.

As soon as the election date became known, David Owen and I were ready to do a hedge-hopping tour of all the major cities in three days, simply to hold press conferences, meet our campaigners in each area and give the necessary television interviews. This was David's idea and it was a good one. Rather than sit around in London in the 'phoney war' before Parliament was dissolved we planned to visit every media centre. To put flesh on the idea, I persuaded Anthony Jacobs, former parliamentary candidate, who was joint Treasurer of the Liberal Party and a good friend, again to lend his executive jet, the one I had used at the previous election and for the visit to Moscow. It is the most comfortable and efficient way to transport a group of people to a number of places. Using this, we were able to cover three centres a day for three and a half days.

I used the plane intermittently throughout the election. David and I indulged in some good-natured rivalry. He used a much larger but slower plane which could carry a busload of journalists. Mine could seat only eight. With support staff and Special Branch, there was only room for an occasional journalist or broadcaster. But my plane – unlike his – was reliable and very fast – and the stewardess produced superior snacks. I was regularly abusive about his plane, even when he gave me lifts on it on a couple of occasions.

The pre-election days gave us time to see and discuss final proofs of the election manifesto and other material. We were in constant touch with Headquarters on our radio telephones – how did we ever run elections before without them?

One event shattered this preparation period. After our press conference at Manchester, a reporter from the *Daily Express* asked if he could have a private word and we went to a corner of the hotel conference room where our interviews had just ended. He had been asked by his editor to put to me a story 'going the rounds' at the Scottish Tory Conference at Perth and which the *News of the World* intended to publish on Sunday, namely that I had been having an affair with the wife of a prominent Scottish Liberal. The story was that their marriage had split up and that she was living in a cottage in the Highlands where I was carrying on the said affair. At first I didn't know whether to laugh or cry. Then I became very angry, realizing the combined provenance of the story from a Tory Conference in a Tory newspaper.

I saw this as a deliberate attempt to smear our campaign before it started.

Gary Hart was known to be a friend of mine and somebody seemed to have hit on the bright idea of trying to knock me out of the campaign as effectively as he had knocked himself out of the Presidential race. I felt almost physically sick.

On the next leg of the plane journey I had to tell David Owen and my staff what I had just been told. I have to say that David Owen was constantly sympathetic and supportive. But the next five days were a complete mess. The chosen timing could not have been more devastating. Instead of completing the 'mugging up' of the details of the manifesto, I spent all my time on the telephone to solicitors, press officers and my offended friend and her husband, both of whom are friends of Judy and me and our children. One newspaper inadvertently published the story and a writ had to be issued. They swiftly retracted, apologized in open court and paid substantial damages. We also obtained a High Court injunction against the *News of the World*, on the hearing of which their Counsel admitted that there was no justification for the story. (This saga did not end until November 1988 when, following Koo Stark's successful court case, News International Ltd settled out of court with substantial damages, all of which I am putting towards the cost of restoring Oakwood Tower.)

Then the election proper started with the opening press conference in the National Liberal Club, after which we departed in our separate battlebuses. Mine was not quite designed as I had ordered and we spent the first two or three days trying to get changes in the interior and equipment which should have been seen to in advance. The 'Ask the Alliance' rallies were a great success. They lacked the rehearsed passion of Neil Kinnock's showbiz events and the carefully stage-managed enthusiasm of Mrs Thatcher's faithful-only rallies. But they were as before open to the public, they drew large crowds and we did spontaneously answer questions from the public, something neither of the other two leaders did. Our manifesto, *Britain United*, received the expected mixed bag of reviews, with favourable responses from the *Financial Times*, *Guardian* and *Today*.

Yet somehow the strategy of the campaign became confused. David Owen and I had already agreed in detail what we would do if we held the balance of power after the election and in a joint letter to our candidates four months prior to the election we had offered the following advice:

You should make clear that, in a balanced Parliament, we are ready to negotiate with other parties to give Britain a period of stable yet reforming government. We shall also insist that any negotiated agreement covers an agreed programme for a fixed period of years .... You will repeatedly be asked whether you want a Labour or a

Conservative Government – Mr Kinnock or Mrs Thatcher as Prime Minister. The answer which we are giving is that we genuinely believe that neither Mr Kinnock, nor Mrs Thatcher, nor the parties they lead, can on their own unite the country or provide good government ... *We shall not allow ourselves, nor should you, to express a preference between working with Labour or Tory* MPs [My italics]. We want a new government to reflect as much as is reasonable of the constructive Programme for Government on which we will have fought the election.

We had discussed the balance of power with the Secretary to the Cabinet, Sir Robert Armstrong. We went to see the Cabinet Secretary under the convention that he makes his advice available to the Opposition as well as Government once a dissolution is announced so that he can make preparations for changes in Government. So far as we know, this was the first time that this advice had been extended beyond the official Opposition, and the suggestion was Sir Robert's. It could have been a rather sticky meeting because both of us had been critical of his role in the Peter Wright affair, especially his 'economical with the truth' evidence in Australia. Yet he was courteous and affable, and reassured us that none of our conversation would be relayed to the Prime Minister. We rehearsed with him our understanding of the constitutional conventions surrounding the different varieties of 'no majority' results. He confirmed the general approach of the private memorandum the two of us had drafted some months before. We had no difficulty between us, partly because we had been on opposite sides in the Lib-Lab pact and knew intimately the advantages and pitfalls of holding a balance.

Unfortunately the balance of power seemed to become a positive objective in David's mind. In vain I argued that, having fought the 1979 election as a survival effort on this theme, I knew all its shortcomings, chief of which is that third parties cannot decree that the two main parties should finish close enough to each other for us to provide the balance.

As if that was not enough, the good Doctor dropped an almighty clanger on our joint *Panorama* interview with Sir Robin Day by expressing a preference between the other two parties, something no experienced third-party leader should ever do and which Roy Jenkins and I had always avoided. Sir Robin asked David which would be the greater evil, a majority Labour government or a majority Tory government. And David replied: 'In the last analysis, the one issue on which I will always judge anyone – and that is somebody who would put at jeopardy the defences and security of this country – unless the Labour Party changes its defence policy, in my judgement they are not fit to govern the country.' The fact that the preference was for Mrs Thatcher lost us Labour support in those key seats we needed to take from the Tories as

279

well as in Labour seats. (A preference for Mr Kinnock would have had different but equally damaging effects.) David realized that he had put his foot in it before the discussion had ended. When I gave a neutral answer, he added that he agreed with it and said that I 'was much wiser in handling your [Sir Robin Day's] attempt to get us to decide'. Afterwards we agreed that that had been a nasty moment but hoped it would not matter too much. I remember saying, 'It's easy for me – I've answered that one so often before, not least to Robin Day.' But the press the next day seized on it, with *The Times* pointing out yet again that 'Owen and Steel fail to agree'.

The reaction to David's gaffe was strong everywhere. Even on the doorsteps in my own constituency, people were saying, 'What is the point of voting for you if you're going to join Mrs Thatcher?' My own attempts to modify this image were less than successful. On a television phone-in I said it was 'unimaginable' that we could join a coalition under Mrs Thatcher. It was a well-chosen word. We had agreed in endless private discussion that a Prime Minister who had been defeated in the polls (that is what losing a majority meant) could not head a new government. She would not wish to, anyway. In a later interview with David Dimbleby, I was asked if I would serve under Mrs Thatcher and replied: 'If she had lost the election, she would be unqualified and almost definitely would not wish to continue. She would have lost the election. She would go. You must give Mrs Thatcher some credit – she's a democrat.' But my efforts only provided a further impression of disunity in the Alliance.

A further complication was that Labour was clearly failing to close the gap to make 'balance' likely. David Owen refused to accept this, interpreting all 'Don't knows' in private opinion surveys as potential voters for us or Labour. My preference for proclaiming Labour as obvious losers and therefore appealing for support to switch to us was not clearly put forward.

Despite these stresses, the campaign was amicable enough. We had a particularly warm and at times entertaining 'Ask the Alliance' rally in Edinburgh at which, in response to a question about future merger, David Owen was positive to the extent of declaring himself an old-fashioned Liberal at heart! On one Sunday afternoon we made a particularly jovial and crowded river trip to support Alan Watson in Richmond.

My main complaint was that two leaders campaigning together conveyed a negative image, making us look like Tweedledum and Tweedledee, especially on 'one camera' local TV interviews. We were both bored silly by listening to each other at these rallies. However, when we were apart the media amused themselves by playing 'spot the difference' with our respective comments.

My former assistant, Stuart Mole, experienced the problems of the dual leadership as an ordinary candidate, lamenting: 'The fatal perception of an Alliance divided came from the different messages emanating from the two Davids. The image was a fragmented one – most particularly and most damagingly through the starkly contrasting attitudes to dealing with Mrs Thatcher. The decision – if it was such – to talk of the balance of power was also a critical error.'

The election campaign on the move was as gruelling as the '83 one. My second assistant, Michael Duncan, was doing an outstanding job taking charge of the Battlebus press corps with the additional hazard of an overflow bus. My secretaries, Ann De'Ath and Nali Dinshaw, alternated in travail on board, as did my political assistant, Graham Watson, and press officer, Paul Medlicott, who returned to help my campaign while the Party press officer, Jim Dumsday, stayed at base. The good Lord Chitnis presided as usual over my personal team.

At one point a spat developed between Paul and Graham when it was discovered that the helicopter taking me from Yeovil to Plymouth was smaller than expected and one of them had to be left behind. Paul insisted that he was needed more to cope with the Plymouth TV programmes and so Graham was left to come with the others by bus. That helicopter journey was the most horrific of three uncomfortable episodes I have had with helicopters over the years. We had just passed the tall spire of Buckfastleigh parish church (I remembered it well because my brother Ian had got married there to his Devonian wife, Jill) when we ran into thick low cloud. Helicopters are usually flown visually, unlike fixed-wing planes which rely more on instruments. They are not therefore permitted to fly at night or in mist or fog. I suppose that, since he was only a few miles away from our renedzvous at Plymouth airport, the pilot thought it might just be a narrow belt of fog. It wasn't.

He then shot straight upwards and emerged above the clouds but could see no holes through which to descend. Plymouth Airport is not equipped with full radar, so although we were in radio contact they could not guide us down. Eventually he decided to try a descent, instructing us all to look out below and shout if we saw land. We descended slowly through the pea-souper and could see nothing. At about 300 feet on the altimeter, I began worrying about the church spire I had last seen, though later people on the ground at Plymouth Airport said they heard us descending. Then the pilot decided it was dangerous to go any lower while unable to see anything, so we shot off to Exeter, leaving David Owen to cover the two television interviews on his own while we made another descent over Exeter Airport assisted by radar. On landing, all very shaken, the Special Branch officer on duty got out and kissed the ground, saying that in all his years in the police he had never been so frightened.

Our Party election broadcasts did not give us the impetus we needed. The first, the much criticized one featuring Rosie Barnes with her rabbit, compared unfavourably with the slick opening effort of Labour, focused entirely on Neil Kinnock. I was asked at the last minute to do the third broadcast myself, face to camera, concentrating on the Alliance as a healer and an alternative to the politics of envy and division. Our advertising agency for the election, Abbot, Meade and Vickers, were much criticized for having a limited comprehension of our parties and, indeed, of politics, while they complained of lack of direction.

But the campaign staggered on sluggishly to the end; the long awaited 'late surge' never occurred. We polled 23 per cent, 2 per cent down on the previous election and emerged with twenty-two MPs in place of our former twenty-seven: Liberals fell from nineteen to seventeen and the SDP dropped from eight to five. Our losses were countered by three gains: Ronnie Fearn in Southport; Menzies Campbell in Asquith's old seat in North East Fife; and Ray Michie in Argyll and Bute. It was a frugal reward for the valiant efforts of so many of our talented candidates and their hard-working associations.

In the early hours of Friday morning, after the results were clear, I spoke to David Owen on the telephone and we expressed mutual regret that the result had not been better, but relief that it had not been worse. I had returned home after the declaration of my own result and was watching the later results on television between 3 a.m. and 5 a.m. He had similarly retired to the privacy of his cottage in Plymouth. I said, 'There is only one thing to do now and that is to get our two parties together.' He neither agreed nor demurred. That afternoon he gave a press conference in Plymouth which, to my surprise, appeared to put a block on merger. He mentioned our telephone conversation and then, according to the *Independent*, 'fired the opening shots in his campaign against merger'.

This came as a shock to me, partly because of his warmth towards the idea during the campaign itself and partly because of his own utterances on the subject of merger before the election. For example, in June 1985 in a radio interview he said: 'After the next election the issue of merger or of a closer relationship will come back on the agenda and rightly so, inevitably so.' In March 1986 on television he said: 'It may well be that we shall merge.' Yet here he was within hours of the election putting up a block.

When I read this on Saturday, together with pro-merger comments from other Liberals and Social Democrats, I realized that a lead had to be taken, echoing Macbeth's 'If it were done when 'tis done, then 'twere well It were done quickly.' My overwhelming mood was not one of despair nor anger but sheer frustration. All through the previous parliament David had dragged his feet on joint selection of candidates, joint parliamentary meetings, joint everything and even now when 'jointery' had proved wanting here, he was putting up more obstacles to unity. David Owen's attitude was well summarized in the Butler and Kavanagh analysis of the election:

If the relationship was to be only an electoral pact, his dislike of joint spokesmen, joint policymaking, and joint selection, his rejection of a single leader, and his veto over clear organisational links, all can be seen as a perfectly coherent political position. Most Liberals never understood that this was David Owen's basic attitude to the Alliance.

One key figure in the policy development of the Alliance, Dr William Wallace, vented the general frustration of Liberals towards the 'Noah's ark principle' which dominated the operation of the Alliance:

Much time and energy which should have been devoted to projecting the Alliance to the electorate was resolved in repeated, and often gruelling, negotiations between the two parties; I spent over fifty hours in meetings on one of these negotiations. Worse, the semi-detached nature of the Alliance weakened both parties.

He pointed out that the SDP leader's attitude towards the Liberal party made it difficult to maintain the status quo in the relationship between the two partners:

One cannot maintain a coalition without a degree of mutual respect between the partners, let alone create a broader political movement. The Franz-Josef Strauss approach to coalition politics, in which the co-operation of partners is accepted provided they recognize the superior intelligence and political dynamism of the great leader, is unlikely to appeal any more in British politics that it has in German.

The debate had already begun. I was especially alarmed that the SDP Executive had been summoned for Monday and I feared that David Owen would use that meeting to get support for blocking merger unless I did something to keep the issue open. After reading a call from Roy Jenkins in favour of merger in that morning's press, I telephoned David Owen at home on Sunday to tell him that I was proposing to write a memorandum for my own Party on merger, with copies to him in time for his Executive and I would make the fact that I was doing so – though not the contents – public. Unfortunately he was out for a long walk with, as it happens, Bob Maclennan and I left the message with his wife Debbie, who was as always helpful and cheerful. I asked her to tell him to call me back if he had any qualms.

But here as so often the cock-up theory of politics prevails over the conspiracy theory. Only months afterwards did I discover from Bob Maclennan that he had been there. When they got back from their walk there was not only my message but one from Chris Moncrieff of the Press Association asking him to comment on my announcement. I had waited an hour or so before phoning the Press Association, but it had not been long enough. So David Owen was able to persuade his SDP colleagues, including Bob Maclennan, and much of Fleet Street, that he had been bounced by me. It was only months later that Bob Maclennan learned from me that my phone call was the second one to David, not the first, and that I *had* already given my views direct to his leader in the first call after the election. The 'bouncing' complaint came ill from someone who on the very same Sunday after the previous general election was arranging his own succession to the SDP leadership.

My phone call to the Press Association was designed to bring the cameras to Ettrick Bridge and ensure adequate coverage for my move. I declined all interviews as I did not want to elaborate beyond the short pro-merger statement. But the statement and the pictures were enough to provide widespread exposure for the start of the merger debate, a start which came as no surprise but had been clearly foreshadowed in the months, indeed years, before the election.

I feel now more than ever that it was right to face the issue of union between the SDP and the Liberal Party as soon as possible after the election. It was unlikely that there would be a wholly smooth path to merger, although the fracas that unleashed itself was unexpected. I saw my job as a leader of the Alliance to urge the membership of both parties to make a clear decision. My own preference was clear. It was for a united Alliance, formed democratically on the basis of a common constitution. The relationship between the two parties could not stand still. The status quo, with its two leaders, two conferences and two organizations had manifested its weaknesses only too clearly during the election campaign itself. It was therefore a choice of moving forward to union or backward to separation.

I issued the following statement on the following Tuesday (16 June 1987):

I have decided to publish this memorandum with the agreement of the Liberal Party's officers in order to demonstrate that no one is trying to bounce anybody into anything and there is no cause for acrimony between the two halves of our Alliance.

The memorandum was to my own party, not to the SDP, who were given one yesterday as a matter of courtesy. I did not expect any decision from them on these fundamental questions so quickly and I have referred to the need to proceed without undue haste.

The words 'democratic fusion' are deliberately used because I believe the SDP's constitution provides in many respects a better model for any united organization. We are not talking about takeover. I hope that the decentralized aspects of the Liberal party would also be embodied in any merged organization.

As an advocate of union I saw the need to spell out the principles that ought to guide members of both parties in thinking about the type of new party that could be created. There were five important points:

- one member, one vote as a basis of legitimacy
- a representative annual conference
- democratic and accountable policy making
- a single leader, nominated by MPs, elected by all members
- one campaigning organization, with a decentralized regional structure.

Whatever hopes any of us had for calm and careful consideration of these and other points were soon shattered. Early signs of problems came when within a week of polling day SDP MPs abandoned our joint Alliance spokesmanship arrangements and opted for a separate Whip and separate spokesmen in the House of Commons.

Two meetings of the SDP's highly divided National Committee considered merger matters in June. The immediate one postponed any decision, having received a proposal from their president, Shirley Williams, which was with hindsight a commendably cautious approach, that the Party's autumn conference should consider the need for a membership ballot.

It was somewhat ironic that at the subsequent meeting a fortnight later, the opponents of merger, who might have been expected to play for as much time as possible, were the ones to press for and succeed in getting an immediate ballot, which would close in early August. At the end of July I used a party political broadcast to assert the case for merger, declaring: 'Six years is long enough for an engagement. It's time for wedding bells.' SDP Chief Whip John Cartwright, playing the reluctant partner, rejoined that they would not be 'railroaded into a shotgun wedding'.

Much haggling occurred over the wording of the SDP ballot; but to general relief the original anti-merger proposals, which to put it mildly were designed to prejudice the outcome, were dropped. None the less the SDP's National Committee did decide by 18 votes to 13 to recommend to the membership a rejection of merger of the two parties. Instead, those opposed to merger urged support for negotiations to create a 'closer constitutional framework for the Alliance', an option without substance in the event. The debate that ensued was clearly one between unionists and separatists. There was in practice, as I had suspected and suggested in my memo, no longer any middle way. Tom

McNally baldly stated the pro-merger case for the SDP:

No coherent programme for an electable centre-left Government can be assembled
on the basis of the separatist case. Of course, there are dangers in trying to construct
too broad a church. For me, however, the rumbustious uncertainties of a wider
movement, which can actually mount a credible bid for power, are infinitely preferable
to a life of certainty and unquestioning obedience in the Plymouth brethren.

It was by any standards a long, hot summer, politically though not in terms
of weather. The ending of the joint MPs meetings meant the end of regular
weekly contact at parliamentary level in the few weeks after the State Opening.
Thereafter David Owen left with his family for America and I came back to
the Borders and the Edinburgh Festival. August and early September really
are nonpolitical periods for politicians. Certainly the month of July belonged
well and truly to the SDP. Liberals, somewhat uncharacteristically, kept silent
even in the face of some fairly harsh and bitter attacks from anti-merger Social
Democrats. The exchanges that occurred took place between 'pro' and 'anti'
SDP groups, much of it heated and nearly all of it in the public gaze. Against
merger, apart from SDP Leader David Owen, lay a majority of the party's
National Committee, its two trustees, and four of the five SDP MPs. Yet the
unity cause boasted the other three founding parents of the SDP – Roy Jenkins,
Shirley Williams and William Rodgers – as well as a clear majority of the
Party's grassroots councillors and parliamentary candidates. Alec McGivan,
the SDP's talented national organizer, resigned to set up and run the 'Yes to
Unity' campaign in his party.

   Coming so soon as it did after the public presentation of a working Alliance
in a general election campaign, this summer bloodbath was both hurtful and
embarrassing to everyone involved. The only comfort was the knowledge that
at the end of the day the SDP founding democratic principle of 'one member,
one vote' was sure to decide the matter. On 5 August it did, with just over
77 per cent of SDP members voting: 19,228 (42.6 per cent of the poll) voted
for closer constitutional links with the Liberal Party; 25,897 (57.4 per cent)
voted to go further and negotiate merger.

   It was a decisive result. Despite the public row, a huge number had voted.
A clear majority wanted to pursue the merger option and even the minority
ostensibly voted for closer links. It left the way open for both of the party
conferences to take matters a step further. Having misjudged the mood of his
party, David Owen suddenly and without warning resigned the leadership of
the SDP.

   The SDP went first to Portsmouth, where the Party's Council for Social

Democracy confirmed the views of the wider membership. A clear majority gave Charles Kennedy's pro-merger motion their support and identified the chief areas of concern in the pending negotiations. They bore a considerable resemblance to the points I had raised in June. Perhaps more significantly, in a counted vote the 'pro' lobby won a handsome victory on how the merger might be carried out, confirming that whatever the SDP democratically decided as a Party, under its constitution, would be a decision for the whole Party, thus making it the policy of the Party. It was an important vote. Anti-mergerites were later to argue that despite democratic defeat in the second ballot, they would ignore the result and continue to call themselves the SDP. Such an approach was firmly rejected by the Portsmouth SDP Council.

Liberals convened twelve days later at Harrogate. The mood was dramatically different. Positively enthusiastic almost to every last man and woman, the Assembly voted overwhelmingly for a new political party in a spirit typified by an inspirational speech by Russell Johnston. There was a real awareness of what it was we were embarking upon. The creation of a new party generated both excitement and some sorrow. It meant that the old Liberal Party, which everyone had grown up with and fought for, would be no more. Whatever our enthusiasm for the new venture, there was an element of sadness for all of us in that debate. In a speech made from the assembly floor I called upon the merger negotiators to get on with their job quickly, arguing that: 'Serious deliberations are necessary and valuable in setting up our new direction, but, I beg you, let them be brief. Let the deliberators be locked in a room for a month if necessary but let them get on with it.'

If only it had been so. Any ideas that it would now be smooth sailing, were premature. The growing strength of the pro-merger cause within the SDP was partly the result of some former opponents and sceptics working now to achieve success in the negotiations. Among them was Robert Maclennan, who had genuinely wanted 'closer links' and believed in accepting the majority decision for merger. Quite understandably they wanted to negotiate as good a 'deal' as possible. Also at Portsmouth the Social Democrats had indicated that they wanted to discuss policy, and Robert Maclennan, my new Alliance partner in leadership, now called for a policy prospectus.

Those seeking an easy passage were not helped either by some developments within Liberal ranks. The Assembly called for a large and, as it transpired, totally unmanageable negotiating team headed with enthusiasm by Party chairman Tim Clement-Jones. Some negotiators were incapable of sighting new party horizons, and arrived at our first meetings determined to preserve all that was Liberal, bad as well as good. My original hopes had been for a small group to devise a package of proposals which would then go to a 'one person, one vote' decision among both the parties' memberships. However, not only did we end up with thirty-four participants, but we got hopelessly bogged down in specific points of detail, hour after weary hour, week after dreary week.

Gradually despite the seemingly endless and often middle-of-the-night discussions, we edged towards an agreement. Such was the give and take, it was clear the draft constitution ought to be acceptable to the majority of members in both parties.

Yet, perhaps predictably, within the Liberal Party a minority began to stir up opposition, requiring amongst other things a visit by me to Northampton the week before Christmas, to try and lift a little the sights of the somewhat unrepresentative Party Council. It met in a cramped and rather squalid part of the students' union. It was an untidy and unhappy meeting, from which I tore myself away early with enthusiasm to attend Shirley Williams' wedding reception. Judy was with me for that purpose and never having seen a Party Council was genuinely shocked. The TV cameras had recorded elder statesmen such as Baroness Seear and Lord Bonham-Carter picking their way through the previous night's session's beer barrels to get to the meeting. It didn't even look businesslike. Needless to say, they passed some motion demanding changes in the negotiations and I was confronted with this when I arrived for Shirley's reception. I resorted to the 'I'm here for the wedding' formula and walked quickly past the cameras and photographers trying to conceal my exasperation.

Beyond the constitution itself there lay only one outstanding matter – the drawing up of a policy prospectus. It might have appeared a relatively straightforward matter to some observers, but it was to prove almost fatal to the whole exercise.

It is still the case that there is no simple explanation for this bizarre episode, the production of a document which I christened subsequently 'the dead parrot'.

The desire for a policy prospectus had come from the SDP, and in particular those Social Democrats who had been sceptical at first, but who now accepted the democratic decision to negotiate. The Liberal negotiating team was not involved and the document awaited an SDP initiative. When the initiative came, time of course was desperately short to meet the deadline of our respective January conferences. The constitutional discussions had dragged on so long that it was only three days before Christmas that Alan Beith, as chairman of our Policy Committee, and I had the first exploratory discussions with Bob Maclennan and his young assistants at my home in Ettrick Bridge. The discussions did not get into precise detail, certainly not for instance into any controversial VAT proposals. Even with hindsight nothing in that first discussion should really have sent alarm bells ringing except that none of us really took on board the terribly short timetable we were setting ourselves, caused by the delays in the interminable constitutional discussions.

Bob Maclennan went off to the United States the next day. By the time he returned, I had departed with Dr Atul Vadher for an exhausting tour on behalf of a charity project in Africa. Behind me there lay with Alan Beith and the two leaders' offices a more detailed draft document and it was a second redraft of this that we rushed to finalize in a twenty-four hour slot we had managed to create before the full negotiating teams met on Tuesday, 12 January 1988.

Other issues – the name we were to use for the new Party and a reference to NATO in the constitution's preamble – had resurrected themselves and were still exercising the negotiators. We had flagged up the release of the policy document for Wednesday, 13 January, but there was no time to do it justice. We ended up trying to produce the document *and* finish the negotiations, and botched the document badly. At one point I was in two meetings at the same time in different buildings.

All might have been well if we'd grasped the nettle the day before our now infamous Wednesday press conference and delayed publication. Indeed Des Wilson and I argued for such a course without success and now realize we should have insisted.

On Tuesday, it was gone midnight before the negotiating teams settled on the 'Social and Liberal Democrats' as the name, thus ditching the now familiar 'Alliance' shorthand, an error made in the name of consultation. Then there began the hopeless task of working throughout the night to discuss the policy draft and to try and get it settled in time for the midday press conference.

A small group of us worked through the night at SDP headquarters until 5 a.m. trying to redraft and improve the document. It was marginally better but not significantly so. Both Bob Maclennan and I were in fractious mood and dead tired. When I got into my office at about 8.30 a.m. after two hours' sleep and a bath, I was still unhappy. So also was Alan Beith, who penned a letter to tell me so; but it was never sent, because events overtook us. The MPs were supposed to have read the document in my office the previous day, but few had bothered to do so and convey any views. However the bush telegraph had been operating since the policy committee meeting the previous evening and they had eventually either seen copies or heard lurid accounts of some of its contents. They made their views properly known to the Chief Whip, Jim Wallace, who at about ten o'clock came to tell me there was open rebellion over it.

'That settles it', I told him, 'I'm not prepared to go ahead with its launch at twelve.'

I telephoned Bob Maclennan and told him I had some grave news which I would rather give him to his face and would he please come across and see me. I asked Jim to leave when Bob arrived at about 10.30. I spoke quietly and sorrowfully to him and said I was not prepared to join him at the press conference to launch the document.

He could either go himself and announce the whole merger was therefore off, or we could postpone the launch and try to rewrite the document. He could have been angry but he was not. We were both exhausted and upset. I told him that in the circumstances I would resign the leadership of my party because merger had failed, and after he left I phoned Judy to tell her the same.

He agreed that a better course would be to postpone the press conference till 5.00 p.m. and meet the MPs at 2.00 p.m. Unfortunately by this time it was too late to prevent journalists and TV crews from assembling in the press conference room at noon. So we sent our respective assistants to announce the postponement to those assembled. Thanks to our still-divided operations, the whole setback was revealed by the SDP press department's distributing the document to the press as they filed in. I thought we had all the copies safely hidden in my room.

When the MPs met at 2.00 p.m. the atmosphere was tense and gloomy. Two of them subsequently revealed that they were prepared physically to prevent an emotional Bob Maclennan from leaving because of the crush of journalists in the corridor outside. They proposed several points for redrafting, while Bob maintained – probably rightly – that this would be useless in view of the circulation of the existing draft. After two hours of anguished discussion, they agreed they would all join us at the 5.00 p.m. press conference when we would simply announce a few days' reflection on what to do next.

That afternoon my parliamentary colleagues loyally rallied round. They said in effect: 'You've got us into this mess and you must now stay at the helm and get us out of it.'

Maybe it was the politician's instinct for survival that pulled us all through. But amid the mess one also had to try and hold on to the fact that outside this ridiculous turmoil we had created at Westminster, our members in the country, in both parties, were still thinking we were on the verge of total agreement. If we had completely failed them, we would never have been forgiven. Union was still the right course, just as it had been the day after the General Election. Somehow there just had to be a way back from the brink.

The immediate aftermath of the issue of the Leaders' Policy Document was grim indeed. But there was no time for wallowing in misery. The danger was that the whole merger process might unravel in general recrimination. Although I could not escape my own share of the blame, I decided that the moment should be treated as a minor setback which could be turned to advantage rather than some sort of final defeat. I did my best to rally the spirits of Bob Maclennan, who was deeply downcast by what he felt to be an exaggerated and unreasonable reaction to the paper. In a strange way the joint calamity brought us closer together.

I secured his agreement to an extensive Policy Agreement exercise designed to replace the Leaders' Document, which was buried swiftly and decisively by my using in a radio interview the terms of Michael Palin's and John Cleese's celebrated *Monty Python* 'dead parrot' sketch. We asked Des Wilson, a former President of the Liberal Party, and a team of five others consisting of Jim Wallace, Alan Leaman, and from the SDP side, Edmund Dell, Tom McNally and David Marquand to come up with a synthesis of existing policy on which the Alliance had fought the previous election and which could provide the initial basis for the launch of our new Party.

This was the sort of document which I, and many other Liberals, had originally envisaged as the only possible starting-point for a new democratic party eager to chart is own future. Perhaps I had allowed myself to be oversensitive to the requirements of the leader of the SDP, Bob Maclennan, who for his part was understandably looking over his shoulder at the shade of David Owen.

One very positive aspect of the almost universally negative reaction to the 'parrot' was the realization on my part that most Social Democrats shared our view that rather than striking out on an uncharted course designed, by out-Owening Owen, to maximize the appeal of the new Party to his section of the SDP, any policy document should rather be of the sort that our group of six now had to produce, and in a hurry. A restatement of existing policy rather than trespassing on the policy-making rights of the new party was the correct approach.

They laboured to considerable effect over the ensuing weekend. By Sunday evening they had agreed on an initial policy statement, *A Democracy of Conscience*, which was ready for submission to the two parties. Their efforts together were precisely the swift and effective kind I had advocated for the whole merger process in my post-election memo.

In parallel, I and other colleagues, particularly Jim Wallace, our Chief Whip, Charles Kennedy, and Shirley Williams, set out to steady the understandably raw nerves of our respective parties, for whom the negotiation process had turned out to be even more harrowing than they could have imagined.

On Monday the new policy statement was agreed without dissent by the parliamentary Party and the policy committees and was sent to the full Negotiating Group. The relief, and elation, were palpable.

As Shirley Williams and I headed for the TV studios to be interviewed on our agreement, Bob Maclennan and Charles Kennedy went to Limehouse in one last attempt to persuade David Owen to join us. Unsurprisingly in the light of his previous pronouncements, he declined.

I was more concerned at this juncture with securing the support of my own Party members for merger. The anti-mergerists were headed by Michael Meadowcroft, the former Liberal MP for Leeds West, and Tony Greaves, the former Political Secretary of the Association of Liberal Councillors. Both men had left it to the last possible moment before departing from the negotiating team, though not over the policy document itself.

The 'dead parrot' had given them precisely the opportunity they needed to appeal to latent suspicions in the Liberal Party of a 'hidden agenda'. Like all anti-authoritarians, Liberals are ever sensitive to conspiracy theories. But although a small and highly vocal group joined them in condemning the agreement, in this instance I felt they underrated the general will and the good sense of the Party.

Nevertheless the Special Assembly at Blackpool, barely more than a week away, loomed as a political occasion of more than ordinary significance. Richard Holme, who over the years has acted as an unfailing source of good advice and practical help, and Alec McGivan, whom I had already appointed my chief assistant, had been maintaining liaison with one of our candidates, Ian Powney, who had set up a grassroots network known as Merger Now. They reported that, after a day or two of depression and confusion, constituencies were rallying round, determined to send their full quota of delegates to Blackpool.

So it proved. The registration for Blackpool approached 2,000 excluding the 'day-trippers' who were coming just for the crucial debate on the Saturday. It turned out to be the most extraordinary and emotional occasion of my entire leadership. From the meeting organized by Merger Now on the Friday evening, addressed by Roy Jenkins and Jo Grimond, and briefly by me, it was apparent that the Party had decided in favour of merger. But what no one could have foreseen was the quality of the debate on Saturday and the overwhelming sense of unity in taking this great leap into the future.

In my own speech, given before the debate, I decided to direct the Party's attention to the external task of providing an effective nonsocialist alternative to Thatcherism. The Assembly responded generously and in speech after speech the same theme was reiterated. I particularly recall Nancy Seear's response to a delegate who had called on the Liberal ancestral gods to make the case against merger: 'After that somewhat selective view of history,' said Lady Seear 'I want to talk about the future.' The final majority, 2,099 to 385, nearly six to one, was a resounding vote for the future of the Social and Liberal Democrats. I have never felt prouder of my Party than I did in February 1988 when, after 120 years of history, it decided in a mature, deeply serious but completely good-humoured way to take this new step forward, together with our friends in the SDP.

They, for their part, one week later in Sheffield, had to secure the parallel agreement of the Council for Social Democracy to put the proposal for merger to a ballot of members. I watched the live television coverage in my study at home and was amazed at David Owen's failure to take his argument personally into the conference hall. He lost a lot of support by conducting press and television interviews outside. In fact, his section of support seemed to have been reduced to about one-third of those present, although the decision of some of them to abstain obscured the precise balance of opinion. Nevertheless the majority was convincing and the way was clear for the final ballot.

As the two conferences had voted, so voted our members a month later. An overwhelming majority in the Liberal Party and a substantial majority in the SDP decided democratically for the permanent union of the two parties. We had plucked success from what had at times seemed the very jaws of failure.

Some have maliciously said that Owen is a Conservative and that he will join them one day. I do not believe that. He has again recently described himself as a Socialist, though the word has largely been expunged from the paperback edition of his policy book, *A United Kingdom*. I am doubtful about that. The truth is that he is and always will be an Owenite. I do not decry that. The fact that what Owenites think on Monday may be different from what they think on Thursday is just something up with which lesser mortals will have to put. Parliament could do with a few more individualist MPs. Fitting them into a team is another matter. Even as far back as the committee stage of the Abortion Bill, David Owen did not join the team but supported it in the way he thought best.

Looking back on the preceding nine months, I tried to strike some sort of political balance of profit and loss in my mind. On the one hand there was no doubt that the spectacle of division where there had been amity had disillusioned many of our erstwhile supporters. Moreover the process of negotiation had been more difficult than we could have imagined and we did not always handle it well.

But, on the positive side of the ledger, was the fact that we had responded decisively to the wish of the electorate that we should 'get our act together'. If a minority of Social Democrats and a handful of Liberals had decided to retreat into the isolation of sectarian self-righteousness that was their own affair. The great majority of us had found the means to realize our common future and, in doing so, had listened to the verdict of the voters in June 1987. Out of the negotiations, moreover, we had constructed a constitution we could be happy with, the most democratic constitution of any British political party. Over the years I had made no secret of the fact that I felt the Liberal Party's constitution was far from being the right structure for that combination of democracy and decisiveness which makes for success, and I am very pleased that the new party is blessed with a better one, including a proper commitment to federalism.

I thought long and hard about whether to put my name forward for leadership of the new party. A majority of my parliamentary colleagues and many of our members urged me to do so. A February *Guardian* editorial offered words of warning on my 'staying on':

To look on the job as continuous, as the thirteenth year of his former leadership, would plainly be disastrous. He would need to engage more actively with the work of the party's influential institutions – though given the tighter, more disciplined constitutional framework with which the SLD is equipped, he may not find that sort of thing as tedious as he did in his Liberal days.

This reflected advice I received from Richard Holme: that I could no longer rely on a coalition of support from the MPs and the mass membership of the Party alone, and that the 'parrot' episode had dangerously eroded my 'political capital' amongst the party activists, with the result that I could only narrrowly expect to win a leadership election.

When in January I repeated that it was unlikely that I would be a candidate I came under pressure from two-thirds of MPs to think again. I did so very seriously during the Easter recess and my fiftieth birthday celebration with family and friends in Brussels. Two or three of my closest colleagues almost persuaded me, against my better judgement, to stand. It was put to me especially strongly by Russell Johnston and David Alton that the prospect of yet another circuit of the same halls may seem an awful prospect, but what had I been working towards since my first leadership speech? One friend advised me not to stand, saying that I should be 'the chrysalis that produced the butterfly, not the sow that rolled over on her litter'.

But I finally decided with Judy in the unlikely setting of a car journey to Windsor Castle for a state banquet for the King of Norway. We then had to keep the decision to ourselves until after the local elections a month later – that was the hardest part of all, denying to friends and colleagues access to my thinking. All along, contrary to press speculation, Judy did not push one way or the other but simply pledged her support for whatever I decided to do.

It was a difficult decision and a deeply emotional moment. One close political friend wrote to me saying simply that I 'had brought to the leadership a feeling of relaxed good nature and a tolerant sanity'. My political mentor, Jo Grimond, wrote: 'I'm sure that David has had his full share of private doubts, irritations and gloom. But in public life he has been a salesman for the politics of hope. I have never seen him fail to make people a little happier than they were before he arrived, or, even more important, than they expecte to be.'

I announced my decision not to stand in a speech in my constituency in Galashiels. It was a highly charged moment when I told my constituency executive:

It is never easy to pit your own judgement against that of friends and colleagues. But I suspect that some of their attitude is summed up by Hilaire Belloc's couplet:

> 'Always keep a-hold of Nurse
> For fear of finding something worse.'

In the House of Commons the parliamentary party is a cohesive and determined group of nineteen able men and women. It should be more and it will be more. But among them are several people well qualified now to lead the party. I intend to remain as an active MP, helping to broaden the appeal of our party and at the service of its new leader and continuing in post until the new leader is elected.

Those who have urged me to stay should not feel let down. I have been party leader now for twelve years – the longest serving in the entire history of the Liberal Party, except for Mr Asquith. It has been a great privilege and I have thoroughly enjoyed it – well, most of it. Judy and I have made a great many friends throughout this country and in other countries. I share our collective frustration at our disappointments, but I am deeply proud of the advances we have made together over these years. Thousand-year Reichs, like empires on which the sun never sets, seem in human history to have enjoyed shorter lifespans than their creators envisaged. I do not believe that the prevailing Thatcherite temper of government can last forever. Thatcherism has not been good for Scotland, nor for Britain. It represents a deadly mixture of private greed, public squalor and creeping authoritarianism which is corrupting our civic life. Our party has much to contribute to creating a credible alternative. I look forward now, even more than when I became leader of the Liberal Party in 1976, to the day which is coming steadily closer when we shall have a government including Social and Liberal Democrats, based on British values of fairness, mutual tolerance and democracy. For us, the best still lies ahead.

POSTSCRIPT

Luck has played a large part in my life, good and bad. The resignation of the prospective candidate for the Borders, the sudden death of the sitting MP and my draw in the ballot for private members' bills were all events over which I had no control but from which I benefitted. Equally, Mr Callaghan's decision not to hold an election in the autumn of 1978, and the Argentine invasion of the Falklands were events which substantially altered the course of political history to our detriment. Even our polling only two per cent behind Labour rather than ahead of them in the 1983 election made a profound psephological and psychological difference.

In two cases, however, events were to some extent within my control and might have been handled differently and to the Party's advantage. I believe that after the major advance of the 1983 election, I should have pressed the argument for merger of the Liberals with the SDP rather than leaving it until four years later. When I did press it in 1987, it was a mistake to have got embroiled in long-drawn out 'negotiations' between party teams. A group of four, taking evidence and producing a report for amendment, acceptance or rejection, would have been more effective and less destructive than the byzantine processes in which we indulged with resulting weariness, attrition and confusion.

As Leader of the Liberal Party I do not think I will ever be awarded full marks for either party management or pioneering policies. Where I believe I made a contribution was in articulating our values and attitudes in a way which brought a huge public response. This is an essential part of leadership. I have never been keen on my face being captured by the camera, unlike Harold Wilson, as a boy, on the steps of Number 10 Downing Street. I therefore feel none of the disappointment which seems to infect so many

297

would-be Prime Ministers on the Tory and Labour benches of the Commons.

I took no part in the new leadership campaign, but I told the two candidates that I would be voting for Alan Beith, both as a friend and neighbour of many years and knowing him as my kind of Liberal. The party made its democratic choice of Paddy Ashdown, whom I did not previously know well. Not only has he flung himself with a verve and gusto I could not have summoned into the demanding tours of the country but, unlike his notorious predecessor, he is engaged actively in the Party's Executive and Policy Committees. The whole Party finds his style and vigour refreshing after twelve years of me, the last in harness with Bob Maclennan. The new party also has a more effective structure than the old, my one regret being that the simple title of 'Liberal-Democrat' was not adopted. It is what I continue to call myself. The grass roots strength of the old Liberal machine was demonstrated in May 1989 when, in spite of poor opinion poll ratings, we held on to 450 county council seats in England and Wales largely gained at one of our highest Alliance points in May 1985.

Meanwhile, I have been writing this book, and have regained the sort of control over my own life which I have not enjoyed for twelve years. I have been resisting the blandishments of those seeking to drag me into other new pastures; but have been pleasantly surprised at the variety of suggestions, ranging from chairing a major charity, becoming the European consultant to an American firm, joining the board of an investment company, down to advertising a chocolate bar on television. Some I have declined, others I will now consider. I also have in hand the presentation of two major television documentaries in 1990.

One venture I did undertake was to stand for the Central region of Italy in June 1989 as a candidate in the European elections. This I was encouraged to do by Paddy Ashdown and Russell Johnston, both as a symbol of solidarity with our Italian colleagues, and as a protest against our outrageous electoral system in Britain. It was another 'first', my being the first parliamentarian in one country to stand for election in another. Italy is the only country where any European Community citizen can stand for election to the European Parliament. Adopted at the last minute and speaking no Italian, I enjoyed a hectic but somewhat chaotic, intermittent three-week campaign. My campaign was effectively organized by an Italian Liberal, Rita Watson, the wife of my former assistant Graham. To my astonishment, I polled 15,500 votes which was very respectable. Encouraged and emboldened by this experience, I may stand for the Presidency of Liberal International in a couple of years' time.

I have also undertaken the joint chairmanship of the Scottish Convention. The aim of the Convention, on which I set high hopes, is to succeed where we failed (as I described in Chapter Six) in producing an effective scheme for internal self-government. The Claim of Right for Scotland reasserts, in a dramatic and forceful way, the sovereignty of the Scottish people over their own destiny. I am in no doubt that there is an overwhelming desire to renegotiate the terms of the 1707 Act of Union, turning our constitutional settlement into a quasi-federal one. If the Convention achieves a broad consensus on such a scheme, then I hope to help bring it into reality.

Another bee in my bonnet remains electoral reform. Here I hope the new party will not prove too purist. I recognize the intrinsic merits of our long-standing policy, but if all we can squeeze out of the Labour or Conservative parties is the alternative vote in existing constituencies, we should go for that as at least a step in the right direction. We may yet again hold a balance of power in the Commons after the next election. The European Parliament, a Scottish parliament and even local government should be the places where the case for reform should be pressed with urgency.

It is astonishing that while proclaiming freedom, the Thatcher government has presided over a tightening grip on our liberties; the power of government has been used and abused ruthlessly. Unhappily, our programme of con-stitutional reforms excites little public interest, but that is no reason for not pursuing it vigorously. Autocratic government has increased under Mrs Thatcher, a lady of astonishingly narrow and blinkered vision who has little capacity to understand, still less to sympathize with, those who have not enjoyed her advantages of wealth and brain. Her good qualities, carried to excess, become bad ones. Determination lurches into stubbornness, conviction into prejudice, and strength into bullying. The tide must, at some point, turn as people grow weary of her style of government and its consequences.

The preamble to the Liberal Party constitution stated: 'The Liberal Party exists to build a liberal society in which every citizen shall possess liberty, property and security and no one shall be enslaved by poverty, ignorance or conformity.' That was as true of the party of the 1950s in its darkest days as it is of the party of the Social and Liberal Democrats of the 1980s, the main difference being that we have now created a mass movement and organization which supports these objectives.

In spite of lingering problems with the breakaway minority from the Alliance, I have every confidence both in the new Party's prospects of success and the public's appetite for our kind of politics. I would still like to serve in government to put our ideals into practice.

How do people define 'success'? If it is only in terms of climbing to the top and occupying supreme power, then along with fifty million fellow citizens, that has eluded me. Yet, by any normal standards I have every reason to be satisfied. I have a blessedly happy and interesting life with Judy and our lively family, and although I shall never be rich I am comfortably off. I have the immense satisfaction of serving a beautiful and fascinating constituency, and I enjoy parliamentary life. I have exercised considerable influence if little power. I have more invitations to travel and lecture than I can possibly accept in the next year or two, and I have undertaken to restore one small part of Scotland's heritage – Aikwood (Oakwood) Tower – over the next few years. I have just passed my half-century with I trust, plenty of years in store.

I would like to achieve more in those areas in which I have fought – to reduce inequalities of opportunity, of race or of wealth within Britain and secure our place in a more just and less stressful world order; to see Scotland have control over her own destiny and Europe bind the old nation states together; to develop a greater industrial partnership in the pursuit of wealth creation and the refurbishing of the welfare state; and to secure a greater priority for what are fashionably called Green policies to nurture the planet we hand on to our descendants.

The Goliath of our two-party system has yet to be slain, but he is now shaky on his feet. I still intend to make my contribution to delivering our promise of a more tolerant, civilized and fairer society in a safer and happier world.

BIBLIOGRAPHY

I have drawn substantially upon the Nuffield election studies series (Macmillan) which has been masterminded for decades by David Butler; *Keesing's Contemporary Archives* have also proved to be an invaluable source when the memory dries up. I have made use of all the major national newspapers and political journals and magazines, as well as party sources such as *New Outlook*, the *Radical Quarterly*, *Liberal News* and *Social and Liberal Democrat News*. I have also raided the *Liberator Songbook* for various scurrilous pieces of verse.

I have used the following books:

JOEL BARNETT, *Inside the Treasury*, Andre Deutsch, 1982.

JAMES BARR, *The Scottish Covenanters*, John Smith and Son, 1946.

PETER BARTRAM, *David Steel: His Life and Politics*, W. H. Allen, 1981.

PETER BESSELL, *Cover-Up: The Jeremy Thorpe Affair*, Simons Books, 1980.

VERNON BOGDANOR, *Devolution*, Oxford University Press, 1979.

VERNON BOGDANOR (ed.), *Liberal Party Politics*, Clarendon Press, 1983.

IAN BRADLEY, *Breaking the Mould*, Martin Robinson, 1981.

JAMES CALLAGHAN, *Time and Chance*, Collins, 1987.

JOHN CAMPBELL, *Roy Jenkins*, Weidenfeld and Nicolson, 1983.

LORD CARRINGTON, *Reflect on Things Past*, Collins, 1988.

LEWIS CHESTER, MAGNUS LINKLATER AND DAVID MAY, *Jeremy Thorpe: A Secret Life*, Fontana, 1979.

PETER CHIPPENDALE AND DAVID LEIGH, *The Thorpe Committal*, Arrow, 1979.

CHURCH OF ENGLAND'S BOARD OF SOCIAL RESPONSIBILITY, *Abortion: an Ethical Discussion*, Church Information Office, 1965.

JO GRIMOND, *Memoirs*, Heinemann, 1979.

KENNETH HARRIS, *David Owen*, Weidenfeld and Nicolson, 1987.

KEITH HINDELL AND MADELEINE SIMMS, *Abortion Law Reformed*, Peter Owen, 1971.

ALICE JENKINS, *Law for the Rich*, Victor Gollancz, 1960.

PETER JENKINS, *Mrs Thatcher's Revolution*, Jonathan Cape, 1987.

ROY JENKINS, *European Diary 1977–81*, Collins, 1989.

JEREMY JOSEPHS, *Inside the Alliance*, John Martin Publishing, 1983.

NEIL MacCORMICK (ed.), *The Scottish Debate*, Oxford University Press, 1970.

PAUL MARTIN, *The London Diaries 1975–79*, University of Ottawa Press, 1988.

ALASTAIR MICHIE AND SIMON HOGGART, *The Pact: The Inside Story of the Lib-Lab Government 1977–78*, Quartet Books, 1978.

A. A. MILNE, *The House at Pooh Corner*, Methuen, 1928.

STUART MOLE (ed.), *The Decade of Realignment: The Leadership Speeches of David Steel 1976–86*, Hebden Royd Publications, 1986.

DAVID OWEN, *A United Kingdom*, Penguin, 1986.

BARRIE PENROSE AND ROGER COURTIOUR, *The Pencourt File*, Secker and Warburg, 1978.

JAMES PRIOR, *A Balance of Power*, Hamish Hamilton, 1986.

NORMAN SHRAPNEL, *The Performers: Politics as Theatre*, Constable, 1978.

MICHAEL STEED, *The Alliance: A Critical History*, Prism Publications 1983.

CYRIL SMITH, *Big Cyril*, W. H. Allen, 1977.

DAVID STEEL, *A House Divided: The Lib-Lab Pact and the Future of British Politics*, Weidenfeld and Nicolson, 1980.

DAVID STEEL, *No Entry*, C. Hurst, 1969.

DAVID STEEL AND RICHARD HOLME (eds), *Partners In One Nation: A New Vision of Britain 2000*, The Bodley Head, 1985.

HUGH STEPHENSON, *Claret and Chips*, Michael Joseph, 1982.

NORMAN TEBBIT, *Upwardly Mobile*, Weidenfeld and Nicolson, 1988.

GEORGE THOMAS, *George Thomas: Mr Speaker*, Arrow, 1985.

DES WILSON, *Battle for Power*, Sphere Books, 1987.

INDEX